If you were born and raised in the South, then you knew someone who worked in a textile mill. But did you really know what their lives were like? Sigmon's book, *Weaving the Heart Threads of a Mill Village: Rhodhiss, North Carolina*, will give you more interesting details and intriguing stories about the lives of people who worked and lived in Rhodhiss textile mills than you could ever possibly glean on your own. Personal interviews, factual statistics and beautiful, wonderful pictures await the reader who is interested in this historic time. A good read and an exceptionally well-researched book.

—Sara Thompson, retired Iredell County teacher

As a second grader who was fascinated with her developing reading skills, Sherrie Sigmon's enthusiasm for words and for books originated. Her excitement for printed materials continued through high school, college, and throughout her outstanding career as a secondary English teacher. Today, Sherrie has shared her talents by writing her first book about a small town--its history, its people, its struggles, and its endurance--located in the foothills of North Carolina. Following years of research, interviews, and countless hours of writing, she has produced a work that will touch the hearts of citizens who lived the events, as well as those who wish to become acquainted with the birth and the growth of the beloved town of Rhodhiss.

—Barbara Jones, retired Caldwell County teacher

Sherrie Hartsoe Sigmon has woven a treasure of interviews, personal experiences, and photos into a valuable history of Rhodhiss, which otherwise might have been lost. I learned so much about the closely-knit community by reading it. The mill provided much more than employment. Workers readily helped with maintenance to the school when needed and offered encouragement to students. An Educational Fund was established to help further opportunities for students, draperies were provided for the auditorium, and necessities were given to the cafeteria. Rhodhiss residents have battled many hardships. Through typhoid outbreaks, impassable muddy roads, soot-covered children and clothes, and many other difficulties, the people were resilient and overcame their challenges. During my years of teaching at Rhodhiss School, 1971-1980, I could see and feel the pride of the community for their school. The children were well-educated and loved by the teachers, staff, and cafeteria ladies alike in a unique family atmosphere. I'll always cherish my memories of the dear people I loved when I was part of the Little Red School.

—Mary T. Laws, retired Caldwell County teacher

I remember a lot of the names. My closest friend back in those days was Thad Elmore's son, and Thad was a policeman, so we walked the straight and narrow. I never got into trouble because I knew anything could get back to my dad. Rhodhiss was considered home to me from the time I was 6 years old until we sold the house after my dad's death in 2011. I still miss the simple town and village we called our playground. Good memories.

—Gerald Jones, former Rhodhissian and son of Calvin and Marguerite Jones.

Weaving the Heart Threads of a Mill Village:

RHODHISS, NORTH CAROLINA

Sherrie Hartsoe Sigmon

For the Town of Rhodhiss

Work with love, it is to weave the cloth with threads drawn
from your heart.
Khalil Gibran

Front cover picture courtesy of Duke Power.

Redhawk Publications
The Catawba Valley Community College Press
2550 US Hwy 70 SE
Hickory NC 28602

ISBN: 978-1-959346-08-1

Library of Congress Number:

Printed in the United States of America

redhawkpublications.com

Layout and Cover Design by: Ashlyn Blake

Edited by Robert Canipe and Melanie Johnson Zimmermann

ScantheQRcodeformoreinformationorvisitusonlineathttps://townofrhodhissnc.com/town-council/

FOREWORD

I often think of things that only someone that has passed on could answer. I remember thinking I'll call mom only to realize I can't soon after her passing. That alone is why this book is so paramount in preserving the rich history of Rhodhiss! In 2023 the town will celebrate 120 years of incorporation; this documentation starts around 1875 and is so well documented with over 600 pictures, 28 chapters, and 60 years of research. We are so fortunate to have Sherrie Hartsoe Sigmon who has unselfishly and voluntarily recorded, researched, interviewed, and traveled to put on displays and represent the Town of Rhodhiss!

Thank you, Sherrie, for your tireless effort; you are the only one who will ever know the struggles you encountered along the way. But the rewards will be left for this generation and generations to come. I cannot think of anything that has been more exciting for Rhodhiss since the landing on the moon, and yes that's in the book.

Rick Justice, Town Manager

DEDICATION

This book is dedicated to the memory of Tom and Frances Ross, who gave their love, support, and inspiration. Frances Ross encouraged me for years to write the town's history. I started collecting information on Sunday, March 20, 1988, and I went to her house to share my findings. She was thrilled, but five days later, Mrs. Ross died of a massive heart attack. I started the interviews within a month of her death, and Tom Ross went with me to help in his grief and to introduce me to some people that I didn't know. This book is also dedicated to the memory of my parents, Boyce and Mildred Hartsoe, who saw the advantages in letting their children grow up in a small town. In addition, this it is dedicated to the memory of Thelma Church, who loved to share her stories of Rhodhiss with me. Furthermore, it is dedicated to the memory of all of those whom I interviewed throughout the years. Their stories have been shared for others to enjoy. Lastly, it is dedicated to my two favorite men: my husband, Michael Sigmon, and our son, Lance Hart Sigmon. Thank you guys, for believing in me and putting up with my passion of preserving Rhodhiss' history.

PREFACE

It is difficult to put into words what writing Rhodhiss' story means. I wrote my first paper on Rhodhiss when I was in the sixth grade at Rhodhiss Elementary after I interviewed Boyd Hollar and Effie Kirby. Almost twenty years later, I started anew. When Burlington closed the Burke Plant in 1983, they gave away boxes of old photos, and I was able to preserve these visual memories. In 1988 I started interviewing people, hearing stories, collecting pictures, and making new friends. In this book I have repeated various stories that were told by different people. For example, I told the story of the first and second depots from several perspectives because I wanted to be certain that I had confirmation. I have tried to cover the 120-year history of Rhodhiss, North Carolina. The twenty-first century information is not as detailed as the early twentieth century history, but my goal was to retain the stories of the early years before those people were no longer here. I heard a quote in grad school that touched me. An old African proverb says, "Every time an old person dies, a library burns." Everybody has a story to tell, and I hope that I was able to save a few libraries in the process of collecting the history of Rhodhiss. As for the twenty-first century information, I hope that there is someone who would like to interview the present generation to preserve this library. At this point, I wrote what was told to me or found in my research. I tried to weave the material into a story that would preserve Rhodhiss' place in history much like the millhands wove their material for the products that were used worldwide. More material is out there for someone else to weave.

I taught in Statesville, NC for thirty-one years. I always told my high school students that I was from Rhodhiss, but few knew where that was. Years later, I ran into a Rhodhiss person who is younger than I am. He came up to me and said, "I must tell you what happened to me. I was making reservations for a hotel in Myrtle Beach. I gave my name and address. When I said 'Rhodhiss,' the hotel reservations clerk said, 'Rhodhiss! Do you know Sherrie Hartsoe?'" Rhodhiss' story is known around the world. Years ago, my friend, Cary Ross, was on a ship in Spain. He started a conversation with a man who asked him where he was from. Cary responded, "North Carolina." The man said, "What town?" Cary replied, "It wouldn't do you any good to hear it." The man retorted, "Where are you from? Charlotte, Raleigh, Rhodhiss." Cary said that after he picked himself up off the floor, he asked the guy how he knew about Rhodhiss. The gentleman explained that his father, Mr. Mayberry, was the Baptist Church's minister years prior. Rhodhiss' legacy has no bounds. Another story was told by Willard Herman. His nephew, Q. T. Curtis, a preacher at a large Baptist Church in Alabama, was conducting a revival in a nearby town, and a woman approached Q. T. after the service. She said, "I heard that you are from a town called 'Rhodhiss,' and I can't find it on the North Carolina map. I went to college at Mars Hill with a woman from there. Her name was Aileen Bumgarner." Q. T. laughed and told the woman that he indeed was from Rhodhiss, he knew Aileen, and he then showed her where Rhodhiss would be on the North Carolina map. Ned Bean also shared a story of Rhodhiss' fame. A gentleman, Harold Oglesby, lived in Rhodhiss prior to World War II, played baseball for the mill team, and worked for the company. During the war, he went to the Army. Later, he married a woman from South Africa whose family was in the diamond business. Ned and Elvie were at a cocktail party on Laurel Hill, and they met a man that was in the diamond business. Ned asked this guy if he knew Harold Oglesby. The man responded, "I sure do. I was at a cocktail party with him in Cape Town, South Africa, last summer." Rhodhiss' legacy continues.

Rhodhiss' story is varied with lots of celebrations and disappointments. The town was hit numerous times by natural disasters and fires, yet the townspeople showed their strength and courage to move forward. Rhodhiss will always be remembered as a village that worked hard to achieve its goals and to do it with an added flair. The town continues this tradition today. Rhodhiss is a great place, and I am so happy that I had the opportunity to experience the love, friendship, and lessons that it had to offer. The hearts of the past and present Rhodhiss villagers have a special component; we all are woven together by love because we are family!

Any profit made from this book will be donated to Rhodhiss. I hope that it can be used for scholarships for students who wish to pursue their educations, or it is used to help families experiencing food shortage or other financial woes.

Sherrie Hartsoe Sigmon

ACKNOWLEDGEMENTS

The Town of Rhodhiss for their willingness to fund this book. The Rhodhiss Staff: Rick Justice, Rhodhiss Town Manager and Town Clerk Julie Byrd; Mayor Allen Spencer; Council members, Mike Phillips, Kendra Edwards, Joyce Karn, and Donna Abernethy Price. Dale Hawkins who took some pictures for icons.

Duke Energy provided over 40 pictures.

Local newspapers who agreed to have their pictures and articles reprinted. The *Lenoir News-Topic*; Sam Erby, owner of the *Granite Falls Press*; The *Hickory Daily Record*, and *The Morganton News-Herald*.

Anita M. Haas, who gave the town permission to use her grandfather's pictures.

Carl Compton, a Rhodhiss citizen and friend. Carl was willing to share stories, identify people, and give many, many photos.

Barbara Jones, my high school English teacher, my friend, and my Hartsoe cousin. She proofread some of the book for me. Barbara, thank you for your willingness to help.

Sara Thompson, my West Iredell English teacher coworker and friend. She proofread most of the book. Sara, thank you for your comments and support.

The people who were willing to read and write blurbs: Barbara Jones, Sara Thompson, Mary Laws, Kathy Tramble, Gerald Jones, Gwen Longshore, and Crystal Feimster.

The picture id team: Carl and Brenda Compton, Bruce Hartsoe, Gwen Longshore, Donna Abernethy Price, Cindy Kirby Rogers, Paul Bright, and Tim and Renita Hartsoe.

Beth Kirby Furman, former Rhodhiss citizen, who wrote a paper in 1982 while at ASU detailing the history of Rhodhiss Mills. This information was destroyed when the plant closed in 1983.

Cindy Hedrick Day, Executive Director at the Caldwell County Heritage Museum.

Burke County History Museum for their pictures that were used for some of the chapter icons.

Burl McCuiston, Instruction and Reference Librarian Assistant Director at Lenoir Rhyne University, Hickory, NC.

Timothy Scott Reeves, Archival Assistant at Columbia Theological Seminary, Columbia, SC.

TABLE OF CONTENTS

CHAPTER 1

TRAINS: A PASSAGEWAY FOR TRANSPORTATION, PLEASURE, AND HARDSHIP

A t the turn of the twentieth century the fastest mode of transportation in America was via train. In western North Carolina horse and buggy along with the rail enabled people to travel for pleasure, work, or entertainment. The soon-to-be village of Rhodhiss, North Carolina saw the railroad travel through in the late 1800s. Located in the foothills, Rhodhiss is named for two gentlemen, John Rhodes and George Hiss, who came to town at the turn of the twentieth century to establish a cotton mill that would be powered by water. The Carolina and North-Western Railroad was primarily the company which used this route, but the people in the area frequently referred to it as the "Can't and Never Will."

Before Rhodes and Hiss arrived in the area, the community was named "The Cliffs." As per Edward Phifer who wrote a history of Burke County, "CLIFFS was the former name for the portion of Rhodhiss which was situated in Burke County. Rhodhiss was settled in 1875 and incorporated in 1903."[1] The Cliffs was where the train stopped to take on coal, and it was also a respite for passengers to have a picnic and enjoy the tranquility. A pavilion provided seating for 1,200 people. Stories have circulated that many people spent their Sunday afternoons in their finest attire picnicking at this grand site. Before the Cliffs became a reality, a bridge was needed that would allow a train to travel into nearby Burke and Caldwell counties from Hickory. In the late 1800s it would have been a difficult task to move equipment and find laborers. The author, Matthew Bumgarner, wrote in his book, *Carolina & NW: The Legacy of The Carolina & North-Western Railway*: "In 1878, the grading from Lenoir to Hickory was completed with the use of convict labor at a cost of $14,000. The convicts were also used to complete the piers of the Catawba River bridge at a cost of $4,500 . . . the railroad construction 'was a Caldwell hobby and included everybody.'"[2] Hard labor was required to construct the route from

Hickory to Lenoir. Bumgarner continued the story: "The largest obstacle to overcome was completing the large bridge over the Catawba River. This bridge consisted of three spans. Each one was 120 feet long and cost nearly $6,900. Over 4,700 feet of lumber was used in the trestle work, and its cost was almost $11,000. On the day this bridge was completed, February 7, 1884, the first train entered Caldwell County."[3] Thus, a train was running through what is now known as Rhodhiss. In the late 1800s having access to a train ride to local cities enabled people to broaden their lives. Alan Coleman added in his book, *Images of Rail: Railroads of North Carolina*, "Chester and Lenoir Narrow-Gauge Railroad (1873-1897): Building upon the work of the Kings Mountain Railroad, this 3-foot-gauge railroad ran from Chester, SC, to Lincolnton by 1880 and to Lenoir by 1884. Of its 109.5 miles, 10 were laid over the Western NC Railroad by means of a third rail. The company was foreclosed and reorganized in 1897 as Carolina and Northwestern Railroad."[4] People were able to travel by rail as opposed to horse and buggy. More opportunities bettered lives with this mode of transportation.

A TRAIN FROM THE EARLY DAYS OF RAIL IN CALDWELL COUNTY.
CALDWELL COUNTY LIBRARY PHOTO

The Cliffs was located between Hickory and Rhodhiss on the Burke County side. This land was often frequented by visitors on their way to the mountains or even people who just caught the train for a Sunday afternoon ride. In a brochure produced by the C&NW Railroad, the Cliffs is described as a beautiful area four miles from Hickory. It is a "'Fisherman's Joy, the Botanist's Paradise, and the Small Boy's Inward Satisfaction.'"[5] Obviously, the C&NW advertisement allowed many people to learn of this area, and this publication enticed them to visit. The pamphlet's information includes:

On a summit overlooking the Catawba River there is a place called the Cliffs. It is full of natural beauty with views of the mountains. It is a temporary resting place for travelers who like to escape 'the din and noise of the busy city life with its never-ceasing push and rush, anxiety and care.' The C&NW has made this a place for its patrons.

'A neat, comfortable passenger station, with waiting rooms for men and women, and well supplied with water, has been built expressly for the company's outing parties. A pavilion with seating capacity of 1,200 crowns the summit of the bluff, where a refreshing breeze may be enjoyed at almost any hour... In this lovely, secluded spot, it isn't anything of a difficult task to throw care and worry to the four winds and give one's self (sic) up to the full enjoyment of nature's own inevitable charms. No need here to quench thirst with the liquid which runs through the rusty pipes of a city, for instead a body can enjoy the living of copious draughts from the clear and sparkling waters which bubble up from the cold springs.' Between Lenoir and the Cliffs there are several small stations. 'Rhodhiss has one industry, Rhodhiss Manufacturing Co., Sheeting, out-put per annum 3,000,000 pounds; capital, $300,000. Round-trip tickets at a low rate are available.'[6]

A PAGE FROM THE 1905 C&NW BROCHURE. PETE SETTLEMYRE PHOTO.

ANOTHER PAGE FROM THE 1905 C&NW BROCHURE. PETE SETTLEMYRE PHOTO.

The railroad company spent many years completing the dream of rail from Hickory to Lenoir, and they were able to make the project aesthetically beautiful for all to enjoy. The description of the Cliffs' area would be a wonderful adventure even today. For the first time people were able to travel by train to neighboring counties and cities.

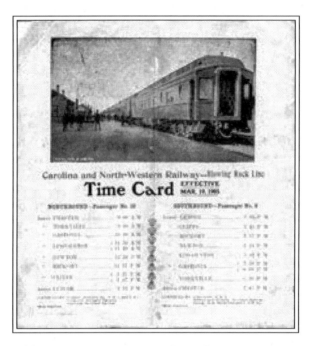

THE C&NW TRAIN SCHEDULE. PETE SETTLEMYRE PHOTO.

THE CLIFFS DEPOT. PETE SETTLEMYRE PHOTO.

During the late 1800s and early 1900s vast amounts of land were available in Caldwell and Burke counties with these areas being primarily agricultural. Matthew Bumgarner describes one passenger's view of the area during an 1884 train ride to Hickory. The Mull Trestle to the Catawba River is specifically mentioned. One account indicates that the granite was taken from a quarry located about ¼ of a mile above the bridge. The passenger says that the Mull Trestle to the Winkler's approximately five miles away is the "'prettiest pieces of railroad scenery in the state.'"[7] This area is described as "two miles from the bridge." The Mull land was near Rhodhiss. Even today the terrain from the Hickory 321 bridge all the way to Rhodhiss is very rocky, and the landscape is beautiful. The Carolina and Northwestern hauled cargo within the area. Matthew Bumgarner says, "Lumber was transported on the C&N-W, but in 1916 there was a 'setback in the low-rate commodity,' but it was 'offset with increased gains provided by the cotton and furniture business. Cotton industries continued to mushroom in Gastonia, Newton, Rhodhiss, and Granite Falls.'[8] Rhodhiss Manufacturing was thriving in 1916 as were other cotton mills.

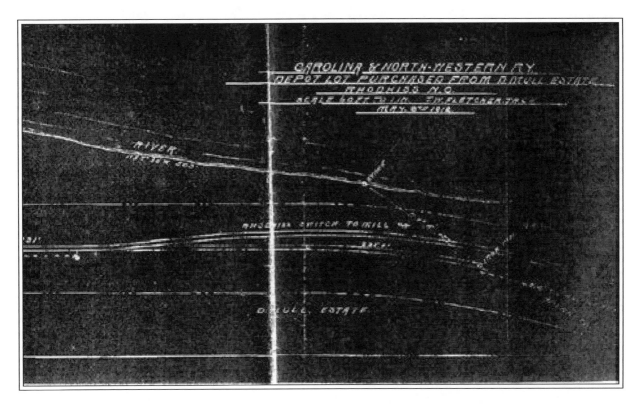

THE MULL LAND AREA 1912. EDDIE SIPES PHOTO.

MULL TRESTLE CIRCA 1882 IN CALDWELL COUNTY. MATT BUMGARNER PHOTO.

The building of the railroad did meet obstacles along the way. A smallpox outbreak stopped construction. Dr. A. A. Kent from Lenoir was the Superintendent of Public Health for Caldwell County. His son, Dr. A. A. Kent, Jr., later practiced medicine in Granite Falls. Senior Dr. Kent sent a letter to the State of North Carolina in 1902 asking who was obligated to pay for the quarantine of the railroad workers who had contracted smallpox and were in Rhodhiss, which was not yet an incorporated community. Dr. Kent's letter to the state and the state's reply follow:

> Lexoir (sic), N.C. April 3, 1902
> Dr. R.H. Lewis,
> Secretary State Board of Health, Raleigh, N. C.

Dear Doctor: -- I have had only the two cases of small-pox in my camp up to this time. I released all but seven yesterday. The ones released had been least exposed--two weeks since last exposure, and everything about them twice cleaned up and disinfected. If no further developments, I will release all very soon.

In the meantime, I wish to understand the law applying to this case: They were all working for wages for the Atlantic Construction Company.... The shanty cars in which I found them were owned by the railroad company and on their track--that is. On the line switch running from the main line to Rhodhiss cotton factory. This switch is owned by the railroad company. The negroes and the two white men were working for wages, in the employ of the construction company.

None of them were citizens of Caldwell County. Small-pox broke out among them before they were sent into Caldwell County. The general manager of the railroad ordered them moved from an adjoining county to the Rhodhiss switch after they knew that small-pox had broken out among them. Although it had been among them for some time, the railroad authorities made no effort to suppress it or to keep them from mixing with the Rhodhiss population. Nor did they report the fact to the health officer anywhere. The railroad has fed the men, but at the expense of the men, as their board was taken out of wages due them. I have met all the other expenses of the quarantine. As it will end soon, I wish to know who should pay all the expenses of it. You referred me to section 8, amended law. Published in February Bulletin 1901. I have not a copy of that Bulletin and cannot find the amended law in the acts of Legislature as published. As I see it, the Atlantic Construction Company is the 'householder' and must pay the expenses of the quarantine. Further, they have violated the law by knowingly bringing into the county a crowd of men, shanty cars and effects infected with small-pox; and have again violated the law that requires the householder to report such diseases to the proper health officer when they break out. In this instance they made no report of it. The community complained, threatened and finally reported it to me. The railroad has not refused to pay the expense, but in case it does I wish to know the law, so as to know just how to proceed. Please send me the full text of the amended law, if it has been printed; if not printed, please send me a copy of the February Bulletin (sic) of 1901.

Any other advice, etc., will be duly appreciated.

Yours sincerely,

A. Kent, M.D.,

Super. Of Health, Caldwell County

Response from Dr. Richard H. Lewis to Dr. A. A. Kent
Richard H Lewis, M.D., Sec., and Treas. A.C. Board of Health, Raleigh, N. C.

My Dear Sir: -- I have the honor to acknowledge the receipt of your favor of recent date, with enclosure of letter of Dr. Kent of Lenoir, relating to the payment of expenses incurred in maintaining quarantine on account of small-pox infection. This matter, as you are aware, is regulated by section 8, chapter 214 of the Laws of North Caro-lina (sic), session 1893. In this section the following language is used:

'The expense of quarantine and of the disinfection shall be borne by the householder in whose family the case occurs, if able; otherwise, by the city, town or county of which he is a resident.' The term 'householder' signifies the occupier of a house or one who provides for the household. Whether this definition of the word is suffi-cient (sic) to embrace the Atlantic Construction Company or the railroad company is not entirely free from doubt. I note that Dr. Kent says that the railroad company has not refused to pay the expenses of maintaining the quarantine, and I am inclined to the opinion that under the circumstances detailed in this letter that the company is liable. Dr. Kent says: 'The general manager of the railroad ordered them moved from the adjoining-county to Rhodhiss switch after he knew that smallpox had broken out among them.' And it also appears from his letter that the railroad company furnished provisions to the men, the cost of which was deducted from their wages. This assumption of control on the part of the railroad company might constitute it a householder... I beg to suggest that Dr. Kent consult with the railroad authorities with reference to the question. It is clear that the county of Caldwell is not liable, for the persons in quarantine had neither acquired a resi-dence (sic) nor settlement in that county. If the railroad company cannot be held responsible under the term 'householder', the resident county is responsible for the cost of main-taining (sic) the quarantine.

> Very respectfully,
> IvOBT. D GILMEH, (sic, Robert D. Gilmer)
> Attorney General [9]

Smallpox would wreak havoc in Rhodhiss on several occasions, but this outbreak of the disease was before the town was fully established, and it is the first documented case. The railroad workers who had contracted smallpox were found in their shanty cars by Dr. Kent. Living in a shanty had to be hard enough, let alone their being infected with smallpox. A shanty would have been an abode that was less than desirable and crudely built. The questions about the quarantine for these workers were sent to the state. The railroad had tried to add to the troubles of these workers by making them bear the cost of their quarantine. Their plight was hard enough, but added problems came from the railroad. However, the State's Attorney General, Robert D. Gilmer, said that the "householder" in this incident was the railroad. No additional information was given as to who took responsibility for these men. Workers during the early 1900s had few rights because labor laws had not been established yet. Because these employees were a minority, their treatment was not of concern to the employer.

TRESTLE IN CALDWELL COUNTY. CALDWELL COUNTY HERITAGE MUSEUM PHOTO.

TRESTLE IN CALDWELL COUNTY, CIRCA 1920. JOHN EDGAR HAAS PHOTO WITH PERMISSION FROM HIS GRANDDAUGHTER, ANITA M. HAAS.

The Cliffs provided peaceful afternoons for many passengers on the C&NW. In addition, the train was able to take on coal from the chutes. This area is presently overtaken by foliage and weeds. It is located on a hill below the trestle on the Burke side.

After Rhodhiss was established, one citizen, Leona Hunsucker, remembered riding the train and going to the Cliffs. She described boarding the train at Rhodhiss' second depot. Leona said:

> You went right across from Joe's old store. The cafe was in that vacant lot. There was a road going down there, and there was a depot, just right down at the railroad. The train stopped all the time for passengers. We'd go to Hickory on the train. We went to the Cliffs, they called it. It was somewhere between here and Hickory. They'd stop and

add water and all that, coal, and things. You'd stay there a little while till they got their supplies.[10]

2012 VIEW OF THE FORMER CLIFFS. EDDIE SIPES PHOTO.

The old store that she mentioned was once owned by Joe Church, and it is presently located at the intersection of Hickory and Caldwell streets. Exie Hand, who moved to Rhodhiss when she was 18 years old, remembered the location of the first depot which was at the Caldwell County mill in Rhodhiss. The old road before the 1972 bridge went between the old Company Store/post office and the Caldwell plant. Exie explained, "The depot was right over there (as she pointed toward the river). It was right down at the railroad there. I walked over there many and many and many a day. This house is right above the mill. The old depot was down here. A mail train came through here. A freight train always came up in here to the coal chute to the mills."[11] When the mill first began operation, it was understandable that the depot needed to be close to its location for the delivery of freight, mail, and commodities. Similarly, the mill company would need the rail for their shipments to customers. The depot was washed away in the 1916 flood along with other buildings, such as the livery stable.

Another longtime resident, Mattie Munday, described going down to the depot near the mill. She recalled, "You could get a ticket to ride the train. I think that it was a dime or a quarter, or something like that. You could go down there and hear that typing. Click, click, click. They would be getting messages, you know."[12] The railroad depot housed the telegraph office as per Mattie. Her recollection of the train's being near the mill is shared by Willard Herman, who explained:

THE DEPOT IN RHODHISS THAT WASHED AWAY IN THE 1916 FLOOD. JOHN EDGAR HAAS PHOTO, WITH PERMISSION FROM HIS GRANDDAUGHTER, ANITA M. HAAS.

Now it was there all during World War I because I went with my mother, and I was just old enough to kinda remember World War I, the end of it. Her brother left to go into service, and he left from the depot at Rhodhiss. I can remember her holding my hand, and her standing there crying when he got on the train. The depot was straight down the river about where what we call 'the little trestle.'

The main railroad goes up, and the road used to go from that old barn to the livery stable, and the road used to go to the bank of the river between the river and the railroad. With all that sidetrack it came up to Rhodhiss. Everything came in by rail.[13]

Thelma Church, another lifelong member of the community, said that the train provided entertainment in those days. "And everybody would go down there on Sunday to see who got off and who got on. People would catch the train to just go to Granite, and then they would walk back." Thelma added the depot's location, "You go straight down from our old store building, and down to the railroad track, and there was a depot there. There used to be an old cafe building across from our store. You could go right by it, and the depot was on down yonder. You could catch the train and go from here to Granite and to Hickory and Lenoir."[14] Thelma's description of the depot is in the same area that Leona described. People found great entertainment in either riding the train or simply going down to the depot to see who boarded or disembarked. Another train story involved two young people who fell in love in Rhodhiss. Earl and Fletcher Lutz shared their parents' adventure. Fletcher said, "Here's a story for you. My mother and dad got married right there at the railroad track in Rhodhiss at the mill. Then they got on the train and went to Hickory for their honeymoon."[15] Mr. and Mrs. William Arthur Lutz (Letha Camilla Julian Lutz) were married in 1914. They would return from their honeymoon to live in Rhodhiss for several years before moving to Hickory.

JOE CHURCH, MARIE MUNDAY,
AND ANOTHER PERSON ON
RAILROAD HAND CART.
REBECCA SIGMON PHOTO.

Eugene Walsh, a Rhodhiss native, explained how his Grandpa Tucker, a train engineer, would throw candy to Eugene when he would travel through Rhodhiss. He stated:

> Grandpa Tucker would always wave if we saw each other. He was very strict and always told us never to get close to the train when it was stopped or moving! On one occasion I remember that the train had stopped, and he tossed a Hersey candy from the window. We were not allowed to get too close to the train, and we never could try climbing on any part. That was his very strict order. There were times when I could hear the whistle, and l would take off running as fast as I could just to get near where I could wave at Grandpa, and he would always wave back. There were a few times when he brought coal. We would stand by and watch how they would park the coal cars to leave off track at the old waste house. Oh, I would be standing on the hillside near the Hambys' or Jordans' house, and near the river. That was the best place to be. Everybody knew when Tom Tucker was the engineer on that train once the whistle was blown! He just had a certain way that he would blow the whistle. I've heard this said by people who knew him in Rhodhiss, Granite Falls, and Hickory.[16]

Eugene, as a young lad in Rhodhiss, had great memories of growing up there and seeing his grandfather engineer the train.

Several young men also voiced their experience with the train, but it involved upsetting the train personnel. Paul Bumgarner, Finn Simmons, Ned Bean, Earl Lingle, and Fred Elmore all discussed their adventures. Fred Elmore stated: "Sometimes we would sneak off and go down to the railroad and soap the rails. You could really hear those train wheels then. We would sit in the woods and watch. The engineer would get out and look. He would leave the engine. They had to shovel dirt under them wheels to get it to go. And they would cuss. We boys sat up there in those trees laughing."[17] Putting soap on the rail was done to slow the train to catch a ride or to simply frustrate the engineer. Finn Simmons declared:

> The old depot down there used to be about where the Rhodhiss Town Garage is. It was a hobo ride. We were 16 or 17 years old, and we would jump that train. Sometimes we'd ride it to Hickory, and then ride it back. We would put soap on the track to slow it down, so we could catch it. Down there at the old depot they used to have to order whiskey out of South Carolina because they didn't have any here. North Carolina was dry. The fellas down there in the mills, the overseers and all 'em brothers that didn't want anybody to know about it; they'd order a big pile from South Carolina. Then they'd meet the train down here at the old depot. Some of the train's workers helped.[18]

Hoboing the train ensured a free ride when fare was not available. Finn was also able to add another element to the story involving alcohol's being transported to Rhodhiss. This was a common practice during Prohibition.

The hobo story was told numerous times. Earl Lingle added, "We used to take oxygen soap down there on Saturday morning and soap that track. Here come that old train up through there, and if he was going pretty fast and hit that soap, it would go choo, choo, choo, and we'd hop that thing."[19] Paul Bumgarner's experience was the same as Earl's, Finn's, and Fred's. Paul explained, "About the time that the train was ready to come by, we would go out there and soap the track. It would come chugging up through there, and about the time that it hit that soap, they would lose all their steam, and the engineers would stick their heads out cussing. Yeah, we would hobo that train."[20] Ned Bean talked about his times of jumping the train fare free; however, one of Ned's rides caused grief. Ned explained, "We always hoboed that train when we had to go to Granite. It would come up through there real slow. One friend Junior got on the train, and he caught the ladder. Junior rode above another guy, and Junior jumped off, and he knocked this guy under the train. It skinned his head and caused his head to come close to the wheel and cut his arm off. I was one box car behind them."[21] Paul Bumgarner added to Ned's story. "We first went to the gas station for help. Then we took him to the hospital. We put an old sheet over it (the arm). He had more guts than I have ever seen. He walked into the hospital, jumped up on that table in the emergency room. The doctor came in there, and he told the doctor to put it back on. The doctor said, 'I don't believe that I can do that, young man.' The doctor sewed him up."[22] These young men had an experience that stayed with them for the rest of their lives. They were able to discuss their friend's being maimed by the train with vivid details. Not all the train's history was enjoyable.

The train played a vital role in the history of Rhodhiss. It began when the trestle was completed for travelers to ride through the area. It is highly probable that John Rhodes' first trip to Rhodhiss was via train. One can only imagine Mr. Rhodes' voyage to the vast area of hills, rocks, and water that encompass the community. His first impressions must have been positive because he purchased land for the passageway of a textile village.

NOTES

1   Phifer, Edward William, Jr. *BURKE: The History of a North Carolina County, 1777-1920 with a Glimpse Beyond.* Burke County Historical Society: Morganton, NC, 2005, p. 263.

2   Bumgarner, Matthew C. Carolina & NW: *The Legacy of the Carolina & North-Western Railway.* Overmountain Press: Johnson City, TN, 1996 p. 13.

3   Bumgarner, p. 17.

4   Coleman, Alan. *Images of Rail: Railroads of North Carolina,* Arcadia Publishing, Charleston, SC, 2008, p.38.

5   "C&NW." Pamphlet by C&NW. 1905.

6   "C&NW."

7   Bumgarner, p. 167.

8   Bumgarner, p. 72.

9   "Public Documents of the State of North Carolina {1903 v.2}. Pp. 1610-1612. https://digital.ncdcr.gov/digital/collection/p249901coll22/id/137279/rec/1 Accessed 27 July 2020.

10   Hunsucker, Leona and Tom Ross. Personal Interview with Sherrie Hartsoe. Granite Falls, NC. 16 May 1988.

11   Hand, Arthur and Exie. Personal Interview with Sherrie Hartsoe. Rhodhiss, NC. 20 May 1988.

12   Munday, Mattie and Louise Keller. Personal Interviews with Sherrie Hartsoe. Rhodhiss, NC. 21 April 1988 and 12 May 1988.

13   Herman, Willard and Tom Ross. Personal Interview with Sherrie Hartsoe. Granite Falls, NC. 26 July 1988.

14   Church, Thelma. Personal Interview with Sherrie Hartsoe. Granite Falls, NC. 19 April 1988.

15   Lutz, Fletcher and Tom Ross. Personal Interview with Sherrie Hartsoe. Hickory, NC. 11 August 1988.

16   Walsh, Eugene. Email interview. 15 May 2022.

17   Elmore, Fred and Martha and Tom Ross. Personal Interview with Sherrie Hartsoe. Granite Falls, NC. 28 July 1988.

18   Simmons, Finn and Pawnee and Tom Ross. Personal Interview with Sherrie Hartsoe. Granite Falls, NC. 29 July 1988.

19   Lingle, Earl and Tom Ross. Personal Interview with Sherrie Hartsoe. Granite Falls, NC. 22 May 1988.

20   Bumgarner, Paul and Helen. Personal Interview with Sherrie Hartsoe. Rhodhiss, NC. 4 August 1988.

21   Bean, Ned and Elvie and Tom Ross. Personal Interview with Sherrie Hartsoe. Hickory, NC. 5 May 1988.

22   Bumgarner, Paul and Helen.

RHODHISS

CHAPTER 2

JOHN RHODES, GEORGE HISS, AND E.A. SMITH

At the turn of the twentieth century John Rhodes found himself in Caldwell and Burke counties seeking land to construct a textile mill. Mr. Rhodes chose this area on purpose because of access to the Catawba River so he could use water to power the machines. John Rhodes who had attended school at Table Rock Academy in Burke County moved to the area in 1900 from Cherryville where he had served as mayor; prior to that he had served as a justice of the peace and register of deeds in Gaston County, along with being the leader of the Temperance Party.[1] Carl Anderson and John Hawkins, who edited *The Heritage of Caldwell County, North Carolina* gave information about Rhodes' purchase of land in Caldwell County with the help of Norma Kirby, Rhodhiss Town Clerk for forty years: Rhodes "made his first purchase of fifty acres from J. M. Bernhardt on August 6, 1900. A few days later, thirty more acres from M. E. and Henry C. Mackie were bought, and within the week seventy-five more acres were added from J. D. Berry."[2] Not only did Mr. Rhodes have a vision for a mill in Caldwell County, but he also set his sights for expansion. He acquired over 200 acres of land in Burke County in June, September, and November of 1900. This land was obtained from James and S. E. Houck; Sarah Houck; G. W. and Blach Houck; W. W. and R. E. Aikin; J. W. and Ida Winkler; Robert and M. A. Sides; and Langdon and Sarah Ann Settlemyre, et al.[3]

Mr. Rhodes started his dream for a mill village on a grand scale. He and his son Caleb Junius had already started a mill in Cherryville, and they found a partner in George Hiss from Charlotte. The area was then named for both men, Rhodhiss. *The Heritage of Caldwell County, North Carolina* explained, "According to records kept by the early mill owners a capital outlay of $500,000 was required to build the mill.... community leaders were successful in having the town incorporated in 1903. Caleb H. Rhodes, son of John, was appointed to serve as the municipality's first mayor, along with his duties as postmaster."[4] The land was purchased in 1900, but the town was not incorporated until three years later. Rhodhiss was no different than any other textile town within the state. These villages were popping up throughout North Carolina. "By 1900 there were 177 mills, 90 percent of them located in the Piedmont," and "From 1900 to 1902 thirty-four mills were built in North Carolina alone."[5]

Many sources agree that 1903 was the incorporation year, but few give further details. A longtime citizen, Boyd Brown said in his 1988 interview, "The town was incorporated in 1903. I don't know the exact date. Caldwell side, only."[6] Mr. Brown, while sitting on his front porch in Burke County on Carolina Avenue pointed to Caldwell County as he made that statement. After further investigation the North Carolina Archives has a 1903 entry which reads, "Chapter 84: An act to incorporate the town of 'Rhodhiss' in the county of Caldwell. Page. 138."[7] Boyd Brown was correct in his assertion that Rhodhiss was incorporated only for the area of Caldwell County. After more research in the North Carolina Archives, the needed information was obtained. In 1919 the Burke County section was included in Rhodhiss' incorporation. The act reads: "Caldwell: To extend the corporate limits of the town of Rhodhiss, and extend the limits of that graded school."[8] Rhodhiss as it exists today was not fully incorporated until 1919. The possible reason is that Duke Power bought the mills for the water rights in 1919, and full incorporation was needed to complete this purchase.

Rhodes and Hiss' first steps in starting a mill village involved building a mill, a dam that would allow the machines to run by waterpower, and a company store that would provide necessities. According to *The News-Herald* in 1902, "The great stone dam of the Rhodhiss Manufacturing company (sic), on the Catawba river (sic) twelve miles below Morganton has been completed at a cost of about $60,000."[9] The dam, which was in the shape of a horseshoe, provided waterpower to run the machinery. Two gentlemen, Willard Herman and Alvis Kelley referred to it as the "coffey dam." Tom Ross suggested that it was really the cofferdam, and the colloquial name had become "coffey." Willard Herman, who lived in Rhodhiss for years, mentioned the first dam and his pride in his grandfather who helped supply the building materials for the mill. Willard stated:

> My granddaddy lived at Castle Bridge, and he moved lumber down. That's way back. Yeah, when they were building the mills, my daddy was born in 1885. The mill was being built around 1900. He sawed the pine columns that went up in the mill. The ones in the weave room were kind of square, but the ones in the card room and spinning room were more round. They floated them down the river. My daddy and my grandpa told this. They'd put them in the river up here about where Castle Bridge is or right above there. They would float them down the river, and they were building what we called the little Coffey dam (coffer) that they run the mills by. That's where they'd pull them out. It sat just below where the Duke Power Dam is now. This is the dam that they used for power for the mills. It wasn't a very high dam at all. They had huge paths in both mills that the water run in. It was built right across from what was known as Devil's Shoals.[10]

Devil's Shoals is an area above the dam and several interviewees mentioned it. Ned Bean, who was born in Rhodhiss, elaborated on how it received its name:

Did you ever hear that the place was called Devil's Shoals? I will tell you where you can see the old road. This was before the dam or anything. This was back when only a few settlers lived there. The depot was at Connelly Springs. People used to go there for the train, from Alexander, too. Old Man Pink Cline told me that they got their first cook stove in Connelly Springs on that road. Behind Nora Annas' house there is an old roadbed that goes through there. You can see where it goes into the lake. There's a spring there. That was all wild. Right there is where that road forded the river going onto Connelly Springs. It was known as Devil's Shoals. The reason it was known as Devil's Shoals is because people would camp there where the spring was, and they said that regardless of what kind of mess they left, it would be gone. So, they were really superstitious and started calling it Devil's Shoal. It was shallow. They could cross, and they made their road. You can see the old roadbed down in there.[11]

Ned mentioned behind Nora Annas' house. This would be toward the end of the present-day Duke Power Road. Only a few older citizens or their offspring were knowledgeable of such a place. However, Edward Phifer mentioned it in his book detailing the history of Burke County. Phifer explained, "Joseph Smith was operating a ferry in eastern Burke in 1846 at or near the Devil's Shoals."[12] After the bridge was built there was no longer a need to ford the river, float the logs, or use a ferry. Willard Herman elaborated more on Devil's Shoals with Tom Ross and me:

SH: Ned Bean said that Devil's Shoals was up behind Nora Annas' house.
TR: That's where it starts. Ned said that the old road starts behind Nora Annas' house up in there.
WH: Well, there used to be a road that went all up the river, you see, before the Duke Power Dam was built. It went all the way to the Connelly Springs Road. Now how I knew about Devil's Shoals part of it, Pink Cline told me about the first cook stove that they ever owned. It was shipped into Connelly Springs. He went with his dad when he was a small boy in a wagon to Connelly Springs to get it. That's where they forded the river at Devil Shoals. He even pointed out to me how he came into Rhodhiss, and Rhodhiss wasn't even built at that time. They came in and went up and went across.[13]

Devil's Shoals was a place near Rhodhiss known either for its haunting aspects or its passageway from one side of the Catawba River to the other before manmade structures were completed.

The Rhodhiss bridge was completed in 1904. The town minutes indicate that four men were hired to serve as marshals for the opening of the new steel bridge in June 1904. The *Lenoir News-Topic* wrote that 1,500 people attended the gala day in Rhodhiss. The bridge was "over 700 feet in length with two central spans of 225 feet each."[14] Edward Phifer who wrote about Devil's Shoals also mentioned the Rhodhiss bridge. Phifer noted, "In 1905 an iron bridge was erected at Rhodhiss by Burke and Caldwell Counties at a cost of $12,000. In late July of the following year, a cyclone 'lifted the bridge from its pillars and dropped it into the river.' The bridge was immediately rebuilt." [15] Phifer's date is a year off from other sources. A newspaper from the Raleigh area reported the cyclone, but the article indicated that the bridge was damaged in 1905 and built in 1904. The article stated:

> A cyclone Saturday afternoon at Rhodhiss, accompanied by hail and rain, did considerable damage to property, including growing crops, for some miles in its course. The greatest loss was the destruction of the new county bridge erected about a year ago by Burke and Caldwell counties at a cost of $12,000. The bridge is all down except its pillars, which represent one-third its cost. It is thought possibly some of the iron can be used for rebuilding. Under the State law the counties will have to rebuild the bridge at once. One corner of the Rhodhiss Mill, rather the upper part, was blown off, but there was little damage to machinery, said to be between one and two thousand dollars. Two or three cottages were damaged, but there was no loss of life so far reported. The crops near the mills in its course were considerably damaged. The gale crossed the Carolina and Northwestern Railroad just above the Cliffs, but did no damage to the track. The loss of the bridge will affect the surrounding county for the time being. The telephone connections are such at this writing that I am unable to get further details. [16]

The cyclone story was confirmed by Beth Kirby in her research paper for Appalachian State University. Beth's research was obtained from the files at Burlington Industries in 1982. In 1988 Ned Bean said that these files were burned when the Industrial Division of Burlington Industries was closed in late summer of 1983. In addition, I tried to obtain documents from the corporate office in Greensboro in 1988, and I was told that no information was available because they had destroyed their files. Regarding the cyclone, Beth wrote, "In 1905 severe destructive storms caused Rhodes and his son to sell out to other stockholders. Rhodes moved to Lincolnton to begin the construction of another mill on the South Fork River and C. J. Rhodes went to Kings Mountain to engage in another mill project." [17] In addition, Frank Cauble's biography of Rhodes indicated that he did indeed leave Rhodhiss in 1905. "On October 22, 1905 he transferred by letter from Bethany Evangelical Lutheran Church, Rhodhiss, N. C. to Emmanuel Evangelical Church, Lincolnton." [18] Another source added that upon the departure of John Rhodes and his son Caleb, their replacements were named. "Mr. Espey of New York is the new secretary and treasurer and Mr. Scruggs of Caroleen, N. C. is superintendent of the mill." [19] John Rhodes left Rhodhiss in the capable hands of his former business partner, George Hiss and stockholders. In reference to the building of the bridge, a former Rhodhiss Elementary School teacher during the 1930s, Mrs. Mary Jones, talked about her mother-in-law's meeting her father-in-law in Rhodhiss, and she alludes to the bridge. In the interview I spoke to Mary Jones about Bessie Hayes Jones:

> SH: I was told that Miss Bessie Hayes was a teacher at Rhodhiss.
> MJ: That's my mother-in-law.
> SH: Yes, the article says Miss Bessie Hayes, now Mrs. M. E. Jones. So, your mother-in-law

taught there?

MJ: Yeah, yeah. She didn't teach when she was married because she started having children.

SH: She met her husband down there though, right?

MJ: Yeah, yeah. He was building the bridge.

SH: I read that she met a man by the name of M. E. Jones, and she then became engaged to him. He was building a bridge across the Catawba River. That's your mother-in-law.

MJ: Yes, she is dead. She was Bessie Hayes. She did teach at Rhodhiss, and she would walk from out on the Dry Ponds Road. Their home was out in the country. She would cut through the woods some way. That must have been a couple of miles. She would walk down there, teach, and walk back home.

SH: Was she from Granite?

MJ: Yes.

SH: Was M. E. from Granite?

MJ: No, he was from Chatham, Virginia, but he was building bridges and dams.

SH: Did he decide to settle here?

MJ: After he met her, they settled here on Main Street where the old Ford garage was. (Downtown Granite Falls).

SH: Do you know how many years she taught there?

MJ: I don't believe that she taught after she married. Not that I know of anyway. Because she had Harold. Then two years later, she had Melvin. Well, she had eleven children. Papa was building dams, and she had the responsibility of looking after the children, tending to them. He would come for the weekend every couple of weeks. He didn't build a dam in Rhodhiss, but he built dams in Pilot Mountain. He did build the bridge in Rhodhiss.

SH: The first one lane bridge?

MJ: Yeah, I reckon. But mother met him. She said that she would walk right by his camp going to teach school and in the evenings. She passed his camp, and he was there. I started in Rhodhiss in '35, I think. Mother taught when they built the bridge.[20]

Bessie Hayes and M. E. Jones married after meeting in Rhodhiss. According to a 1941 newspaper article written by J. M. Laxton, a Rhodhiss principal:

In the fall of 1903, however, the first free school in Rhodhiss was provided at the expense of the Rhodhiss Mills company (sic). Miss Bessie Hayes taught this school which lasted for either seven or eight months. Classes were held in the present lodge hall until cold weather and then in a commissary building which stood on the Caldwell side of the Catawba River just a few years (sic) above the present bridge. Even though the commissary building was provided with a stove, heat was not always satisfactory because a stove pipe would give trouble occasionally. It was during such stove pipe trouble that a young man by the name of M. E. Jones, then engaged in constructing a bridge across the Catawba river (sic) nearby, proved very helpful to Miss Hayes. From that experience developed an acquaintance, then a romance, and marriage.[21]

The union of Bessie Hayes and M. E. Jones produced many children, but most people will recall their sons, Dr. M. E. Jones who practiced medicine and Melvin Jones, who owned several businesses in Granite Falls.

Ned Bean said that his aunt, Victoria "Vic" Mundy Bean, "pulled the handle on the first loom that ever started up in Rhodhiss."[22] This is possible since Manuel and Victoria Bean lived and worked in Rhodhiss. Victoria was born in 1886.[23] Child labor was very common during the early 1900s, and Rhodhiss was no exception. Two dates have been given as to the actual opening of the first plant. Many interviewees suggested 1902, but Anderson and Hawkins mention 1901.[24] The *Lenoir News Topic* does list it as one of the twelve textile plants in Caldwell County in 1902.[25] Furthermore, the *Lenoir News Topic* indicated in June 1902 that machinery was being placed in the Rhodhiss Mill to prepare for the opening.[26] Willard Herman explained some of the early years of the first mill through the eyes of Mr. Luther "Shorty" Elmore:

Fred Elmore's daddy told me about helping to carry the machinery up the steps in number one mill to the third floor because they didn't have the elevator yet to take anything. He said, "The spinning frames and all were tearing up the steps." They had to be put back together after putting the frames up there. He also talked about grading out the hill by the mill and company store. They used shovels and wheelbarrows. He said that the black people that helped just hummed the same song all the time. They would fill the wheelbarrows up and dump them, and here they would go again. This was in plant one.[27]

Hard labor was required to build the mill, dam, bridge, and company store. Singing or humming would make the job more endurable. Working to the rhythm of a song would also enhance productivity.

In 1912 new construction began on a second plant across the Catawba River from the Caldwell Plant. As per the *Lenoir News-Topic*, "A 15,000 spindle cotton mill opposite the present Rhodhiss Mills in Rhodhiss will be built soon. An estimated cost is $500,000. The contract says that work will be completed within six months."[28] The exact date of opening was in 1913 or 1914 depending on the source. As per Boyd Brown whose information had been accurate before, "The first bale of cotton that went through on this side (Burke) was in February 1913."[29] Boyd Brown proved to be very valuable with his information. Another source says 1914. *The Heritage of Burke County* indicates, "In 1914 E. A. Smith, John Rhodes, and George Hiss built another cotton mill, the E. A. Smith Manufacturing Company, on the Burke County side of the river."[30] Rhodhiss had two mills in the town by 1913 or 1914; however, information stated earlier indicated that Mr. Rhodes left Rhodhiss in 1905. *The News-Herald* reprinted an article from *The Charlotte News* which stated:

The *Charlotte News* of the 18th contains the following, which will be read with interest in this section: Mr. E. A. Smith of this city, and one of the most widely known manufacturers of the South, has purchased the entire holdings of the Charles A. Hiss estate of Baltimore, Md., in the Rhodhiss Mfg. Company, Rhodhiss, North

Carolina, and after having given most careful consideration to a large number of suggestive locations, has finally decided to locate his new mill, which will be built by the E. A. Smith Mfg. Company at Rhodhiss. The site selected for this mill is on the Burke county side of the Catawba river (sic). Rhodhiss is located in the foothills of the Blue Ridge Mountains, where the rhododendrons bloom in profusion, and the air ladened with mountain ozone and embraces parts of both Burke and Caldwell counties, the Catawba river (sic) being the dividing line, between the two counties. It is an incorporated town, the boundary of which embraces only the property of the Rhodhiss Mfg. Company. The town has the advantage of an excellent water power, and is supplied with adequate railroad facilities by the Carolina & North Western Railroad. Mr. Smith being desirous of locating his new mill on water power, has displayed his usual good judgment in locating at Rhodhiss. Co-operating with Mr. Smith in the Rhodhiss Manufacturing Company and the E. A. Smith Manufacturing Company will be: Mr. C. S. Child, of Philadelphia, Pa., and Mr. W. J. Fullerton, of Ridgewood, N. J., (who constitute the firm of Wilson & Bradbury, well known dry goods commission merchants of Philadelphia and New York). Mr. John M. Miller, Jr., vice president, the First National Bank, Richmond, Va. Mr. Robert Lassiter, president and treasurer, Middleburg Mills, Batesburg, S. C. and treasurer of the Oconee Mills Company, Westminster, S. C. Mr. Walter S. Taylor, secretary, the Rhodhiss Manufacturing Company, Rhodhiss, N. C. Mr. Geo. B. Hiss, president and treasurer, the Rhodhiss Manufacturing Company, whose residence is in this city. A meeting of those interested in the E. A. Smith Manufacturing Company was held in the private office of Mr. Robert Lassiter in this city this morning and the following organization was perfected: Directors: E. A. Smith, C. S. Child, John M. Miller, Jr., W. J. Fullerton, Robert Lassiter, Walter S. Taylor, Geo. B. Hiss. Officers: President and Treasurer-E. A. Smith. Vice President-C. S. Child. Secretary-Walter S. Taylor. Executive Committee: Geo. B. Hiss, chairman; E. A. Smith, C. S. Child. All of the officers and directors were present at the organization meeting. Building and machinery plans have been prepared by the Shand Engineering Company, of Columbia, S. C. The mill will be operated by water power, direct drive, and will be equipped with 15,000 spindles and 450 looms, making export and domestic sheetings and drills.[31]

Rhodhiss had quite a reputation throughout the state as a mill that was successful; therefore, the investors wanted to add another facility that would be profitable.

Many people from surrounding areas came to find employment in the town. Violet Curtis, who came to Rhodhiss in 1912, described the land where the Burke plant was constructed:

Before they ever built a bridge there, at number two mill the one on the Burke side, at the E. A. Smith Plant, Cec Settlemyre, the Settlemyres owned a house. They sold the land for plant two to be built. Cec showed me and Old Man Settlemyre, John who was Cec's daddy. Mr. Settlemyre used to pick him up and take him up about Granite and all. He was always showing me where the boat landing was and how they crossed the river. It was right about where the bridge is right now. That's where they kept their boat tied up. Now Old Man Lang Settlemyre sold all that land to them for the Rhodhiss Mill. There was a log cabin down where the cloth room was is where they were raised. He took the money that he got and built his house, and I've heard him tell it. He was an old man. The day that World War I ended, he walked and tried to go to the Company Store. His daughter come down to our house and stood on the back porch and watched him…. He died that night. My daddy went up there. They called him, and he went. You know, back then they didn't take them to the funeral home. They called people to come. He left that house. I've heard him say, 'Oh these hardwood floors.' It was a fine house then. He built it for $500. $500! He built it with the Rhodhiss money that he got for the land that he sold to the mill to be built. There were no houses on Middle Hill. It was a great big old house up there. I can remember when we first moved there, it sat kind of up in the square, a big old house.[32]

The Settlemyres owned the land that encompassed what was often referred to as Plant 2. John Rhodes' vision of mill companies on both sides of the river had now been realized; however, Rhodes and Hiss found another partner in E. A. Smith. Ned Bean and Tom Ross discussed the Smith Mill.

NB: The bricks for the plants were made down the river. Somewhere near the big trestle. Now E. A. Smith is the guy that built plant 2 in 1912 or 1913. He built Number 2 plant. Rhodes and Hiss built Number 1 plant. Then in 1912 Smith built Number 2 plant and started it up. Now all the houses on the Burke County side were his. He built those. Caldwell County side was Rhodhiss. Burke was called the Smith Mill.
TR: Yes, Smith Manufacturing Company. You know that safe that we had in the office said 'E. A. Smith Manufacturing Company' on it.[33]

Tom Ross and Ned Bean worked at Rhodhiss many years. Tom came to Rhodhiss when Pacific Mills bought the two plants. Even during the 1940s and 1950s the old E. A. Smith safe was still used. Willard Herman gave the reason for Smith's desire to establish a mill in this location, "Well, they operated the mills by waterpower. Both mills were operated by waterpower. That's why Mr. Smith built the one on the other side of the river so that he could use the same dam."[34] Mr. Smith left Rhodhiss in 1917, but he retained some ownership of Plant 2. "E. A. Smith has resigned the presidency of two manufacturing companies in North Carolina. One is located in Rhodhiss, and the other is in Paw Creek. George Hiss will replace him at Rhodhiss. Mr. Smith will move to the Phenix (sic) Manufacturing Company in Kings Mountain."[35] The two Rhodhiss plants were founded by John Rhodes, George Hiss, and E. A. Smith.

Like many textile entrepreneurs throughout the South, John Rhodes and George Hiss started a mill village. Their desire to do so resulted in the making of a town that has been in existence for over 120 years. Mr. Rhodes and Mr. Hiss brought their families with them when they moved to Rhodhiss. Earl Lutz, whose dad worked at the Company Store, was the first person to say that Dr. Voigt Cromer was born in Rhodhiss. Earl said that he liked to tell people that three good men came from Rhodhiss: Jerry Townsend, his co-worker at Bass Smith Funeral Home; Dr. Voigt Cromer; and himself.[36] John Rhodes' grandson, Voigt was born in Rhodhiss on July 31, 1906, and his parents were the Reverend Joseph Cromer and Lillie Mae Rhodes Cromer. Joseph Cromer was the minister at the Lutheran Church that was built in the Rhodhiss village. Voigt Cromer, too, went into the ministry as a Lutheran pastor, and he later held the longest running tenure as the President of Lenoir Rhyne University (1949-1967). As a matter of fact, the Cromer Center is named for him.[37] The book written for the 100-year anniversary of Lenoir Rhyne College, now University, says that Voigt was a "native of Rhodhiss."[38] In addition, Caleb Rhodes, John's son, later became the first postmaster and the first mayor for the town of Rhodhiss. Caleb married Minnie Ida Plonk Rhodes, and their son and grandson were well known doctors in Raleigh, North Carolina. One account read:

> In 1990, the Rhodes Family established the John Sloan and John Flint Distinguished Professorship for the UNC School of Medicine Department of Urology. Dr. John Sloan Rhodes graduated from UNC CH School of Medicine in 1927; Dr. John Flint Rhodes graduated from the UNC CH School of Medicine in 1962 and was second in his class. The two practiced urology in Raleigh, NC at a private practice that they began in 1970. The senior Dr. Rhodes retired from the practice in 1980. The Junior Dr. Rhodes continued practicing until his retirement in 2001, and he also served as associate clinical professor of urology at UNC CH School of Medicine.[39]

CROMER CENTER AT LENOIR RHYNE UNIVERSITY 2022. SHERRIE HARTSOE SIGMON PHOTO.

The Rhodes family obviously did well in their chosen professions and in aiding mankind. When the 1976 Bicentennial celebration was held in Rhodhiss, Voigt Cromer and John Rhodes represented the Rhodes family, and they served as guest speakers.

George B. Hiss did have an unsuccessful bid for Congress in 1902.[40] Ned Bean detailed more information about the Hiss family. "Well, you know when we had our Bicentennial in Rhodhiss, a Hiss from Connecticut came. Alger Hiss was related to the Hisses from Rhodhiss."[41] This story was told to me during the 1970s by Sinclair Deal at Granite Falls High School. Alger Hiss was convicted of perjury for lying during an investigation into accusations of his being a post-World War II spy; however, he was never convicted of espionage. He served five years and spent a great deal of time trying to clear his name.[42] More research was required for verification of the relationship between Alger and John Hiss. The University of North Carolina at Chapel Hill's Southern Oral History Program from 1977 provided that. In an interview with Margaret McDow MacDougall, she discussed her Uncle Robert Moore's involvement with Rhodhiss. Mr. Moore was the principal stockholder in the mills from 1919 to 1945. Ms. MacDougal stated:

> My uncle Rob Moore started working when he was thirteen to help to support his mother. He was a delightful person, you never would have known he hadn't had anything but a grade school education. A delightful gentleman if you ever saw one. And he worked his way up, and he became, I think it was president or owner of the Rhodhiss Cotton Mills. I think he must have had several. But Mr. Hiss was Alger Hiss's uncle. I think the mills were in Rhodhiss, North Carolina. I know they were not in Charlotte although Uncle Rob lived in Charlotte. I thought it was so funny about Mr. Hiss being Alger Hiss' uncle, because Uncle Rob was so reactionary.[43]

The Rhodes and the Hisses had prominent family members. In 1972 a *Hickory Daily Record* article said that Mr. Hiss' only living relative was a niece, Mrs. John P. Rabb.[44] Rhodhiss' unique name and history can be attributed to its founders, John Rhodes and George Hiss. The first mill later became known as the Hiss Mill since John Rhodes left in 1905. The old Hiss Mill burned in 2005, but the former employees and citizens remember it fondly.

North Carolina was full of textile mills during the twentieth century. Textiles provided jobs for people who were migrating to these areas from farms. The millhands went from tending the soil to tending machines.[45] North Carolina was built on textiles and tobacco, and the people who worked in either of these fields were hard, dedicated workers. John Rhodes and George Hiss founded Rhodhiss, but the millhands also deserve recognition for their work ethic.

JOHN M. RHODES, FOUNDER OF RHODHISS.
CARL HOLLAR PHOTO.

GEORGE B. HISS, FOUNDER OF RHODHISS.
CARL HOLLAR PHOTO.

EARLY 1900S OR BEFORE. SETTLEMYRE LAND. BUTLER MONTEITH PHOTO

A BURKE COUNTY CORNFIELD. LOOKING INTO CALDWELL COUNTY.
BUTLER MONTEITH PHOTO.

BURKE COUNTY LOOKING INTO CALDWELL COUNTY.
BUTLER MONTEITH PHOTO.

1902 HORSESHOE DAM. RHODHISS MANUFACTURING PHOTO.

THE MILLSAPS SISTERS AND A DOG AT HORSESHOE DAM. JOHN EDGAR HAAS PHOTO WITH
PERMISSION FROM HIS GRANDDAUGHTER, ANITA M. HAAS.

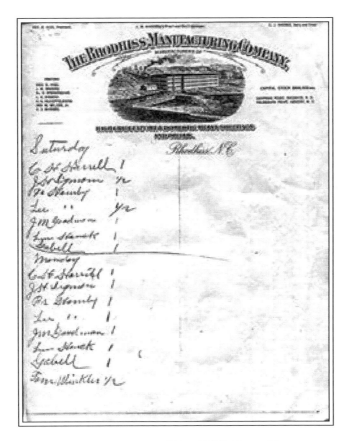

COMPANY STATIONERY FROM 1901-1905. FRED ELMORE PHOTO.

1908 POSTCARD OF RHODHISS. TOWN OF RHODHISS PHOTO

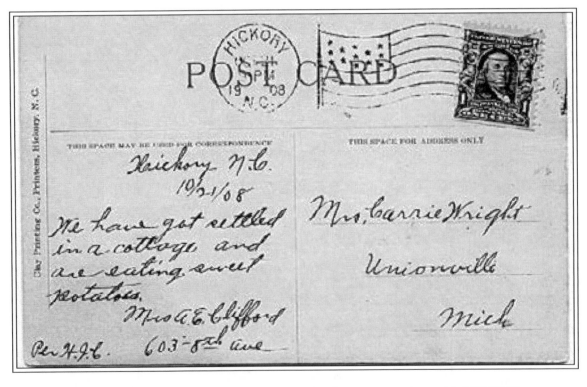

BACK SIDE OF RHODHISS POSTCARD WITH MESSAGE, DATE, AND ADDRESS.
TOWN OF RHODHISS PHOTO.

CIRCA 1910 RHODHISS WITH DAM. TOWN OF RHODHISS COPY.

AN EARLY BRIDGE IN RHODHISS, CIRCA 1910S. TOWN OF RHODHISS PHOTO.

THE STEEL BRIDGE CIRCA 1910S.

1912 CONSTRUCTION OF PLANT 2 IN BURKE COUNTY. HORSESHOE DAM IS VISIBLE AS WELL AS
THE BRIDGE THAT WASHED AWAY IN 1916. THE HOUSE ON CALDWELL SIDE WASHED AWAY, TOO.
RHODHISS MANUFACTURING PHOTO.

HORSESHOE DAM AND MILL. JOHN EDGAR HAAS PHOTO WITH PERMISSION FROM
HIS GRANDDAUGHTER, ANITA M. HAAS.

RAILROAD THAT WENT TO MILL. BRIDGE AND MILL COMPANY IN THE BACKGROUND. JOHN EDGAR
HAAS PHOTO WITH PERMISSION FROM HIS GRANDDAUGHTER, ANITA M. HAAS.

MILL DURING THE 1920S.

1924 HORSESHOE DAM. DUKE POWER PHOTO.

1924 HORSESHOE DAM. DUKE POWER PHOTO.

RHODHISS CALDWELL PLANT. DUKE POWER PHOTO.

Rhodhiss willows

CLOSER TO THE POWERHOUSE, FISHERMEN CAN BE DETECTED. DUKE POWER PHOTO.

IN 2005, PLANT 1 BURNED. TOWN OF RHODHISS PHOTO.

THE LENOIR NEWS-TOPIC COVERS THE 2005 PLANT 1 FIRE.
LENOIR NEWS-TOPIC PHOTO.

THE LENOIR NEWS-TOPIC GIVES MORE INFORMATION ON THE PLANT'S FIRE.
LENOIR NEWS-TOPIC PHOTO.

NOTES

1   Cauble, Frank. *Biography of John Melanchton Rhodes*. Hickory, N.C.: Lenoir Rhyne University Special Collections, 1975, p. 14.

2   Anderson, Carl and John O. Hawkins, editors. Written by Norma Kirby. "Rhodhiss." *The Heritage of Caldwell County, North Carolina*. Vol. I. 1983, pp. 181-182.

3   Burke County Online Records. http://burke.courtcompsys.com/burkeNC/. Book J2. Pages 580, 583, 283. Year 1900.
        Accessed 10 October 2019.

4   Anderson, p. 180.

5   Hall, Jacquelyn, et. al. *Like a Family: The Making of a Southern Cotton Mill World*. Chapel Hill, NC: The University of North Carolina Press, 1987, p. 26 and p. 107.

6   Brown, Boyd and Cora. Personal Interview with Sherrie Hartsoe. Rhodhiss, NC. 1 May 1988.

7   Private Laws of the State of North Carolina Passed by the General Assembly at Its Session Of. . . 1903." *North Carolina Digital Collections*. https://digital.ncdcr.gov/digital/collection/p249901coll22/id/215443/rec/6. Accessed 2 July 2021.

8   "Journal of the Senate of the General Assembly of the State of North Carolina 1919." North Carolina Digital Collections. https://digital.ncdcr.gov/digital/collection/p249901coll22/id/591809/rec/61. Accessed 3 April 2022.

9   *The News-Herald*. 20 February 1902. https://newspapers.digitalnc.org/lccn/sn84001806/1902-02-20/ed-1/seq-3/#words=Rhodhiss. Accessed 28 July 2022.

10   Herman, Willard and Tom Ross.

11   Bean, Ned and Elvie and Tom Ross.

12   Phifer, p. 180.

13   Herman, Willard and Tom Ross.

14   "Gala Day at Rhodhiss." *Lenoir News-Topic*. 10 June 1904, p. 2. https://newspapers.digitalnc.org/lccn/sn97064560/1904-06-10/ed-1/seq-2/#words=Rhodhiss. Accessed 28 July 2022.

15   Phifer, p. 181.

16   "Cyclone in Catawba." *The Caucasian*. 3 August 1905. Clinton, N. C. Edition 1, p. 1. https://newspapers.digitalnc.org/ lccn/sn91068245/1905-08-03/ed-1/seq-1/#words=Rhodhiss. Accessed 11 July 2022.

17   Kirby, Beth and Susan Robinson. *A History of the Rhodhiss Mills*. Spring 1982.

18   Cauble, p. 32.

19   *The News-Herald*. 21 September 1905. Vol. XXI. No. 24, p. 1. https://newspapers.digitalnc.org/lccn/sn84001806/1905-09-21/ed-1/seq-1/#words=Rhodhiss. Accessed 11 July 2022.

20   Jones, Mary. Personal Interview with Sherrie Hartsoe. Granite Falls, NC. 18 April 1988.

21   Laxton, J. M. "Rapid Progress at Rhodhiss." *Lenoir News-Topic*. September 1941. Reprinted for *Centennial of Caldwell County*, September 1941.

22   Bean, Ned and Elvie and Tom Ross.

23   "Bean, Victoria M." https://www.findagrave.com/memorial/82820127/victoria-e-bean.

24   Anderson, pp. 181-182.

25   "Textile Mills in Caldwell County." *Lenoir News-Topic*. 2 January 1902. Reprinted for *Centennial of Caldwell County*, September 1941.

26   *Lenoir News-Topic*. 13 June 1902, p. 3.https://newspapers.digitalnc.org/lccn/sn97064560/1902-06-13/ed-1/seq-3/#words=Rhodhiss. Accessed 28 July 2022.

27   Herman, Willard and Tom Ross.

28   "Contract to Build Big Cotton Mills Was Let in 1912." *Lenoir News-Topic*. 20 April 1912. Reprinted for *Centennial of Caldwell County*, September 1941.

29   Brown, Boyd and Cora.

30   Hildebran, Abbie Seals. "Rhodhiss." *The Heritage of Burke County.* Burke County Historical Society, 1981, p. 50/ section 27.

31   "Big New Mill At Rhodhiss." *The News-Herald.* 21 March 1912, p. 1. https://newspapers.digitalnc.org/lccn/ sn84001806/1912-03-21/ed-1/seq-2.pdf. Accessed 11 July 2022.

32   Curtis, Violet, Willard Herman, and Tom Ross. Personal Interview with Sherrie Hartsoe. Granite Falls, NC. 2 August 1988.

33   Bean, Ned and Elvie.

34   Herman, Willard and Tom Ross.

35   "Cotton Goods." *Women's Wear.* 27 June 1917. Vol. 14, Issue 149, p. 10.

36   Lutz, Earl. Personal Interview with Sherrie Hartsoe. Hickory, NC. 27 May 1988.

37   "History." North Carolina Lutheran Synod. https://www.nclutheran.org. Accessed 22 July 2019.

38   Norris, Jeff L. and Ellis G. Boatmon. *Fair State: A Centennial History of Lenoir-Rhyne College.* Brookfield, MO: Donning Company Publishers, 1990, p. 101.

39   "In Memoriam: Dr. J. Flint Rhodes of the UNC Urology 'John Sloan and John Flint Distinguished Professorship.'" UNC School of Medicine, Urology. www.med.unc.edu/urology/in-memoriam-dr-j-flint-rhodes-of-the-unc-urology- john-Sloan-john-flint-distinguished-professorship. Accessed 13 November 2019.

40   "George B. Hiss For Congress." *The Asheville Times.* 5 September 1902, p. 4.https://newspapers.digitalnc.org/lccn/ sn84020684/1902-09-05/ed-1/seq-4/#words=Rhodhiss. Accessed 28 July 2022.

41   Bean, Ned and Elvie and Tom Ross.

42   "Alger Hiss." https://www.fbi.gov/history/famous-cases/alger-hiss. Accessed 6 July 2022.

43   MacDougall, Margaret McDow. Interview. April 1977. Atlanta, Georgia. By Mary Fredrickson.Transcribed by Jean Houston for the Southern Oral History Program. Southern Historical Collection Wilson Library UNC CH, Chapel Hill, NC. Interview number G-0037 in the Southern Oral History Program Collection (#4007). pp. 33-34.

44   Greene, Nell. "Old Bridge To Become Rhodhiss History Soon." *Hickory Daily Record.* November 1972.

45   Hall, Jacquelyn, p. 3.

Chapter 3
Mill Company Rentals

Most employees in textile mills had previously tended the soil. These agrarian laborers had motivation, determination, and a strong work ethic. Lawrence Brady discussed his being in the field tending to the mules when Glenn Stephens came to ask him to work for the mill company. Lawrence told Stephens, "'I don't want a job. I'm satisfied with what I'm doing." Stephens kept pleading with him, and Lawrence agreed to help him for a few days. Forty-three years passed, and Lawrence was still there.[1] There were many stories like this. These workers came to town from nearby areas, and the mill company provided the necessary housing. Jacquelyn Hall states, "At the turn of the century 92 percent of southern textile families lived in villages owned by the men who gave them work....A typical village consisted of a superintendent's residence, a cluster of single-family dwellings, one or more frame churches, a modest schoolhouse, and a company store."[2] Katherine Townsend indicated that her dad, Mr. Decker, helped build the original houses in Rhodhiss.[3] The cost of building a house at the turn of the twentieth century is reflected by Butler Monteith's comment, "When the mill company built the houses, I believe, that they said that they were built for $400 a house."[4] In order to live in a mill house, someone in the family had to be employed with the mill company. Management liked to rent to large families ensuring that many workers would be available. Mill villages across the South provided housing for their employees, and Rhodhiss was no exception.

Not only was it a common practice for textile companies to offer houses, but they also provided pastureland for rent, sources of heat, and a company store. Ned Bean told me that his granddaddy sold lumber to the mill company to build the first houses.

NB: Yeah, my grandfather brought lumber from Cajah's Mountain, and he came down the road that is now covered by water. He brought lumber to build the houses and the mill. He would come down in the wintertime and work. He would go back and farm in the summer. In

1907 he moved down permanently and sold his farm.

SH: Maybe that's what Margie Hand Cowick was talking about. Her grandfather would ford the river bringing lumber across to build the mill houses.[5]

Building the mill, houses, company store, and a dam within the first two years had to be a daunting task for Rhodes and Hiss, but it was necessary for the success of the company. Village houses were built in Caldwell County in 1900, 1904, and 1914, and housing in Burke County was done in 1912, 1913, and 1935.[6] This information was available at the Burke plant until the summer of 1983, and then it was destroyed with the closing of the Burke County mill. Jacquelyn Hall indicates that an investigation of mill communities by the federal government in 1907-8 found "'all the affairs of the village and the conditions of all of the people are regulated entirely by the mill company. Practically speaking, the company owns everything and controls everything, and to a large extent controls everybody in the mill village.'"[7] The mill company did own the housing, the company, the store, and the school in Rhodhiss.

CIRCA 1929 MAE HILTON WITH HER DOLL AT HER MILL HOUSE HOME ON MIDDLE HILL. MAE HILTON YOUNT PHOTO.

The houses had four to seven rooms. The larger seven room houses were split between two families. The dwellings did not include inside bathrooms until Pacific Mills constructed them in the late 1940s. There were outhouses for their personal needs, and community wells provided water from which tenants carried water to their houses. In the 1920s they had spigots that were closer to each individual house. While sitting at her house on Walnut Drive, Exie Hand remembered the early days, "We had to carry water from that spring down yonder under the hill. Way down under that hill. We had to carry water from there for a long, long time. Then they put a pump in and put the pump out yonder near that yellow-looking tree. There was a well out there. When they put that pump in, they closed up the well."[8] Doughton Beshears, Butler Monteith, Tom Ross and Shelley Teague also discussed their renting houses from the mill company:

BM: I will tell you another thing that was good about the mill company. You could rent one of these four-room houses for fifty cents a week. A three-room house was forty cents a week. I believe that it was seventy-five for a seven-room house.

ST: Later, it went to 25 cents a room.

DB: I rented one of the newer houses right over here near the Methodist parsonage, and that cost me $1 a week.

TR: Was power furnished?

BM: Well, it was when we first got power. They only let power on one day a week in the daytime.

ST: There wasn't any water in the houses. Plumbing and water came with Pacific. They had a spigot out between houses, and we all shared the same spigot. At one time they had wells.

BM: The ladies did their ironing on Thursday afternoons. They turned the power on for them.

TR: I think that the spigot that you are talking about Mr. Massie Mullinax devised that system. Didn't he?

ST: I don't know who did it. Every house had an outhouse.

BM: When I was really small, all we had was wells. The house that I used to live in was right below the post office. I was just a small kid, and right across the street there was a well there. We had to go down there and draw water.

DB: Everybody had to draw water.

TR: They drew water from the back porch on this house.[9]

Tom Ross mentioned that water was on the back porch of his home. He lived at 202 Church Street. Electricity was not installed in the houses until 1926. Massie Mullinax came from Gastonia, and he was hired by the mill company to install electricity in the houses in 1923 according to his daughter, Pawnee Mullinax Simmons; however, Duke Power did not complete the project of providing electricity to the homes until after the hydroelectric plant was completed in 1925. According to Arthur and Jack Edwards and Edna Edwards Laney Stilwell, the superintendent's and plant manager's houses had running water from the early days. They said, "The Cobbs had an inside bathroom, as opposed to bathing in a horse tub."[10] Mr. H. C. Cobb was a superintendent during the 1920s and 1930s. He lived at the end of Church Street in a huge white house beside the present-day Church Street Baptist Church. Those days were hard for everyone, but some families had advantages. Bathing in an indoor tub would be a luxury compared to bathing in a horse trough outdoors.

DEWEY AND NORA ANNAS, FLORA ANNAS, A MOFFITT WOMAN, AND OTHER UNIDENTIFIED. HOUSES NOT UNDERPINNED AND ON STILTS, OUTHOUSE. CALDWELL STREET. JOANNE PROPST PHOTO.

The people who lived during the early 1900s did not have the advantages of electricity to cool their houses. The summer heat would have been oppressive. A 1904 newspaper article revealed the danger of summer storms. "At Rhodhiss mill Tuesday evening lightning set fire to one of the mill cottages. The hands turned out with buckets and after a lively fight subdued the fire before very much damage was done. Mr. Geo. B. Hiss came down that night and said that the storm was heavy and that there was a great deal of lightning. Mr. John Sigmon lived in the house that was damaged."[11] Many forces of nature would wreak havoc in Rhodhiss for years to come.

Staying warm in the houses was difficult because the houses were not underpinned. In a conversation among Violet Curtis, Willard Herman, and Tom Ross, they discussed how people lived during the first few decades of the twentieth century:

WH: I was telling them about how people kept pigs under the houses. Many older people told me about that. It must have been before my time because I don't remember it.

VC: I don't remember that either.

WH: I know that we did have between the water tank and where the Settlemyre house was, I guess, a dozen people had pigs and hogs in there.

VC: The houses weren't underpinned. That wind would blow. Back then we just had a linoleum rug. Sometimes that rug would blow up. There was no insulation.

WH: No underpinning until Pacific Mills bought it.

TR: How did they keep warm?

VC: I don't know.

WH: They didn't.

VC: We thought that we were warm.

TR: We'd freeze to death now.

VC: Oh, I know it. My daddy he would cut wood. Mr. Lowman, a man from out in the country, he'd come with stove wood to burn in the kitchen. He'd put in a big old chunk of pine to start his fire. Mr. Lowman would bring that wood for the whole winter. He kept us warm. We were never without wood.

TR: The mill company sold wood, too. Didn't they?

VC: Yeah. They sold wood. My daddy bought his from Mr. Lowman.[12]

During Rhodhiss' early years pigs were able to live under the houses because these dwellings did not have underpinning; however, that would cause sanitary problems, plus issues with heating. Those days were difficult ones for the people of Rhodhiss.

RHODHISS MILL VILLAGE IN THE 1920S SHOWING SUPERINTENDENT HILL. DUKE POWER PHOTO.

Gladys Barker who was born in 1904 talked about families helping each other cope during the hard days of no electricity and no running water. Gladys said, "People had more time then to visit and help each other. They helped each other can, and they took care of each other's children on wash day. We had to go to the well, draw the water and carry it. The wells weren't in the yards, but they were nearby. There were three big iron pots for washing: a wash pot, a rinse pot, and a bluing pot."[13] Wash day would have been a strenuous task because there were no modern conveniences. Indoor toilets were out of the question without running water. Matt Munday described the outhouses. "When the outhouse would get about full, they would move them somewhere else. They called them toilet pits."[14] With today's modern luxuries, it is difficult to imagine the perils of those days. In addition, electricity was turned on in the homes for only a short period of time. Exie Hand explained to me:

EH: Yeah. They cut off our power every night at 9:00, and we got power one day a week to iron.

SH: If they turned it off at 9:00, what time did they turn it back on?

EH: They turned it on before people got up the next morning, and they turned it off when it got daylight. When ironing day would come, you couldn't get enough power to heat the iron. It was so aggravating, and I got to where I'd wash early enough to get mine done before they cut it off at 9:00.

SH: So, you got to iron one day a week?

EH: Yeah. Unless you would iron before they cut it off at 9:00.

SH: Did you buy coal or wood from the company?

EH: Coal and wood both. I had a wood stove. Daddy hauled me most of my wood. You couldn't keep coal. You'd buy a ton of coal, and in two or three weeks, you didn't have any coal. One winter I bought eight tons. When they underpinned the houses, we got to locking it up, and we didn't even burn about 2 ½ tons of coal.[15]

RHODHISS VILLAGE. CALDWELL STREET. DUKE POWER PHOTO.

Exie's family was able to use less coal because the houses held heat better with underpinning, and the coal was locked up which prevented theft. The mill company provided all the utilities that were available for the time. Water was included in the rent. Coal or wood were bought at an extra expense. After 1926 electricity was provided with no expense to the renter. The citizens depended on the mill company for their survival.

JANUARY 21, 1965 — THE GRANITE FALLS PRESS

One cannot help being envious of Mr. and Mrs. C.F. Kirby's home at 54 Church Street Extension. Many improvements inside assure easy heating of that area most lived in during cold weather. In warm weather the entire home may be opened for good ventilation. Gallons and gallons of paint certainly have done wonders to the exterior. Mr. Kirby is in the process of rebuilding a wall and restoring a well-situated terrace high up overlooking the town of Rhodhiss and the Catawba River.

THIS WAS THE HOUSE FOR THE
SUPERINTENDENT AND HIS FAMILY. LATER
CHARLIE KIRBY AND HIS FAMILY LIVED
THERE. IT WAS ON BIRCH STREET. GRANITE
FALLS PRESS PHOTO.

In addition to renting mill houses, the mill company owned a hotel and a boarding house. Some people referred to both as boarding houses, but most referred to the one on Caldwell side as the "hotel," and the one on Burke side as "the boarding house." The hotel sat off Magnolia Street at the end of Oak Street. This area was referred to as "Hotel Hill." Matt Munday remembered, "There were two. They called one the hotel, and the other a boarding house. Don't you know that Mrs. Church run the hotel? She had all those girls. Joe Church's mother ran the hotel."[16] Lonie Smith verified that Mrs. Church ran the hotel. Lonie said, "Mrs. Church ran the hotel for a while, and yeah, Mrs. Sims used to run it, too."[17] After Mrs. Church ran the hotel, the Sims family took the job. Alvis Kelley explained, "Well, when we come here, the Simses ran the boarding house. A lot of people would stay there during the week, and on Friday go home at quitting time and come back on Sunday evening.

Yeah, I remember Mr. and Mrs. Sims. He was a big ole fellow."[18] Alvis referred to the Caldwell facility as the boarding house, but Leona Hunsucker called it both. "Mrs. Sims run the hotel. It was a nice hotel up on that hill. She ran a boarding house, and they boarded up there. They would come to church, the ones that just stayed here. Now some lived a way and could drive back and forth, but a lot of them, the young men just stayed, and they took part in the activities, church, and whatever public things that you had. They were nice."[19] There were various types of lodging provided by the mill company, a hotel, a boarding house, and houses. In a conversation among Hans and Katherine Townsend and Tom Ross they discussed the facility in Burke County.

TR: Kat, I never knew that the big house on the hill on the other side was a hotel or boarding house.

KT: Yeah, they tore it down and Jones Decker and his wife built a house there.

TR: That's on this side, Caldwell. I am talking about Burke.

HT: It was a boarding house at one time. Yeah, Charlie Kirby lived in it across the river for a long time. Then Charlie moved over here.[20]

This structure is a large house at the top of the hill in Burke County at the end of Shelby

Street. Doughton Beshears said that he had lived in the boarding house, and Tommie Rhea said that she had lived in the hotel at one time. Doughton lived there when he first arrived in town. Arthur Edwards said that he lived in the boarding house at one time, and his friend Palmer Franklin lived there at the same time. In addition to these dwellings provided by the mill company, several families opened their homes to boarders. Shelley Teague said that his family kept boarders in the big house on the hill that was known as the superintendent's house. It burned a few years ago, and it was on Birch Street in Caldwell County. Shelley explained, "Kurt Smith and his wife used to board with us down in the big house when we were down in there. We kept boarders. We also kept teachers. There were two teachers that stayed with us. That was a big ole house. They stayed upstairs and had their own room."[21] Not only did Shelley's family board people in the big superintendent house, but Thelma Church said that her mother took in boarders when her father died:

> Yeah, that's what they call Hotel Hill. You see Mrs. Sims run a boarding house there because people had to come from other places to work, and they had no transportation, so they would board and stay with you during the week and go home on the weekend. My mother kept boarders. That's the way that she made a living because she didn't draw Social Security. There wasn't Social Security in those days. And she kept a milk cow, and she kept chickens, and she made a garden.[22]

People were able to increase their incomes by boarding workers in the town. The need for extra money would allow them to meet their financial obligations.

A GLIMPSE OF THE HOTEL ON THE HILL. PICTURE TAKEN FROM THE DAM AREA.
SHERRIE HARTSOE SIGMON PHOTO.

Violet Curtis mentioned that her husband stayed with the Cloningers as a boarder before they married. She said that the Cloningers lived "on down the river."[23] Rhodhiss was such a thriving town that various forms of lodging were needed. Tom Ross told Katherine Townsend, "Kat, they told me that there was a woman that lived in Taylorsville who walked here to work in the spinning room. She walked here on Sunday evening, boarded here during the week, and walked back to Taylorsville at the end of the week."[24] This story was repeated many times throughout the interviews. Taylorsville is approximately twenty miles from Rhodhiss. People would work during the week in Rhodhiss and return to their former homes for the weekend. The hotel in Caldwell County ceased to exist after Pacific bought the mill company. Calvin Jones, Tom Ross, and I discussed the end of the hotel:

> SH: Calvin, when you came to town was the hotel still here? Up on the hill over here where the Deckers live now.
> CJ: I was trying to think.
> TR: Yeah, it was because I remember the talk of their repairing the porches. The porch was going to cost more than the house was worth. Twelve hundred dollars is what that porch was going to cost, so they decided to tear it down.
> CJ: Yes, I remember Hotel Hill.[25]

According to Tom Ross, repairing the hotel was not cost effective, and it was torn down. After it was removed, a mobile home was placed there that housed the principal of Rhodhiss School. I recall that Mr. and Mrs. Parker lived there when I was quite young. Then when I entered elementary school Mr. and Mrs. Doug Tolbert lived in a mobile home where the present post office sits on Church Street. Mr. Tolbert was the principal of Rhodhiss School during that time.

LAND DEED INFORMATION FOR HOTEL.
EDDIE SIPES PHOTOCOPY.

In addition to rental houses the mill company also leased pastureland for the employees. The Edwards family said that there was a pasture behind the Baptist Church that was kept by the mill company.[26] Fred Elmore discussed two areas where cows were allowed to graze:

> We raised cows. Everybody had a cow. One time up on the hill where the Deals live now that was one big whole field. It was beautiful because everybody raised their cows up there. In the spring of the year those Shasta daisies bloomed. That field was

white with daisies. In the summertime by 7:00 that whole field would be full of kids grazing their cows. When we crossed the bridge and went straight up the holler behind Charlie Kirby's house to go to school, that was all cow pasture.[27]

The area in Burke County where the Deals lived is presently on Jones Drive. The pastureland behind Charlie Kirby's house would most probably be the Walnut Drive area in Caldwell County. Since most of the employees had previously lived on farms, the mill company wanted to provide an area where they could keep their farm animals.

Violet Curtis and Willard Herman discussed the problems faced by both the Earley and the Curtis families while grazing cows in Rhodhiss:

WH: It cost twenty-five cents a month to keep a cow in the barn.

VC: My boys used to keep the cows. For fifty cents a week they'd take cows, graze them, and take care of them down the river there. I remember that. They finally built a pasture there on Strawberry to put their cows in. We had two or three cows to tend to. Joe Bill and all of them milked the cows in the morning. Down the road they'd go. One of my boys would ride the cow, and he told their daddy about it, and he got after him.

WH: Tell you a little story about grazing the cows. This was back before Duke Power dam was built. Ruth and Grady had the cow down grazing her by the river. It was above where the coffey (coffer) dam used to be. There was quicksand there. The cow got in it and mired up all the way up to her stomach. Well, Mr. Earley was in the store. Gene Glass was a young boy, a couple of years older than my wife Ruth. She didn't know what to do, so she went up and told her mother, and mother told her to go to the store to get her daddy. There wasn't anybody in the store when she went over there. She wouldn't tell Gene what the problem was. She just told him to tell daddy to come home. He was delivering groceries in the village somewhere. He came riding up on his horse scared to death because he was afraid that something happened to one of the children. He was about to give Ruth a spanking after he found out. She was so embarrassed. She was a pretty good size girl. She wouldn't tell Gene, you know. Gene told him, 'Mr. Earley, they want you home right quick. I don't know what the trouble is.' That is what it was, so he got the cow.

VC: We were always afraid that something might happen to one of them grazing cows. One time a cow swam out in the river. Charles told Betty to run home and tell me that the cow was in the river. He knew that he could swim. All of them could swim like ducks. He said that he did that because he wanted to take off his clothes so he could swim in the river and go get the cow. He had to pull the cow back out of the river. Down the road I went with Betty. Here came Charles around the curve with the cow. I said, 'Betty, what did you tell me?' Charles said, 'Ah, mama. I knew that I could get her out. I wanted her to get away from me so I could get my clothes off and swim to get her. I didn't want to go in with my clothes on.'[28]

The mill company provided various areas for people to care for their cows. Many children were the ones responsible for this task. During those days children grew up fast, and chores were a daily routine. They helped the family by carrying their own weight. Pawnee Mullinax Simmons told the story of the pasture catching fire:

> I remember that I was about 7 years old, and we still lived over in Burke. When we first came to Rhodhiss, we lived in Burke. A lot of people had their own cows or chickens. Somehow the field where the cows were grazing caught fire. Talk about being scared. I can't recall a lot of those things, but I recall some. Talking about screaming, we did. Mama and Effie Kirby went up there and got buckets of water. That was the biggest fire that I ever saw.[29]

Again, there were many problems that could arise with the grazing of cattle, whether it be the pasture catching on fire, a cow going out into the river, or a cow getting caught in sinking sand.

Fred Elmore and Frank Byars discussed cattle grazing near the river. They talked about the child's responsibility:

> FB: Well, we used to graze the cows. Everybody had a cow back in those days. It was down the river on the other side. My job was to go down and graze the cows all day. These thunderstorms would come up. The kids would run out to round up the cows to take them to this rundown barn. As quick as it came up, I would head to the barn. Of course, I would be dry, and the other kids would be drenched. I would have to fight the kids because they were mad at me. My cow would follow the other cows, and I didn't get wet at all.
>
> FE: Like Frank said everybody had a cow. And the kids had to graze them. Well, each fellow had his own cow.
>
> FB: The mill company did have a cow shed.
>
> FE: After Number 2 was built, they made cow pastures for people to put their cows in.
>
> FB: Number 2 mill had just been built for two or three years at the time that I am talking about. [30]

The company was in the rental business for several reasons. They wanted to keep their employees happy and have them live locally. In addition, they wanted the workers to stay in town and not seek employment elsewhere. Lastly, the mill company was making money by renting homes, pastureland, and barns.

The mill company owned the mill, the dam, the Company Store, the houses, the pastures, and everything else in the town. The employees rented homes and grazing areas. They did own their livestock, but the millhands retained possession of little other property. Even with their hard work and dedication, the millhands were not privileged to own real estate.

1940S, HOUSES AND OUTHOUSE. PACIFIC MILLS PHOTO.

NOTES

1   Brady, Lawrence and Nancy and Tom Ross. Personal Interview with Sherrie Hartsoe. Hickory, NC. 3 May 1988.

2   Hall, Jacquelyn, et. al. *Like a Family*, p. 114.

3   Townsend, Hans and Katherine and Tom Ross. Personal Interview with Sherrie Hartsoe. Granite Falls, NC. 28 April 1988.

4   Beshears, Doughton, Butler Monteith, Tom Ross, and Shelley Teague. Personal Interview with Sherrie Hartsoe. Rhodhiss, NC. 20 April 1988.

5   Bean, Ned and Elvie and Tom Ross.

6   Kirby, Beth.

7   Hall, *Like a Family*, p. 114.

8   Hand, Arthur and Exie.

9   Beshears, Monteith, Ross, Teague.

10   Edwards, Arthur, Jack Edwards, Edna Edwards Laney Stilwell, and Tom Ross. Personal Interview with Sherrie Hartsoe. Rhodhiss, NC. 22 July 1988.

11   "Catawba." *The News-Herald*. 23 June 1904. Vol. XX. No. 12, p. 1. https://newspapers.digitalnc.org/lccn/sn84001806/1904-06-23/ed-1/seq-1/#words=Rhodhiss.

12   Curtis, Violet, Willard Herman, and Tom Ross.

13   Barker, Gladys. Personal Interview with Sherrie Hartsoe. Rhodhiss, NC. 2 May 1988.

14   Munday, Matt and Louise Keller.

15   Hand, Arthur and Exie.

16   Munday, Matt and Louise Keller.

17   Smith, Lonie and Boyce and Mildred Hartsoe. Personal Interview with Sherrie Hartsoe. Granite Falls, NC. 20 November 1988.

18   Kelley, Alvis and Precious and Tom Ross. Personal Interview with Sherrie Hartsoe. Granite Falls, NC. 10 May 1988.

19   Hunsucker, Leona and Tom Ross.

20   Townsend, Hans and Katherine, Tom Ross.

21   Beshears, Monteith, Ross, Teague.

22   Church, Thelma.

23   Curtis, Violet, Willard Herman, Tom Ross.

24   Townsend, Hans and Katherine.

25   Jones, Calvin and Tom Ross. Personal Interview with Sherrie Hartsoe. Rhodhiss, NC. 26 May 1988.

26   Edwards, Arthur, Jack Edwards, Edna Edwards Laney Stilwell, and Tom Ross.

27   Elmore, Fred and Martha and Tom Ross.

28   Curtis, Herman, Ross.

29   Simmons, Finn and Pawnee and Tom Ross.

30   Byars, Frank and Jo, Fred and Martha Elmore, and Tom Ross. Personal Interview with Sherrie Hartsoe. Granite Falls, NC. 1 May 1989.

CHAPTER 4
THE COMPANY STORE AND OTHER MERCANTILE

For Rhodhiss to thrive the mill company provided a store where the town's residents could shop for all their necessities. The Company Store was a given in mill villages throughout the South. Rhodhiss' Company Store was the hub of all the activity within the town. Locals could either shop in person or place orders for delivery. Most of the interviewees shopped there at different times; however, some shopped at other businesses that were nearby. Some of the local stores were owned by various people, such as Joe and Thelma Church, Mr. Icard, Berry and Ethel Annas, Nate Monteith, Mr. Lutz, Will Branch, Mr. Killian, Mr. Stephens, Mr. Pritchard, Pappy Church, Everett Teague, Ann and June Austin, Mart Wilson, the Stephenses, and the Knoxes. Even though it was a small town, Rhodhiss had the Company Store within the city limits and various other businesses outside the village.

The Company Store started when the first plant opened in 1902. From all indications the mill company leased it to various people, and these store owners stocked it with their own merchandise. An article found at the North Carolina State University Hunt Library indicated that a store burned in Rhodhiss in 1914; however, the information was not validated by the interviewees. *Women's Wear* stated, "The store building owned by Marvin Starnes burned in Rhodhiss, NC. A loss of $8,000 to the building and there was no insurance. The general store of H. W. Price occupied the building and there was a loss of $6,000 in merchandise with insurance covering $4,000."[1] The first known lease holder mentioned in interviews was Wade Shuford. Both Earl Lutz and his brother Fletcher mentioned that their dad worked for Mr. Shuford. Fletcher said, "My dad worked at the old Company Store when Wade Shuford owned it. Dad looked after caskets upstairs."[2] Wade Shuford was also confirmed by Willard Herman and Violet Curtis:

WH: The first person that I remember running it was Wade Shuford.
VC: Yeah.

WH: Do you remember who operated it before him?

VC: That's the one when we came to Rhodhiss.

WH: I know that your daddy, Mr. Earley, worked for Wade Shuford in the store there, along with Ellis Glass, Horace Rector, Claude Rector, and Astor Peeler. They did a lot of business because everybody that lived in Rhodhiss went there.

VC: That is the only store that there was. We called it the Company Store.[3]

According to the town minutes Wade Shuford still held possession of the store in 1922. In the early years Rhodhiss Manufacturing Company issued a coin for payment to the employees that could be used only in the Company Store. It is unclear how long this coin was used, but according to Willard Herman it was called the "doogaloo," which is the same term used for the currency at Henry River Mills which is another village about seven miles from Rhodhiss.[4] Willard explained, "Yeah. Now, I can't remember anything about it, but they said that at one time they had this doogaloo system. They would issue you so much in advance, and you could spend it. Just like money. They took that out of your wages. I don't know a lot about that."[5] Mill companies all over the South issued their own type of coins to make sure that the employees were buying from the Company Store and no other merchants. The money needed to stay in the owners' pockets.

MILL COMPANY CURRENCY, THE DOOGALOO. WAYNE CLINE PHOTO.

MILL COMPANY DOOGALOO. WAYNE CLINE PHOTO.

The Rhodhiss Company Store carried a large array of items according to many citizens. Thelma Church talked about her dad, Will Branch, working at the Company Store as a butcher. Thelma added, "That used to be the Company Store. Wade Shuford ran it. He sold caskets, cloth, and all kinds of things. Well, I think that he individually owned it, but the company rented him the building. He sold all kinds of groceries, clothes, towels, and shoes, and he sold furniture."[6] Butler Monteith and Shelley

Teague agreed that the company leased the store, and that the store sold caskets.[7] Matt Munday and Louise Keller were able to tell more items that were sold at the Company Store, and Louise said that her daddy delivered groceries when another man owned the store.

> MM: Yeah, they sold shoes, hats, and cloth. About anything that you got, you got there. Men's shirts.
> LK: Daddy worked for them for years. He delivered groceries.
> SH: Yes, that's right. Tom Ross told me yesterday that Raym Munday delivered groceries for the Glasses.
> LK: See Glass ran that store.
> MM: Well, he wasn't the first one.
> LK: Well, I don't remember anybody before that.
> MM: Well, I do, but I can't remember their name, and they had a girl named Virginia, and that is who Virginia Hollar is named after. Oh, Ballengee was his name.
> LK: I can't remember that.
> MM: The post office was down there in that building. The store. The first pair of nylon panties that I ever bought was in that store. I paid $1.50 for them. I remember that just so good. Brought them home and there was one of my husband's aunts and her husband here. They had one daughter, and she saw them and said, 'Daddy, I got to have a pair.' We went down there and got her a pair. Had elastic in them with lace. I can remember them. Wade Shuford run the store. Shuford ran it; then Ballengee. I used to walk up there for fun.[8]

The Company Store was the place for commerce and entertainment. Many people talked about just sitting on the front steps, drinking a soft drink, and watching the town's citizens enter and exit. Matt Munday's first personal undergarments were purchased there. Gladys Barker added more items that were sold at the store:

> They sold shoes, cloth; it was the only place to buy things. Once in a while, you might make it to Hickory to shop. During the 1920s they might take the bus for fifteen cents to Hickory. They called it the Jitney. The Company Store was also a gathering place on Saturday afternoons. I bought my first pair of high-top boots there. Some had laces, and some had buttons. My dad would sew our shoes with leather and tacks that he bought at the Company Store while I held the lantern.[9]

Gladys was able to add more about the entertainment the store provided on Saturday afternoons. The Town Minutes indicate that Mr. Shuford was in control of the store in 1922, but in 1923 it is listed in the minutes as Homer Ballengee's store.[10]

THIS BUILDING HOUSED THE COMPANY STORE AND POST OFFICE AS WELL AS OFFICES. EARLY
1900S. RHODHISS MANUFACTURING PHOTO.

The Edwards family (Arthur "Ott," Edna, and Jack) gave details about the store, too. Jack said that his dad would send him down to the store to tell them to come see the eggs for purchase. Jack added that vaccinations were administered there, and oftentimes children could be heard screaming. Ott remembered that the store sold medicines, soap, and salve. Edna stated:

> I have heard Dad (Finley Edwards) say that Grandma Edwards knew everybody and their needs, even if they were sick. Dad said that she tended to everybody's business on this side of the river (Caldwell). She was like that. If people needed anything, Grandma was there. She was a social worker. She went down here to the store and told Mr. Ballengee or Mr. Glass that people needed food. She would tell them that this here family has to have this now; they need food because of the children.[11]

Edna described her grandmother as a compassionate woman who made sure that children's needs were met. The owners of the Company Store were asked to help starving families. Leona Hunsucker talked to Tom Ross and me about Mr. Ballengee.

> LH: The post office was on one side of the Company Store. Lawd, that woman from Morganton was the postmaster. Mr. Ballengee run the store. He was a big old man.
> TR: That was before the Glasses then.
> LH: Yeah, that was before the Glasses.
> TR: How do you spell that name?

LH: B-A-L-L-E-N-G-E-E

LH: Virginia was their daughter's name. What was his? I haven't thought of him in so long. He owned the store. You know they rented it. He owned everything in there. It was a big store. Real nice, about like Winn Dixie, but not quite as big.[12]

Ellis Glass took over the Company Store from Mr. Ballengee; however, Finn Simmons and Willard Herman confirmed that Mr. Glass owned his own store prior to going to work at the Company Store. Finn explained the location of the original Glass Store to Tom Ross and me:

FS: You know that Ballengee had the Company Store down there. Ellis Glass owned a store up there, you know, about where Deal lives now. Right out that ridge there he had a store.

TR: Sherrie, are you hearing Finn? Where Richard Deal lives now right out the ridge from there he says the Glasses started a store.

SH: I didn't know that.

FS: Ellis Glass bought Ballengee out.

SH: But he started out on Dogwood Drive area?

FS: Yeah. Well, the building used to be where you went right up there and turned around, right up in there. Where Calvin Jones lives now. That was a curve where you turn back down in there to go to Henry Smith's. They built those new houses up in there where Calvin lives.[13]

Finn was talking about the present Dogwood and Jones drives. Ellis Glass was a fixture in Rhodhiss from the early days. According to town records he was appointed to oversee voting registers during a 1909 election.[14] In addition, an article in *The News-Herald* revealed that fire destroyed the store and stock of Ellis Glass in 1916.[15] This would account for Ellis Glass' starting to work at the Company Store.

Willard Herman and Violet Curtis in a joint interview were the first people to tell Tom Ross and me that no other store was allowed within the town's limits for fear of competing with the Company Store. Their story follows:

WH: Up on the hill, of course you can't remember, Pappy and Mammy Church ran a store up there, you know. Mart Wilson run one up there at one time. Anyway, Ellis' first store sat up on the hill just going toward Valdese just to the left of where Arlie Church lives now. It was at the top of the hill. It was a wooden weatherboard building.

SH: Finn said out by Calvin's though, didn't he?

TR: I guess that he was talking about Calvin's direction. Up where Richard Deal lives now.

WH: It was right close to, but out from Richard's place. That was all woods back then. Ellis Glass ran it at one time. Mart Wilson ran it at one time. Walt Icard was in it at one time.

TR: The Company Store was it going at the time?

WH: Yes, these were just small stores that were right outside of Rhodhiss city limits at the time. You couldn't have another store within Rhodhiss' city limits.

SH: Ohhhh!

VC: Because of the Company Store.

WH: It couldn't be in the city limits.

VC: That was the store where you bought clothing and everything.

WH: Ellis Glass took it over.

TR: Obviously, the Company Store must have had a good business at that time.

WH: Oh, it did.

TR: It must have made money.

WH: Tom, people couldn't go anywhere else. They bought their clothes, furnishings, groceries, and everything else there. If you went to Granite, you had to walk or take the train.

TR: They sold on credit, too, I guess.[16]

The mill company wanted to make sure that the Company Store was profitable. First, they required that the doogaloo money was used, and then they would not let anyone else have a store within the city limit that could interfere with their business. Most of the stores did hold accounts for their customers; however, several people elaborated that their wages were diminished because the mill company deducted from their pay what they owed the Company Store. Yes, they sold on credit, but they made sure that their money was collected before the employee was paid.

A lot of people talked about how well they were treated in the stores, whether it be the Company Store or one owned by someone outside of Rhodhiss. Katherine Townsend was pleased with the Glass family and their running the mill's store. In her conversation with Tom Ross and me, she stated:

TR: The Company Store, Joe Church's store, and Annas' store put out a lot of groceries.

KT: Gene and Buddy Glass took orders and delivered as did Joe Church and the Annases. We traded with the Glasses for years. You know back when food was rationed, there weren't a lot of bananas and chewing gum. Whenever we ordered our groceries, if Gene Glass had any bananas or chewing gum, he would put them in the bags. We couldn't order them. He was a fine man. They were certainly fine people. They treated everybody alike.

KT: I bought Kay's first bra there. I was at the Granite Drug one day and Kay whispered to me, 'Kat, I still have that bra that you bought me.' She was tickled to death when I first gave it to her, but she was so shy about it.

TR: Gene carried just about everything down there. I remember shoes. He had a big supply of shoes.

SH: Now, he just rented that building, right? He had his own company though.

KT: I think that his daddy was the first to have it. Ellis Glass was his daddy. Ellis got disabled to work, and his sons, Gene and Buddy, took over.[17]

The Glass family maintained a store in Rhodhiss for many years. They moved to the building that housed the post office and mill company offices in 1928. They stayed there until the late 1950s or early 1960s, and they then moved to the location beside the old Rhodhiss Town office building on Burke Street in Burke County.

Tom Ross and I also talked to Fletcher Lutz about his dad's working in 1915 at the Company Store. Fletcher explained:

TR: Who else was working in the store with your dad?

FL: To tell you the truth, I don't remember.

SH: Will Branch worked down there.

FL: That is correct.

TR: Did Wade Shuford stay out at the store any on the weekend or any other time?

FL: Yes. He stayed at the store just about all the time.

TR: So many people know about Wade Shuford and the store. Most people remember him for the textile and banking business. The store must have had tremendous business.

FL: It had all the business. Some people from Granite Falls even came down there.

TR: Later they took orders by phone. They delivered the groceries.

FL: They went out and took orders every day. You knew who your customers were. They filled it and delivered it.

TR: They were doing that when I came in '46. Glass was doing that.

FL: Ellis Glass.

TR: Yes. He, Gene, and Buddy. Ellis must have made some money there.

FL: Evidently, he did. There is a lot of history around Rhodhiss. You just have to find the right people to dig it out.

TR: That is what we are doing.[18]

Ellis, Gene, and Buddy Glass were proprietors of the Company Store for many years. My mother, Mildred Hartsoe, often talked about living on Catawba Avenue when she and daddy first moved to Rhodhiss. Mama mentioned that Zollie Hamby would take his boat across the river to Glasses' Store to purchase groceries. He would put them in his boat and come back across the river. The Company Store provided many necessities for the mill people.

There were many other mercantile facilities outside the city limits. Another store belonged to Joe and Thelma Church, and it was in Caldwell County at the intersection of Hickory and Caldwell streets. For years this area was dubbed "No Man's Land." It was neither in Granite Falls nor Rhodhiss, but during the early 1970s it was annexed by Granite Falls. Thelma Branch Church talked about her dad, Will Branch, owning the store at the corner of Hickory and Caldwell streets. Thelma said, "My Grandpa Icard owned a lot of land from Annas' Store to clear down here to Rhodhiss on both sides of the road. He owned it all. He had a building down there, and my daddy rented it. He ran the grocery store till he died from the flu in 1918. Then they sold it out."[19] Thelma's grandfather, John Icard, owned all the land from this store on both sides of the road to Duke Power Road. Many people ran business out of this building before Joe Church did. Matt Munday and Louise Keller gave their thoughts to me:

MM: I went to Rockett's Store, too.

SH: Now, I don't know about Rockett's Store. Where was it?

MM: There where the furniture store is. It was beside it. Rockett's Store.

SH: Where Joe Church's Store was?

MM: Yeah, then Walt Icard and Mr. Branch ran the store.

SH: So, it was the Rockett's store first, and then the Icard and Branch Store?

MM: As far as I can remember, it was the Rocketts first. After Mr. Branch died, the Icards ran it because they owned the building. Then I don't remember who took it after that.

SH: Did Thelma and Joe take over then?

LK: No, Glenn ran it before them.

SH: Glenn?

LK: Glenn Church, Joe's brother.[20]

Matt and her daughter Louise were able to discuss the building where Joe Church had his store. They recalled previous owners prior to Joe. Willard Herman and Violet Curtis told their memories of this store:

WH: Talking about Joe Church's store. It used to be an old wooden building that sat there, and they had rooms upstairs that they rented. Downstairs was a grocery store. Gus Rockett run the store in the early years. He married one of the Teague girls. Walt Icard ran it, too. That building was built by, I am assuming, Old Man John Icard. It was on his property. His oldest boy Robert owned it. Rob moved over to Longview and built a building over there to run a grocery store. Later he rented it to a Walsh, and he ran a grocery store.

VC: Yeah, Icards owned that.

WH: He owned the building and Robert Icard lived with part of his family in that house right beside of it. That's where Thelma and Joe's store building is now. There used to be a weatherboard house, pretty good size house.

VC: Yeah, Rob moved to Hickory.

WH: They moved to west Hickory.

VC: I traded there because we moved to Hickory at one time. In Long View down there. Robert Icard run a store.

WH: There were two stores there together. Will Branch that we were talking about, Mary Bumgarner's daddy and Thelma's daddy, he had one that he was running there when he died. Mrs. Branch continued to run the store a while after he died. Then they went out of the grocery business and rented the store building to Mart Wilson. Mart ran the store there for a long time. I guess Old Man John Icard owned all that land in there or he owned it then. I have to tell you about the old store. I can remember it. There was no ice to be had. They did haul ice around so many days each week. They had what they called spring houses. That's where people put their milk and butter. Old Man John Icard had one that sat off down in, I'll try to tell you where this was. You know where Ann Austin lives? It was off down 700 yards from her house.[21]

Willard's recall of the spring house at Ann Austin's house is on Hickory Street near the intersection of Cedar Street. Willard and Violet named John Icard, Walt Icard, Robert Icard, Gus Rockett, Will Branch, Mr. Walsh, Mart Wilson, and Joe Church as former proprietors of the store just outside of the city limits of Rhodhiss at Caldwell and Hickory streets. Finn Simmons agreed that Mart Wilson ran a store in this location. Finn said, "Oh, yes. Everybody took orders back then. Mart Wilson had a store right there where Joe Church's store is now."[22] Lawrence and Nancy Brady added that a Pritchard man ran the store when they first moved to lower Duke Street. They said that they shopped at the stores owned by the Pritchards, Joe Church, and the Annases. They said that they didn't shop at the Company Store often.[23] Fletcher Lutz also mentioned the Pritchard man running the store, and he added that Mr. Pritchard was also a preacher. Lawrence Brady said, "Joe and Thelma Church kept us from starving," and Nancy added, "A babysitter cost $1.25 per week, and we borrowed the $1.25 from Joe Church to pay the sitter."[24] Joe Church probably held the longest tenure at this site on lower Duke Street. Beatrice Branch and her daughter, Betty Jean Branch Terry, reflected on Joe's store. Betty said, "And we bought our groceries, there wasn't no Dixie Store, at Joe Church's. We kept Joe Church up. Yeah, right out here. His store had the only phone here. You had to go upstairs to go to the phone. The store didn't have the phone. The phone was upstairs on that porch."[25] Rebecca Church Sigmon said that Joe sold the store a couple of times, only to buy it back later. At one time he sold it to Floyd and Boyd Kirby who were twins. They lived in the upstairs of the store when they owned it; however, they sold the store back.[26] Joe's store building dates to the beginning of Rhodhiss in the early 1900s. The white wooden edifice with the apartments on top was torn down in 1951. The town minutes indicate that on December 5, 1950, Joe Church negotiated the sale of his old store building on the highway right-of-way that was creating a hazard.[27]

JOE CHURCH'S STORE BUILDING IN 1949. THELMA CHURCH PHOTO.

Thelma Church discussed the sale of the old building, "Yeah, we tore that store down. The state gave Joe $500 to tear it down; then the guy that tore it down gave him $500 more because it had a lot of good lumber in it. That guy built a brick house out of it. All that was bad is what was on the outside. The inside was good. It was a big building. There was a barbershop on one side. People lived upstairs."[28] Shortly after it was torn down, Joe and Thelma built the store back in brick at the same location, but the store was moved farther from the road. Carl Compton would have been a customer at Joe's brick store. Carl recalled a story from his childhood:

> When I was very young, I sneaked down to Joe's store with two of my friends and set them up with a BIG cream roll and a banana. We went up in the pine trees below the Methodist Church to eat them, thinking we were hidden. Can you imagine that? I told Joe to charge them to my dad. The next time dad went to the store, Joe told him what I did and WOOOO! Did I get my hide tanned! Needless to say, I didn't try that again.[29]

Carl's story is humorous because many children enjoyed their purchases at various stores in town, but Carl was willing to treat his friends at his dad's expense. On a more serious note, many years ago while attending a funeral, I met a Rhodhiss gentleman, and he told me that had it not been for Joe and Thelma Church his family would have starved to death. Joe was willing to extend credit numerous times to his single mother who had four children. She was a very hard worker, and Joe and Thelma provided food to this family during difficult times. When Joe closed the store, she came to pay off the debt. Joe told her that he did not know how much she owed because the records were gone, and she said, "Well, I do." She paid him the amount that she had tallied herself. Thelma and Joe ran the store until the late 1960s or early 1970s.

JOE'S FOOD SHOP CALENDAR.
REBECCA SIGMON PHOTO.

JOE AND THELMA CHURCH. REBECCA
SIGMON PHOTO.

Finn and Pawnee Simmons discussed the store owned by the Annas family. It was located at the intersection of Duke Power Road and Duke Street.

> FS: Then I went out there to Annas' Store to haul groceries.
> SH: You hauled for Annas' Grocery?
> FS: Lawd, I was raised there.
> PS: That's why he knows so much about Rhodhiss. I think that he was in everybody's house.
> FS: I used to know everybody in Rhodhiss.
> SH: Well, if you worked 12 hours a day, how did you have time to deliver groceries?
> FS: Well, back when I worked the 12 hours, I worked when I was a sophomore in high school till I was a junior. I went back to school. Then I hauled groceries in the meantime. I was only 12 years old when I was at Annas' Store.[30]

Pawnee and Finn shared their memories of the Annas' Store, which was owned by Berry and Ethel Annas. Finn had such a deep affection for this building that he later purchased it. Another store that was close to the Annas' Store was the Monteith Store. It was farther out Duke Power Road toward the end. It was owned by Hattie Mae Butler Monteith and Nathan Monteith. Louise Keller and her mother, Mattie Munday, discussed the Monteith Store and its location:

> LK: The Monteiths had a store up around where Doughton lives. We used to go up to Annas' to get our milk and stuff, and we traded up there at Mr. Monteith's Store. I remember that they ran that store.
> MM: Raym worked at the Monteiths' Store.
> SH: Well, I knew that he worked for Glasses, but not there.
> MM: He didn't work up there much, but Jim Hemphill worked there.[31]

Leona Hunsucker verified this information when she stated, "Yeah, Mr. Monteith ran the store before he started working at the mill or maybe it was after. Kinda there where Doughton's garage is."[32] A third confirmation of the Monteith Store was provided by Arthur "Ott" and Exie Hand when I interviewed them:

> SH: I know that there were three grocery stores. Well, four counting Monteiths' Store.
> EH: Yeah, there were four. Butler Monteith's dad's. Ott delivered groceries for him.
> SH: The Annas Store, the Glass Store, the Monteith Store, and the Joe Church Store. Somebody told me that there was a Lutz's store over on Strawberry Hill.
> EH: A what?
> SH: Lutz's
> EH: Yeah, there was one over there.
> SH: Did Ott like delivering groceries?
> EH: Oh, yeah. Now that was fun to him.

SH: I bet so. He got to see people.

EH: He got to go a long way. He used Mr. Monteith's truck.

SH: Ott, tell me about delivering groceries.

AH: Oh, I did. That was for old man Nathan Monteith.

SH: I just found out last week that he had a store near Doughton's house.

AH: Yeah. Had it over there where that shed is where that other building is beside his house.

SH: Did he do well?

AH: Yeah, he done all right.[33]

The Rhodhiss community was full of options for groceries. Another store in the Caldwell County area of Rhodhiss was located near Joe Church's Store. Betty Branch Terry and her mother Beatrice said, "Ev Teague had a store where Frankie Price lives now."[34] Rebecca Church Sigmon confirmed that Everett Teague did indeed have a store at this location at one time.[35] This would have been at the intersection of Duke Street and Bumgarner Road. In addition, Billie Sue Laney said that she grew up on Hickory Street in Rhodhiss, and she recalled going to Ann and June Austin's Store to buy things. This store was at Ann and June's house.[36] This location would have been on Hickory Street just past the intersection of Cedar Street. There is a small block building on the right. The Austins lived there for many years.

Moving to more stores in Burke County, Tom Ross asked Fletcher Lutz about the Lutz Store located off Carolina Avenue (Strawberry Hill). This store would have been before 1925. Mr. Lutz replied, "You wouldn't exactly call it Strawberry Hill. We called it Settlemyre Hill. The old store building was near the Settlemyres, turn right there, and it was on a hill. It's torn down now."[37] Lawrence and Nancy Brady talked about Arley Church's granddaddy's store in the Rhodhiss area of Burke County. Willard Herman had already mentioned Pappy and Mammy Church's Store. Paul Bright said that he had a newspaper route in 1940, and he delivered 102 papers on a bicycle to various customers for fifteen cents a week. He went from lower Duke Street at Clete Walker's house all the way to Pappy and Mammy's Store on the hill in Burke County.[38] Tommy Elmore said that he recalled going to Pappy and Mammy's Store when he was a small child. That would have been in the mid to late 1930s.[39] Lawrence and Nancy also mentioned that the Knox family had a store near Rhodhiss on the Burke side.[40] The last store alluded to was the Stephens' Store. Violet Curtis and Willard Herman explained to Tom Ross and me:

TR: Is that the Stephens that ran the store up there?

VC: That was their grandpa. Buster Stephens is the one that lived in the house after that. Mr. and Mrs. Stephens always called him Buster.

WH: They were related to the Settlemyres.

VC: Yeah, they were Settlemyres.

WH: Buster Stephens had three children. Two girls and one boy. Grace Hayes is still living.

VC: They had another little girl that died.[41]

At any given time Rhodhiss citizens had a variety of choices for their grocery needs. In 1988 Thelma

Church was thankful for the loyalty of their customers. Thelma said, "Yeah, they patronized their neighbors. I will tell you, Sherrie. There were three grocery stores here in Rhodhiss at that time. That goes to show you that they really patronized their merchant. We had a grocery store here; Annases had one up here; and Glasses had one at the foot of the hill. We all made a good living. Now, there are not any."[42] When more transportation became available, people started traveling to the nearby towns of Granite Falls and Hickory for their purchases; thus, the grocery store businesses in Rhodhiss ceased.

The mill company had a Company Store that provided for their employees. At first, they paid the workers in currency that could be used only in the Company Store. Later, they stopped this practice. The company also made sure that no other stores could operate within the city limits of Rhodhiss. They again wanted the villagers to use their store. The mill company owned the entire village, and the laborers gave their hard work, money, and dedication to the mill company.

NOTES

1   "Fires, Floods, Etc." *Women's Wear*. 19 January 1914. Vol. 8, Issue 15, page 16.

2   Lutz, Fletcher.

3   Curtis, Violet, Willard Herman, Tom Ross.

4   Callihan, Nicole and Ruby Y. Keller. *Henry River Mill Village*. Charleston, SC: Arcadia Pub, 2012, p. 35.

5   Herman, Willard, Tom Ross.

6   Church, Thelma.

7   Beshears, Monteith, Ross, Teague.

8   Munday, Matt and Louise Keller.

9   Barker, Gladys.

10   Rhodhiss Town Minutes. 1922 and 19 March 1923

11   Edwards, Arthur, Jack Edwards, Edna Edwards Laney Stilwell and Tom Ross.

12   Hunsucker, Leona, Tom Ross.

13   Simmons, Finn and Pawnee, Tom Ross.

14   Rhodhiss Town Minutes. 1909.

15   "Brief Notes of Recent Happenings in North Carolina." The News-Herald. 13 April 1916, p. 1.https://newspapers. digitalnc.org/lccn/sn84001806/1916-04-13/ed-1/seq-1/#words=Rhodhiss. Accessed 28 July 2022.

16   Curtis, Violet, Willard Herman, Tom Ross.

17   Townsend, Hans and Katherine, Tom Ross.

18   Lutz, Fletcher and Tom Ross.

19   Church, Thelma.

20   Munday, Matt and Louise Keller.

21   Curtis, Violet, Willard Herman, Tom Ross.

22   Simmons, Finn and Pawnee, Tom Ross.

23   Brady, Lawrence and Nancy, Tom Ross.

24   Lutz, Fletcher.

25   Branch, Beatrice, Betty Jean Branch Terry, and Mildred Hartsoe. Personal Interview with Sherrie Hartsoe. Granite Falls, NC. 8 May 1988.

26   Sigmon, Rebecca Church. Personal Interview with Sherrie Hartsoe Sigmon. Hudson, NC. 21 May 2022.

27   Rhodhiss Town Minutes. 5 December 1950.

28   Church, Thelma.

29   Compton, Carl. Email Interview with Sherrie Hartsoe Sigmon. 20 January 2015.

30   Simmons, Finn and Pawnee and Tom Ross.

31   Munday, Mattie and Louise Keller.

32   Hunsucker, Leona and Tom Ross.

33   Hand, Arthur and Exie.

34   Branch, Beatrice, Betty Branch Terry, and Mildred Hartsoe.

35   Sigmon, Rebecca Church.

36   Laney, Billie Sue. Telephone Interview with Sherrie Hartsoe Sigmon. 28 December 2021.

37   Lutz, Fletcher and Tom Ross.

38   Bright, Paul. Personal Interview with Sherrie Hartsoe Sigmon. Rhodhiss, NC. 19 May 2022.

39   Elmore, Tommy. Personal Interview with Sherrie Hartsoe Sigmon. Boone, NC. 13 May 2022.

40   Brady, Lawrence and Nancy and Tom Ross.

41   Curtis, Violet, Willard Herman, and Tom Ross.

42   Church, Thelma.

CHAPTER 5
OTHER BUSINESSES

Many businesses have been successful in Rhodhiss throughout its 120 years of history. These establishments offered the hard workers of Rhodhiss the chance to relax, eat, get a snack, take a shower, or be entertained. Some enterprises are still open today, but most have long since left town because their usefulness has dwindled. The citizens of Rhodhiss supported the small businesses that blanketed the town.

Within the town on the Caldwell side the mill company leased a house to various people for a barbershop. This would have been during the early decades of the town's existence. Several barbers served the community at this location: Astor Peeler, Mr. Roseman, Joe Lail, Cletus Hunsucker, Willard Herman, Mr. Sims, and Everett Roberts. This old house was located behind the old post office/Company Store building. Later several houses were torn down in that area when Pacific bought out the mill company. This would have been at the lower end of Magnolia Street going toward the bridge. The barbershop offered the citizens a chance for a shave, shower, and haircut. Many people commented that they were thankful for this business.

Fletcher Lutz talked about his first haircut, "I got my first haircut in Rhodhiss from Mr. Astor Peeler. The barbershop was near the post office."[1] Fletcher was born in 1917, so this must have been around 1920. Hans Townsend explained to Tom Ross and me the benefits of the barber business owned by Clete Hunsucker:

HT: The barbershop was upstairs, and he had a place downstairs where you could take showers. He charged you a quarter to take a shower. There were five or six shower stalls in there, and he furnished the soap and a towel.

TR: So, he had the whole building.

HT: You could see people walking from their homes to go down there to take a shower. They didn't have showers in their homes. A lot of them did it on Saturday so that they could go to town. A shave was fifteen cents. A haircut was a quarter.[2]

Hans explained the expression, "He's going to take his Saturday bath." Hans even added that the Saturday bath was a prelude to a day or evening on the town. Mr. Hunsucker was at Rhodhiss as the barber for approximately twenty years. His wife Leona discussed in detail her husband's establishment:

LH: There was a Roseman. That was his surname. I don't remember his first name. He stayed a while, but he sold his part to Joe Lail. I believe it was 1922 when Clete bought it. One of the houses down there had been converted to a barbershop. It was a nice place. This will be interesting to you. You know way back then you didn't have a bathroom in the house. There was a bath downstairs in the barbershop with stalls, and people paid twenty-five cents to come and take a bath. Well, a shower. There were four or five of them. He furnished the towels and the soap. I thought that was odd. Then there was too much business for one person, but not enough for two. So, Clete later took up the dry-cleaning business. He would go through the mills then and ask the people if they had any dry cleaning, put down their names, what they had if they knew, and then he went around and picked it up. He did it and delivered it. He had a press in the back of the barbershop. He would have the laundry in Granite Falls to do his dry cleaning, and he would bring it down there and press it. Pick it up and deliver it.

TR: Right behind the office.

LH: Yeah, right behind the office down at Rhodhiss. It was, well the road is a little different now, isn't it Tom? It comes around.

TR: Yeah.

LH: It used to come right by the barbershop. It was right in that curve off the road a little bit between the office and the first house up on the hill. It doesn't look like one could be there, but they had plenty of room. You know it was downstairs where all those bathrooms were. Then the top floor had steps that you came up. It was a nice barbershop.

TR: Yes, it was. I remember it.

LH: He had the furnishings changed one time. I have two cabinets out there on the porch that I talked him out of. Then he had mirrors all the way around that one side. They had big ole wood frames. Then the cabinets were all the way across. Then there was marble on top of the cabinets. Then those pretty mirrors which just lined the walls. I have one mirror up in the attic. I can't use it because it's big. He gave me one piece of marble. I wanted more than one. Yeah, so many people now say, 'Oh, Clete used to cut my hair.' Girls then went to barbershops. All over in the country, even Gene and Buddy Glass way over there in Icard came there. People up at Granite even, he had a lot of customers from Granite. All through here. I will never forget John Story. Clete told him, 'John, I am going to quit being a barber. You'll have to get you a new barber.' He said, 'Clete, I can't let anybody else cut my hair. You have cut it ever since I can remember.' Clete said, 'Well, I will take you out in the woods and let you sit on a stump, and I will cut it.' He was just kidding him, you know. I forgot to tell you that the chairs that people sat in all across one row, those were captain's chairs, antique captain's chairs. I didn't get a one of those. I would give anything for just one. Everett Roberts bought the business from Clete. Now when Everett quit working, he let his children have those chairs, and they got some of the other things, too. Clete was not going to tear up that barbershop any of it. He wanted to leave it just like it was. It was an unusual shop for that little town. It was pretty.

TR: Was there any beauty shoppes around or anything?

LH: No, that's the way that I met Clete. I went to the barbershop to get my hair cut.[3]

Leona's description was full of information. She said that Mr. Roseman owned the barbershop before Clete, that Joe Lail was in business with Clete, that Clete also did dry cleaning, and that Clete sold the business to Everett Roberts. She gave details of the inside of the business and its beautiful furnishings. She talked about the showers and the cost. It was very interesting that women had to go to a barbershop if they chose to have their hair cut. Clete's dry-cleaning service was apparently needed because he left to pursue that business full time during the 1940s in Granite Falls. Jack Edwards also mentioned that he obtained his first haircut in Rhodhiss when the business was owned by Joe Lail and Cletus Hunsucker.[4] Many Rhodhiss men and women used the services of the barbershop.

AN EARLY BARBER WHO WORKED AT THE RHODHISS BARBERSHOP. SEVERAL PEOPLE FEEL THIS IS ASTOR PEELER. JOHN EDGAR HAAS PHOTO WITH PERMISSION FROM HIS GRANDDAUGHTER, ANITA M. HAAS.

Shelley Teague talked to Ann Austin and me about the barbershop. He said that it was at the bottom of Magnolia Street, too. Shelley said, "Right below that last house where they got a dead end. It was a mill house, but they made it into a barbershop. It had showers. It was the only place in Rhodhiss that you could get a shower. He pressed clothes. He had haircuts and shaves."[5] In 1928 someone deemed the business profitable enough to break in and try to steal various things. As per the town's minutes: "Town paid $10 to Mr. Hunsucker for his expenses in securing bloodhounds to trace robbers of the barbershop which occurred Thursday night, December 20, 1928."[6] This company provided several benefits for the mill village. Finn and Pawnee Simmons also talked about this establishment to Tom Ross and me:

PS: Rhodhiss even had a barbershop. It had a shower. A lot of the boys would go down on Saturday night and get a shower.

FS: I shined shoes for Clete Hunsucker and Joe Lail at the barbershop. Joe Lail was just a little short fellow.

TR: He was a barber, wasn't he?

FS: Yeah. Clete and I would collect dry cleaning. He took it to Granite to get it cleaned; then he brought it back down to the barbershop to press it. All of the ball players and anybody else that wanted took a shower in the bottom of the barbershop. The barbershop was on the hill. It was practically over the branch. Clete Hunsucker, when he first came here, boarded with Mrs. Branch whose kids were John, Pee Wee, Kathleen, Mary, and Thelma.[7]

Finn Simmons was able to add more information by saying that the barbershop also offered shoe-shining services. Before Cletus Hunsucker went into business with Joe Lail, Willard Herman tried his hand at barbering, but he said, "I give it up pretty quick."[8] Obviously, Willard was not interested in this profession. Several people discussed the barbershop's burning down, and it was mysterious because it burned during the night and was on fire twice. Toward the end of my interviews, Fred Elmore was able to give the answers to the questions about its demise. Fred stated:

FE: The mill company wanted to get rid of the old barbershop, so the shop men set it on fire. It was kept hush hush. Then Will McGuire saw it and put it out. We set it on fire again, and Will McGuire put it out again. The last time though he didn't have a chance.
TR: They just wanted to get rid of that building to rearrange that road.
FE: Yeah, yeah. Get it out of the way. Take too long to tear it down.[9]

Fred Elmore smiled when he told this story, for the mill company kept this a secret. There was a barbershop near Joe Church's Store that Leona Hunsucker said she went to first, but the barber refused to cut her long, pretty hair. Clyde Keller and Everett Roberts also had a barbershop in Joe Church's wooden building, and it was located to the side; however, after the Church Store was built back in brick, the barbershop was downstairs.[10]

Another business in town was the slaughterhouse which was located off Hickory Street past the intersection of Cedar and Hickory. It was behind Marie and Flowers Austin's old house in the woods. The slaughter pen was available for anyone that needed to butcher their cows or pigs. Leona Hunsucker said: "They had a slaughterhouse over here in the woods, and they killed their own beef. Yeah, right up in there near the Flowers and Marie Austin house, somewhere up in those woods. They had this big ole building. Then they had, what do you call it, a rove and tackle? They draw them up, killed them, and threw them up there. They butchered them and sold them."[11] The slaughter area would have been beneficial to the grocery stores in the area and people who just needed to butcher their livestock. Apparently, the slaughterhouse was quite a spectator activity. Mattie Munday voiced her experience:

I used to go back over in the woods kind of like where Marie Austin's house was to the slaughterhouse to watch them. They would kill beef and throw their heads and all the waste down the hill. The dogs would go eat it. We youngins would go up there and watch it. They had a springhouse where we kept our milk. We just played in them woods all the time. There wasn't anything for you to do. I was brave enough to go watch them kill those old cows. One time a cow died, and they had to bury it. I would stand and watch things like that.[12]

Mattie said that she and her childhood friends would watch as the slaughterhouse work was being done. Killing livestock must have been commonplace. Finn Simmons commented on watching the slaughter, "Back in there where Flowers Austin lived, right there where Flowers Austin's house is there was a slaughter pen. See, they killed hogs or cows. Mitch Church, Garland Annas, Old Man Icard, or anybody that had one to kill went there. I went over there, and they would give me the leftover parts. I'd take them to sell."[13] Not only did Finn go to watch, but he was able to make a profit. Fred Elmore also talked about this business. Fred said, "You know there used to be a big slaughterhouse out there where they slaughtered beef and pork. It was privately owned. Mr. Hollar, the outside man who cared for the community, lived in that big house out there. The slaughterhouse was catty cornered from that house. Go by the service station and turn right. The big house was on the right, and the slaughterhouse was catty cornered to that."[14] The last people to comment on the slaughterhouse were Arthur, Jack, and Edna from the Edwards family. They said that the mill company used the slaughterhouse so they could sell food in the company store.[15] Rhodhiss was a small town with several grocery stores that used the services of the slaughterhouse.

Another nearby business was the café run by Thelma Branch Church's aunt, Julia Icard Winn. This food establishment was across the street from the Icard Store (later Joe Church's Store). The present-day location is at the intersection of Caldwell and Hickory streets. Willard Herman described this diner:

> WW: It sat right across from Thelma and Joe Church's store building there. Mrs. Winn owned it.
> TR: That's Harvey Winn's mother?
> WH: Yes, Harvey Winn's mother. It had living quarters on one side. That used to be the place. It would be full on the weekends. It was a big ole building. They had a couple of pool tables in there.
> SH: So that was beside of the gas station?
> WH: The gas station wasn't there at the time. Nobody had cars then to have a gas station.
> SH: Oh, okay. That later became the gas station?
> WH: That's right. You had to go up about ten concrete steps to get into it. There was a bank there, and it had never been leveled.[16]

Many people discussed this early café. Mattie Munday agreed that it was run by Thelma's aunt, Mrs. Winn. Matt said, "They made homemade ice cream. You could go up there and get homemade ice cream out of the freezer. You got a big ole dip of ice cream for a nickel."[17] Many citizens were enticed by the café because of its food, ice cream, and pool tables. Leona Hunsucker called it "a nice café, real nice."[18] Lastly, Finn Simmons went as far as to call it a restaurant. He also described it as being across from the Icard Store.[19]

1920S, THELMA BRANCH CHURCH AT HER AUNT'S CAFÉ WITH JOHN AND NINA ICARD. REBECCA SIGMON PHOTO.

This café would later become a gas station per Willard Herman. He told Tom Ross and me about George Starnes' gas station:

WH: George Starnes ran the old service station in Rhodhiss. George died, and Rufus Holt rented the service station building from Mrs. Starnes and bought stock. Well, you can't remember the old service station before they tore it down at Rhodhiss.
SH: Is this the Starnes' station that you were talking about?
WH: Yeah.
SH: Where was it?
TR: Across from Joe Church's old store?
WH: Yes. Back behind there they had gambling going on. George Starnes built that service station along about 1929, and he operated it. He had some kind of shoulder problem. Anyway, he had to go to Johns Hopkins in Baltimore, and they operated on his shoulder. George had a small café in there, too, but all that he had was just an oil stove that he cooked on, and he had a counter. We would get off at the mill on Friday night at 12:00. I got old enough that I could work on the night shift then. He would stay open, and they'd stew oysters. He'd sell you a bowl of oysters with crackers for fifteen cents. He'd stay open till about 1:00 on Saturday morning. About ten or fifteen of us from the mill would go up there to eat oysters on Friday night. You didn't get a premium for working third shift, but you worked five or six hours a week less. I think that we got off at 11 or 12 on Friday night. If you worked first shift, they were still on eleven hours a day. If you worked first shift, you had to work five hours longer than you did if you worked night shift.[20]

Willard was able to give information about the gas station, gambling, eating oysters, and working the night shift at the mill. His memories proved to be very helpful and informative. Also, Finn Simmons elaborated on the Starnes' gas station with Tom Ross and me:

FS: Old man George Starnes' gas station was pretty wild. Cec Bumgarner later bought George Starnes' station. It burned. Cec and Mary worked in the mill. Both of them worked in the spinning room. He helped June and Paul buy the station. They worked at the service station. When the old building burned up there, that's when he got the other filling station. Tynce Munday, Tynce's daddy, Cec, June, and Paul were all just one fine group of people together.

SH: Paul told me one time that there was a gas war.

FS: A gas war?

SH: Yes, Paul told me that it got down to eleven cents a gallon.

FS: Well, Paul would know about that. There was a pool room up there beside of Annas' Store. It burnt here a while back.[21]

RHODHISS GAS STATION AFTER A CAR RAN INTO IT. GRANITE FALLS PRESS PHOTO VIA EDDIE SIPES.

Finn added that there was a pool room beside the Annas' Store. Later, Finn owned the building where the pool room was. George Starnes' gas station was apparently the first one in Rhodhiss because Willard had said previously that there weren't any cars, so one was not needed. Finn mentioned that the Bumgarners bought the station. Paul Bright ran that station in the early 1940s because Paul and June Bumgarner were in World War II. Paul Bright said that Cec offered him $22.50 a week to run this station while his sons were involved in the war. Paul Bright was making $15 a week in the mill, so he took the job and worked until he was drafted.[22] The Bumgarner station was located first at the intersection of Caldwell and Hickory. It burned and was moved up the street to the intersection of Duke Street and Bumgarner Road.

June and Paul Bumgarner ran this company for many years. They were instrumental to the success of the community because they provided gasoline and repaired automobiles. Their station was Rhodhiss Shell, but it later changed to Rhodhiss Gulf. Jim Huffman ran a gas station at the site of the first Bumgarner station during the late 1960s and early 1970s. Another gas station located at 170 Duke Street had various owners.

COY LUNSFORD IN CAFÉ AT 183 DUKE STREET IN THE 1960S. DONNA PRICE PHOTO.

CEPHUS LUNSFORD AND BOYD HOLLAR OUTSIDE CAFÉ IN 1960S. DONNA PRICE PHOTO.

Many other businesses would come and go in Rhodhiss. In the 1950s and 1960s there was a beauty shop in the basement of Joe Church's Store. At one time Becky Estes worked there, and Tommie Haas Rhea did, too. It was beside Clyde Keller's old barbershop. In the 1970s Doug Cowick had a shop called the "Nic Nak" in this same area. In the early 1980s Joe and Gail Kirby had an ice cream parlor called Two Sons in this same building. Cindy Kirby Rogers, their daughter, said that they sold ice cream and hot dogs. Frankie Price came in daily to buy several hot dogs because he loved the chili. Cindy added that when she and her husband Julian came to Rhodhiss to visit, they would go to the ice cream shop. When she answered the phone, she would say, "Two Sons. . .and a Daughter!"[23] Other businesses prospered in this area. Beside Joe Church's Store there was a laundromat at one time which Rebecca Church Sigmon said was run by Jack Caldwell and Wade Church. Rebecca added that Troy Yount had a hosiery mill in that same building years prior. Jack Caldwell also had a furniture business beside Joe's store for several years. The small building located at the intersection of Duke Street and Bumgarner Road, (183 Duke Street) housed a café in the 1960s which was owned by Rob and Betty Hand. This building was owned by Joe Church.[24]

George Keller ran a small store on Magnolia Street for several years, and he mostly sold candy. On the riverbank in Caldwell County a company opened during the 1990s that derived its name from the dam. It was dubbed "The Dam Tool Store." Another store that was popular was Buck's Dollar Store, and it was located at the intersection of Duke Power Road and Duke Street. Van Foxx operated a shop located on lower Duke Street that had used appliance parts, and he also serviced appliances. In Burke County, Barry Oxford ran a gas station and convenience store across from the former town office on Burke Street. He purchased the premises from the J. L. Owens' family (J. L., Betty, David, Mike, and Lori). The Owens family ran this store on several occasions. According to the Secretary of State's Office online data, one stent for The Ole Store was from 2012 to 2017.[25] Select Caterers also had a business in the old Glasses' Store beside the former town office on Burke Street. Data indicates that this business was in vogue from 1986 to 1989. The Owens family also had a store going toward Friendship Methodist Church, which is presently called "Market Basket." Mike Owens was the company agent for a business on Burke Street called Lake Rhodhiss Fish Camp from 1981 to 1986, and it was located beside the current fire station.[26] On Catawba Avenue along the river a restaurant opened in the late 1980s or early 1990s. Later, George's on the Lake took this same space in 2009 to 2014.[27] It then became The Village Inn Pizza for a brief period. It is currently operating as The Copper Penny, and it opened in April 2022. The Settlemyre family had a bait shop on Carolina Avenue. Grady Settlemyre and his son Pete provided supplies to many people in the area. Also, Pete ran a speedway for several years, and the Secretary of State's information indicated that it ran from 1995 to 2002. In the same area Pete's sons and grandson have provided recreation at Halloween at their establishment, Lake Hickory Haunts, which opened business in 2012.[28] Presently, Ryan Settlemyre runs this establishment. A few years after Lake Hickory Haunts opened, Rhodhiss obtained a Dollar General that still thrives at 301 Burke Street. John Yount had an automotive repair shop in the 1970s, and Rick Justice opened a similar venture in 1996 after he moved his business from Granite Falls to Rhodhiss; however, when he became the Rhodhiss Town Manager in 2020, he left this enterprise with his daughter. Rhodhiss has been full of businesses from the beginning.

GRANITE FALLS PRESS AD FOR VARIETY
DISCOUNT JUNE 1, 1967

MIKE OWENS' FISH CAMP ON BURKE
STREET. GRANITE FALLS PRESS PHOTO.

Throughout the years Rhodhiss had many opportunities for its citizens, whether it was food, entertainment, gas, recreation, or service. These entrepreneurs worked hard to ensure the success of their businesses. In the earlier years it was important to have all these companies within the town because transportation was limited; however, with the large number of automobiles available today, people can drive to nearby locales for their needs if Rhodhiss doesn't provide.

NOTES

1   Lutz, Fletcher and Tom Ross.

2   Townsend, Hans and Katherine, Tom Ross.

3   Hunsucker, Leona and Tom Ross.

4   Edwards, Arthur, Jack Edwards, Edna Edwards Laney Stilwell, Tom Ross.

5   Austin, Ann, Thad Martin, Shelley Teague. Personal Interviews with Sherrie Hartsoe. Rhodhiss, NC. 12 July 1988 and 3 August 1988.

6   Rhodhiss Town Minutes. 29 December 1928.

7   Simmons, Finn and Pawnee, Tom Ross.

8   Curtis, Violet, Willard Herman, Tom Ross.

9   Elmore, Fred and Martha, Tom Ross.

10   Sigmon, Rebecca Church.

11   Hunsucker, Leona and Tom Ross.

12   Munday, Mattie and Louise Keller.

13   Simmons, Finn and Pawnee, Tom Ross.

14   Elmore, Fred and Martha, Tom Ross.

15   Edwards, Arthur, Jack Edwards, Edna Edwards Laney Stilwell, and Tom Ross.

16   Herman, Willard and Tom Ross.

17   Munday, Mattie and Louise Keller.

18   Hunsucker, Leona and Tom Ross.

19   Simmons, Finn and Pawnee, Tom Ross.

20   Herman, Willard and Tom Ross.

21   Simmons, Finn and Pawnee, Tom Ross.

22   Bright, Paul 19 May 2022.

23   Rogers, Cindy Kirby. Telephone Interview with Sherrie Hartsoe Sigmon. 24 July 2022.

24   Sigmon, Rebecca Church. Personal Interview. Hickory, NC. 22 April 2022.

25   "North Carolina Secretary of State." https://www.sosnc.gov/search/index/corp. Accessed 8 July 2022.

26   "North Carolina Secretary of State." https://www.sosnc.gov/search/index/corp. Accessed 8 July 2022.

27   "North Carolina Secretary of State." https://www.sosnc.gov/search/index/corp. Accessed 8 July 2022.

28   "North Carolina Secretary of State." https://www.sosnc.gov/search/index/corp. Accessed 8 July 2022.

CHAPTER 6
THE POST OFFICE

The post office in Rhodhiss started two years before the town's incorporation in 1903. Communication would have been essential for the mill company to keep up with their customers. Mail was vital for the townspeople, too. A letter was the easiest form of communication in those days. The mail arrived via train, and its route came to the mill. Caleb J. Rhodes, the son of John Rhodes, was the first postmaster for Rhodhiss. According to the postal records, "Rhodhiss' post office was established 16 April 1901."[1] The post office was housed in the Company Store building along with the company offices. This area was across the street from the manufacturing company on the Caldwell side. The post office served a vital role in Rhodhiss' success.

Violet Curtis was a young child when her family moved to Rhodhiss in 1912. She said that she recalled the post office: "I went to school with Sidney and Ralph Sims. Sidney was later a postmaster. I remember a Triplett man running the post office."[2] Mr. Adolphus Triplett did indeed serve as postmaster from 1915 to 1919. Violet's dad, Mr. Earley, worked at the Company Store, so she probably would have visited there on occasion. Violet's mention of Sidney Sims was paralleled by Ned Bean. Ned stated, "I remember Mr. Sims. He had an old dog named Rowdy. It was a big old dog. His son, Sidney Sims, ran the post office. Mr. Sims would send the dog to the post office to get his mail from Sidney."[3] Sidney Sims was postmaster from 1932-1941. Similarly, Shelley Teague said that his mother was the postmaster when the Southern (later Duke) Power dam was being constructed. Shelley added, "I used to keep a king pole and some worms in the post office. The post office was in the old Company Store. Right in the corner next to the railroad tracks. You would go in the door there on the right-hand side."[4] Shelley's mother was Jennie Teague, and she worked at the post office from 1922 to 1928.

1953 1 CENT STAMP WITH RHODHISS
POSTMARK. SHERRIE HARTSOE
SIGMON PHOTO.

1960S 2 CENT STAMP WITH RHODHISS
POSTMARK. SHERRIE HARTSOE
SIGMON PHOTO.

Helen Hemphill came to Rhodhiss from South Carolina when her husband, James "Jay" Hemphill, went to work for Duke Power. Mrs. Hemphill ran the post office for twenty-one years. An old article in the *Granite Falls Press* detailed her retirement:

> Helen Hemphill was appointed 4th class postmaster, December 10, 1941 and took over her duties from Acting Postmaster, Estelle Teague, January 1, 1942. The post office because of increased receipts was declared 3rd class, July 1, 1944. Mrs. Hemphill was appointed 3rd class Postmaster, September 23, 1944. The PO quarters were enlarged in 1946, but larger quarters are now needed to carry on the steadily increasing business. Mrs. Precious Keller was substitute and Career Clerk from October 1944 to July 6, 1958, she then resigned and took a position with Burlington Mills, and now works in the office there as Mrs. Precious (Verdis) Whisnant. Mrs. Nora Annas who has assisted Mrs. Hemphill since July 1958, will continue work in the PO as Career Clerk. Mrs. Ruth Beshears will be assisting Mrs. Annas. An acting postmaster will be put in charge. Mrs. Hemphill expresses that she has enjoyed her time working with kind and cooperative citizens of Rhodhiss.[5]

Mrs. Hemphill said that she enjoyed her job in Rhodhiss, and she especially liked the people. In my interview with Helen Hemphill, she spoke highly of Rhodhiss:

> HH: I started in 1942. January 1, 1942. I liked the people. I didn't have a bit of trouble. The people were good people. I say that the working people are the best people in the world.
> SH: Nora Annas worked with you, right?

HH: I started her off. She was just working a few hours a day. I made the highest grade on the postal test. Estelle Teague fell and broke a bone, so I got the job. The political party at the time put me in.

SH: So, you were there when Pacific bought out the plants.

HH: Yeah, and Burlington, too.

SH: How did they treat you?

HH: They treated me well. I had to cross the bridge to get the mail because we had a box over on that side. Some people think that Rhodhiss is only on this side of the river (Caldwell).[6]

I had been told for years that federal jobs were political, and I found this to be true from Mrs. Hemphill and Precious Keller Kelley. Helen's description of the Rhodhiss citizens, "Working people are the best people in the world" is a good portrayal. This statement is very true of the community's men and women. Their hard work ethic was the reason for the mill company's success. The Hemphills lived in the Duke Power Village which was on Duke Power Road. Her husband Jay died in 1956, and she was told that she had to leave the Duke Power Village. Just like the mill company, someone living in the village had to work for Duke. She moved to the Methodist Church parsonage that was on Magnolia Street, and she later purchased a house on Park Avenue.[7] During her twenty-one-year tenure, Helen met a lot of people and served the town well. When she retired, Senator Sam J. Ervin wrote her a nice letter.

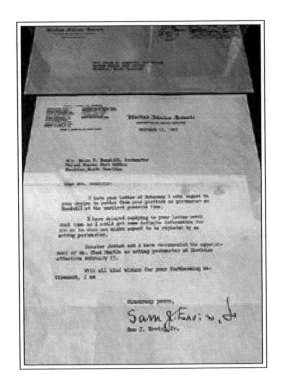

1963 LETTER TO HELEN HEMPHILL FROM SENATOR SAM J. ERVIN, JR. ELAINE KIRBY DOCUMENT WHICH WAS DONATED TO THE TOWN OF RHODHISS.

Precious Keller Whisnant Kelley also worked at the post office, but she was never a postmaster in Rhodhiss. She went to work for the postal service when her husband, Clyde Keller, was in World War II. After they divorced, Precious went to work for Pacific Mills, but she later returned to the post office in Lenoir. Precious stated:

PK: I went to work in the Rhodhiss post office in 1944. I took the examination for postmaster at Rhodhiss in the early 1960s.

TR: It wasn't politically motivated?

PK: It was political.

AK: At that time Jim took the test, too.

PK: Jim made the highest grade. He didn't get it because he was not the correct political party. At that time, I was registered correctly, but I didn't have as much political pull as Ann did, so Ann got it, which I am glad that she did.

PK: Whenever I was a child, I used to turn old-timey chairs upside down, and mama would give me her old circulars and old mail, and before I was old enough to go to school, I used to play post office.[8]

Here again is a story of the political involvement in postal jobs. Ann Austin took over at the post office in 1964. Precious had a long postal career. She enjoyed her time working with the people, especially those of Rhodhiss. She commented that she knew everyone in the village, and they were very kind to her. Paul Bright said that he most remembered Precious as the woman who ran the post office.[9] Tommy Elmore said that he received his Social Security card at the post office in Rhodhiss. He said that was where everyone went to obtain a card.[10]

THE OLD ROAD RAN BETWEEN MILL 1 AND THE POST OFFICE AND THE COMPANY STORE. SHERRIE HARTSOE SIGMON PHOTO.

THE OLD ROAD BETWEEN THE MILL AND POST OFFICE.
SHERRIE HARTSOE SIGMON PHOTO.

THE OLD ROAD BEFORE THE 1972 BRIDGE WAS COMPLETED.
SHERRIE HARTSOE SIGMON PHOTO.

Ann Austin had the longest tenure as postmaster in Rhodhiss. She started in 1964, and she left in 1992. She served the people for 28 years. Ann was the only postmaster who worked in both the old Company Store building and the new office on Church Street. According to the town minutes on December 20, 1965, Ann attended a town meeting to see if the town would sell the lot beside the Baptist parsonage for a new location for the proposed post office. Then almost two years later a building permit was granted on October 9, 1967, to Baylor Incorporated out of Miami, Florida for a new post office building, which would be located on Church Street. The proposed cost was listed at $18,000.[11] The new post office opened in the summer of 1968. I recall going over there, and the first piece of mail that we had in the new location was my fourth-grade report card. Ann Austin was able to give some information that included the founding father, John Rhodes. His grandson was Voigt Cromer who was born in Rhodhiss. Ann elaborated:

> I received a letter from Mrs. Cromer, and she said, 'I want you to postmark my Christmas cards with Rhodhiss on them.' This is how I got to know her. Just out of the blue she contacted me. This was before the Bicentennial. I wrote back and told her that I would be glad to do that. She sent me her boxed Christmas cards, and I postmarked them Rhodhiss. When Ben Pearson and David Hollar were getting things together, I told them about these people. That's how they contacted them to have them come.[12]

Ann's story was very interesting in that the Cromers' Christmas cards had the Rhodhiss postmark since Voigt's grandfather founded the town, and Dr. Cromer was born there. Dr. and Mrs. Cromer were both proud of this heritage, and they wanted to commemorate that fact at Christmas. Ann was the postmaster during most of the time that I lived in Rhodhiss. She was helpful, knowledgeable, and hard working.

GRANITE FALLS PRESS ARTICLE JULY 13, 1967, ON NEW POST OFFICE. GRANITE FALLS PRESS.

The following are two different accounts of people who served in the capacity of postmaster at the Rhodhiss Post Office. The first is from Cecil Hayes' information in "Caldwell County Postal History," and he gives more detailed information. The second account is from a website entitled "North Carolina Postal History." This website also includes various pictures of postmarks from the Rhodhiss post office.

Rhodhiss Postmasters

Caleb J. Rhodes		16 April 1901
David M. Cloninger		3 November 1905
Sydney L. Thompson		3 December 1907
Ellis S. Glass		4 February 1909
Adolphus Triplett		2 February 1915
Pearl M. Mullis		24 September 1919
Jennie W. Teague		14 June 1922
Joseph G. Benfield	Acting	7 November 1928
Fred D. Laxton		23 February 1929
Sidney J. Sims	Acting	28 July 1932 (assumed charge)
Sidney J. Sims		30 July 1932 (acting)
Sidney J. Sims		22 November 1932 (confirmed)
Estelle P. Teague	Acting	3 June 1941 (assumed charge)
Estelle P. Teague		18 July 1941 (acting)
Helen B. Hemphill		8 November 1941 (confirmed)
James Thad Martin	Acting	15 February 1963 (assumed charge)
Mary Ann Austin		22 April 1964 (confirmed)
Mary Ann Austin		22 May 1964 (assumed charge)
Lee L. Revis	Officer-In-Charge	2 October 1992
Alice Smirch		20 March 1993
Alice McCullough	(marriage)	25 May 1996
Deborah P. Sanders	Officer-In-Charge	25 October 1999
Deborah P. Sanders		29 January 2000
Debbie Lunsford	Officer-In-Charge	4 February 2010
Kay Vaughan	Officer-In-Charge	8 April 2010 [13]

"North Carolina Postal History": Rhodhiss

Caleb J. Rhodes		16 April 1901
David M. Cloninger		3 November 1905
Sydney L. Thompson		3 December 1907
Ellis S. Glass		4 February 1909
Adolphus Triplett		2 February 1915
Pearl M. Mullis		24 September 1919
Jennie W. Teague		14 June 1922
Joseph G. Benfield	Acting	7 November 1928
Fred D. Laxton		23 February 1929

Sidney J. Sims	Acting	28 July 1932
Sidney J. Sims		22 November 1932
Estelle P. Teague	Acting	3 June 1941
Helen B. Hemphill		28 November 1941
James Thad Martin	Acting	15 February 1963
Mary Ann Austin		22 April 1964
Lee L. Revis	Officer-In-Charge	2 October 1992
Alice Smirch		20 March 1993
Alice McCullough	(marriage)	25 May 1996
Deborah P. Sanders	Officer-In-Charge	5 October 1999
Deborah P. Sanders		29 January 2000
Rachel Duncan		28 August 2013
Converted to Remotely Managed Office of Granite Falls		23 August 2014[14]

Many men and women have served as postmaster in the Rhodhiss community. The Rhodhiss post office started in 1901, and it is presently located on Church Street. The town's citizens appreciate the postal service provided to them.

NOTES

1   Haynes, Cecil L. *Caldwell County Postal History*. 6 April 2016. Caldwell County Heritage Museum.

2   Curtis, Violet, Willard Herman, Tom Ross.

3   Bean, Ned and Elvie and Tom Ross.

4   Beshears, Monteith, Ross, Teague.

5   "Mrs. Helen Hemphill Rhodhiss Postmaster Retires After 21 Years." *Granite Falls Press*. 1963.

6   Hemphill, Helen, Jim, and Mae Hemphill. Personal Interview with Sherrie Hartsoe. Granite Falls, NC. 29 July 1988.

7   Hemphill, Helen, Jim, and Mae Hemphill.

8   Kelley, Alvis and Precious, Tom Ross.

9   Bright, Paul.

10   Elmore, Tommy.

11   Rhodhiss Town Minutes. 20 December 1965 and 9 October 1967.

12   Austin, Ann, Thad Martin, and Shelley Teague.

13   Haynes, Cecil L. *Caldwell County Postal History*. 6 April 2016. Caldwell County Heritage Museum.

14   "North Carolina Postal History." http://www.ncpostalhistory.com/wp-content/uploads/2020/06/ PostmarkCatalog_caldwell_county--20200615.pdf. Accessed 15 December 2020.

CHAPTER 7

POLICE, TOWN OFFICIALS, AND JUDICIARY PROCEDURES

It is inevitable that where a large group of people live or gather there is a need for law and order. Rhodhiss was no exception. With the opening of the mill company in the early 1900s, police protection was needed from time to time. According to the town minutes the first event was on June 1, 1904. Mayor Caleb Rhodes, the son of John Rhodes, said that the purpose of the town meeting was to elect four marshals to preserve order on the following day on which there was to be a picnic to celebrate the opening of the new steel bridge at Rhodhiss across the Catawba River. The following were elected as marshals at a rate of $1 per day: H. C. Detmas, W. H. Dennis, George Burgess, and Robert Miller.[1] The town minutes also indicate that the board would get together and appoint various men as police officers as the need arrived. In addition, the mayor could make this decision on his own if needed.[2] The town's minutes are incomplete regarding policemen. Also, minutes are missing from 1914 to 1919. When going through the minutes for the early years, I found information stating that a person resigned, but there was not a mention of when he began. For this reason, it is possible that someone served as an officer, but his name is not included in the list. The minutes would be the only place where police officers were logged. Many people have served Rhodhiss as police officers or town officials.

The town minutes document the first event where police officers were hired, and they also discuss the need for a guard shack's construction on the mill property. On February 12, 1904, a motion was made for the building of a guard house, and the mayor was asked to oversee this project. In addition, there was a need for protection during the holiday on December 16, 1905. Mr. R. E. Lineberger, who was the constable, was given extra help for the weekends. The board ordered that G. F. Smith and T. W. Smith "go on duty until 12:00 noon on Saturday, December 23 and remain on duty until 12:00 midnight and receive $1.00. They will be relieved, and that person will stay on duty until 12:00 noon on Sunday.... It was ordered that one policeman be on duty every Saturday night and Sunday night until 12:00 midnight."[3] During the early 1900s the police were protecting the town.

Several people have expressed their pride that they or their relative served as a police officer in Rhodhiss. This fact was especially true in the interview with Doughton Beshears, Butler Monteith, and Shelley Teague:

> SH: So, who was the first policeman?
> ST: God, I don't know.
> BM: I think my granddaddy. Billy Butler.
> DB: They didn't call them a policeman then. What did they call them?
> ST & BM: Constable
> ST: We lived in that big house, Kirby house now, when dad was a policeman. Dad looked after Rhodhiss and the county, too. Dad was both. We got our rent and everything free. He was policeman, and they didn't pay him. We just got our rent.
> SH: What was your daddy's name, Smokey (Shelley)?
> ST: Everett. EET.
> DB: They paid me when I was chief, they paid me $10 a month. I was chief of police, and it paid $10 a month.
> TR: But you had a job in the mill, too.
> DB: Yeah, I was working. That's all they paid the chief was $10 a month. Now, I don't think they paid your daddy anything, Smokey. They just gave him his rent.
> ST: That's right.
> SH: Was your dad a constable?
> ST: No, he was a Caldwell deputy. [4]

Butler Monteith's granddaddy served as a constable in 1906 as he suggested, but his relative was not the first policeman. Tom Ross asked an important question of Doughton Beshears that needs clarification. All the policemen prior to the early 1960s held jobs in the mill, too. They served as police officers and worked for the mill company. They were on company payroll and worked in two capacities. When Burlington Mills bought the company in 1954, they gradually phased out many of the former procedures. The first full time police officer who was not on company payroll was R. A. Bowman in 1962; however, the first police chief as per town minutes was R. D. Beshears. Doughton served in this capacity several times. These men elaborated even more regarding police work:

> BM: Right there where Earl Bumgarner lived between those houses there was a
> wagon road that went down in there.
> ST: That's where we used to do our courtin' way back then. Parking places. We used to drive in there with our girlfriends and spark. Right there where Earl Bumgarner's house and the town maintenance man live.
> BM: Clarence Burns.

ST: Yeah, Burns. The houses weren't there then. There was an old road in there.

DB: When I was a policeman, they told me that there was parking down in those woods.

BM: You could go over to Henry Smith's area and get you a $1 liquor. That's where you came back and divided it up.

SH: Doughton, what year were you police chief?

DB: I don't remember what year it was.

ST: I was around '64 and '65.

SH: I have a picture of when they purchased the first police car. Did you have to drive your own car?

DB: Yeah, you furnished your own car.

ST: I didn't. They had a car when I was a policeman.

DB: When did you move out of the big house down here, Smokey (Shelley) because when your daddy quit policing, I took over.

ST: I was about 22 years old, I guess. That was 50 years ago.

DB: Well, it was about 50 years ago then. Then I came back and took the chief job again. Tom, what date did I come back?

TR: I don't have any idea. I can't remember.

DB: I went with the sheriff's department in '46. I stayed there 8 years. In '54 I came back to take the chief's job back. I stayed another 8 years.

TR: That's when they sort of divorced the policing from the company.

DB: Yeah, the town took over. Before the company paid the police salary.[5]

First, the location of the "sparking" as Shelley called it is off the present-day Dogwood Drive. Secondly, Doughton was correct as per the town minutes. He was the first police chief in 1939 after Shelley's dad, E. E. Teague was a policeman. Doughton left this post in 1943. He then returned in 1954 for eight years. When he left in 1962, the town began paying for police protection instead of the mill company. In addition, Doughton said that he had to drive his own car during patrol, and according to the town minutes on July 18, 1962, a bid for a police car from Fox Tolbert Chevrolet in Granite Falls was accepted at a cost of $1,995.[6] Shelley said that he used this car for patrol. The *Granite Falls Press* posted a picture in 1962 that said that Rhodhiss was experiencing three firsts: the first female mayor who was Evelyn "Tommie" Haas Rhea; the first full time police chief, R. A. Bowman, (not on company payroll); and the first police car.

1ST PICTURE, TOMMIE RHEA, FOX-TOLBERT REPRESENTATIVE, R. A. BOWMAN, 1962. 2ND PICTURE, 1962, ROY TUCKER, ARLEY CHURCH, VAN FOXX, TOMMIE RHEA, NORMA KIRBY, R. A. BOWMAN, JOHN RHEA, AND THAD MARTIN. GRANITE FALLS PRESS PHOTO.

Although most interviewees expressed the sentiment that Rhodhiss was a safe place, crime did take place within the area, so law enforcement was needed. According to the *Hickory Daily Record* in 1922 a man was alleged to have broken into several stores and the post office at Rhodhiss, and he then broke out of jail. A $175 reward was offered for his return.[7] In 1917 Justice of the Peace, Calvin Hollar, confiscated nine gallons of whiskey in Rhodhiss. He arrested two men according to the *Lenoir News-Topic*.[8] One man was charged for criminal carelessness in the shooting of a woman within the town. He "was handling his pistol carelessly in the presence" of two women, "when the pistol went off, the ball striking" one below her eye "ranging downward through her neck and shoulder and inflicting a serious wound." The man served twelve months.[9] Ned Bean also mentioned the Justice of the Peace, Mr. Hollar. Ned stated:

> Old Man Calvin Hollar was the outside superintendent, Boyd Hollar's daddy. He used to walk around at night, and all of us boys were scared to death of him because quite a few boys at one time or another got put into reformatory school, and he was the justice of the peace, and he was the one responsible for getting them there. Often boys would shoot the streetlights out with slingshots. He would walk around and check the streetlights. Every night before he went to bed, he walked the hill.[10]

Mr. Hollar walked softly around the town gathering the ones who needed extra guidance in obeying the law.

Pawnee Mullinax Simmons discussed her dad's serving as a mayor in Rhodhiss; M. T. Mullinax served as mayor in 1927-1928, and he held a job in the mill as the master mechanic. I was told that this man was well before his time, and that he could fix anything. He was instrumental in wiring all the houses in Rhodhiss. Pawnee talked about his role as mayor and that he had to hold Mayor's Court for various disputes, crimes, or problems. Pawnee stated:

> Daddy was the mayor. I don't remember any of the details, but as sure as Monday morning come, he had to have a hearing. People had gotten into fights, between one man and another or a man and his wife. I remember daddy telling some of the awfullest and funniest things about his Monday mornings. He'd get the people settled down, and then the next week, it would happen again. It was the same thing over.[11]

Mayor's Court took place often in the early days because it is documented in the town minutes. This practice occurred into the 1960s. Tommie Haas Rhea told me about one particular man that would come to her house frequently to discuss his arguments with his wife prior to court because he wanted Tommie to hear his story without his wife's being present, and he could not do that in Mayor's Court.[12] The town minutes read that on "July 1, 1964 Ordinance #27 states that the Mayor will be paid $4 for each case that is tried in Mayor's court," and on August 10, 1964, "Six arrests were made in July, and four will be tried in Mayor's Court."[13] The mayor's job was already hard enough in that he/she had to listen to the citizen's complaints, but having the duty of holding court with fellow townspeople would only add more stress. Perhaps, that is why this practice no longer exists.

Mattie Munday did not call it Mayor's Court, but she called it Magistrate Court. Her terminology indicated the same thing as Mayor's Court though. Mattie explained:

> MM: Yeah, I know my girlfriend was pretty, blonde headed, and I don't remember what she was doing now, but this man was doffing, and they got into it, and he slapped her. She took him to court. And after the mill closed down that night, I went out there with her to have the trial. They fined him $5.
> SH: Who was the judge?
> MM: Well, the magistrate or whoever tried her. Mr. A. C. Hollar was the one who tried her. You know Boyd Hollar's daddy. He charged the man $5 for slapping her. The man said, 'I can say that it was well worth it.'[14]

Mr. A. C. Hollar was the mayor in 1913 and then again from 1920 to 1924. This was most probably Mayor's Court, too. The man that was tried by Mr. Hollar was charged $5 for the assault. He could have spent time in the jail that was in Rhodhiss, but that was not part of the sentence. The town minutes list several times that people had to pay jail fees. The jail was near the company offices as per conversations with former citizens. On December 7, 1920, Mr. A. C. Hollar also signed an ordinance that stated that explosives were not allowed within a certain distance of buildings, and guns could not be fired within 300 feet of a dwelling.

1920 GUN ORDINANCE. FROM RHODHISS TOWN MINUTES.

In the 1920s the town found that nearby towns were collecting sand from the riverbanks to take to their homes and/or companies. The town was forced to start charging for the sand because the riverbanks were looking bare.

LETTER TO BROOKSHIRE AND FRAZIER STATING THE TOWN'S SAND POLICY.
FROM RHODHISS TOWN MINUTES.

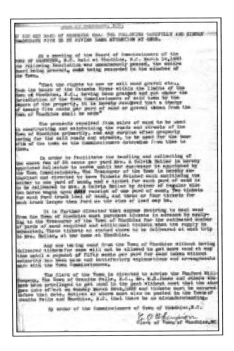

SAND ORDINANCE. FROM RHODHISS TOWN MINUTES.

During the 1927 mayoral term of L. A. "Shorty" Elmore, he felt the need to write a letter to the citizens to inform them that he represented everyone, rich or poor. At the same time the board drew up 33 ordinances that the people should observe.

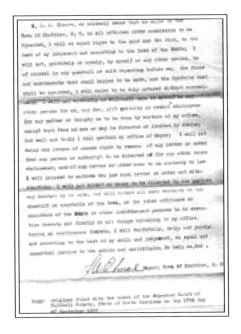

1927 MAYOR L. A. "SHORTY" ELMORE'S
LETTER TO THE TOWN.
FROM RHODHISS TOWN MINUTES.

1927 TOWN ORDINANCES. FROM TOWN
MINUTES.

During 1945 the Town Minutes suggest that some teenage boys were causing problems because they were loitering past a reasonable hour. "The policeman reported that he was having a good deal of trouble with boys under 16 loafing around the streets and buildings at the mill. The Mayor will talk with the Clerk of Court and Solicitor about passing an ordinance requiring those 'under age' boys be at home by a certain time."[15] Law enforcement had quite a job then. In 1945 Pacific Mills bought out the mill company, and their positive changes probably helped to maintain order. During Pacific's tenure and prior to that, the office manager for the company also served as the town clerk. The conversation between Calvin Jones and Tom Ross explained this idea:

CJ: Whoever was the office manager was the town clerk.
TR: And was on the school board, too.
CJ: Right.
SH: Till the 1960s when Norma Kirby took over as town clerk?
TR: Yeah.
SH: Then she was a paid town clerk; paid by the town and not the company?
TR: Yeah.[16]

While observing the attached list of Town Clerks and Town Managers, people must note that until 1960 the town clerk was on company payroll, served as the office manager, and also was on the school board. The mill company was able to fill three positions with one job title.

Presently, the Town of Rhodhiss is patrolled by Tim Anthony who has held the position since 2006. According to a March 17, 2006, article in the *Lenoir News-Topic*, "Rhodhiss has been operating without a police force, but Tim Anthony was hired as part-time Rhodhiss Police Chief. Mayor Jimmy Wilson introduced Anthony at its most recent town meeting, but Anthony was hired on March 7, 2006."[17] Officer Anthony has been a blessing to the town. On March 13, 2012, Chief Tim Anthony was recognized for Distinguished Service because on February 14, 2012, Chief Anthony entered a burning home and rescued the resident before the fire department arrived.[18] In addition, another Rhodhiss notable found his picture and story on the front page of the *Hickory Daily Record*. Mr. Larry Hendrix retired from police work in 2012. Here is his story:

Larry Hendrix grew up in Rhodhiss where his parents both worked in local mills. His cousin, Ken Hamby, who was 13 years older, influenced his career choice the most. He and Hamby worked on cars and spent a great deal of time together. When Larry was 14, he started pondering career choices. Hamby was a Longview policeman and Larry's Uncle Jack Hendrix was a Rhodhiss Police Chief. Larry started hanging out at the Longview Police Station with Hamby. Hendrix many years later retired from the Catawba County Sheriff's Office in September 2012. He was also an SRO at Fred T. Foard High. Hendrix started out as a dispatcher at the Granite Falls Police Department when he was 18. It was on his birthday, April 26, 1981, that Hendrix became a full-fledged police officer in Rhodhiss. Back then, folks could be officers before they were

21 years old. A year later, Hendrix joined the Longview Police Department. Several years later, opportunity knocked again, and Hendrix became the youngest police chief for the town of Rhodhiss. He stayed put until someone talked him into going to work for Pepsi in Granite Falls. He missed police work so he went to Longview. In 1992 he joined the Catawba County Sheriff's Office.[19]

Rhodhiss has been fortunate to have so many people who cared about the town to serve as policemen.

MR. BENFIELD, A POLICEMAN IN THE LATE 1930S.

PINEY RANDALL, A POLICEMAN IN
THE 1940S.

LES WEAVER, A POLICEMAN IN THE
1950S. RUTH WEAVER PHOTO.

R. A. BOWMAN, A POLICEMAN IN THE
1960S. BETTY BOWMAN PHOTO.

DOUG COWICK, DOUGHTON BESHEARS, AND THAD
ELMORE SERVED AS POLICEMEN IN THE 1960S.
MARGIE COWICK PHOTO.

MARVIN ABERNETHY WAS A
POLICEMAN IN THE 1970S.
DONNA PRICE PHOTO.

JACK HENDRIX, WALT FOX, AND JAMES CHURCH. JACK
HENDRIX WAS A POLICEMAN FROM 1969 TO EARLY 1980.
RHODHISS FIRE DEPARTMENT PHOTO.

Pfc. Joe Munday is stationed at Myrtle Beach, S. C. after finishing basic training at Ft. Jackson. Formerly with the Rhodhiss Outside Crew, his parents, Raymond and Mattie Munday, work in No. 2 Spinning.

JOE MUNDAY WAS A POLICEMAN IN THE EARLY 1980S. PACIFIC TRUTHS PHOTO.

Rhodhiss Council Takes Oath

The new Rhodhiss town council was sworn in Tuesday night during a special meeting. The transition of government occurred when Alene Dale administered the oath of office to the municipal officials. Pictured from left, are commissioners R.D. "Doughton" Beshears, Thad Martin, Ernest Church, Bruce Hartsoe, mayor R.A. Bowman and Ms. Dale. Martin was named mayor pro-tem. Mayor Bowman appointed the commissioners to the following committees — Beshears, police commissioner; Church, street commissioner; Hartsoe, fire commissioner and garbage committee; and Martin, water-sewer commissioner. The next meeting will be Monday, Dec. 14 at 6 pm. (GFP Photo)

RHODHISS TOWN BOARD 1980S. DOUGHTON BESHEARS, THAD MARTIN, ERNEST CHURCH, BRUCE HARTSOE, R. A. BOWMAN, AND ALENE DALE. GRANITE FALLS PRESS PHOTO.

RHODHISS OFFICIALS AT THE 2012 SCHOOL HISTORICAL SIGN DEDICATION. JOE KIRBY, COUNCILMAN; RICK JUSTICE, MAYOR; DIANE ECKARD, TOWN CLERK; MIKE PHILLIPS, COUNCILMAN; AND BARBARA HARMON, TOWN MANAGER. CARL COMPTON PHOTO.

Norma Kirby held the position of town clerk the longest. Her 40-year tenure started in 1960 and ended in 2000. Norma was the epitome of an honest, hardworking person who served the community. In an article in the *Lenoir News Topic*, Norma described herself as "just an ordinary person with just an ordinary job." She knew all the town's citizens, and her job in 1960 started as a temporary assignment replacing Ben Pearson as town clerk. At first, she worked only on Saturdays because she was the mother to two small boys, Allen and Ray, and because Saturdays were a good day for the town citizens to pay their water bills. Next her schedule changed to Saturdays and two hours on Tuesdays. By this time, she had added a daughter Beth to her family. Then two hours on Tuesdays became a full day, and later she added Wednesdays, too. Norma was responsible for council meetings, minutes, town transactions, water and tax notices, voter registration, collecting mail at the post office, and conducting transactions at the bank. The citizens felt as if they could talk to Norma. She served the town well, and in addition, she helped with the United Fund, worked for the Rhodhiss Baptist Church as a secretary, sang in the church choir, and helped with training union.[20] The town council resolved to have a Norma Kirby Day in 2000 in honor of her forty-year service to the town.[21] Barbara Harmon has also served the Rhodhiss community the longest as town manager. She has returned on several occasions to fill in as an interim when a manager left. Barbara, too, has served the community well, and her tenure as town manager has allowed the town to have continuity and professionalism because she, too, is honest and hardworking. The townspeople benefited immensely from her leadership. Presently, the town manager is Rick Justice, and he has served in this capacity for two years.

NORMA KIRBY, RHODHISS TOWN CLERK
FOR 40 YEARS. CARL HOLLAR PHOTO.

Rhodhiss made history in 1980 when Mike Owens served as mayor. He was the youngest mayor to serve in the state of North Carolina. Whether people served as a policeman, a constable, a mayor, a town clerk, or a town manager, they deserve gratitude from all the former and present citizens. Working in any of these capacities shows a dedication to the community. Their service is greatly appreciated. The lists of police officers, mayors, town clerks and town managers follow.

Rhodhiss Town Sheriff, Police, Constable, or Marshal
(Taken from Town Minutes)

Date	Name(s)	Notes from Town Minutes
February 12, 1904	H.G. Moon	given 2 pairs of handcuffs
June 1, 1904	H.C. Detmas W.H. Dennis George Burgess Robert Miller	picnic to celebrate opening of the new steel bridge across the Catawba River at a rate of $1 per day
June 18, 1904	W.H. Dennis	
September 9, 1904	T.R. Miller	
November 1904	Henry Lowery	
June 25, 1905	R.E. Lineberger	$1.50 a day (10 hour day)
December 16, 1905	G.F. Smith T.W. Smith	Added to help Lineberger during holidays
May 28, 1906	W.E. Butler	Badge and handcuffs purchased Note: Butler Monteith's granddad
October 4, 1907	G.H. Morgan	Salary $15 a month
September 2, 1909	S.L. Thompson	Salary $10 a month
February 25, 1910	Various men	Appointed by Mayor from time to time because Thompson resigned
October 11, 1910	Gus Poovey	Paid him $20 for police service
February 2, 1911	Gus Taunt	Paid him for police duty

January 13, 1913	Jess Mundy Tom Statin	$50 for police duty $1 for police duty
1914-1919	No minutes available	
May 31,1920	L. Smith	
August 2, 1920	J.D. Kirby	
August 26, 1921	W.H. Barker	
March 19, 1923	W.A.L. Dagenhart	Salary $12.50 per month
October 20, 1926	Various men	Appointed by the Mayor from to time; salary at a minimum
May 27, 1930	J.P. Kaylor Robert Moore	Resigned Replaced J.P. Kaylor
March 1, 1932	W.L. Mathis D.L. Tolbert	Resigned (no start date) Replaced W.L. Mathis
May 15, 1936	E.E. Teague	
May 25, 1938	E.E. Teague and C.P. Benfield	To receive the same salaries Benfield resigned on 2-1-1939
September 8, 1939	Doughton Beshears, Chief	$10 a month salary; later Increased to $15; Mayor will hire an assistant policeman from the Burke County side at $5 monthly.
July 29, 1943	E.M. Randall, Chief	$15 a month; later increased to $20.
May 8, 1946	E.M. Randall, Chief Lester Weaver, Assistant	Chief: $25 a month; $25 a month car allowance
December 9, 1946	E.M. Randall, Chief	Police required to patrol at

	Lester Weaver, Assistant	least 500 miles per month; allowance increased to $50 a Month. Ordered 2 uniforms; pay monthly phone rental for the chief and his assistant.
April 19, 1951	Lester Weaver, Chief	Death of E.M. Randall 4-14-1946 and Weaver named chief. Randall had been chief since July 29, 1943. Weaver's salary: $25 month; routine auto expense of $50 month; $2.19 per month telephone expense.
April 25, 1951	Lester Weaver, Chief Thad Elmore, Assistant	
May 26, 1952	Lester Weaver, Chief James Austin, Assistant	
June 10, 1953	Lester Weaver, Chief Arley Church, Assistant	
October 5, 1953	Lester Weaver, Chief Earl Bumgarner, Assistant	
November 10, 1954	Arley Church, Chief	Lester Weaver died on 10-31-1954; Arley appointed by the board
November 16, 1954	Doughton Beshears, Chief	
July 14, 1956	Doughton Beshears, Chief Arley Church, Assistant	$33.00 per month $30.00 per month
September 29, 1956	Doughton Beshears, Chief	Board voted to have only 1 Police officer; $66 per month

July 8, 1958	Doughton Beshears, Chief Thad Elmore, part-time	$40 per month
July 9, 1962	Doughton Beshears, Chief R. A. Bowman	Town purchased complete Summer uniforms. Two temporary officers were hired for a week with Chief Beshears on vacation: Hans Townsend and Bill Eckard; 38 Colt police revolver was purchased for R.A.
August 13, 1962	R. A. Bowman, Chief Van Foxx, Deputy	Winter pants and jacket purchased for R.A. and 3 shirts and a jacket for Van.
March 11, 1963	R. A. Bowman	
March 18, 1964	Wayne Mullinax, Chief Homer Goodman, Deputy	Purchased 2 shirts 1 pants Both resigned 6-30-1964
July 1964	Thad Elmore, Temporary Hansel Townsend, Temporary	
July 21, 1964	Van Foxx, Chief Doug Cowick, Assistant	Salary $85 weekly Salary $50 per month, but increased to $75 on 10-31-1964.
May 10, 1965	Thad Elmore, Chief Doug Cowick, Assistant	
September 14, 1965	R.A. Bowman, Chief Doug Cowick, Assistant	$90 per week; he will work school crossing twice daily, read water meters, clean catch basins 2 times monthly, read water meters, check and replace street lights.

June 23, 1966	R.A. Bowman, Chief Homer Goodman, Assistant	$70 per month
January 13, 1967	Shelley Teague, Chief	$85 per week; purchase him a raincoat
September 11, 1967	Shelley Teague, Chief Ralph Powell, Assistant	
April 9, 1968	William Blanehard, Chief Ralph Powell, Assistant	$90 per week; clean town offices; cut grass at municipal building; read water meters; check and replace streetlights; work school crossings twice daily; give gas and mileage report
June 4, 1968	Thad Elmore, Chief Ralph Powell, Assistant	$90; duties as those above
April 19, 1969	Plez Rash, Temporary	$70 per month; till a police chief hired
April 28, 1969	Billy Hicks, Chief	$90 per week
June 16, 1969	Billy Hicks, Chief Larry Nichols, Assistant	30-day trial; $70 per month; officially hired after 30 days July 14, 1969
November 10, 1969	Jack Hendrix, Chief Larry Nichols, Assistant	
June 25, 1971	Jack Hendrix, Chief Marvin Abernethy, Assistant	Weekend duty $85/month
July 1, 1972	Jack Hendrix, Chief Gary Ray Helton, Assistant	

July 9, 1973	Jack Hendrix, Chief Michael E. Melton, Assistant	
August 19, 1974	Charles Beshears Michael Melton, Assistant	Special Office Fill in for Chief Hendrix who is hospitalized. Beshears agreed to do this for no pay.
September 1974	Jack Hendrix, Chief Michael Melton, Assistant	Return
April 14, 1975	Jack Hendrix, Chief Coy Long, Assistant	
March 14, 1977	Jack Hendrix, Chief Ken Yarber, Assistant	
December 10, 1979	Jack Hendrix, Chief Joe Munday, Captain	Joe was lieutenant prior to this; however, minutes do not say when he began the job.
April 21, 1981	Joe Munday, Chief Jack Hendrix, Part-time Chief	
December 14, 1981	Joe Munday, Chief Larry Hendrix, Assistant Jack Hendrix, Auxiliary	Larry may have started before this date, but no indication in minutes.
July 12, 1982	Joe Munday, Chief Keith Edwards, Assistant	Retired 2-15-1985 Resigned 11-14-1983
February 17, 1985	J. Mel Rhoney, Chief	
July 7, 1986	Larry Hendrix, Chief	Resigned 11-29-1988
December 19, 1988	Michael Hennessee, Chief	

June 14, 1993	Jack Holsclaw	laid off 2-25-94 budget deficiency
March 17, 1994	Tommy Madron, Acting Police Chief	Temporary, Became full time June 29, 1994
May 22, 1995	John Larue, Part time	
June 10, 1995	John Larue, Chief	
May 13, 2002	John Larue, Chief Terry Campbell, Assistant	
February 10, 2003	Terry Campbell, Chief Tim Anthony, Part-time Barry Pruitt, Auxiliary	
January 11, 2004	Terry Campbell Chief, Tim Anthony, Assistant	
March 8, 2004	Terry Campbell, Chief Tim Anthony, Assistant Jenny LeBeau, part-time Barry Pruitt, Auxiliary	
January 11, 2005	Terry Campbell, Chief Tim Anthony, Assistant Jenny LeBeau, part-time Michael Kirby, Reserve	
May 11, 2005	Turned over to Burke County for 40 hours a week of service.	
December 13, 2005	Officer Brandon Crotts	
February 23, 2006	Tim Anthony, Part time Chief	
August 2006	Tim Anthony, Part time Chief Steve Deal, Reserve Officer	

August 14, 2007	Tim Anthony, Part time Chief	
	John Pierce, Reserve Officer	Pierce Resigned 4-8-2008
	Mike Boston, Reserve Officer	
	Tim Sawyer, Reserve Officer	

January 12, 2010	Tim Anthony, Part time Chief	
	Roger Phillips, Reserve Officer	
	Anthony Talton, Reserve Officer	Added on 11-9-2010

December 11, 2012	Tim Anthony, Chief	
	Scott Warren, Field Training Officer	
	& Background Check Officer	
	Barry Halter, Reserve Officer	Added on 8-13-2013
	Officer Milton, Reserve Officer	Added on 2-11-2014

| October 2018 | Tim Anthony, Chief | |
| | Barry Halter, Assistant | |

| June 2021 | Tim Anthony, Chief | |
| | Kirby Anderson, Assistant | |

| 2022 | Tim Anthony, Chief | |
| | Barry Halter, Reserve officer | |

Mayors of Rhodhiss (Taken from Town Minutes)

Name	Years
C. J. Rhodes	1903-1904
C. E. Nabors	1904-1905
J. M. Rhodes	1905-1905
C. E. Nabors	1905-1909
F. S. Mosher	1909-1910
L. W. Kirkman	1910-1911
G. F. Smith	1911-1912
W. S. Taylor	1912-1913
A. C. Hollar	1913-1913
W. W. Byars	1913-1914
No minutes for years 1914-1919	
A.C. Hollar	1920-1924
L. A. Elmore	1924-1927
M. T. Mullinax	1927-1928
A.C. Hollar	1928-1930
L.A. Elmore	1930-1933
T. B. Smith	1933-1936
A. L. Fox	1936-1940
Claude Barker	1940-1950
Fred Elmore	1950-1954
W. M. Childers	1954-1962
Mrs. John Rhea (Tommie)	1962-1963
Arley Church	1963-1968
Charlie Kirby	1968-1970
Odell Tramble	1970-1972
C. J. Munday (Bud)	1972-1979
Charles Beshears	1979-1980
Mike Owens	1980-1981
C. J. Munday (Bud)	1981-1981
R. A. Bowman	1981-1983
R. D. Beshears	1983-1989
R.A. Bowman	1989-1993
Naomi Burns	1993-1998
Doug Cowick	1998-2003
Jimmy Wilson	2003-2007
Rick Justice	2007-2020
Allen Spencer	2020-present

Town Clerks (Taken from Town Minutes)

Years	Name
1904-1904	C. E. Nabors
1904-1904	S. L. Thompson
1904-1904	J. D. Rudisill
1905-1906	S. L. Thompson
1906-1907	D. M. Cloninger
1907-1910	James W. Espey
1910-1913	J. C. Harrill
1913-1914	W. N. Stroupe
1914-1919	No minutes
1920-1933	C. O. Champion
1933-1935	W. W. Hinson
1935-1946	Clarkson Jones
1946-1953	D. O. Cook
1953-1955	L. E. Lee
1955-1958	T. H. Ross
*1956	Floyd Kirby, Assistant
1958-1960	Ben Pearson
1960-2000	Norma Kirby
2000-2002	David Hollar
2002-2004	Julie Jarvis Trivette
2004-2007	Rose Waldroup
	Became manager in 2005
2017-2019	Barbara Harmon
	When she wasn't an interim Town Manager
20019-present	Julie Byrd

*1956 Floyd Kirby became an assistant town clerk because villagers now had to pay water bills for the first time. When the houses were rented by the mill company, the water was included in their rent. Also, water meters had to be installed on the houses for the first time. Floyd worked only on Saturdays. The office manager of the mill company served as the town clerk until 1960.

Town Managers (taken from Town Minutes)

2005-2007	Rose Waldroup
2007-2007	Larry Bowman, Interim
2007-2014	Barbara Harmon
2014-2016	Art Delaney
2016-2016	Barbara Harmon, Interim
2016-2017	Benjamin Turnmire
2017-2017	Barbara Harmon, Interim
2018-2019	Chris Wagoner
2019-2020	Barbara Harmon
2020-present	Rick Justice

NOTES

1   Rhodhiss Town Minutes. 1 June 1904.

2   Rhodhiss Town Minutes. 25 February 1910.

3   Rhodhiss Town Minutes. 16 December 1905.

4   Beshears, Monteith, Ross and Teague.

5   Beshears, Monteith, Ross, and Teague.

6   Rhodhiss Town Minutes. 18 July 1962.

7   "Saw Out of Jail." *Hickory Daily Record.* 10 January 1922, p. 1.

8   "More Whisky (sic) Cases Added To Calendar." *Lenoir News-Topic.* 23 February 1917, p. 1.

9   *The Hickory Democrat.* 12 March 1914, p. 1.

10   Bean, Ned and Elvie and Tom Ross.

11   Simmons, Finn and Pawnee, Tom Ross.

12   Rhea, Tommie Hass. Personal Interview with Sherrie Hartsoe Sigmon. 3 May 1988.

13   Rhodhiss Town Minutes. 1 July 1964 and 10 August 1964.

14   Munday, Mattie and Louise Keller.

15   Rhodhiss Town Minutes. 19 September 1945.

16   Jones, Calvin and Tom Ross.

17   Payne, Linda. "Rhodhiss Hires Police Chief." *Lenoir News-Topic.* 17 March 20016, pp. 1A and 5A.

18   Rhodhiss Town Minutes. 13 March 2012.

19   McBrayer, Sharon. "Former Police Chief Says Career Was His Calling." *Hickory Daily Record.* 14 January 2013, pp. 1A and 3A.

20   "Norma Kirby: She's the Pulse of Rhodhiss." *Lenoir News Topic.* Spring 1983.

21   Rhodhiss Town Minutes. 13 March 2000.

CHAPTER 8
WORKING CONDITIONS

Textile mills began in the northern states, but around 1900, they started moving southward. Northerners came to the South to find workers who were used to being treated as family.[1] Southern workers were loving, friendly people, and they were devoted to their work. Oftentimes, they felt as if they were married to their jobs. Northern mill owners also came southward because Southerners were considered more "docile."[2] The workers in Rhodhiss took their jobs seriously and honored management. They left the hard life of farming to start operating machinery in the textile mills. People came from all over North Carolina to seek employment in textiles; however, their jobs were hard, and the working conditions caused a lot of frustration and strife.

Mattie Munday talked with her daughter, Louise Keller, and me about the problems that faced mill workers. Will Knight was her boss man when she went to work at the age of 14 in 1921. Matt explained:

MM: Well, I worked barefooted because your feet got tired, and you just took your shoes off. I would get splinters in my feet, and my boss man would set me up in the window and pick them out. The windows weren't closed up; they kept the windows open. I went with my brother down there and messed around, but when I got 14, I could go to work. I was little, and I had to climb up on a rail to reach. So, I stayed in there, and you didn't make money for learning. But I stayed in there until I could run a half a side. Then they kept adding another side. They kept adding like that. I made $2 a week.

SH: How many hours a week was that?

MM: Sixty. We worked eleven hours a day and five hours on Saturday.

LK: But they would come home during the day.

MM: Yeah, I would. We later moved up on the hill where Roam Bowman died. There's a trailer there now. But we lived there in a house below that. I would go home for lunch. If any of them would get hungry during the day, they would watch my side and let me go up there to get a biscuit. Mama always had biscuits; you know. She might cook streaked meat. I would go up there and get it. I would put it in a paper bag because you didn't have paper towels.

SH: What's streaked meat?

MM: Fatback. I got some that I can show you. You know we raised our own, everything we had nearly. I would go up there and get us some biscuits for the ones that were hungry. Then we would go home at dinner. We got an hour off for dinner.

SH: You worked from 6 to 6?

MM: Yeah, 6 to 6. Then sometimes when everything got into such a mess we had to stay until 7:00, eat supper, and come back. And then we would start up frames. We were running cotton, and it's a terrible mess. But there's where I got to courtin' Raym.

SH: In the mill?

MM: Yeah, we done our courtin' there in the mill. He lived here, and I lived up on the hill. Getting back to working in the mill, you never wore shoes. They would take the thick cloth, quill like stuff, heavy, and they would take and cut that and make us shoes out of it. We would wear them a lot. I have had my boss man set me up in a window and put them on me. That would keep me from stepping in the spit. People spit all in the floor. Everybody dipped snuff. They had a well right along where the railroad tracks were right up from the mill, and they had what they called the water boy. He swept and carried water. We had two big ole water buckets and a dipper. They had a place where those water buckets sat. They hung the dipper up over it, and everybody drank out of the same ole dipper.

SH: Thelma Church said that in the card room there was so much dust that the water had so much dust on it that you had to blow it off.

MM: I guess that it was like that in the spinning room, too. Then the toilets had old wooden seats with a hole cut out in them. You would go in there and sit down and chinches would bite your butt before you could get up. I used to go in there and take a piece of bread and put it on the cracks just to see them run out, you know. They were starving, I guess. Those chinches would run out toward your hand. The first year that they ever gave a Christmas bonus, they gave the boss man about $25, but not the millhands. I don't remember what year that was, but I was working down here, and I remember. When the hands found out about it, they really got upset, you know. They had a meeting, and the owner, Mr. R. C. Moore, came. I remember him talking and apologizing, and I don't know or remember what the excuse was that they did that for them. He was just trembling, you know. I think that he was scared that we would jump on him or something.[3]

Mattie's description is very thorough. She had splinters in her feet from working barefoot. They constructed their own shoes to avoid the spit and tobacco juice. Everyone shared the same dipper for the water bucket. In several areas within the mill the water pail would have dust on top, and it had to be blown away. Mattie did not receive any pay for learning her job. She had to learn from going to the mill to help her brother. She made $2 a week for a 60-hour week, which is a little over three cents per hour. She was only 14 when she started. The mill company liked child labor as was heard in various interviews. Romance also was commonplace within the mill. With people working sixty hours a week, they had few places to meet a mate. Matt also described the owner's knowing that it was unfair for the boss men to receive bonuses, and the laborers to be shunned. The people doing the hardest job were not rewarded. Lastly, the bathrooms had wood bugs that would attack the person on the toilet. These details explain many hardships that the mill worker had to endure. Child labor was often not reported by the southern textile companies. "The 1907-8 Bureau of Labor study found that an astounding 92 percent of the mills in South Carolina and 75 percent in North Carolina ignored child labor regulations.[4]

Exie Hand also talked about the hazards of working in the mill. She and her husband Arthur "Ott" worked for Rhodhiss Mills, Pacific Mills, and Burlington Industries during their time at Rhodhiss. They started there in 1927. Exie said, "Oh, Lord, I've had splinters taken out from under my fingernails plumb down to there. See I spin, and I would reach up on the quill, the top of the quill to get a bobbin, and the quills were kinda rotten. Splinters would run down under your fingernails. When they'd get ahold of them, then a piece would break off. Lord, I've had my fingers hurt me so bad."[5] Two women, Exie and Mattie, discussed the handicaps of working in the mill.

Many other people have said similar things. Thelma Church talked about being a young child and carrying lunch to her mother's boarders. She would leave school and walk to the Caldwell plant to provide these people their meal. Thelma described her chore in 1919, 1920, and 1921.

Back in those days they didn't have things to make sandwiches out of. They didn't have bologna and all that stuff. Everything was bought in big buckets and big things, you know. Out here at the school at 11:30 they let me go home. Well, my mother had this big basket like a picnic basket. She would put their lunches in that basket. What she did is that she had beans, and potatoes, and all this, and she would put them in little bowls in the basket. She would have a pie or something for dessert, and then I would carry the basket to the mill. It was up on the third floor where all these people worked. They would stop off all the spinning frames and everything during lunch hour. They just had a well down there. They didn't have running water, and this guy you might remember, Ross Triplett. Well, it was his father. He carried water, and they would go down there and carry water and bring it up there and set it on a table. They just had one dipper, and everybody drunk out of that one dipper. There was so much dust in that spinning room that on the top of that water they would have to blow the dust off the top before you could drink it. Well, all the help then would go sit down in the windows. They had the windows pushed up because there was no air conditioning or anything, and they would go sit down in the window and eat their lunch. They might drink the water, or sometimes they sent out to the Company Store for cold drinks. Then they would eat their lunch. While they were eating lunch, they would have me go through the spinning room, and me only about 9, 10, or 11 years old, I was somewhere along in there, I would pick their slats. I don't know if you know what that is or not.

They are on the spinning frames. I would pick slats while they ate their lunch, and they would give me a dime for doing that, you know. Well, that just tickled me to death because you could come back by the store, and you could buy a big bag of candy for a dime or anything that you wanted for a dime then. Then I would take their basket back home, and I would go back to school about 1:00.[6]

Thelma was able to give more details on the water, the dust, and the one dipper for all to share. She also discussed pulling slats from the machine to help the people that boarded at her home. Her job for her mother was to walk from the school at the top of the present-day Church Street to her house on Bumgarner Road. Then she would have to walk to the mill which was near the present-day bridge. She had to return home to Bumgarner Road to deliver the basket. She would have time to stop at one of the area stores to buy candy and make it back to school by 1:00. Even at the age of 9, 10, or 11, children were helping their parents. Thelma also mentioned that the workers sat in the window to feel cooler. The mill did not have air conditioning, and that fact was discussed by several people. Willard Herman went to work in Rhodhiss in 1929 when he was 14. He told Tom Ross and me:

> WH: It was hot, humid, and uncomfortable, Tom.
> TR: Nobody says anything about it.
> WH: They carried the water because when I went to work you didn't have running water. They kept about three buckets of water sitting there. They had a well over at number one mill over near the railroad track. They would fill the buckets up, and that's where we got to drink from. From number two mill they didn't even have a well. They carried it from that spring in the holler. There was so much lint a flying all the time that you'd go to get you a drink of water, and you had to skim cotton lint off.
> TR: That lint made the water taste like metal is what they told me.
> WH: Well, I was young and didn't know any better. I just didn't know any other kind of life.
> TR: Well, I guess that was the same way with everybody. It was their job, earn money, and it wasn't any better anywhere else.[7]

Tom and Willard added an element about the water tasting like metal; however, their concluding words explain that it was like that in any mill village throughout the South.

Violet Curtis agreed with Willard about the uncomfortable heat. Violet went to work in Rhodhiss in 1921 when she was 15 years old. Violet said, "It was hot. There was no air conditioning. It was all cotton, so there was lint. It was dusty. The lighting was bad. It was so hot in there."[8] Interviewee after interviewee detailed the plight of the mill worker. When asked about the mill's source of heat and cooling, Exie Hand said, "Nooo! no air conditioning or anything in the mill. They heated with steam, and they kept it pretty warm."[9] At least the wintertime provided warmth within the mill, but the summer heat was apparently unbearable. Doughton Beshears, Butler Monteith, Shelley Teague, and Tom Ross discussed the heat and the water situation:

TR: Someone was telling us about the dust in the mill. You were talking about the water and the sewer. The rats used to be so bad they told me when I first came up here. Even after we (Pacific) came here before the equipment was changed out, they said that you couldn't see from one end of the card room from the other because it was so dusty. The air was full of dust. You see they used to run what they called low grade cotton, which was unclean and caused the dust.

ST: Snakes were in the mills, too.

TR: They told me that people couldn't keep their lunches sitting out because the rats would eat it.

ST: There were windows. There weren't any air conditioners. It was hot.

DB: I worked in the weave room. We carried our drinking water from up above the mill. There was a spring up there.

ST: There was a spring up there at the playground.

DB: We would take two buckets. We would set them up in the window. We used the same dipper.

BM: Everybody drank out of the same dipper.

ST: You had to scrape the cotton off the water to drink it.

TR: That is what someone else told her.

DB: It wasn't so bad dusty in the weave room.

TR: The card room was what I was told was bad.

BM: Oh, yeah, it was. I did work one summer in the spinning room.[10]

These gentlemen were able to add more to the hazards of working in the mill. Rats and snakes were crawling around inside. Conditions continued to weigh on the workers. Butler went to work at Rhodhiss in 1926 when he was 14 years old, and he worked 45 years. He labored for three mill companies: Rhodhiss Mills, Pacific Mills, and Burlington Industries. Doughton worked for all three, too, but he left on several occasions to work for Caldwell County. Shelley also worked for the three companies, and he went to work in the 1930s. He worked in Rhodhiss for 30 years. Tom Ross didn't come to Rhodhiss till 1946, and he worked for Pacific Mills in South Carolina before he was transferred to Rhodhiss. He worked for 43 years for Pacific and Burlington. These men knew the companies and their operations.

Gladys Kirby Barker went to work in 1917 when she was 13 years old. She said that they passed a law, and she had to go back to school until she was 14. She worked eleven hours a day for five days a week from 6:00 AM to 12 PM; she had an hour for lunch and returned at 1 PM and worked till 6 PM, and she worked 5 hours on Saturday (6 AM-11 AM). That was a sixty-hour week for $2 as a spinner at the Burke County mill, and she walked that bridge four times a day.[11] Gladys indicated that she was stopped from working at the age of 13 because of child labor laws. Oftentimes these laws were overlooked or enforced minimally. Thelma Church talked about her working in the mill in 1927 for a brief period when she was 15, and she indicated that her husband Joe went to work in the mill in 1911 when he was 9 years old. Thelma stated:

TC: People made very little. I know when Joe and I got married, I went to work down there in the cloth room. I just worked three or four months.

SH: In Caldwell or Burke?

TC: Caldwell. I worked down there and made $10.80 for 55 to 60 hours a week. Joe went to work down there at 9 years old. He made $2.40 a week.

SH: He went down there to work, and he was 9 years old?

TC: Yeah

SH: Child labor.

TC: Yes. He went down there. He would go to school, and then go down after that and work. Then in the summertime he worked. Sherrie, back then at 9 or 10 years old, they would let them work. In the summer he made $2.40 a week for 60 hours. Can you imagine? I never heard tell of their giving a bonus or anything.[12]

Many children worked in the mill, and the mill companies throughout the South depended on them. At the turn of the twentieth century one fourth of the mill workers were under 16 years old. Children did all sorts of jobs within the mill. They were defined as youngsters up to eight; then this increased to twelve, and then fourteen, and lastly sixteen.[13] This is most probably why Gladys Barker had to stop working at 13 and wait till she was 14. The age requirement kept increasing. Similarly, Violet Curtis, Tom Ross, and Willard Herman discussed child labor:

WH: How old were you when you started working in the mill, Violet?

VC: I was 15.

SH: Did you go to work full time?

VC: Well, no they let me work only 8 hours because of my age. My brother Werd went to work when he was 12 years old. He ran four looms. Then child labor laws came in. They cut him out. I worked only 8 hours when I went to work.

WH: I'll tell you a guy that could tell you some things. Conrad "Connie" Woodie. He came to Rhodhiss from Wilkes County. He went to work in the mill when he was about 10 years old. The head doffer would whistle for the children to fill the batteries. You had to whistle good.

VC: Yeah, I remember that, too.

SH: Is that Glenn Woodie's daddy?

WH: It's Glenn's daddy's brother. He worked in the spinning room. He never wanted to do anything but doff.

VC: I've heard children say that they had to climb up on something to run machines. They said that they were barefooted.

SH: I read that some women took their babies into the mill in a box because they couldn't find babysitters. I heard that happened in Marion.

VC: Mrs. Curtis, my mother-in-law, told me about that at the old mill in Granite, that old mill down there. She'd fix a box for her two little boys, and she'd go to work at night, and she'd let them sleep in those boxes. Then she'd take them home the next morning, just little boys. I've heard her tell about that. She worked in a mill at Granite.

WH: I went to work in '28 or '29.

The story involving the Marion Mill stated, "'she used to put her baby in a little box and tie him in there to the framer while she worked so he couldn't get hurt.'"[14] Violet Curtis was also able to add more information about her mother-in-law's taking her children to work with her in Granite Falls at the old mill and letting them sleep in a box while she worked. Violet herself went to work in 1921. Her older brother Werd started working in Rhodhiss prior to that. He had to stop working just as Gladys Barker did because the child labor laws changed. Paul Bright told me of his dad's responsibility as a child. His dad, Clifton Bright, had two brothers, Clarence and Clyde. Clifton's chore was to take Clyde to the mill for Mrs. Bright to nurse him. Then Clifton returned home with the baby.[15] The times were hard for these women and children.

The Edwards children, Arthur, Jack, and Edna explained their father Finley's coming to Rhodhiss from McDowell County in 1907 with his parents. Finley went to work at the age of 12. The Edwards siblings said that there were more than fifteen of their family members working at the mill at one time.[16] It was a common practice during the early 1900s in mill villages to hire families that had a lot of children and/or relatives who would come to town to work, too. Jacquelyn Dodd Hall explained that "southern mill owners quickly settled on the family labor system. Rather than hiring individual workers, owners purchased family labor as a package, paying adult workers less than a living wage and offering employment to children."[17] Rhodhiss was no different than the rest of the South. Ned Bean and Tom Ross explained:

TR: One other comment that needs to be said about Rhodhiss. The superintendent would hire families that had multiple workers within the family. They liked families where they might could get three or four workers, too, out of one household.

NB: That's like when my friend's grandfather moved to Rhodhiss. He had eight or ten kids. He put all the kids to work in the mill, and he sat on the front porch and talked to people walking up and down the street. I guess that is what they were looking for. Someone with eight to ten kids so that they could work them to death. They came home and gave the daddy the wages. They worked eleven hours a day for nothing.[18]

Lastly, Fred Elmore mentioned that his family had the payroll ledger from 1902. He said that some people made as little as five cents per hour.[19] Fred must have been talking about five cents an hour for the adults because children were making less than that. As previously stated by Thelma Church, Joe was nine years old and made $2.40 for a 60-hour week.

Arthur and Exie Hand started their jobs at Rhodhiss Manufacturing in 1927. Arthur was 20, and Exie was 18. They talked about their wages:

EH: We worked twelve hours for a long, long time. Well, till they changed the law.

AH: We worked till 12:00 and was off. Then at 1:00 we went back to work.

SH: If you don't mind, may I ask you how much you made when you first started down here?

EH: When we first went to work, we just made $4 a week. Then they raised us to $6 a week. Then after about a year they raised it again.

AH: We both worked for cheap wages.[20]

These textile workers endured low wages and many hardships while at their jobs. Doughton Beshears, Butler Monteith, Shelley Teague, and Tom Ross discussed some of the obstacles:

DB: I stayed in the weave room the whole time.

TR: I am sure that the weave room was noisy.

DB: Oh, yeah. So many of the machines and the overhead drive. You talked because you learned to read lips. You couldn't hear a body talk. You just read lips.

ST: You would throw a quill down an alley if you wanted somebody to look up.

BM: That was after they fixed the floors. There was barely enough room to pass down there. If somebody came by, you had to try to squeeze by.

TR: So, they had it full of looms, did they?

BM: 450 of them.

TR: That's right.

SH: On Burke side?

BM: That's right.

SH: 450!

ST: They were all run by line shafts and belts, too.

TR: Did they have what they call a motor on each loom?

BM: No, they had what they called a motor drive, and it was on the upper end of the mill.

ST: But before that they had water wheels.

BM: I can remember the water wheels.

ST: I don't remember the water wheels.

BM: During heavy rains they would have to close the mill down to get the trash out of the water wheel.

ST: I worked the second shift from 6 to 6. They would blink the lights at midnight and stop the looms off, and you took off to eat.

BM: Yeah, they would stop the machinery all down.

DB: I worked from 6 in the morning till 6 in the late afternoon.

SH: How many days a week?

DB: Five.

BM: Five and a half

DB: Yeah, we worked half a day on Saturday.[21]

Doughton Beshears explained that the noise was so loud in the weave room that employees had to learn to read lips, or Shelley said that throwing things drew attention. Butler Monteith was able to recall when the looms were run by water wheels. This would have been before 1924. He was able to elaborate on the hazards of heavy rains on this machinery. After the water-wheel-run looms, the company advanced to a motor drive that was not on the machine.

Fred Elmore was able to elaborate on the hearing problem that Doughton mentioned. Fred explained to Martha, Tom Ross, and me:

> TR: Doughton Beshears was talking about the weave room was so noisy that they had to learn to read lips in order to communicate.
>
> FE: That's what's done that (pointing to hearing aids).
>
> TR: Martha, everybody that we've talked to has a hearing problem. Some just accept it and don't do anything about it.
>
> FE: If you were standing on one end of the weave room, you could talk to someone through the alley by hand motions. The noise was so loud that people communicated that way, by motions. We shop people knew what they wanted in the weave room by hand motions. Everybody could whistle, too, but you couldn't hear that over the weave room noise. You could in the spinning room or the card room, but not the weave room.
>
> FE: Yeah, it was so dusty that you couldn't see anything in the card room. We drank out of a bucket, and someone came in and set it down, and that dust would collect on top.
>
> ME: It is a wonder that they didn't smother to death.[22]

Not only did the employees have hardships to face while on the job, but some of these caused problems with their health. Martha Elmore was correct in asserting that it was amazing that they could breathe.

Mary Settlemyre Darty worked at Rhodhiss for forty-five years. She lived nearby in Burke County off Carolina Avenue. Mary discussed her life at Rhodhiss with Tom Ross and me:

> MD: I worked in the weave room. I started out filling batteries. Then I filled unifills. I worked on the Burke side.
>
> SH: You worked down here how many years?
>
> MD: 45. I started in 1937.
>
> TR: Let's see. If you went to work in '37, then your rate of pay was what, 30 cents?
>
> MD: Well, we were making $12 a week.
>
> SH: How many hours a week was that?
>
> MD: Eight hours a day. They had gone on eight hours a day.
>
> TR: Yeah, that was in '32 and '33 that change came in.
>
> SH: So, you worked for Rhodhiss Mills, Pacific, and Burlington.
>
> MD: Clarkson Jones was the first superintendent and Luther Elmore was, too. Luther used to live right down the road there.[23]

Mary said that she liked her job, and she was proud to have worked there. She gave 45 years to the mill company.

Another Mary worked at Rhodhiss for over 48 years. Mary Bolick gave a lot of detailed information to Mr. Ross and me:

MB: Well, I liked working there. I can remember, and I don't know if any of them told you about not really having drinking water. In the plant they had water for the toilets. They would carry water from a spring for you to drink, and they had this dipper. It's a wonder that everybody didn't die drinking from the same dipper. I never did drink too much water. Sometimes I used to take me some water because I couldn't stand it. Like the Coca Cola drinks they sent somebody over to the Company Store to get it. They had them in a sack, and by the time they got back, they were hot. Like if you wanted anything like cookies or cakes or anything like that, of course they didn't have that much back then, but they would dump it in a big sack. Most people just took what they ate. You didn't really have the money to buy like they do now.

TR: You were talking about flushing the toilets, I think that they used river water for that.

MB: Yeah, that's what I say. They had it to flush the commodes, but they didn't have drinking water. They used to have these light bulbs that hung down with a bulb and socket. You know, you thought that you were seeing good then, but when they started putting these fluorescent lights around, we thought that it was daylight in there. With the bulbs part of the time they were burned out, half of them were. Some people would complain, and I told them that they should have been there when we had a bulb hanging down.

TR: How did you happen to get your job, Mary?

MB: You know what. I don't remember how. It just happened. Somebody said something about going down there, so we went. We had to train ourselves. I mean you didn't get paid. Like when you start filling batteries I would go so many hours a day, and work a while and come home till I learned it. Then when you learned, they put you on the job. I did have some pictures of those looms, but I don't know whatever happened to them. They were round. They put these bobbins of yarn about this long, and you pulled it off, and you wrapped it. The shuttle would go around.

TR: What kind of looms were there when you first started working? Did they have Oakdales over there?

MB: I believe they did. I believe that's what it was. You know they had belts on them instead of the motors. Then they got into the motors.

TR: Yeah, the loom was full of belts.

MB: Yes, and those belts would come off.

TR: They were dangerous really.

MB: They were, and sometimes they would break. You had to be so careful, and if you got up close to those things, they'd jerk you in them.

SH: Did you ever see anybody get hurt from them?

MB: No, not really. I know one time my dress, that's been a long time. There were no pants for women. That's something that women didn't wear. You had to wear these dresses with big aprons around you to keep you from getting greasy. I know my dress got caught, and one started to pull me in, and we stopped the loom off before it pulled, but it could have pulled me in. Somebody was telling about somebody over at number two that got caught in one way or another. It just stripped her dress off her, but I forget now who that was. That's been years ago.

TR: It's a wonder that more people weren't hurt.

MB: Well, now that's the truth.

TR: Yeah, because you had so many belts. They went from the ceiling down, you know.

MB: The shuttles would fly out.

TR: There was always that fear.

MB: Well, I had one to come out and hit me on the leg and cut my leg. I was standing there, and it just come out. You can't stop it when they do it. I had just started to start the loom up, and that thing had popped out. A man was killed back when Clarkson Jones was there. It was along the elevator, you know; well, it was about at the same place. You know they remodeled and did all that. He was, well back then the elevator was different than like the one we did have. He was going up to bring the yarn down. We had big wooden boxes to put it in. I saw him go up before he got killed. Some way or another he stuck his head out, and I think that it pulled him and mashed and crushed him to death.

SH: Was that in Number 1 or Number 2?

MB: Number 2.

TR: They used ropes, didn't they, to operate the elevator?

MB: Yeah, he must have stuck his head out. I remember back then we went to work from 2 to 10. I was working on the second shift. Clarkson Jones came down there, I remember that. I believe that they shut the plant down. That's the only person that I remember hurt. What's that Franklin man's name?

TR: Palmer?

MB: He was Palmer's brother. So, we didn't see anything after it happened. It just scared me to death. After that I was even afraid to ride on the elevator. I never did ride on it, but one time they did something, and we had to go up on it. I stayed clear of that thing.

SH: There was nobody ever killed at Plant 1 was there?

TR: Not that I know of.

MB: Now that's the only person that I really know of that was killed. I know when I first started work, of course, I just worked part of one summer, then I finished school in '34 and went back. I know that I made $7.20 a week back then.

SH: How many hours a week was that?

MB: That must have been about what? Sixty?

TR: Yeah, it must have been.

TR: You've always been in number two, haven't you?

MB: Yes. Well, no I started in number one. I went to work in '34.

TR: Oh, you did.

MB: I worked there till 1940. They wanted me to go over to number two to smash for a couple of weeks. I got over there, and I stayed.

TR: What different jobs have you done, Mary?

MB: Well, I started off filling batteries. Then I smashed for a long time. Then I went out to the IE Department (Industrial Engineering), and I worked out there till they closed.

SH: So, you were there when they closed the plant.

MB: Well, the last that I worked was in January. I forget exactly when they finished out.

SH: It was in the summer.

MB: I left in January because my job involved the layouts. Everybody used to go to the old Company Store to get their check cashed. Yeah, but they used to put it in an envelope. I believe that Dewey Milstead was working there. There were only three people working in the office, I believe.

TR: Dewey, Mrs. Anderson, and Mr. Walter Moore?

MB: Yeah, I believe it was.

TR: You were paid off in cash, too.

MB: Yeah, you had to go out there to get it at the office.

TR: Mary, people used to kid me about the fact that it took so few people to run the office back then, but later, it took fifteen to eighteen people to run the office.

MB: Yes. People would say, 'Well, they used to just have three people.' Of course, there weren't as many people, but they did have a lot of employees.

TR: They must have been running with 900 employees.[24]

Tom Ross alluded to the mill company using river water to flush the toilets. Calvin Jones said, "We had to stop it because the health department made us stop it."[25] Calvin and Tom mentioned that river water was no longer used to flush toilets after Pacific came to Rhodhiss in 1945. Mary Bolick discussed the dangers of the jobs in the mill company. Shuttles could fly loose from the looms. The machines were hazardous, and even the elevator caused a casualty during the 1940s. Yates Franklin was killed in 1943 at the Burke plant when he was 16 years.[26] Gladys Barker said that he was the same age as her daughter.[27] Exie Hand described Yates as "the funniest little ole boy. He sung all the time. He danced, and he was so friendly. They thought that maybe somebody in the card room had hollered at him, and had him look down, and the elevator was coming up. It caught him. They closed the plant down, and Virgil came home to tell us about it."[28] Mr. Franklin's death at such a young age had an impact on the community. There were stories of several others who died while working for the mill company; however, these people's deaths could not be confirmed. One man drowned in the early years as per Lonie Smith, "You know, old man Hallman (or Holman), he backed a team of mules in and drowned. I forget what his name was. He was Edie's daddy. They used to haul that stuff from over there from number 2 you know to number 1. Some way he was backing a load off the wagon, and the mules and he drowned."[29] Boyce Hartsoe, my dad, who was present in this interview said that he had heard that same story. Similarly, Thad Martin told of a man that was killed at the plant. Thad said, "Pearl's brother got killed working in the mill."[30] Willard Herman told of another man that was killed while working for the mill company while working with coal. Willard said, "A man got killed on a company truck. Well, they were delivering some coal. He was standing on a running board on the truck that they had. Somehow when they turned, he fell off the truck and was killed."[31] Again, there was no confirmation of Lonie's, Willard's, or Thad's stories. Another death was described in a local newspaper:

> Mr. John Teague of Rhodhiss who sustained fatal injuries in a fall from the steps of the Hiss mill there Thursday afternoon, and who was hurried to the Richard Baker Hospital here last night, died at 5 o'clock this morning. Details of the accident were not obtainable, but it was said that Mr. Teague, who was a machinist, fell from the steps, and sustained a broken arm, several broken ribs and internal injuries. His liver was pierced by a rib and while he was conscious most of the time in the local hospital, there was no hope for him. He is survived by several children and was about 45 years old.[32]

This industrial accident happened at Rhodhiss' Caldwell plant before the government mandated stringent rules for employers.

Hans Townsend went to work in Rhodhiss in 1934. He worked there for 48 years, 11 months, and 10 days. He ran the slashers, which was a machine that could not be left. His wife, Katherine Decker Townsend, worked in town for 31 years. Kat liked to tell everyone that when Plant 1 closed, she was "sent overseas" to work at Plant 2.[33] Tom Ross, Hans and Kat Townsend discussed working with inferior cotton and machines:

TR: That stuff was hard on the looms, wasn't it?

HT: Yeah, it would tear a loom all to pieces.

TR: They used a low-grade cotton. The card room was dusty. I've heard Roy Tramble say that you couldn't see from one end of the card room to the other. There was so much dust in the air. It had to be the quality of the cotton creating that much dust. It was cheaper and unclean because it was low grade cotton. They ran a lot of Osnaburg fabric. It's a glorified burlap, but the yarn in it was coarse and didn't have to have as much twist as a better fabric.

HT: Yeah, that's right. It had dirt and everything in it. I've seen them bring cotton in down there, and it was already dusty. It wasn't even white.

SH: Did that get better after they upgraded cotton, as far as dust?

TR: Well, Pacific changed over to synthetics.

HT: Well, you know the cotton got better there at the last. The quality was better.

TR: It depends on where you bought the cotton. The dirty cotton was machine picked. If it was hand-picked, it wasn't that dirty.

HT: You were talking about tearing looms up. We couldn't get parts back then for the looms, and they really had a time.

TR: I know that was critical. I had heard that some of the looms were tied together with hay bale wire. That was the best thing to do, I guess.

HT: Yeah, the only thing to do.

SH: Did you like your job?

HT: It was work.

KT: He liked it so good that he never got a job anywhere else.

HT: Everybody down there treated me right, supervision, management, and all.[34]

Using a machine that was tied together with hay bale wire was an obvious safety hazard, and the dirty cotton only added to their woes. Willard Herman described to Tom Ross the difficulty in trying to weave:

WH: Rhodhiss wove just plain drill cloth. The drill was 300 weave. Plain cloth was 200. Three hundred was as much as you could work on those old looms that they had.

TR: Still that's heavy quality. What was it used for?

WH: It was a heavy cloth, Tom. It was used mostly for some bedding. You didn't weave anything like bed sheets or anything like that. It wasn't real high-count cloth. I know most of the cloth went somewhere in West Virginia. It was shipped out of Rhodhiss. Most of it was shipped out in big bales in boxcars. I do remember a couple of big trucks from West Virginia coming in. Most of all the cotton and coal came in by rail.[35]

Willard was discussing the early days when he went to work in 1929. Later, the mill company shifted to synthetics when Pacific came in 1945.

Doughton Beshears discussed the stress of working the mathematical aspects of the job during the 1930s. Most people think that textile workers were not intelligent; however, that is not true. Textiles required higher level math and thinking skills. Although some employees lacked formal education, they were able to obtain instruction and an education while on the job. Doughton talked about this with Tom Ross, Shelley Teague, and Butler Monteith:

DB: They had school down there in the hall of the company office. I went to school, and I don't know how many went to school down there. Cornfield was the teacher, and he was as pig-headed as they come. They just taught textiles.

TR: That was extra teaching. You aren't talking about public school. A training kind of.

DB: Yeah, a training. It was all about the mill. They would teach you about yarn.

TR: Textile industry is all math. Many things were done with mathematical equations.

ST: You would be surprised back then that some people couldn't read and write.

TR: Everything really, looms and spinning frames, doffing, everything had math in it. The spacings. The ratios.

BM: The ratios in the stretching of the yarn. On the cards and stuff like that.

ST: When I was in spinning, I would have to change gears, you know. The hardest thing for me in that was the square root. That was rough.

DB: Yeah, the square roots were rough.

ST: As long as it was an even number, I was all right. It was those odd numbers that messed you up.

DB: I got a diploma for finishing square roots down there. It was square root school. At the end of school, they took me and Grady Hamby to make the speech at the graduation exercise. All the boss men, Clarkson Jones, R. C. Moore, Walter Moore, the whole outfit, were there. That was about the hardest thing that I did was to get up there and make that talk.[36]

Doughton Beshears served as a Rhodhiss police chief and a Caldwell County Magistrate, yet he found it difficult to speak in a public setting when he graduated from square root school. Millhands had to be smart to figure out the mathematical equations that were necessary to complete their jobs. Joe Aldridge stated, "Work was a schooling for me--an education."[37] The employees saw their work life as a learning experience.

The working conditions in Rhodhiss were no different than any other mill community in the South. *Working Lives: The Southern Exposure of History of Labor in the South* states that "To be honest, sober, and hardworking was their way."[38] Laborers in Rhodhiss saw vermin inside the company walls along with spit and tobacco juice on the floor. Wood bugs could easily infiltrate various places, especially toilets. Dust caused lung conditions and unbearable problems. Many employees suffered hearing loss because of the loud machinery. Lastly, poor lighting, sluggish machines, and hot, humid conditions only added to the daunting life of a millhand; however, most of the workers in Rhodhiss were dedicated to their jobs, almost married to them. Most of the people interviewed served the mill company for decades. Their devotion was unparalleled. The mill company was fortunate to have these hard-working people.

SOME OF THE FIRST EMPLOYEES. MANY OF THEM WERE CHILDREN. JAKE CURTIS AND HATTIE BUTLER (LATER MONTEITH) ARE IN THIS PICTURE. BUTLER MONTEITH PHOTO.

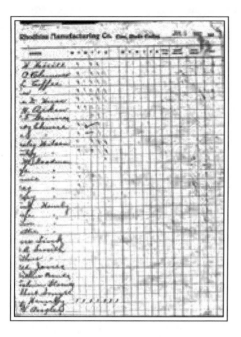

PAYROLL LEDGER 1902.
FRED ELMORE PHOTO.

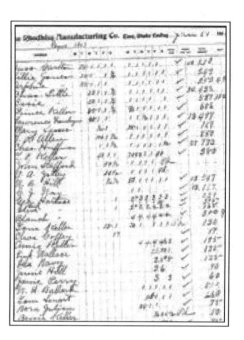

PAYROLL LEDGER 1903.
FRED ELMORE PHOTO.

PAYROLL LEDGER 1903.
FRED ELMORE PHOTO.

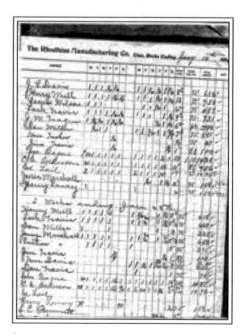

PAYROLL LEDGER 1905.
FRED ELMORE PHOTO.

SOME OF THE PEOPLE ARE NOTSIE LANEY RASH, BONNIE FRAZIER, BESS COOPER, PEARLINE LAIL, VIRGIE NELSON, HESS BOWMAN, VERNIE LAIL, MARIE AUSTIN, DOVE JONES, PEARL HAAS COOPER, EXIE HAND, __ MOORE, ___ SMITH, VAN BUTLER, THEODORE HOYLE, ROAM BOWMAN, BUD HAAS, WERD EARLY, MR. KELLEY (THE BOSS MAN), OTT HAND, LEE BOWMAN. TOMMIE RHEA PHOTO.

SOME OF THE PEOPLE ARE KURT SMITH, PAWNEE MULLINAX SIMMONS, LEONA HUNSUCKER, RUTH EARLEY HERMAN, MARTHA BYARS ELMORE, JETER POARCH. PAWNEE SIMMONS PHOTO.

THIS WAS THE WHISTLE THAT BLEW
TO INDICATE LUNCH TIME. JENNIFER
FULBRIGHT PHOTO.

PEARL MUNDAY SAUNDERS AND FLOYD
KIRBY, LATE 1930S OR EARLY 1940S. TOMMY
AND PHYLLIS HIGH PHOTO.

KELLY FULBRIGHT WORKED IN THE SHOP,
1930S OR 1940S. PHOTO OBTAINED FROM
CARL COMPTON.

MAE HILTON YOUNT, 1940S. MAE HILTON
YOUNT PHOTO.

JOHN LANEY IN 1951 AT THE
SLUBBERS. PACIFIC MILLS PHOTO.

1940S, VIRGINIA JONES HOLLAR.
VIRGINIA JONES HOLLAR PHOTO.

1940S, TOMMY MULLINAX AT THE MILL PARKING AREA. SHERRIE HARTSOE SIGMON PHOTO.

NOTES

1   Cox, Annette. "The Loray, North Carolina's 'Million Dollar Mill.': The 'Monstrous Hen' of Southern Textiles." *North Carolina Historical Review*. 89.3. (July 2012): 241-275, p. 244.

2   English, Beth. "Global Women's Work: Historical Perspectives on the Textile and Garment Industries." *Journal of International Affairs*. 67.1 (2013) 67-82. p. 73.

3   Munday, Mattie and Louise Keller.

4   Hall, Jacquelyn, *pp. 56&58*.

5   Hand, Arthur and Exie.

6   Church, Thelma.

7   Herman, Willard and Tom Ross.

8   Curtis, Violet, Willard Herman, and Tom Ross.

9   Hand, Arthur and Exie.

10   Beshears, Monteith, Ross, Teague.

11   Barker, Gladys Kirby.

12   Church, Thelma.

13   Hall, Jaquelyn, p. 56.

14   Conway, Mimi. *Rise Gonna Rise: A Portrait of Southern Textile Workers*. Garden City, New York: Anchor Press/Doubleday, 1979, p. 26.

15   Bright, Paul.

16   Edwards, Arthur, Jack Edwards, Edna Edwards Laney Stilwell, and Tom Ross.

17   Hall, Jacqueline Dowd, p. 52.

18   Bean, Ned and Elvie, and Tom Ross.

19   Elmore, Fred and Martha, Tom Ross.

20   Hand, Arthur and Exie.

21   Beshears, Monteith, Ross, Teague.

22   Elmore, Fred and Martha, Tom Ross.

23   Darty, Mary Settlemyre and Tom Ross. Personal Interview with Sherrie Hartsoe. Hickory, NC. 9 May 1988.

24   Bolick, Mary Starnes and Tom Ross. Personal Interview with Sherrie Hartsoe. Granite Falls, NC. 19 May 1988.

25   Jones, Calvin and Tom Ross.

26   "Franklin, Yates." Find a Grave. https://www.findagrave.com/memorial/18490311/yates-franklin.

27   Barker, Gladys.

28   Hand, Arthur and Exie.

29   Smith, Lonie, Boyce and Mildred Hartsoe.

30   Austin, Ann, Thad Martin, and Shelley Teague.

31   Curtis, Violet, Willard Herman, and Tom Ross.

32   "Dies From Injuries Sustained In Fall." *The Lenoir News*. 27 March 1917. Vol. XVIII. No. 82, p. 1. https://newspapers.digitalnc.org/lccn/sn84024879/1917-03-27/ed-1/seq-1/#words=Rhodhiss.

33   Townsend, Hans and Katherine and Tom Ross.

34   Townsend, Hans and Katherine, Tom Ross.

35   Herman, Willard and Tom Ross.

36   Beshears, Monteith, Ross, and Teague.

37   Aldridge, Joe and Olive. Personal Interview with Sherrie Hartsoe. Rhodhiss, NC. 17 May 1988.

38   Miller, Marc S., ed. *Working Lives: The Southern Exposure of History of Labor in the South*. New York: Pantheon Books, 1974, p. 7.

CHAPTER 9
LIVING CONDITIONS

Working conditions were not optimal in the manufacturing companies in Rhodhiss, and the living conditions were also bothersome. A story recently detailed that one family had to bury their stillborn child in a shoebox near their millhouse in Burke County during the 1920s because they lacked funds for a burial. Many areas of the millhands' lives could have been more fulfilling. It was not until the mill company was sold to Pacific Mills in 1945 that life became somewhat easier for the people who were employed in the mills and for the people living in the community. The employees endured hardships at work and at home.

Mattie Munday and Shelley Teague both talked about the bathroom facilities in the mills. The sewage went into the river. Matt said, "Where we used that bathroom, we did have toilet paper though. I guess we did. It would go out in the river."[1] It goes without saying that this was a health hazard for the townspeople. Shelley Teague added: "Every time it would come up a rain, they used to dump the sewage from the mill into the river. Yes, sir. Every time it would rain, the sewer came out of the mill. I would go down there and fish. When the sewage came out, the catfish would just bite."[2] The unsanitary conditions prompted many outbreaks of typhoid in the town. Willard Herman stated to Tom Ross and me:

WH: We lived on what they called Pee Ridge, right along where Harley Woods lives now. We lived in the house where Harley Woods lived in before Jim Kirby ever moved down there. I had typhoid fever when we lived in that house. I believe I was 7 years old. I know a lot of people in Rhodhiss had typhoid fever, and I was one of them. There was Mrs. Matt Munday's brother Thad. He and I were the same age, and they lived in the next house. The dad's name was Walt Hilton, and he had typhoid fever at the same time. Old Dr. A. D. Jones was here in Granite Falls. I can remember him so well. He wore a little black derby hat all the time. He was our doctor. He'd come every day to see us, and a lot of people died with typhoid fever, but we got through it.

SH: We haven't heard about typhoid fever.

TR: I haven't heard that either.

WH: A lot of people had it.

SH: About what year was that?

WH: About 1919 or 1920 because I was about 7 years old.

SH: So right after the flu epidemic.

WH: There were quite a few people in Rhodhiss that had typhoid fever. I remember one of Lawrence Rector's, no Claude Rector's daughters. They lived across the road in front of us. We didn't call them streets then because they were dirt. They had twin girls that were about my age. One of the girls had typhoid fever at that time. In that section there were at least four or five that had typhoid fever.

TR: How did they treat typhoid fever?

WH: Tom, I think that it was mostly sulfur or something like that. I can remember a big ole glass bottle of old brown pills that I had to take after I got out of bed. I remember that when I had it, mother had a sewing machine sitting beside the bed. All you had was a bed stand and a few straight chairs and things like that. I can remember that Dr. Jones sat his little black satchel up on the sewing machine. He'd sit down in a chair there beside the bed when he was checking me, and he got up one day, and he was fixin' to leave. He was looking around and looking around. I asked what he was looking for, and he said that he was looking for his hat, and he had it in his hand.[3]

Typhoid fever is predominately passed through contaminated water. At this time there was a community well, and many of the children on this same street contracted the fever. Fred Elmore added to this, "Well, typhoid was coming from the outhouses and public wells. There was a lot of that in Rhodhiss."[4] Violet Curtis was able to elaborate more when I interviewed her and Willard Herman. Violet and Willard said:

WH: I was telling them the other night about having typhoid fever just shortly after the flu epidemic. I had it. It was treated.

VC: On down below the old Baptist Church there was this hill. There was a family that lived there that two of their children died of typhoid fever. Two of them.

WH: There was a lot of it in Rhodhiss.

VC: Oh, yeah.

WH: Now, it never did hit any of our family besides me.[5]

Arthur and Exie Hand also talked about typhoid fever in Rhodhiss:

EH: This used to be the awfullest place for typhoid fever. The last people that I remember having it was Mrs. Hamby that lives right there. She came right near dying, and Perry Weaver's two kids. They lived across the river. One was a girl, and one was a boy. Just about everybody took typhoid fever over here. So many of them never did get over it. Doc Copening (Corpening) was the doctor. They never did get it before it got so bad until they started giving typhoid fever shots. Oh, after two of my kids was born, Mrs. Hamby liked to have died with it right there. Perry Weaver's kids had it. He lived down the river. Right down the river.

AH: That last house on the right as you go down.

EH: You had to quarantine anybody with typhoid. That's the last family that I ever heard tell had it.[6]

Typhoid was a serious health condition in Rhodhiss during the first forty years because of the sharing of the water at a community well; later they added spigots that were shared within the community.

ARTHUR "OTT" AND EXIE HAND, 1930S. EXIE HAND PHOTO.

Many other health problems surfaced during the early days. Stewart Munday, who was the father of Raym Munday, worked and tried to care for his wife who was an invalid. Matt explained, "See Raym's mother was an invalid. She had rheumatoid arthritis, and she sat there in a chair. His daddy would come home from work and care for her. She had a big ole long handle spoon that she fed herself with. Someone had to comb her hair; they waited on her for 21 years. They didn't have anybody to come in to do anything."[7] Mr. Munday managed to work his job and check on his sickly wife. Willard Herman and Violet Curtis also discussed Mr. Munday's devotion:

WH: The grandpa that we were talking about, Stewart Munday, he was over the machine shop before Mr. Massie Mullinax. He was Raym's dad. They used to have a machine shop in each mill. Gladys Barker's daddy, Eli Kirby, was the machine shop man at number two, and Stewart Munday was over number one as well as I can remember. The mother was in a wheelchair.

VC: Yeah, Stewart went home to take care of her.

WH: That's right. You could tell when 9:00 came because you could see Stewart taking off to go home to check on his wife.

VC: Yeah.

WH: He'd go back at dinnertime. Then again in the afternoon, and then when he got off in the evening.[8]

Gladys Barker said that people were more willing to help others and their own families in the early days of Rhodhiss. Mr. Munday did this.

Alvis Kelley also discussed health hardships within his family. Alvis went to work in Rhodhiss in July 1927 when he was 14 years old. He told Tom Ross, Precious, and me of his own turmoil after moving to town:

AK: We moved here the 10th day of June, and my dad fell dead the 7th day of September.

PK: He fell dead in the mill.

SH: How did he die?

AK: He asked me, and I was just a boy, 15. He had weak spells. He said to me, 'Was there anything left from dinner?' We always carried our meal down there. I said, 'Yeah, I left a few Irish potatoes and a little piece of cake.' I left it especially for him, and he ate it. He came back in, and he didn't have a watch. I had one. He asked me what time it was. I believe that I told him that it was five minutes after five. We quit at 6:00. He said, 'You know I come the closest to fainting a little bit ago that I ever come in my life.' He went back then, and I went to look out the window down the river because we lived in the last house down the river, the one that Thad Martin lives in now. The company owned the house, and we rented it. I heard a noise, and I saw the cotton piling up. I went to turn the lever off. I saw him lying there on the floor. They wouldn't let me help him. I always thought that I could have brought him back to life, but that was just my way of thinking. Marlin Mitchell was working over him.

PK: Now, you and your daddy had not been working in the mill very long.

AK: Oh, no. Just from June to September. He had worked in a mill before where we lived in Ridgecrest until they closed it down and built another one.[9]

Alvis was only 15 years old when he lost his father. He talked about how the family went back to the mountains after his dad's death. The town minutes also tell a story of a family that was left in a hopeless situation. On December 29, 1928, the town paid $10 for railroad fare for a woman and her three children who were left destitute.[10] Previously, in Chapter 4, Edna Stilwell mentioned that her grandmother would go tell the superintendent and the proprietor of the Company Store that certain people were in need. This apparently happened more often than people knew.

One person that was interviewed told of the hardships endured during the early years in Rhodhiss. This person's name will not be divulged, but I discussed the story with Tom Ross and Calvin Jones:

> TR: Calvin, some people don't have good memories.
> SH: In this family the dad drank. He would beat the mother. The child would have to run to get the police. The dad took his child's tricycle and traded it for a bottle of whiskey. The dad took the child to the pool room with him when he was supposed to be babysitting.
> CJ: Is that right? How sad.
> SH: I guess that type of thing you really wouldn't record; however, I was told that I could use the story, but not the name.
> CJ: I understand protecting the name.
> SH: I was told many things like that from this person. The mother was inside the plant working and looked out the window and saw the father with the child on the river in a boat, and the father was drunk. She saw her child out there with a man that was not able to take care of himself much less a child.[11]

Children grew up fast in the mill village, whether they went to work early or simply had to face other hardships. The Edwards family praised Mrs. Estelle Powell Starnes. They said that "Estelle Starnes got underclothes, clothes, and glasses for needy children."[12] Mrs. Starnes was a teacher at Rhodhiss Elementary for several years. She was loved and praised by many. Some women bore the brunt of the load within the village. One story was told several times by Tom Ross. A single mother who had four children was forced to forfeit the family's cow. Mr. Ross discussed this with Ned and Elvie Bean and me:

> TR: There were four children. The mother raised four by herself.
> EB: I remember Ned's talking about that. He said that they had a hard time.
> TR: A man from a nearby town loaned her money, and she gave him mortgage on their cow. He took the cow away from her when she couldn't make the payments, and she was trying to raise four children. Many people did not like him because of that, and neither did this woman.
> EB: He probably needed that cow like he needed a hole in the head. The rich get richer, and poor get poorer.[13]

The mother had nothing else to mortgage because in those days the millhands did not own anything except their animals. They rented their homes, and few people could afford cars. The single mother did the best that she could at the time. According to Mr. Ross and the Beans, the children in this family grew up to be lovely people who cared deeply for their mother, each other, and Rhodhiss. Many families suffered from food shortage at one time or another. One former citizen, Quincy Curtis (Q. T.) recalled his days of hunger during the Depression. He detailed his life's story, including his time as a

World War II soldier, and it is archived at the University of North Carolina at Chapel Hill.[14] Quincy represented Rhodhiss well as a former citizen, patriot, and preacher.

In Chapter 3 the details of cold weather and trying to stay warm were discussed. Another problem that the villagers experienced was poor road conditions. Ned Bean said that the only paved road was Caldwell Street. Ned told Elvie, Tom Ross, and me:

> NB: They paved the main road on Caldwell side because I got into the hot pavement and got it all over my feet.
> EB: So, if it was the 1930s, you might have been 6 years old.
> NB: I was 6 or 7 years old when I got into the tar.
> EB: It wasn't any later than '31 probably.
> NB: '31 or '32.
> TR: Caldwell Street in Caldwell County coming into the mill must have been paved then, but nothing else was paved.
> NB: Right. The main street through there was known as Sand Clay Road.
> SH: I have never heard that.
> NB: When they paved it, that was the only street in Rhodhiss that was paved until Pacific came.[15]

The roads were muddy and often impassable. Many people discussed what a problem this caused. Ned was able to give the name of the main highway coming into Rhodhiss, Sand Clay Road, but today it is Caldwell Street. The roads were so bad that for years Lawrence Brady drove his tractor to work and picked up riders along the way. He put boards in a wagon for seats and pulled it with his tractor. Lawrence would not charge his friends for the ride. He said that he would not think of collecting money from his coworkers and friends.[16] Exie Hand also discussed the muddy roads with me:

> SH: The roads weren't paved when you came to town either, were they?
> EH: Oh, there wasn't anything but mud this deep. You couldn't get anywhere. In the wintertime it was so bad, I declare to goodness. You'd be halfway up to your knees in mud. And then when they got to fixin' the roads, before they got them fixed, it would go up to your knees because they had it plowed up. Oh, Lord. If you walked, you had to get in the ruts where the wagons and cars run.
> SH: Your daughter Margie told me about walking to church. She said once you got to church, you had to go to the bathroom to wash your shoes and feet.
> EH: I'll tell you that it was a muddy mess. This here road hasn't been fixed long. It was a dirt road.[17]

The roads were in poor condition for decades. In 1949 Pacific Mills paved most of the streets. Fred and Martha Elmore talked about the area near Rhodhiss Beach with Tom Ross:

TR: Reconstructing that road took two years, and in the winter it was horrible.

FE: Yeah, Lawrence Brady went over there with his tractor and pulled them up the hill. Mud was knee deep in the 1940s. Mud was knee deep all over Rhodhiss at one time.

TR: The only paved street was the river back up to Caldwell. They told me that kids couldn't ride their bikes on the streets of Rhodhiss because of the briars that hit their legs.

ME: They used to have a road straight to the lake. Lanny was school age. He had boots on walking one day. Instead of walking the good road he went the old road. He came home with mud all over him and the boots. He came in barefoot because he stepped out of his boots because they were stuck.[18]

Adding to this Violet Curtis said, "When we moved to Rhodhiss, the roads were so muddy on Strawberry. They dug and worked on that road. They said that they just hit rock. We went to the door to watch them dig. We had never seen anything like that. Every time that they tried to dig a well over there, they just hit solid rock. I don't think that they ever did get it fixed on the hill."[19]

The roads were in such horrible condition that Calvin Jones had difficulty getting his sick daughter to the doctor. Calvin discussed this with Tom Ross and me:

CJ: The roads were so bad one time, and I couldn't get the car out of the yard for six weeks because the roads were that bad. Then it started raining. They started building this road across the bridge. See it was dirt all the way out. There weren't any paved roads on the other side of the river. The only paved road when I came to Rhodhiss was down to the mill. In the rest of the village the roads were dirt. Rita got sick during that time. The doctors wouldn't come out into that mud. I called a Granite Falls doctor, and he wouldn't come out. So, I got the old six-wheel air compressor that we shuffled around between the two mills, knocking out walls, you know. I plowed through that mud and picked up Marguerite and Rita and borrowed a car from Alan Dameron and took her to Lenoir. We were about ready to leave here at that time.

TR: I didn't know about that.

CJ: We almost went back to Greenville then.

TR: Oh, man. I am sure that Marguerite wanted to after that.

CJ: Yeah. We couldn't get the doctor to come out. Rita was sick. Marguerite was worried to death.

TR: Yeah, yeah.

CJ: But we weathered the storm. We got the roads straightened out, and everything was nice ever since.

TR: Yes, the roads were bad for a while.

CJ: Well, everybody had to walk. Do you remember Charlie Lee? All of us had to walk down to the mill. We couldn't drive.

TR: See we used to park up here at the filling station.

SH: You parked up here and walked home?

TR: Yeah. We started out wearing low overshoes. Then we got to high top boots.

SH: Who came in and paved the roads? The state? The town? The mill company?
CJ: Pacific.[20]

Calvin explained that his family felt compelled to return to South Carolina, but they endured this problem, and things did work out. Calvin Jones and Tom Ross also mentioned the storage of their cars because they couldn't drive them home. The Edwards family said that there were sheds near the mills to park cars because the roads were so muddy.[21] Hans and Katherine Townsend also discussed the bad roads with Tom Ross and me. They said:

HT: Back when the streets down there were dirt, Rhodhiss Mills had car garages
built down there because in the wintertime, you couldn't get up the hills. I think that there were about ten cars in the whole of Rhodhiss. The first car that I bought was a '40 Chevrolet. I had to leave it down there in front of Glass' Store in the wintertime about all the time.
SH: It wouldn't go in the cold?
KT: The roads were so bad.
HT: The roads were dirt, and they were muddy.
KT: They were terrible.[22]

Hans and Katherine were not able to drive their new 1940 Chevrolet to their mill company house because the roads would not allow it.

HANS AND KATHERINE TOWNSEND
IN THE 1930S. KATHERINE
TOWNSEND PHOTO.

Willard Herman was able to add that the cost to rent shed space was twenty-five cents a month, and the money was paid to the mill company.[23] Several people mentioned the car sheds. My dad came to Rhodhiss in 1946, and he said that the sheds were still there then. Doughton Beshears, Butler Monteith and Shelley Teague explained:

BM: They had car sheds there, too. Mr. Calvin Hollar had a little ole office in there along with supplies. He mostly had that one across the river.
ST: They had car sheds across the river.
DB: They had them on both sides.
ST: Yeah, along the main road up there. It was along the parking for the mill over here. It was along, of course, it was along on farther. You used to could drive cars down there, back then in the river and wash them.[24]

Shelley was able to add to the story by saying that they used the river water to wash their cars. The car sheds were used to house the cars because of the horrible road conditions, but the mill company did collect the rent.

Another problem involved the use of coal to heat the school and the homes. Arthur Edwards explained, "At school there were coal stoves in each room; the wind would blow black soot all over the students. One teacher marched us to the town hall to show the mill company the soot."[25] Management was notified of the problem, but little could be done. Willard Herman declared:

WH: We didn't have school like we have now. We had a potbellied stove.
There was a flue. There was soot.
TR: We just heard that.
SH: Ott Edwards told us about that. He said that the teachers would march them down to the office building and show them.
WH: I never did get in on that, but I know that it was done. I was in school when they would let us go home because of the wind blowing soot all over us. I never did march down to the office.[26]

The school children would go home dirty from the soot, and there were no indoor bathrooms for them to clean themselves.

Fred Elmore gave more information, "There was a potbellied stove. As students, me and Odell Tramble were janitors there at Rhodhiss, and we had to fire those potbellied stoves. It was cooler in the summertime with no underpinning in the house, but the winters were cold. It's harder to heat. That old school didn't have partitions in it, but there were folding doors, and it was cold."[27] Thelma Church also discussed the potbellied stove:

When I went up here to this school, they had a big ole potbellied stove, and the boys would have to take care of it. I think that they used coal back then. We would go in there and half the time it was nearly freezing. Sometimes it would smoke, and we had to go out. We would get to go home lots of times. Like I say, we just had outside toilets. We had to drink out of the same cup. A lot of people carried their lunches. Well, they had to carry their lunch, those that lived close enough went home and ate. But those that didn't brought a sandwich.[28]

The elementary children had to face more than difficult lessons or stern teachers. They encountered outside toilets at the school which was located where the present Boy Scout facility is on Church Street (the old Methodist Church). They had to go outdoors if the stove smoked too much. The conditions inside were cold, and outdoors would be even colder.

Not only was soot a problem at school, but it was also an issue within the community. Calvin Jones explained the situation:

Burlington changed the mills to oil heat and stopped using coal. The first one that we put in was across the river (Burke). Then later we put the oil burners in on this side (Caldwell). There's no doubt about it. People, especially around the mill, we'd have to blow the soot out of the flues of the boiler three times a day, and when you did that, the soot would go up through the stack and settle out all around. People would have their clothes hanging out from washing, and it would fall on their clothes, and they'd fuss and raise Cain all the time. This had to be done because if you didn't, you couldn't fire the boiler. The soot would clog up so that you couldn't get any heat because it would insulate from the tubes and you couldn't make steam.[29]

People had all types of problems with using coal as a source of energy at school, in the mill, or at their homes. Calvin Jones explained, "Well, power was included in the rent to begin with, but when we put meters on the houses, then we started reading meters and they'd take it out at the office. They'd take out whatever it cost out of the paycheck once a month. Anyway, Fred Elmore was reading the meters, and he ran across one house that had a bathtub full of coal. They were using it as a coal bin."[30] One family did not use the bathtub for its intended purpose once plumbing was installed in the homes. Storing the coal indoors prevented theft, and it would be handy to locate. Tom Ross added, "I remember that when Pacific came to town, the nurses would go to the houses and talk to people about cleanliness and things like that. The nurses would try to guide them and improve their housekeeping and cleanliness, cooking and whatever."[31] Pacific wanted to help the people in the late 1940s, so they provided additional help from the company nurse.

The company had a lot of control over the millhands' lives. To live in a mill house, someone within the family had to work at one of the plants. Doughton Beshears discussed with Shelley Teague how one superintendent believed that employees needed to be in church:

> DB: When old man Joe Edwards was superintendent down here, you better be at church on Sunday if you wanted to keep your job on Monday. You better be in church on Sunday! That's why I started going to the Methodist Church. I didn't want to lose my job.
> ST: That's right. He did. After McIntyre, an Edwards man took over. He lived in that big house, too.
> DB: That is right. I came to work here when Edwards was there.[32]

The mill company often had control of the citizens' personal choices. Ned Bean discussed the workers' behavior and possible consequences with Elvie, Tom Ross, and me:

> SH: Now, who was the man that Doughton Beshears said that if you wanted to keep your job, you better be at church on Sunday?
> TR: Joe Edwards.

NB: I have heard that name, but I don't know him.

TR: He was an outside foreman or something like that. He fired you if you didn't go to church.

SH: That's when Doughton said that he joined the church.

NB: Oh, really? He wanted to keep his job.

EB: Well, not too many years ago if you were caught drunk or fooling around with somebody else's wife, you were fired.

NB: Yes, you were fired. If you went out and got drunk on Saturday or got in jail, you need not come to work on Monday. It was just that simple.

TR: That sort of held over till I came here.

EB: That's what I said. It hasn't been that many years ago that they abandoned that.

NB: Well, you lived in a company house, so you better not go out and get into trouble. You would lose your house.[33]

This information was also confirmed by the Edwards family. They said, "If you were caught drinking on the weekend, you were fired on Monday."[34] The mill administration exercised a lot of power over the mill workers.

One of the other problems experienced within the town caused concern after Pacific took over the company. According to the town minutes, On December 5, 1950, the minutes read, "The village is badly infested with wharf rats seeking food and shelter caused by oncoming winter weather. Mr. T. H. Ross will see if the residents would be willing to pay $1.00 or $1.50 per family for poison for an all-out rat ridding campaign."[35] Eliminating vermin took place several times.

Money was very tight for these mill workers. Gladys Barker told me that her husband had to sell his first car to buy furniture when they married.[36] Claude had to give up his automobile to have the comforts in a home. The Edwards family talked about being poor:

TR: Do you all agree that it was a wonderful place to live?

ES: It was a wonderful place to live, and as we learned of things that were taking place in larger cities, we were glad that we were here. We had one or two town drunks, but that was the worst that we had. You didn't lock the doors. Nobody broke in and took anything. If there weren't screens on the windows, your friends just came in the windows or opened the door and walked in. Nobody starved. I remember sitting with my coat on right at the fire, freezing to death. There was a wood stove in the kitchen for heating and cooking. At night we all huddled up over that stove and froze.

JE: We went to bed and couldn't turn over because there was so much cover piled over us.

AE: The houses weren't insulated and had no underpinning.

ES: At that time, it would be that cold, and mama would just up and yell, 'Look at that youngin out there with short sleeves or that youngin out there with no shoes.'

AE: We didn't know that we were poor because we always had eggs. Dad had chickens. He ordered chickens every year. The first thing that you did when you got in the door was take off your school clothes.

ES: I had a pair of white shoes one time, even for the winter. Those shoes had to be polished every night. Every Saturday night we got our clothes ready for church the next morning. Yeah, we were poor, but clean.

AE: When I was little, I would pick berries all the way around the river up on beach road. That was my first job for the mill company. Then I had to walk all the way home. I got paid fifty cents a day.

JE: Nobody ever retired back then.

AE: You worked just as long as you were able to go.[37]

Children started to work early, even if it was just picking berries for the mill company.

Few people were able to retire during this time because they did not have savings, and Social Security was not established until 1935. The people who lived and worked at Rhodhiss endured conflict, hardships, and turmoil, but they frequently said that they would not have changed their lives. They lived among family within the mill village. They learned from their experiences and benefited from them, and they valued the hard work that made them the self-reliant people that they were.

NOTES

1   Munday, Mattie and Louise Keller.

2   Beshears, Monteith, Ross, and Teague.

3   Curtis, Violet, Willard Herman, and Tom Ross.

4   Elmore, Fred and Martha, Tom Ross.

5   Curtis, Herman, and Ross.

6   Hand, Arthur and Exie.

7   Munday, Mattie and Louise Keller.

8   Herman, Willard and Tom Ross.

9   Kelley, Alvis and Precious, Tom Ross.

10   Rhodhiss Town Minutes. 29 December 1928.

11   Jones, Calvin and Tom Ross.

12   Edwards, Arthur and Jack, Edna Edwards Laney Stilwell and Tom Ross.

13   Bean, Ned and Elvie, Tom Ross.

14   "Curtis, Quincy." https://catalog.lib.unc.edu/catalog/UNCb10216428.

15   Bean, Ned and Elvie, Tom Ross.

16   Brady, Lawrence and Nancy, Tom Ross.

17   Hand, Arthur and Exie.

18   Elmore, Fred and Martha, Tom Ross.

19   Curtis, Violet, Willard Herman, Tom Ross.

20   Jones, Calvin and Tom Ross.

21   Edwards, Arthur, Jack, and Edna Edwards Laney Stilwell and Tom Ross.

22   Townsend, Hans and Katherine, Tom Ross.

23   Curtis, Herman, Ross.

24   Beshears, Monteith, Ross, Teague.

25   Edwards, Arthur and Jack, Edna Edwards Laney Stilwell, and Tom Ross.

26   Herman, Willard, Tom Ross.

27   Elmore, Fred and Martha, Tom Ross.

28   Church, Thelma.

29   Jones, Calvin and Tom Ross.

30   Jones, Calvin and Tom Ross.

31   Jones, Calvin and Tom Ross.

32   Beshears, Monteith, Ross, Teague.

33   Bean, Ned and Elvie, Tom Ross.

34   Edwards, Arthur and Jack, Edna Edwards Laney Stilwell, and Tom Ross.

35   Rhodhiss Town Minutes. 5 December 1950.

36   Barker, Gladys.

37   Edwards, Arthur and Jack, Edna Edwards Laney Stilwell, and Tom Ross.

CHAPTER 10

EDUCATION/OLD CLAPBOARD BUILDING-
1900 TO WPA-1938

In 1941 J. M. Laxton, who was a principal at Rhodhiss School, wrote an excellent article for the *Lenoir News-Topic* detailing the history of Rhodhiss School. Mr. Laxton's story began with the year 1900 with information obtained from L. A. Elmore, H. C. Cobb, (both from Rhodhiss) Mrs. M. E. Jones, Mrs. E. E. Teague, (both from Granite Falls), and Mrs. Etta Wilson (from Hickory). This article was written for the Centennial anniversary of Caldwell County. His history concluded with the 1941 school year.

As per the article Rhodhiss was one of the youngest schools in the county, if not the youngest. In 1900 as houses were finished, and families migrated to the village, the need for a school became evident. John Rhodes, one of the founders of the textile company and general manager of the mill, was boarding with Mrs. Etta Wilson. He asked her to consider teaching a subscription school in the boarding house. Since Mrs. Wilson had some teaching experience, she agreed. The school term was for two months, and the hours were from 8:00 to 4:00. Her pay was fifty cents per student each month, and she stated that she had fifteen students. She taught the traditional 3 R's (reading, writing, and arithmetic) along with spelling. In 1901 the same subscription school was taught by Mrs. Wilson. In 1903 Miss Bessie Hayes taught the first free school for a seven- or eight-month term. This school was financed by Rhodhiss Mills. Classes were taught in the lodge hall which was on the top floor of the company offices, which also housed the post office and Company Store. When the cold weather started, classes were moved to a "commissary building which stood on the Caldwell side of the Catawba River" just a few yards above the old steel bridge. Mr. M. E. Jones met Miss Bessie Hayes in this area, as was discussed in Chapter 2. In 1904 it is uncertain whether the children continued school in this building or if they went to Granite Falls. If the children stayed in Rhodhiss, they were taught by the minister of the Rhodhiss Lutheran Church, the Reverend Joseph Cromer, who was also John Rhodes' son-in-law. Most likely the children stayed in Rhodhiss because transportation would have been limited to walking or horse and buggy. In 1905 it is with certainty that Pastor Cromer taught school in either the lodge or hotel. During the same year the Granite Falls principal, Professor White, tried to get the children to come to Granite. At this point John Rhodes became even more adamant that Rhodhiss would have its own school. Mr. White and Mr. Rhodes went to Raleigh to plead to the legislature. Rhodes was successful and received a special charter district for Rhodhiss.[1]

Mr. Rhodes decided that a school building was necessary since he was awarded the charter. A facility was not completed until 1907, and in the meantime, school was taught by Mr. Tolbert in the hotel. The new structure was a two-room building. School started in October. In 1907 Miss Jennie Shelley served as principal along with Miss Bettie Watson. Jennie Shelley later became Mrs. E. E. Teague, and her son is Shelley Teague who was interviewed in 1988. Misses Shelley and Watson taught again in 1908, and their school included grades one through nine. Their session was for about seven months, and they were supplemented from the special tax levy of about one tenth of one percent. Rhodes' special charter lasted until the state took over the schools in 1933. The special charter tax levy was paid by Rhodhiss Mills from 1905 to 1923, and then Duke Power Company started paying since they owned the town. Children in both Burke and Caldwell counties attended Rhodhiss Elementary even though the school was in Caldwell County.[2]

Additional rooms were added to the 1907 building. When there was an overflow of students, a nearby dwelling was provided by the mill company to house students. Before 1920 one room was attached to the 1907 structure. The building was excavated for a basement addition in 1920. In 1932 two more rooms were completed. In 1934 the County Board of Education attached another basement room. John Rhodes' dream of educating the children of Rhodhiss was fulfilled. Other people who were instrumental in the success of the school in the early years were the men who served as chairmen of the local school committee. W. S. Taylor, 1906-1919; Eli Kirby, 1920; the Rev. J. C. Benfield, 1920; J. G. Wolfe, 1921-1922; D. S. Walker, 1923-1929; J. O. Edwards, 1930-1931; and Clarkson Jones, 1932-1941. Other committee members who served a long tenure were M. T. Mullinax with a 16-year service and H. C. Cobb served 24 years as secretary.[3]

John Hawkins added that a "library was established within the school for teachers in 1910."[4] A library for students was not added until much later. Education is costly but choosing not to educate children can be even more costly; thus during "1910, the school population had expanded and a house next to the two-room school was rented to make space for the students. Byrd Bush was the upper grade teacher and head of the school. Teachers used a blue back speller and children played marbles or old field baseball."[5] However, Mr. Laxton's list of principals indicated that Mr. Bush was not a headmaster until 1921. Gladys Barker attended Rhodhiss School from approximately 1910 to 1916. She said that Bettie Watson was a teacher and principal. Katherine Taylor was a teacher, and Katherine's father was a supervisor at the mill. He is the W. S. Taylor that Mr. Laxton mentioned in his article for the newspaper. Gladys added that there were three teachers, and each one taught two grades. She said that the school was a three-room structure when she went. Gladys commented that children went to work at 13 or 14 years of age, so they went only to the sixth grade. She indicated that children worked hard at school, at home, and at the mill. At the school they would have to stoke the stove to keep warm.[6]

Shelley Teague and several other people said that there was another school in Burke County which was on the present-day Cape Hickory Road. It was for the people who lived in that area and whose parents did not work in Rhodhiss. Shelley recalled, "The old Aiken school. My mama taught there for a few years. It was an old log school. They had two buildings. One of them was log, and the other one was board. She taught John and Lacy Aiken and Will McGuire and most all those older people over there."[7] In the early days of Rhodhiss to attend Rhodhiss Elementary, someone in the household had to work for the mill company. Willard Herman discussed this with Tom Ross and me:

> TR: What about that school that used to be over in Burke County? Smokey (Shelley Teague) told us about it.
> WH: That was what I always heard called Sourwood School or Aiken. It was a weatherboard building. Do you know where that Turner farm was? It was right across the road.
> TR: Yeah.
> WH: Grady Reece bought the old school building and turned it into a house. Thad Elmore eventually bought it from Grady and lived there a while after Grady.
> SH: Is that building still standing then?
> WH: Some of the house is, I believe. It was just a one-room school.
> SH: That's over near Lawrence Brady's.
> TR: Smokey's (Shelley Teague) mother taught over there. Why did they have to have a school there?
> WH: Well, I guess kids outside of the mill village had to have a school. Outside the mill village couldn't go to Rhodhiss. Now Ivey Stephens, Grace Stephens Hayes, and Buster Hayes and some of them lived right outside the city limits of Rhodhiss. He always worked for the mill company, but they went to school at Rhodhiss. There were three boys from over in there that I played ball with.[8]

Willard explained the location of Aiken School. It is close to the present-day Ray Childers School, but it would be on the opposite side of the road. When Violet Curtis and Willard Herman were interviewed together a few days later, they continued the discussion:

> WH: You asked me the other night about that little school building. It was called Aiken.
> VC: Grace and Ivey Stephens went to that school. That's where they had to go to school.
> WH: My wife Ruth went with Ivey one day, and they sent her back to Rhodhiss.
> VC: I went down there one time with Estelle. I remember. That's Mrs. Stephens' daughter. She's about my age. I was about a year older. We thought that we had a fine school at Rhodhiss because we had big ole potbellied stoves, and we had things like that. We didn't have much heat. We had to pull slide doors between our rooms, you know. We pulled the doors. We had a good school. Fat, Babe's boy, he started to school at Rhodhiss. They said that he could go. So, they found out that he wasn't supposed to go to Rhodhiss because his parents didn't work

at the mill, and he came home. He stopped at mama's. He was hot and he was upset. He must have been about 8 years old or something like that. He was a heavy-set boy. He said, 'Mrs. Earley, they sent me home and said that I couldn't go to that school.' Somebody told 'em that he wasn't supposed to go to school there.

WH: I think that they got away from that because Ivey went to school there later because I went with him.[9]

The mill company paid for the teachers starting in 1903, so that must have been why they allowed only mill children to attend Rhodhiss. Shelley Teague and Butler Monteith discussed this school further:

BM: Well, you used to go to Philadelphia School, didn't you? Didn't your
mother teach over there?

ST: That's the old Aiken School. No, I never did go over there.

BM: You didn't.

ST: No, I was over there only to visit. I was only 4 or 5 years old. It was the old Aiken School; do you know where Turner's Dairy is?

SH: That's over in Burke County, right?

BM: Yeah, at the top of the hill, turn left and go about half a mile or more. Or three quarters of a mile.

ST: You know where the old Settlemyre's Store is. Cut to the left and go on around there. There's a road that goes straight, and one curves around. Right before you get to the curve on the left there's a log building. That's the one that mama taught in.

SH: It's still there?

ST: Lord, no. There was a wooden building. There were two buildings. Bess Hart taught in one of them, and mama taught in the old log building. They had a long stove that they burned cord wood in. In there where mama taught, she taught two or three different grades in that same one room.

TR: Did Rhodhiss people go over there to school?

ST: Ivey Stephens and that bunch did. Settlemyres did, too.

SH: Burke County side people mostly?

ST: Not all of them.

BM: The people that lived in the village went to school over here in Rhodhiss.

ST: Old Will McGuire, Lacy Aiken, John Aiken, and all of them went to school with mama. The Warlick boys, too. All the Warlicks went to school with mama. Ralph and Fred Dale. You know Fred's the mayor in Long View. He went to school with my mama over there.

TR: Is that right?

ST: He went to school here, too.

BM: He finished grammar school right there in that house across from the Methodist Church in the seventh grade with me.[10]

Shelley (Smokey) and Butler were able to give more details about the Aiken School. Mrs. Teague and Bess Hart were the teachers there for a while. Lastly, Fred Elmore was able to give his memory of the school in this area, but he called it Pumpkin Center School. Fred also discussed the school buses in Burke County.

TR: We found out about the school that was over there in Burke County near your family's farm. Martha, did you know about that school over there near the farm?

ME: No, I am learning so much tonight. Fred has never told me all of this.

SH: Smokey (Shelley) Teague said that his mama taught at that school.

FE: The old school was there, and they consolidated it with Hildebran, and that was before, well the story is that it consolidated with Hildebran. That was before I started driving a bus in that area. I drove a school bus from Rhodhiss to Hildebran to Rutherford College. That was when they were doing that consolidating.

SH: So, where did you go to high school?

FE: Rutherford College.

TR: That school that I am talking about was it just a one teacher school?

FE: Yes, just a one teacher. That Pumpkin Center School.

SH: But you went to Rhodhiss?

FE: Yes, for elementary school, then Burke County for high school.

SH: Well, you are the only person that I talked to that didn't go to high school in Granite Falls.

FE: Well, I was in Burke on the farm at that time. See, we moved from Rhodhiss to outside the city limit. We had already moved from Rhodhiss to out on the farm. The school buses were owned privately. One man might own a half dozen buses, and he had to hire the drivers. The state didn't own the buses then.

TR: Did the kids have to pay to ride?

FE: No, no. The county paid that to the man that owned the buses.[11]

Fred would have driven a bus for Burke County children during the 1930s. He did call it the Pumpkin Center School, but he told me that Pumpkin Center was near the old Settlemyre Store on Cape Hickory Road. Aiken and Pumpkin Center must be one in the same. At this point the Aiken School had consolidated with larger schools in Burke County as per Fred's recollection.

Leona Hunsucker explained that when students graduated from Rhodhiss Elementary in the seventh grade, they went to Granite Falls High School, but they had to walk. She would have gone to Rhodhiss from about 1914-1921. The distance to walk to high school in Granite Falls would have been approximately two miles. Leona explained:

LH: We walked to Granite Falls High School every day till we finished high school up there. My brother and two sisters. Where the Methodist Church is now is where the Rhodhiss school house was. You had two grades in all rooms. You had a desk large enough for two people to sit in. Well, they were having my class to recite, and then you just sat there and worked on your lesson or whatever. Then the other side would recite. Well, I would listen to what the others were saying, and I learned the sixth grade. Preacher Sylvester Benfield was our teacher from North Catawba, I believe. He had two sons that became ministers. They were a nice family of people. He told me, 'Leona, don't you go in the sixth grade.' I said, 'Well, I will. I can't go to the seventh grade from the fifth grade.' We had a seventh grade over there where Mike Owens lives. In that house they started having the seventh grade in that little house. It's been remodeled. It was a four-room house. I believe Burgs Bush was the teacher at that time. Anyway, Mr. Benfield went to my parents and said, 'Don't let her take the sixth grade. She knows it. Just let her go up to the seventh.' So, they did. I got along all right. It was hard, but I got along and made good grades and went on through. That way I caught up with my brother. We both finished in 1925 up at Granite Falls. I played basketball, and the goals were out in the front yard. You didn't have grass, just dirt. We had these uniforms, white blouse with a sailor collar with black braid on it and black sateen bloomers.

TR: Rhodhiss School must have been above average.

LH: It was. It really was. Because we went to Granite and finished school. There were just eleven grades back then. We walked and everybody else did. Now, Mr. McIntyre was the superintendent then and lived up there where Charlie Kirby did. That was the superintendent's house. My brother and me would be walking, and the McIntyres were the only ones that had a car. They had a nice car. There were three boys and two girls, I believe. So that was a car full. But if they would pass us along the road, they would stop, and one of those boys would get out and walk with my brother, and they would make me get in there and ride. That's the kind of people that you had down there. I didn't care anything about riding, but they wanted me to ride. Some people used to make little sly remarks about Rhodhiss because it wasn't fixed up so fine, but there were a lot of nice people, good people, good churches, good school. The school was accredited and had good teachers. People have made good that have lived down there.[12]

Leona was able to explain her education at Rhodhiss Elementary and Granite Falls High. The school was on present-day Church Street where the Boy Scout hut is today. The additional house used for the seventh grade is the first house across the street from the Scout building at 201 Church Street. Leona had words of praise for her education and her community.

Similarly, Thelma Church had the same sentiments as Leona. Thelma was a few years younger than Leona, so her years at Rhodhiss would have been from 1918 to 1925. Thelma recollected:

TC: You see they just had to the seventh grade down here, and I went from here to Granite. They didn't have a high school in Rhodhiss. I just went to high school one year and got married. There were no school buses then. When we got out of school here, we had to walk from here to high school. Yeah, we did.

SH: Now did you go to school in the old wooden building?

TC: Oh, yeah.

SH: Where the Methodist Church is now?

TC: Yeah, yeah. I sure did. Right up there in the corner where Mike Owens lives, they had classrooms there.

SH: So, they had two buildings. Where the Methodist Church is and where Mike Owens' house is.

TC: Yeah, that's right. The old Methodist Church was our schoolhouse, and then out there on the corner. I don't know why unless we didn't have enough classrooms. We used that old mill house, and the kids went out there. I think that Miss Carrie Starnes was my teacher out there.

SH: Was the Ross house the teacherage? They housed some teachers there.

TC: Yeah, I think that some teachers lived there. Yes, I think so. Then my aunt out here moved in this house, and my uncle took that house out there, and a lot of teachers stayed out there during the winter. They gave them a bedroom and provided them with lunch. Like I said, nobody had cars or transportation. There was just horse and buggy.

SH: Did you go to school about eight months or less than that?

TC: I think that it was about seven to eight. Not over eight. The teachers boarded around here in places. Teachers had no cars. We had plays in the old school. We didn't have an auditorium until the new school was built. What they had to do, Sherrie, was they had partitions that used to move back and forth for the classrooms to be bigger or littler. Then they would fix a stage with different things that we had. On Fridays we had plays, commencement, or all this stuff. When I was in about the fifth grade, we had contests, you know.

SH: What kind of contests?

TC: I don't know. They had them for every school. You know, like in Rhodhiss, Granite, Hudson, all this Caldwell County. A lot of times, it would be reciting poems or different things to see who could recite them the best. Down here, they would take every grade and put them together for competition. I won in Rhodhiss. I had this dress especially made for me, and I had long curly hair. But my teacher had taught me to put action into what I did. Every time Epaminondas, the character in my poem, made these pies and put them in the window, she would have me take them and put them in the window. When he stepped in every pie, she had me step in a pie. When all of these others did theirs, they just recited. But my teacher was up in the balcony, she was pointing at me, 'You can do better. You can do better. Yours is better than that.' You know, I got up there, and I thought, 'Oh, gosh, I don't know if I can do it or not.' I did, and I did well. I got the blue ribbon for the county.

SH: You did!

TC: I beat the county schools out. Rhodhiss really did put me on the map, you know. Other teachers were upset at how their kids did it, and how I did mine. That shows that we were getting better training than other schools. Yeah, Annie High taught down here. They had some good teachers down here. Well, they had some good teachers at Granite Falls, too. Sometimes, I think that the teachers were better in Rhodhiss. When I left here and went to Granite, I did as well as those in Granite. It was like I had been in Granite the whole time. I went down here through the seventh, you know.

SH: So, when you graduated, was that in the eleventh grade?

TC: Yeah, yeah. After you left Rhodhiss, you had four more years to go at the school in front of the old Dixie Store. That's where the school was. They had the grammar grades and the high school all together in just one building. They taught the smaller ones in the lower floors, you know. As you aged, you got a little higher. We walked from here to Granite, and we took our lunch. When I was up there in eighth grade, they had an economics class where you learned how to cook and sew. All they had up there was to show us how to cook and serve lunch, but as far as serving lunch, they didn't when I was going. You had to carry your lunch. I know that I would carry peanut butter and raisins. I would put bananas on peanut butter.

SH: Raisins on peanut butter?

TC: Yeah, that's what we ate. Something that wouldn't run, you know. You didn't have much meat. You had to eat peanut butter and jelly or whatever. People had plenty of jelly. We ate jelly sandwiches, too. You would get up there and half the time, you would switch sandwiches. Somebody else would have something that you wanted, and you had what they wanted. You would just divide or swap with them.

SH: What did you drink? Did they have a well there?

TC: I guess that they did. I just can't remember. I think that they had running water and had these fountains. When they built these new buildings, I believe that they had running water, but in the old building up there we had to carry water. We had outside toilets. That's right. A lot of these big towns put on a big front. Granite tried to snub Rhodhiss. They didn't want to have anything to do with us. Still yet when they went up there to school or to play ball or whatever, Rhodhiss could come up to their par in anything.[13]

Thelma talked about walking to high school in Granite as Leona did. She also detailed winning a blue ribbon in a speech contest. She gave further details about the school in Granite Falls. According to a 1923 article in the *Lenoir News-Topic*, Thelma won first place along with several other winners from her school. A group of students achieved first place for "The First Thanksgiving." These scholars included Hazel Beshears, Colean Kline, Christine Wright, Catherine Moody, Pauline Colvard, Louise Dale, Ruth Earley, John Church, Bruce Kline (sic), Pennel Hice, Robby Minda, Henry Marlow, Richard Marlow, Noah Lunsford, and Howard Curtis. Another Rhodhiss winner was Ralph Kirby for his recitation of "Spartacus, the Gladiator."[14] Rhodhiss School was able to compete within the county and bring home the gold.

Thelma attended the old clapboard school as did Willard Herman. Both went from about 1918 to 1925 or 1926. Willard explained to Tom Ross and me that he and his wife were in the same classroom and that the school moved locations with the building of the WPA building:

WH: Well, when I went to Rhodhiss School, you had the fifth, sixth, and seventh grade all together. I went one year in second or third grade there. We moved, and I went to school somewhere else. Before mother died, we came back to Rhodhiss. I don't know just how long. We shifted around. I don't remember too much about how we did do it. I know that my wife and I were in the fifth and sixth together or the sixth and seventh together. She was younger than I was, but she was in my same class at school. We didn't have school like we have now.

TR: I wondered if the mill company helped the schools out any back when they were talking about, they were having trouble with the stoves?

WH: I am sure that they did, Tom. They had to.[15]

Rhodhiss Manufacturing paid for the schools until Duke Power took over in 1923. This was because Duke bought the plants for the water rights. Doughton Beshears, Butler Monteith, Shelley Teague, and Tom Ross discussed this further:

TR: I told Sherrie, Doughton, that the mill company has always been involved in the town.

DB: Yeah.

TR: And in the schools and the churches, really. They supplemented the churches and the schools. And the office manager was the town clerk, and he was on the school board. It was automatic. That's how it worked.

DB: Yeah, yeah. I remember that. That's the way that it was.

ST: My mama used to teach up here in this old school where the Methodist Church is now. Where the Owens boy lives that used to be a school room.

BM: They had the seventh grade there.

ST: I don't know what grade.

BM: Yeah, it was the seventh.

ST: It was a house for the employees, but they needed it for the school.

TR: This house used to be a teacherage, didn't it?

DB: Yes. Mr. Keller was the last principal to live here.

SH: Who is he, and when was he here?

ST: He was there after mama.

DB: Keller was the last to live here. You know he's still living. He's 90 years old.

TR: Goodness gracious.

DB: Yeah, the principal used to have to teach, too.

ST: My first year of school was that old wooden school there in the basement.[16]

Shelley and Butler would have attended Rhodhiss School in the 1920s. Shelley said that his mother taught at Rhodhiss and Aiken. According to Malcolm's article in the newspaper, Mrs. Teague did indeed teach at Rhodhiss in the early years, but she later served as a postmaster, when the Duke Power dam was being built.

Arthur and Jack Edwards, and Edna Edwards and Laney Stilwell said that Rhodhiss was a good school. They told of many of their adventures during the 1920s and 1930s. Edna walked to Granite Falls to go to high school. A watermelon feast was provided on the first day of school in Rhodhiss. Edna elaborated that no matter where children lived on the hill, they walked home at dinner time since there was no school cafeteria. Jack said that was a treat because sometimes his mother would pack his lunch, and he stayed at school. Arthur explained that he went home for lunch because beans couldn't be packed. Mr. Ross said that he carried ham and eggs every day for his lunch in South Carolina. Jack indicated that by the time he came along most of the kids still went home for lunch, but the ones on Burke County side would stay at school. Edna explained that she used to fly down that hill at lunch time, get a bite to eat, and fly back. They felt as if they had a luxurious life when the school got a library. Arthur said that "whenever that bell rang for lunch, you better not get in the way. Kids were going in every direction." Edna remembered that they went at 8:00 and had an hour for lunch. Arthur said that they got out at 5:00. Edna did not agree that they stayed that long. Jack said that it just seemed that they stayed till 5:00. Arthur elaborated, "By the time you got out, it was time to go to bed." Edna added, "By the time you got the wood in and the water, it was bedtime."[17] Edna was the third person to say that she had to walk to high school in Granite Falls. Many children quit after the seventh grade and went to work in the mill instead of walking to high school.

Fred Elmore went to Rhodhiss School in the 1920s. He told of a trick that he played on his friend and an encounter with the principal, Mr. Keller, that Doughton mentioned:

FE: I know that you know Jack Hendrix. He and I went to school together. We lived in Burke County. We crossed the bridge and went straight up the holler behind Charlie Kirby's house to go to school. That was all cow pasture. Anyway, one afternoon on the way home from school, to show the tricks we played on each other, I knew that I was immune from poison oak and poison ivy. There was a big old poplar tree. I went over to the tree and got the vine and rubbed it all over me and threw it down. Jack said we don't want to go to school, so he reached over and got a handful and crossed his face. The next morning, I went to Jack's house. He didn't come to the door. His mother came and said, 'I don't know what's wrong with Jack. He can't go to school. His face is so swollen that he can't see.' It dawned on me what I had done. He remembers that to this day. Well, Jack paid me back for that poison. I don't know if it was that same year or the next. We were going to school one morning, and he had already done it. There was frost all over the old steel bridge rail. Jack said, 'How about sticking your tongue on that, boy. That's alright.' I ran my tongue down on it, and it about stuck me to it; it almost froze to it. I got off it, and Jack just laughed.

SH: What did you think about Rhodhiss School?

FE: Good school. I remember one time the principal, Mr. Keller, lived in your house, Tom. It was snowing. I made a big snowball and tried to hit another kid, but it hit the principal and knocked his hat off and knocked him upside the head. He went after a hickory, but he never found out who threw it.

ME: Fred must have been a tyrant.

FE: After a while they added a school across the road for the bigger kids.

SH: But your teachers were good?

FE: Oh, yes. They were good.

SH: What were your school hours?

FE: About like they are now. About 8:30 to 3:30 or 4:00. As well as I remember we went to school later in the morning than they do now.

TR: You had an hour for lunch though, right?

FE: Yes, you went home for lunch. They had these cups that folded. You could mash it flat. If you didn't have one of those, you could make one out of a piece of paper.

SH: Mrs. Jones said that the mill kids were well behaved kids. She had a problem only once.

FE: Yes, they were good kids. Mischievous as the dickens, but not mean. You know, you had to do something rough to be in serious trouble. I will tell you that if you got in trouble at school, that teacher took care of you right then. I tell you what's the truth if you got into trouble at school and that teacher blistered your hind end with a switch about that long and about an inch thick, you might as well say that you were going to get another one when you got home.[18]

Fred described Rhodhiss' children as good, but mischievous. Their school days were spent at the old clapboard building and the addition across the street.

Pawnee Mullinax Simmons was born in 1918, and she went to school in Rhodhiss from 1924 to 1930. She also had to walk to Granite High to continue her education; however, Pawnee was able to explain when the bus started coming to Rhodhiss to transport them:

PS: Well, Rhodhiss was like any other school except it wasn't big. The third, fourth, and fifth grades were combinations. Sixth and seventh grades were combinations.

SH: So, you went to the old school?

PS: Yes. It was a wooden building. There where the Methodist Church is now.

SH: Did Finn go to school in Rhodhiss?

PS: No, I don't believe that he ever did. Did you go to school in Rhodhiss?

FS: I went one year, the first grade. That's what I was telling Tom. John Gaye and I were about the same age. His aunt was a teacher. My daddy had to pay for my brother and sister to come up here to Granite to go to school. That's why a lot of the people over near the river migrated here was for them to go to school.

SH: Now you told me a minute ago, what year you came.

PS: 1923. My parents were very strict. Well, I was way up in high school before I went to the movie. I walked to high school every day. The year (around 1935) that I graduated they had the first bus to Rhodhiss from the high school.

SH: How were Rhodhiss kids accepted in Granite?

PS: Well, I couldn't tell any difference, but sometimes people would say, 'They're from Rhodhiss.' I think it was because there were so few of us. The year that I went to high school, I think that there were only five of us. They came from Grace Chapel, Dudley, and all in there. Then as far as Granite goes, it's a mill village, too. It was just bigger. They had more plants. I didn't feel any different than anybody, but I don't know how everybody else felt. They didn't show it to me. We just had a good time. There weren't too many cars. Then, of course, when I got old enough to really know about things, the Depression came along.[19]

Pawnee's information was helpful in establishing a school bus route to Rhodhiss. Similarly, Fred Elmore said that the route in Burke County began around the same time since he drove a bus.

Another element to the Rhodhiss School was that it burned one time. Nancy Brady lived on Duke Street (presently 166 Duke Street) which is the major pathway to Rhodhiss in Caldwell County, and she stated that she stood at her kitchen window and watched the school burn one morning.[20] In addition, Norma Kirby stated in *The Heritage of Caldwell County* that the school burned in 1930, and it took a couple of years for it to be rebuilt.[21] The town's children had a brief respite from school because of the fire.

Zeno Crump who was later a teacher and principal in Burke County recalled his school days in Rhodhiss quite fondly. He attended school there from 1932 to 1939. Zeno said:

Well, I started attending Rhodhiss Elementary School, and I had to be almost 7 years old at the time because my birthday is in December, and they wouldn't let me start when I was 6. We lived on the Burke side, and we had lived on the Caldwell side for a while, but one of the little houses on River Street came open, and my dad requested that we move over there, and we did. So, I walked across the bridge every morning and every evening to get to the school over on the Caldwell side. We walked up through a cow pasture. I had to go behind the old Company Store building and walked up through a cow pasture to get to the school. I remember that old wooden building. It seems to me that there weren't over four or five classrooms, and it was one big building, and they had petitioned off the classrooms with folding doors, and it looked like as I remember that those doors hadn't been opened many times. I don't ever remember their being opened when I attended school there. It was heated with a great big old wood stove, or coal burning stove in the middle of the room, and I suppose that each one of those rooms had one of those stoves. I do know that one that I attended in most of the time had a big coal burning stove in the middle of the room and usually the teacher would appoint some of the stronger and bigger boys to keep the fire, and I specifically remember Arley Church. He usually kept the fire going in our classroom. Now, I remember Mrs. Melvin Jones, Mary Whitley Jones. She was one of the best teachers that I think that I ever had in my life, and certainly one of the best in the early years of my going to school. She took a real interest in us, and she talked about things to get the children's attention. She could get your attention. The first movie that I ever saw Mrs. Jones took all the kids to a movie. I don't remember whether it was in Granite Falls or Hickory. It probably was in Hickory because I don't think that there was a movie house in Granite Falls at that time. I remember that she told us one time how much money she made. I think that one of the children asked her how much money she made. She said that she made $90 a month that year. Mr. and Mrs. Jones had made a trip to the World's Fair in New York City. I think that it was the year that I was in the sixth grade. She told us all about the World's Fair. It just came alive to us. I think that she was the one that got me interested in English grammar. I learned more just old-fashioned English grammar under her than I did from the other teachers. There were a lot of good teachers, but she just stood out. She was always interested in the personal things of the students. She saw that everybody in the class had a toothbrush. She gave us the first tube of toothpaste that I ever had. Mrs. Jones gave me that little tube of toothpaste. Well, we all carried our lunches. Most of them carried in a little syrup bucket, or that's we called it. A little bucket with a lid on top of it. Most of the families were large enough that they bought the syrup in a little half a gallon bucket, and it made a perfect little lunch pail. Everybody carried your lunch. It seems to me that I finished the fifth grade in the old wooden building. Those were some happy days for me. I got inspiration.[22]

Mrs. Jones was very kind to give children toothbrushes and toothpaste. Zeno gave a great compliment to his favorite teacher, Mrs. Mary Whitley Jones. He said that she inspired him. Certainly, that was true because Zeno later influenced many children in the eastern section of Burke County when he became a principal. In addition, Paul Bright had a memory of Mrs. Jones, too. Mary Jones took him the farthest he had ever been out of Rhodhiss when he was in her class. She took him and others to Hickory to see a movie for perfect attendance. They saw a Charlie Chaplin movie.[23]

One of Zeno and Paul's friends, Ned Bean, lived in Rhodhiss and went to school there. Ned attended the same years as Zeno and Paul. Ned, Elvie, and Tom Ross discussed their experiences with education:

> EB: The school used to be, Ned has told me, in the basement of the old Methodist Church.
> NB: No, no. There was a school building there, and I started to school in the basement.
> SH: That's where your classroom was?
> NB: Yeah, they had two classes in the house on the corner.
> SH: Yes, the sixth and seventh grades were in that house. That's what Mary Jones told me.
> NB: Mary Jones was my teacher in the third and sixth grades.
> SH: So, what did you think about coming through Rhodhiss School?
> NB: Oh, it was great. I don't think that there was a better school. You didn't find teachers like ours. Miss Starnes, Miss Powell, Mrs. Jones.
> SH: Mr. Ross, you said that there was a well at your house.
> TR: It was on the back porch.
> NB: That was the principal's house and the teachers' rooming house. When we lived in the house where Boyd Yount did live, the principals and teachers lived there in Tom's house. In the summers there would be nobody over there, and I know that's when we were closed for school.[24]

Again, the teacherage was at Tom Ross' house even in the 1930s. This house today is owned by Betsy Ross Adkins and Katie Ross, and it is on 202 Church Street. Ned and Zeno both mentioned Mary Jones who was their teacher. Mary was born in Morganton, and she was in Rhodhiss in the mid to late 1930s. Mary reflected on her time:

MJ: First, I was in that old wooden building where the Methodist Church is. That was my first year. I think that I just taught there for one year. Ann Whitener was teaching there I know that year. Estelle Blair and Ruby Courtney were teachers there. They lived in the Ross house. Dermont Moore from Collettsville roomed there, too. He lived in the Ross house, too. The three of them lived there. The Rosses live in the old teacherage. Yeah, it was just the three of them: Dermont Moore, Ruby Courtney, and Estelle Blair who later married Addie Flowers' brother, Brown. Mr. Laxton was there when I was there. I remember that Alan Laxton was the heavy one. J. M. was the slim one. They were cousins.

SH: How large was the school building that you were in?

MJ: The first old wooden one? I think that it had first, second, and third. Then I think that there were combination classes. Fourth and fifth and then sixth and seventh were combinations.

SH: So, that building was big to have all those rooms in it.

MJ: Well, it had a basement, and a lot of the rooms were in the basement. Ann Whitener taught downstairs, and Powell taught in the basement. Powell taught first grade, Estelle Powell. Ann taught second; I had the third. Ruby had fourth and maybe fifth or fourth probably. Blair had the fifth, I believe. Malcolm had the seventh, I believe. I taught two or three of Charlie Kirby's children. Charlie Kirby that lived up on the hill in that big house. He had a lot of children. Well, I taught several of those children. That's been about fifty years ago. All the Rhodhiss children were so polite and nice. Oh, if you would tell them to do something, there wasn't sass. One boy did give me some trouble. He was in trouble a lot. One day I told him to get his book out, and he wouldn't. So, I switched him. His daddy came the next day and said, 'I am gonna go down and see Clarkson Jones and have you fired.' I said, 'You go right along, and I will tell Clarkson how your son has been acting.'

SH: So, Clarkson Jones had the ability to fire you?

MJ: Well, that was just the dad's thought. Clarkson was on the school board. Mr. Mullinax was on the committee and Clarkson and H. C. Cobb. Cobb worked in the mill. His wife was in my bridge club, and they came to our church. I taught his daughter Mary. There was also Peggy Cobb, and there was Jimmy Cobb, H. C., and Lucy. Well, Lucy is dead now. H. C. is dead, too. Jimmy lives in Ohio, and he is president of the Lily something paper company. This big box came in the mail one day to the garage. So, Mel tried to get it in the door of the car. He wedged it in there. I couldn't wait to open it because I thought that it was a mistake. It said on the front that it was from Jimmy Cobb in Dayton, Ohio. The note said, 'Fond memories of you as a teacher.' It had six dozen paper plates, six dozen little pie plates, and six dozen paper cups. The whole box was just full. He was the company president. I started teaching in '35, so I must have taught two years in the old building. I do remember a lot about Rhodhiss. I remember that some of the children went home for lunch. We didn't have a lunchroom. I remember going into the new building. I often had a party on the farm for the children. (Her farm was in Granite Falls.) One dad told me that I had to have his child back home by 8:00 on the dot, and

I had to come to get him. That was sixth grade. They were 12 years old. Some of them wanted to walk to my farm. I can't remember that little boy's name, but I remember that he could write so pretty. I promised to come get him and get him back, and I did. I asked the other children if they wanted a ride back to Rhodhiss, but they wanted to walk.

SH: Well, you were helpful. You told me what the kids were like.

MJ: Oh, they were such good children.

SH: Were the parents interested in what their children were doing at school?

MJ: Well, we would have plays, and the parents really did support us. The parents were there when they were needed. After school was out, I visited every child in my room. I also taught Thad Martin.[25]

Mary Jones was able to give the perspective of a teacher. She talked about how well behaved the children were. She mentioned the school board and the old school building. The students knew that she was devoted to her job as mentioned by Zeno Crump.

Paul Bumgarner attended Rhodhiss School in the old building from approximately 1930-1937. He had fond memories of his time there. Paul said, "I had the best bunch of teachers here that I have ever seen. You take Gordon Starnes' wife, Estelle Powell Starnes. The two Starnes from up there at Granite, Miss Kate and Miss Carrie. You couldn't beat them. Mrs. Williams, too. Couldn't beat them."[26] This is high praise from Paul, and many others have voiced the same sentiment. Earl Lingle also had accolades for Rhodhiss. He went to school in both the old building and the new brick 1938 WPA one. He attended from the late 1930s to the early 1940s. Earl reflected:

EL: Oh, well. Rhodhiss School was great. I started over there where the Methodist Church is now. I went there, and they started building the school. I started in the third grade in the new building. The school was an older frame building. I'll tell you what. Those guys from other towns would rub you too far, you know, and you'd have to work on 'em. Those guys used to come down there riding their bicycles. They'd go up there on Schoolhouse Hill courtin' the gals. We'd pile us up a bunch of drink bottles and rocks and things. They'd come down that hill at the Methodist Church. We'd let them have it. I remember this one guy. I threw an RC Bottle. I must have knocked half of his spokes out. He went up that road, 'shup, shup, shup.' He wouldn't stop.

SH: So, the girls were pretty?

EL: Oh, yeah. Pretty.

TR: Those are some good stories, Earl.[27]

Earl was able to add some zest to life around Schoolhouse Hill. It appears that Rhodhiss girls were indeed some of the prettiest girls around, and guys came from all around to attract their attention.

The Caldwell County Directory listed these people at Rhodhiss in 1936-1937: Allen Laxton, Principal and 7th grade; Mrs. Addie B. Flowers, 6th grade; Kate Starnes, 5th grade; Ruby Courtney, 4th grade; Mrs. Melvin Whitley Jones, 3rd grade; Estella Powell, 2nd grade; Lexie Williams, 1st grade.[28] Rhodhiss Elementary School was blessed with excellent teachers.

Rhodhiss has always taken great pride in their community and their school, even when the school was in the clapboard building on Church Street. The school was the hub of all activities. Not only was it a site for education, but it also hosted many plays, musical events, watermelon feasts, and commencements. The students had respect for their teachers, and a value was placed on education. While the parents worked hard in the mill company, the students worked hard at school.

OLD CLAPBOARD SCHOOL CIRCA 1907. CALDWELL COUNTY
HERITAGE MUSEUM PHOTO.

CIRCA 1914 CLASS PICTURE. KATHERINE TAYLOR
CLASS. BOYD HOLLAR, PEARL HAAS COOPER,
MARY BRANCH BUMGARNER, GLADYS KIRBY
BARKER IN FRONT OF RHODHISS SCHOOL.
GLADYS BARKER PHOTO.

RHODHISS ELEMENTARY 1929, GRADE 1A.
EDDIE LUNSFORD (2ND ROW 4TH FROM LEFT).
KENNETH LUNSFORD PHOTO.

RHODHISS ELEMENTARY 1929, GRADE 1B. CHARLIE MUNDAY.
TOMMY AND PHYLLIS HIGH PHOTO.

RHODHISS ELEMENTARY 1929, GRADE 3.

RHODHISS ELEMENTARY 1929, GRADE 4. FLOYD AND BOYD KIRBY.

RHODHISS ELEMENTARY 1929, GRADE 5. LEFT TO RIGHT, ROW 1 EDA MILLS, TOYE HERMAN, EULA FOWLER, IRENE MCRARY, IRENE COFFEY, VERGIE NELSON ANNAS, MABELLINE PACK, RUYEE BEANE TRAMBLE, IRENE MASK WILLIAMS; ROW 2 PAUL WITHERSPOON, HARLEN NORMAN, FRED FOSTER, GUY BENTLEY, FLAKE MOFFITT, DOUG ANNAS; ROW 3 ANNIE MAE FOX, PAWNEE MULLINAX, BEATRICE PACK, EULA RATHBONE, DOROTHY ADKINS; ROW 4 ODELL TRAMBLE, PAUL PADGETT, CLYDE RINEHART. PAWNEE SIMMONS PHOTO.

VALENTINE FROM ZENO CRUMP TO MAE HILTON, CIRCA 1930S. SUSAN YOUNT PHOTO.

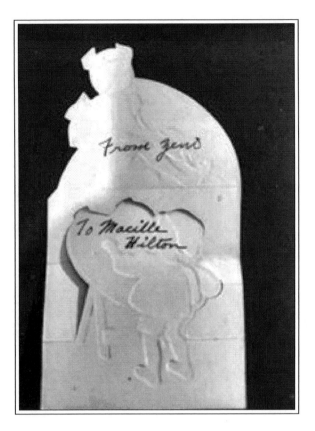

VALENTINE BACKSIDE. SUSAN YOUNT PHOTO.

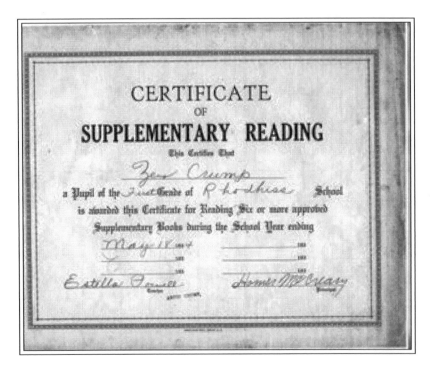

ZENO CRUMP CERTIFICATE. ZENO CRUMP COPY.

1937-1938 RHODHISS SCHOOL GRADE 3,
BETTY HENDRIX, ___ CURTIS (MAYBE JOE), FLORINE STILWELL, MAYBELLE JEAN BRYANT, TOMMIE HAAS RHEA, BAINE HELTON, FRED CARPENTER, WILBUR BARKER, TED BRADY, ROB HAND, RUTH ANNA HOLLAND, INEZ MUNDAY, RUTH HAAS, ANN FAYE COOK, JACK MULLINAX. ADDIE FLOWERS IS THE TEACHER; MARY WOODS WHO IS NED BEAN'S SISTER, LILLIE MAE MUNDAY, STARLENE TOWNSEND, A FRANKLIN GIRL, WANDA TRIPLETT, KATHERINE CHURCH, INEZ HOLLAR, THELMA BUMGARNER, CLARA RIMMER, FAYE POPE, MELLON ANNAS, A PRITCHARD, AILEEN CURTIS, DOUG HOYLE, RAY STORY, CLYDE POWELL, FRANK WOODS, JAMES HOYLE, EARL LAIL, AB HEAVNER, GEORGE BROWN, GLENN WOODIE, J.C. CHURCH, RUEL HEAVNER, A FRANKLIN, FRED HENDRIX, ARCHIE HENDRIX. TOMMIE HAAS RHEA PHOTO AND HER RECALL OF NAMES.

1937-1938 Rhodhiss School Grade 4 with Bill Childers, Ralph Tolbert,
Grady Hamby.

Rhodhiss Elementary Students 1937

The above photo was taken in 1937 of the fifth grade Elementary students standing beside the old wood-frame structure school that stood where the First United Methodist Church now stands in Rhodhiss. Students shown left to right are: (Row 1) Kate Starnes, teacher; Edith Hoyle, Maycill Helton, Grace Burnett, Fred Helton, Zeno Crump, Georgellen Triplett, Earl Keller, Ruth Pritchard and Mary Lou Childers. Row 2, Tommy Gusly, Guthrie Curtis, Ritt Munday, Louise Mundy, Nina Tolbert, Paul Bright, Less Bowman, Ernest Church, Faye Lingle, Dorothy Smith; Third Row, Burleen Blue, Katheryn Laxton, Ray Fox, Evelyn Harris, C. J. Bumgarner, Jr. Jennings Franklin Arley Church, Ned Bean, and Odell Holeman.   Photo Submitted By Paul Bumgarner

RHODHISS SCHOOL, GRADE 5 IN 1937-1938,
ROW 1 KATE STARNES, TEACHER; EDITH HOYLE, MAECILL HILTON, GRACE BURNETT, FRED HELTON,
ZENO CRUMP, GEORGELLEN TRIPLETT, EARL KELLER, RUTH PRITCHARD, MARY LOU CHILDERS.
ROW 2 TOMMY GUSLY, GUTHRIE CURTIS, RITT MUNDAY, LOUISE MUNDAY, NINA TOLBERT, PAUL
BRIGHT, LES BOWMAN, ERNEST CHURCH, FAYE LINGLE, DOROTHY SMITH. ROW 3 BURLEEN BLUE,
KATHERYN LAXTON, RAY FOX, EVELYN HARRIS, C. J BUMGARNER, JR., JENNINGS FRANKLIN, ARLEY
CHURCH, NED BEAN, AND ODELL HOLMAN. GRANITE FALLS PRESS PHOTO.

1937-1938 RHODHISS SCHOOL. GRADE 6,
ROW 1 TOY CHILDERS, NOREEN KIRBY, ELOISE TOLBERT, NINA KAYLOR, MARION COBB, DOROTHY HOLLAR, LEONA MINTON, GRADY CHURCH, JUNIOR MULLINAX. ROW 2 VIOLET TRIPLETT, VIRGINIA JONES, MYRTLE HEAVNER, ALLEN BEANE, WANDA MCCALL, MARY ABEE, ELIZABETH BUTLER, G. S. CHURCH, ROSTOR JONES; ROW 3 HOWARD CARPENTER, JR., ROY WOODS, VERLA MAE ANDERSON, BETTY KEMP, AGNES GREENE, D. W. CHILDERS, RAYMOND PRITCHARD, ____ BROWN, PAUL BUMGARNER. MRS. MELVIN (MARY) JONES, TEACHER. VIRGINIA JONES HOLLAR PHOTO AND HER RECALL OF NAMES.

1937-1938 RHODHISS SCHOOL. GRADE 7. ROW 1 6TH PERSON ELOUISE TOLBERT; LAST ROW FIRST PERSON IS SHIRLEY CHURCH AND LAST PERSON IS THAD MARTIN.

NOTES

1   Laxton, J. M. "Rapid Progress at Rhodhiss." *Lenoir News-Topic*. 12 September 1941. Centennial Edition. Reprint.

2   Laxton.

3   Laxton.

4   Hawkins, John O. *The Most American Thing: A History of Education in Caldwell County, North Carolina*. Lenoir, NC: The Education Foundation of Caldwell County, 2001, p. 161.

5   "Two Teachers, Six-Month School Term: Rhodhiss Opened Doors in 1900." *The Communicator of the Caldwell County Schools*. June 1975. Vol. 1 No. 2. Lenoir, NC.

6   Barker, Gladys.

7   Austin, Ann, Thad Martin, Shelley Teague.

8   Herman, Willard and Tom Ross.

9   Curtis, Violet, Willard Herman, and Tom Ross.

10   Beshears, Monteith, Ross, Teague.

11   Elmore, Fred and Martha, Tom Ross.

12   Hunsucker, Leona and Tom Ross.

13   Church, Thelma.

14   "County School Notes." *Lenoir News-Topic*. 3 April 1923, p. 8. https://newspapers.digitalnc.org/lccn/sn92073196/1923-04-03/ed-1/seq-8/#words=Rhodhiss. Accessed 28 July 2022.

15   Herman, Willard and Tom Ross.

16   Beshears, Monteith, Ross, Teague.

17   Edwards, Arthur and Jack, Edna Edwards Laney Stilwell, and Tom Ross.

18   Elmore, Fred and Martha, and Tom Ross.

19   Simmons, Finn and Pawnee, Tom Ross.

20   Brady, Lawrence and Nancy, Tom Ross.

21   Anderson, Carl, pp. 181-182.

22   Crump, Zeno. Personal Videotape Interview with Sherrie Hartsoe Sigmon. Hickory, NC. 14 April 2012.

23   Bright, Paul.

24   Bean, Ned and Elvie and Tom Ross.

25   Bumgarner, Paul and Helen.

26   Bumgarner, Paul and Helen.

27   Lingle, Earl and Tom Ross.

28   Caldwell County Schools 1936-1937. *Directory and Suggestive Materials*. Caldwell County Board of Education. Lenoir, NC. Pamphlet, p. 9.

CHAPTER 11
EDUCATION/WPA BUILDING-1938 TO PRESENT

J. M. Laxton's 1941 article in the *Lenoir News-Topic* stated that the old clapboard school building was used until 1938. A new facility was needed badly, and the Works Progress Administration (WPA) was able to construct it for approximately $41,000. This new brick building contained seven classrooms, a library, and an auditorium.[1] Grades one through seven were still taught at Rhodhiss in 1938, and the high school was in Granite Falls. Rhodhiss retained pride in their school whether it was a wooden building on Church Street or a brick one on Magnolia.

Laxton explained that in 1941 "there were enrolled 236 students with an average membership of 223 and an average daily attendance of over 218. Particularly outstanding was the record of the seventh grade which had a perfect attendance, the only one reported thus far in North Carolina this year. Library circulation for the year totaled 8,237 books and 1,488 magazines." Some of the teachers included Lexie Williams, first; Estella Powell Starnes, second; Kate Starnes, third; Ruby Courtney, fourth; Mary E. Laxton, fifth; Dermont Moore, sixth; J. M. Laxton, seventh and principal.[2]

The Communicator of the Caldwell County Schools suggested that the construction began in 1938, and the school opened a year later. In 1975 as per this same article, the school had nine classrooms, a library, a lounge, a supply room, an auditorium, a principal's office, a secretary's office, and a cafeteria. Malcolm (J. M.) Laxton was the first principal in the new brick building. Mary Fagerstrom was the first full-time principal, meaning that she did not have to teach. In 1975 the school had ten full-time staff. The student population stayed at approximately 200 from the 1950s.[3]

Willard Herman's children attended Rhodhiss Elementary School as did he and his wife, Ruth Earley Herman. Willard and Ruth were active in the PTA where they tried to get the new school built. Willard discussed with Tom Ross how the building became a reality:

> I'll tell you how we got the school building that is there now. We had one rough time a getting that school building. My children started school in that building. You see part

of the village is in Burke County and part of it was in Caldwell. We had been trying to get a new building. My wife and I tried to be active in PTA and stuff like that going on. We just couldn't get anything done. I made several trips in front of the county commissioners, both counties. Burke always wanted Caldwell County to pay more than they did because the building was going to be in Caldwell County. So, Clarkson Jones lived over where Richard Deal does today. The way that we finally got this ball a rolling. We got a place in politics. Ruth's daddy was very influential in the Democrat Party around over there at that time. His oldest boy Werd was, too. They had me working around in it. We got Clarkson Jones nominated as a county commissioner from Rhodhiss. We got him elected. Clarkson got on the board of commissioners, and we got a school in Rhodhiss.

TR: Is that right?

WH: They got things worked out between Caldwell County and Burke County. I understand that Caldwell County paid more toward building the school than Burke did. Burke offered to do the same thing if they had put it in Burke.[4]

Politics was involved in getting the new brick building in 1938. The twentieth century saw a lot of political influence in state and federal operations.

The new brick building was a win for the community. The citizens took great pride in the school. Zeno Crump explained his involvement in a play at the new auditorium.

> The WPA under Roosevelt started building buildings. They built the new brick school building at Rhodhiss. We moved over there the last two years that I was in elementary school. I attended in that brick building, and I remember that we had an auditorium. I remember that I was in a little play there. It was one of the first plays that they gave. If I'm not mistaken, the name of it was Cinderella, and I played the part of Prince Charming, and I don't know how I got that part. My mother made a little blue suit for me to wear in the play. I remember that little blue suit. I think that is the only time that I ever wore it was in the play.[5]

Mr. Crump was smiling from ear to ear when he told this story. He was quite proud of his Rhodhiss days. He was happy to say that he attended Rhodhiss Elementary School. The town minutes indicate that the community was so excited about the new school that they helped purchase the school's Venetian blinds.[6]

Fred Elmore worked in the maintenance shop at Rhodhiss. The mill company gave the principal of the school a job for the summer to supplement his income. Mr. J. M. Laxton was hired to work with Fred and his coworkers in the mill's maintenance department. Fred told a humorous story about Mr. Laxton's first day on the job for the company. This would have been during the late 1930s to early 1940s. Fred explained:

I'll tell you a story about J. M. Laxton, the principal. It was a practice in the shop that we had pigeonholes that we put our lunch buckets in. We all had a habit of going around and looking at everybody's lunch, and if there was anything in there that we wanted, we ate it. It was a common thing. Everybody did it. If it was good enough, help yourself. The principal of the school was put to work at the plant during the summer. Mr. Laxton came in with his bag lunch and put it in a pigeonhole. Later, I opened his bag. I ate his sandwich, and it was awfully good. It had apple sliced on it. I put the bag back in the pigeonhole and watched to see whose it was. I didn't know it, but I ate the principal's lunch. I told him what I did. The rest of the fellas divided with him. I told him that mine was over there if he wanted it. He was a good fellow, nice guy. I was the one embarrassed. He wasn't.[7]

Mr. Laxton was probably accustomed to schoolboy pranks, but he was not looking for it to happen at his summer job at the shop.

Ruth Walsh Kiziah discussed her Rhodhiss school days. She really liked Rhodhiss, and she was happy there. Ruth states:

We moved to Rhodhiss in 1942 after my father passed away, and I started Rhodhiss Elementary, and I enjoyed going there. I enjoyed all the classmates and the teachers that we had. When I was in the seventh grade, I got rheumatic fever, and I was out of school a few months and couldn't be promoted. So, at the beginning of the next year my mother and I went to the principal, Mr. Cagle. He decided to go ahead and put me in the eighth grade. That year I did very well and made all A's, and A+s. I was so happy to be back in school. I enjoyed all the classmates. We enjoyed living in Rhodhiss. We had great friends, and I did a lot of babysitting. I babysat Carl Compton and his sister Ann Compton. Then after I graduated from Rhodhiss, I went on to Granite Falls High.

SHS: Who was your favorite teacher?

RWK: Annie Mackie High. She was wonderful. I had her in the eighth grade. I remember mainly history because it was my favorite subject. If I had been a schoolteacher, that would have been what I wanted to teach. She was my favorite teacher, and like I say Principal Cagle was great. I just enjoyed living in Rhodhiss.[8]

Ruth's move to Rhodhiss was because of her father's death. Then she got rheumatic fever; however, her relocation to Rhodhiss brought her happiness after these two sad events. She praised Annie Mackie High for being such a great teacher. Annie taught at Rhodhiss for a number of years. Annie gave me a picture of her with the other teachers and principal during the 1940s. She specifically told me that if I ever showed that picture, I had to tell people that she was wearing bobby socks because it was during the war, and nylons were too difficult to find.

1940S STAFF OUTSIDE RHODHISS SCHOOL WITH ANNIE MACKIE
HIGH AND MR. CAGLE AS PRINCIPAL. ANNIE HIGH PHOTO.

The town continued to support their little red schoolhouse. During 1941 the town council voted to give money to the seventh-grade class for their trip to Raleigh. This was in recognition of their perfect attendance for eight months.[9] Rhodhiss continued to support the school with many projects. According to the town minutes in 1943 the town voted to purchase a moving picture machine for the school.[10] A projector would have been an asset to the school, students, and teachers.

Charles Laney was a student at Rhodhiss from approximately 1946 to 1954. Later, he returned to teach there. He discussed his years as a student. Charles said:

Some of the people that I remember at Rhodhiss Elementary are either teachers or principals. The two ladies that I remember the most were Kate and Carrie Starnes. They were sisters to Mr. Richard Starnes who was the principal at Granite Falls High School/Middle School for years. Everybody said that Miss Kate was mean, but I spent a whole year in there, and she was fine. She did well. Mr. Dockery, I learned a lot of history from him. He was the fifth-grade teacher, and he was at Pearl Harbor when it was attacked, so he knew what was going on. Mr. Barnett was my favorite person, principal, and teacher. He was a principal and taught eighth grade. Several times during the year, you know, they would say, 'Well, it's 8:00, time to get started.' Here would come Mr. Barnett, and he had his pajamas on and a bathrobe. He'd say, 'I'm sorry. I overslept. Give me 10 minutes, and I'll be back, and I'll get started. So here read this chapter.' Mr. Barnett loved to play sports outside during PE period. We had a bank there at Rhodhiss, and we played football, and if something happened and we'd get too close to the bank, he'd say, 'You better watch out because you're going over that bank.' He treated everybody the same, too, whether you were rich, poor, or whatever. We had a class of about 20 to 22 students, and over half of them went to college, whether it was State, Carolina, or whatever. They were a very good group of people. I lived within walking distance of the school. I walked until I got into high school. One day I was walking from Burke County side on the old bridge with the steel frame on my way to school, and low and behold, a bird decided that it was bathroom time on my head. Rather than go back home, I just walked down to the river and washed my head, cleaned it off. Nobody even knew except that it was wet.[11]

Charles had a unique experience on his walk to school. He was proud of his eighth grade graduating class, and he talked fondly of his teacher. Mr. Barnett was remembered by many people who attended Rhodhiss Elementary School during the 1950s. He was admired and respected. Carl Compton, a resident for most of his life, reflected on his time at Rhodhiss and Mr. Barnett:

> Mr. Barnett was my favorite teacher in elementary school. He always made sure that the kids had activities to do after school and in the summer. He was a firm believer in keeping the school maintained inside and outside. He did a lot of work himself. Andrew Tramble and I worked with him a couple of summers, painting the foundation of the school with whitewash, and we trimmed the shrubs around the school. He always set us up with a Pepsi, sandwich, and a Moon Pie. Fond memories, for sure![12]

Mr. Barnett held the longest tenure as principal at Rhodhiss. He was a principal and teacher for ten years before he went to work for Don Davis.

It was not until the late 1940s that the school was able to have a cafeteria. Gladys Barker said that the women in the community were instrumental in getting the necessary equipment, and they even went to Asheville to get it. Mrs. Culclasure was the first cafeteria manager, and Mrs. Frances Ross helped her.[13] Tom Ross had already told me this earlier. Tom said, "Jim Barnett made sure that the school was taken care of, too. The Woman's Club started the lunchroom. That must have been the first one in the county. The Woman's Club got the equipment together."[14] The students took their lunches to school or went home for lunch until the late 1940s. Cora Brown assumed the job as cafeteria manager in 1957 when Jim Barnett asked her to take it until he could find somebody. She said that she stayed there 27 years. Cora and Boyd Brown discussed the cafeteria with me:

> CB: Oh, yeah. I liked it or I wouldn't have stayed there 27 years. It wasn't an easy job though. I can tell you that. Have you heard anything about the Woman's Club?
> SH: I have heard of it, but I don't really know everything.
> CB: Okay, the Woman's Club was started right after we moved here in '45 or '46. It must have been '46. Mrs. Frances Ross helped us organize. The Woman's Club had a fundraiser, and we raised $1,000. They didn't have a cafeteria at the school when we moved here. The Woman's Club started the cafeteria. Pacific Mills gave us some cane chairs, and with the $1,000 we bought a stove, a hot water tank, and the tables. They had two workers. I can't think of the woman's name.
> SH: Mrs. Culclasure.
> BB & CB: Yes.

CB: Mrs. Culclasure was the manager. I am not sure if Mrs. Ross worked with her or not. That's how it started. All the other years the cafeteria was supposed to be self-supporting. The state did not pay any money into the cafeteria. The staff's salary, well we weren't considered state employees until, Boyd, do you remember what year that was?

BB: No.

CB: It was about ten years before I retired. It was self-supporting until the county hired a food service director, and then my salary was raised. Before that the staff's and manager's salaries had to be taken out of what you took in. The state only allowed you a certain percent for your labor, and you had to use a certain percent for food and a certain percent for miscellaneous items, like electricity and stuff like that. That was until they got the food service director, and I can't remember what year that was. If I look through some of those certificates that I have, then I might be able to remember. The managers at Granite Elementary, Granite High, and Lenoir made twice as much as I did. Sherrie, when I started to work over there, I made $100 a month. That was all.

SH: That was 1957?

CB: Yeah, 1957. We were feeding 210 students a day, plus the adults. I worked eight hours a day, and a lot of times I had to work on weekends when I had my records to do. That was the reason that I worked. I really meant to retire when I was 65, but I worked till I was 70. I said that I was making a fair salary, but not in comparison to what others made. It was a fair salary then. Most of the time it was 20 to 23 days in a month. When we had those dinners for the parents and everything, we usually had to work on the weekends, and we didn't get anything extra for it either. Mr. Barnett told us that he would pay us extra. Then the principals did all the money part, you know. When I quit, I had to do the taxes and everything.[15]

The Woman's Club worked hard to provide the children of Rhodhiss a fully functioning cafeteria. Cora Brown was able to discuss the cafeteria and her long tenure as the food service manager.

CORA BROWN SERVED AS CAFETERIA MANAGER. FRANCES ROSS PHOTO.

SOME OF THE EQUIPMENT PURCHASED BY THE WOMAN'S CLUB, LATE 1940S.
FRANCES ROSS PHOTO.

Calvin Jones came to Rhodhiss in 1946 to work for Pacific Mills. He would maintain the shop for years. Calvin and Tom Ross talked about the mill company's dedication to the school:

CJ: I'll tell you right now, this little Rhodhiss School up here was one of the best schools that you'll find anywhere. When our kids went up there, that was a good school. The teachers were good. They took an interest in your children, and this is something that you don't see everywhere. I am so glad that my children went up here. I'm glad that they went up here to Granite Falls. Both places, the children were just good children. I am sure that the teachers had a part in that. No doubt. The mill company supplemented the schools. We got Jim Barnett up here.

TR: We supplemented his summer employment with the summertime recreation program. We promised him that.

SH: Tell me the story of how you got Jim Barnett here.

CJ: Yeah. This principal that was here was a little man. A parent went to the school and beat the tar out of the principal for whipping his child. So, D. L. Cook was on the school board. I was on the school board. I forgot who else. Were you on then, Tom?

TR: No, not then. I wasn't involved in that.

CJ: Anyway, we sat down and talked and said that we had to stop this from happening. We came up with the decision that we needed to hire somebody that was rough and tough and could take care of himself. So, we started looking around in Greenville, and we found ole Jim Barnett down there teaching school at Greer out of Greenville and coaching football. He played football at Furman. Jim was a tough boy. So, we approached Jim about it, and we added this supplement that the company was going to give him. He was interested in it. We got Jim Barnett up here as principal, and nobody touched him.

TR: He stayed a good long while.

CJ: Don Davis hired him. I'll tell you that was a good little school.

TR: It was a pleasure to go up there and work there.

CJ: Yes, it was. They had some dedicated teachers. Yeah. The children in Rhodhiss really excelled at Granite Falls. You can look at them and count them. They excelled in everything. In athletics, in everything. I don't care what you mentioned. The Rhodhiss children excelled in everything at Granite Falls. Talking about the school, Mary Fagerstrom would call me. I've been up there to that school a lot of times that the county should have been maintaining it and didn't.

SH: But you maintained the school at times when something needed to be done?

CJ: Oh, yeah. I worked on that boiler. A lot of times they couldn't get them to come down here. The clock system, Mrs. Fagerstrom said that the county wouldn't touch those. She called me. I'd go up there and work on that time clock system that rang the bells.

TR: The playground equipment? Didn't you build some of it?

CJ: Yeah, we did.

TR: Nobody thought anything about it. It wasn't an obligation. You just did it.

CJ: Yes, it was a community effort.

TR: I don't think any other generation will see something like that. We started the Preacher Lay Educational Fund with the money that we made putting on shows at the school.[16]

The mill company happily helped the little red schoolhouse when it needed repairs. Calvin Jones had rave reviews for the teachers, the students, and the staff.

Tom Ross mentioned the Educational Fund that was established. According to the town minutes, an educational foundation was started on March 17, 1953, for worthy Rhodhiss citizens. Thomas Ross served as representative, and Bill Childers was an alternate. In 1954 this educational foundation became known as the L. B. Laye Educational Fund.[17] This money was used to help needy youth who had the desire to attend college. L. B. Laye was the minister of Rhodhiss Methodist Church during the period that the fund was available. Tom Ross discussed his role in helping to distribute money when it was needed, "I wired a college student $200 one Sunday afternoon. He was landing in New England. He was going to Middlebury College. He wanted to take Russian. He had to have the tuition money before he could go. So, I wired him the money to pay his tuition. It was out of that education fund that we had there in the community."[18] Rhodhiss people really came through and helped young college students with loans and/or scholarships. Not many communities have a fund that enables deserving scholars to pursue their dreams.

The *Pacific Truths* Magazine which was written and published by Pacific Mills saluted the eighth-grade graduates in 1953. The school had 28 students to graduate in late May 1953. The article reads:

Medals were presented by Personnel Manager, James Culclasure. The Citizenship medal for outstanding leadership went to Loretta Hendrix and the medal for best speller went to Densel Walker. Mr. Leonard Lee presented diplomas to: Denzel Walker (different spelling from above), Theresa Munday, Christine Freeman, Loretta Hendrix, Wilma Fox, Doras Ann Elmore, Doris Deal, Gail Hendrix, Shanda Bowman, Doris Jean Elrod, Lucy Jane Elmore, Carol Deal Hollar, Barbara Ann Lunsford, Nancy Jean Johnson, Billy Joe Porch, Becky Moffitt, Loretta Smith, Doris Walsh, Clara Hollar, Dean Kirby, Aaron Compton, Cecil Munday, Billy Ray Johnson, Willie Griffin, Kenneth Church, Paul Tramble, Harold Franklin, and Jimmy Woods.[19]

Pacific Mills was involved in presenting diplomas to the students during this time. As the years progressed, the responsibility fell to the principal.

According to the teacher handbook produced by the Caldwell County School system, the telephone number for the Rhodhiss School in 1952-1953 was 164-R. James Long Barnett taught eighth grade and was the principal; Paul Ranson Frye, seventh; Dewey Eustice Broome, sixth grade; Clarence Monroe Cook, fifth grade; Carrie Starnes, fourth grade; Kate Starnes, third grade; Estella Powell Starnes, second grade; Lexie Williams, first.[20] This pamphlet listed all of the schools in Caldwell County. The 1956-1957 teacher handbook listed some of the same people as staff, but some were different. The phone number for Rhodhiss School in 1956-1957 was 6423. Mr. Barnett was still the principal and eighth grade teacher; Paul Frye was again the seventh-grade teacher; Miss Carrie Starnes taught a combination class of fifth and sixth; Miss Mary Beth Baker taught fourth; Miss Kate E. Starnes was the third-grade teacher; Mrs. Estella Powell Starnes remained as second grade teacher; Miss Pauline Bailey taught first grade.[21]

In 1963 the United Fund and the Ruritan Club worked hard to ensure that Rhodhiss did not have combination classes. An article from the *Granite Falls Press* stated, "The Rhodhiss United Fund knew the need for another teacher at the Rhodhiss Elementary School. The United Fund gave $276 to this need. The organization feels that this is a worthwhile project and children will reap the benefits for years to come. The Reverend Harold Brown, representing the Rhodhiss Ruritan Club, accepted the donation from Luther Sigmon."[22] Ned Bean confirmed this information; he said, "I worked in the Ruritan Club over there, and we worked hard to get an extra teacher up there to keep from having split classes."[23] Also, during this interview Elvie Bean raved about the library at Rhodhiss. She said, "Oh, I tell you. That is one of the things that kept us there, too. Our daughter Beth went there. It was one of the best libraries for a school anywhere. Anywhere."[24] Rhodhiss was proud of its little red schoolhouse. The people loved the cafeteria, the auditorium, and the library. The children were fortunate to go to school at this wonderful facility.

The cafeteria hosted many meals for the community whether it be a pancake supper, spaghetti supper, or just a nice dinner. Many organizations used the facility. Cora Brown talked about the fact that the school did not own any coffee cups because children would not be using those. Burlington Industries solved this problem because meals for adults were held there. Mr. and Mrs. Brown explained:

CB: Now, he was a fine fella, Mr. Craven was. He bought us some equipment for our school, for the cafeteria one time.

BB: Now, if you talked to him first, before any other person or any organization, he would help.

CB: You know the government didn't allow you to buy any equipment that you didn't use to prepare the food for the children. You know our dinners that we had honoring our teachers or parents, you know, well, we had one and invited Mr. Craven. We didn't have any coffee cups. He said, 'Well, I will just buy you some.' He gave me enough money to buy, I don't know how many dozens. He bought us water glasses, too. You weren't supposed to spend any money for anything that wasn't used to prepare the food.[25]

Bill Craven was plant manager for Burlington from 1959 to 1970.[26] Many people discussed what a wonderful person he was. He was willing to help the school, the community, and the people of Rhodhiss.

The first full-time principal of Rhodhiss Elementary School, Mary Fagerstrom, had words of praise for the students, the community, Burlington, parents, and the staff. Full-time means that the principal no longer had to teach a class and be the principal. I was also told that Mary was the first female principal in Caldwell County. Mary was at Rhodhiss from 1966-1969. Part of the interview with Mary follows:

MF: At the time that I went down there, I felt like it was a community that really took such pride in its school. I was just so happy to get the opportunity to get to the school and get to know the people. I found out that was true. They were a community that really loved their school, and nothing that school needed was too much for them to try to get. At the time that I was there, I felt like it was the best school in the county. They had a perfectly marvelous library for a little ole school like that. I thought for myself that it was interesting to work with the whole elementary school in that one building. That proved to be a wonderful experience for me, and I felt like that was another thing that pointed to how much pride they had in their school because it was always whatever I asked for they tried to get it. I felt like it was more of a prize to get to go down there. I would have rather gone to that school than any school in the county because it had everything. I got to experience not only grades one through eight, but there was a special education program there, too, which was an education in itself.

SH: Were the parents supportive?

MF: Yes, I felt like that was a real plus in my favor because you can't do much if you don't have that. The attendance was good. I had very few times that I had to call the truant officer to come to find out about children. Anything that the PTA did, it was so well attended. There would be a whole auditorium full of people. That had not been my experience many times in prior years, so I felt like the parents really supported the school, and I felt some of them took such pride and wanted the children to know that they were proud of what they did. They would come out. It was just a wonderful experience.

SH: How long were you there?

MF: I was there only three years at that time. I had more personal problems than I could handle, and I knew that I couldn't continue in that job because it was too time-consuming. I took Doug Tolbert's place. He's probably the one that told Mr. White (the superintendent) to give me a try. I will never forget I went up to talk to Mr. White about something else, and just out of the blue he dropped that bombshell on me. I had never thought about doing anything in administration. I was going to be the first full- time administrator.

SH: Was the mill company supportive?

MF: Oh, yes! Gracious. I felt like I was the luckiest person in the world to have that situation because I felt like Burlington was interested in seeing that school was the best that it could be for that community.

SH: I know when I was in the 7th and 8th grades, both years that we had our end-of-year dance, they bought all the girls a corsage.

MF: Oh, how wonderful! They did just so many wonderful things that made you feel special. If the school needed anything, and we didn't have the money, they would either help us or suggest something, or they would match what we could get. They were just so supportive of whatever. That just meant so much. I think that most of us felt like Rhodhiss was something special because of Burlington. We all had that feeling. It was a wonderful experience. I wouldn't take anything for the years that I was there. I just wish that I could have stayed longer. Mr. White, when I resigned, said, 'My goodness, I thought that you were settled for the rest of your life.' He just didn't believe that I meant it because he waited and waited until school was almost ready to start before he got anybody down there because he thought that I would go back.

SH: Is that when Charles Camp took over?

MF: Yes, but I just didn't feel as if I could.

SH: You were there during the teacher shortage, weren't you?

MF: Yes, mercy. We certainly were. I declare. I got to keep the teachers that I had. I don't remember replacing too many teachers while I was down there. I remember Barbara Price. I remember she came and wanted to be the janitor. She just kept on working. Her husband Frankie would come help her. Then all of a sudden, she was just eaten up with cancer. I felt so bad because the woman really wasn't able to be working at all, but she just wanted so much to do, and she did. It was a miracle that she was able to do as much as she did. She was an inspiration. I did have a time lining up teachers for that first fall because when I first went down there, I had to hire four. I believe that there were four vacancies. I know Mrs. Sox, did you remember her?

SH: Yeah, Dorothy Sox. She was Tim's (my brother) third grade teacher.

MF: Was she? She was a dream. I just felt like I was so blessed. She had already retired. She felt so sorry for me that she came back. She was just such a lovely person and a marvelous teacher.

SH: Is that when Mary Simpson was hired?

MF: After she left. Yes, I hired Mary. She is a dream, too. Oh, she is a lovely person. Let's see. Who else did I hire? I hired Joe Fowler that summer. He was a good teacher. I felt like he was.

SH: He died several years ago. He was at Rhodhiss for quite a while and was beloved.

MF: Let's see. Who else did I hire? I can't remember. Was there a Stephens?

SH: Mr. Henry Stephens was there for a few years.

MF: That Mr. Barton.

SH: Edwin Barton was my fifth-grade teacher, and Mr. Stephens was my sixth grade. Mr. Fowler was my seventh.

MF: Now, Mr. Cooke was already down there. Yes, I am sure that he was there my first year.

SH: I think that he and Mrs. Yount left at the same time.

MF: Yes, that's right. Then Mrs. Hickman did the special ed. I had a good staff. Whose place did Mrs. Terry take?

SH: I'm not sure.

SH: Is that when Mrs. Justice came back?

MF: Yes, that's right.

SH: She was Tim's first grade teacher.

MF: Let's see, I was trying to think.

SH: Can you remember any specifics that Burlington did for the school?

MF: I ought to be able to. I always felt like whatever we needed that they would help us get it.

SH: Did you just call them and tell them your needs?

MF: Most of the time I went to speak to someone at the office. Lots of times I went through Ilze Deal. She was such a worker in the PTA. Burlington gave books to the library. We built up the library, yet the county penalized the school because we built it up. I thought that was tacky. That was their attitude. They said that we didn't need funding because we had books. They said, 'You got all that you need down there.' Burlington furnished us with flags.

SH: I remember at one point some draperies were brought in down there, and I was told that Burlington furnished those.

MF: Yes, weren't they put in the auditorium?

SH: I think so, yes.

MF: I believe that they were. I think that Mrs. Deal was behind getting that done. They did come from the mill. That is exactly right.

SH: What about athletics did they help with that? Either the football or basketball teams?

MF: I am almost sure that they did. I guess that Mr. Joe Fowler and Mr. Charles Laney would know. Charles was a very fine teacher. I bet Burlington did help financially with the teams. Mr. Brown might know something about that. I just can't really remember. It seems like they would ask me about it, and then go to Burlington. They would go ahead and make contacts themselves. I am sure that they had a lot to do with getting athletic equipment.

SH: Were most of the children mill children?

MF: That is one of the things that surprised me because a lot of the children's parents didn't work for Burlington, yet they supported the school. Do you think that most were mill children?

SH: I think that by the time that I came along, only about half of the children's parents in my class worked at Burlington. With generations before, it was a higher percentage because if you lived in a mill house, someone had to work in the mill.

MF: Right. I was surprised when I first went down there that more parents didn't work for Burlington. I thought that it was just about 100%, but it wasn't. As I remember there were a lot of people who didn't work for Burlington. I tell you that was the lifeblood of that community.

SH: No doubt. I wrote Burlington a letter to their corporate office in Greensboro asking for history. Six months ago, they got rid of everything that they had on Rhodhiss Elementary School when they consolidated their files.

MF: No! No!

SH: Can you think of anything else?

MF: Well, you had small classes there. You were able to have more individual attention. To me, that school is what I have always preached is needed to really teach children in all classes. The morning shows have been talking about that. Smaller classes lead to better scores.

SH: Were Rhodhiss' scores on state testing good?

MF: They were very high scores. I was very proud of that because a lot of the children came from homes that had few reading materials, and even at that the small class size accounted for how well Rhodhiss did on testing. I was really proud of the scores and what the children did.

SH: I am glad that you have such fond memories of Rhodhiss.

MF: I certainly do. That is one of the greatest experiences of my working life. I just never would have gotten to know so many things about the education system if it had not been for Rhodhiss. It was certainly a great experience.[27]

Mary's husband became ill with kidney disease, her mother had dementia, and her brother died while she was working at Rhodhiss. For those reasons she felt that she couldn't dedicate the time that was needed for the school to thrive. Mary's description of Burlington as the life blood of the community held true for Pacific Mills, too, as well as Rhodhiss Manufacturing. Had it not been for John Rhodes' decision to provide a free public education to all children in Rhodhiss in 1903, the school would not have been there.

Mary mentioned Charles Laney, who was a student at Rhodhiss during the 1950s. He returned in the 1960s to teach. Charles recalled:

CL: Mr. Pope was the janitor, and he kept those rooms well kept, clean as a whistle. Nobody messed his floors up. He would get mad. Oh, he would get mad.

SHS: Now, was that when you were a teacher, a student, or both?

CL: That was when I was a teacher. When I was a student, it didn't matter to me. As a teacher, it was a little different. We had a little bit of a sports program. We had softball and basketball that we played outside. Then when I went back to teach, I also coached. We started a little football program there. We nicknamed ourselves 'The Rhodhiss Warriors.' We did okay.

Charlie, my brother-in-law, helped me out a lot.[28]

Charles Laney is the one who set the mascot for Rhodhiss as the Warriors. He was proud of his school as a student and as a teacher. Mary Fagerstrom also mentioned Joe Fowler and that she hired him. Paul Bumgarner talked about Joe Fowler's wisdom. Paul said, "That one year they wanted Yvonne (Paul's daughter) to skip a grade. Mr. Fowler said, 'Paul, I wouldn't do it. She's gone to school with all of these kids. She would have to make new friends. It might do more harm than good.'"[29] Rhodhiss Elementary School was indeed blessed with good teachers.

Another principal, Charles Camp, explained the athletic program while he was at Rhodhiss. Mr. Camp said, "I was principal at Rhodhiss for five years, 1969-1974; the colors were red and white. Ed Barton was the coach 1969-1972 and Brent Helton in 1972-1974. Granite Falls had two football teams and Dudley Shoals had one. We played each other twice for a six-game schedule. The basketball teams played Granite Falls, Dudley Shoals, and scheduled games with other schools such as Whitnel, Sawmills, and Hudson, no regular conference."[30] The school also had cheerleaders to lead the boys to victory. The games were not held at Rhodhiss because we did not have an adequate football field, nor did we have an indoor gym. Our basketball goals were on an asphalt court. Rhodhiss produced many good athletes even though our school lacked the facilities.

Following is the list of the former principals of Rhodhiss School:

Principals:

Jennie Shelley and Bettie Watson	1909-1916
C. C. Beam	1917
Miss Lillian Michael	1918
H.G. Benfield	1919
J.G. Benfield	1920
R.B. Bush	1921
Mrs. Elizabeth Scarborough	1922
C.B. Privette	1923
C.A. Keller	1924-1932
H.A. McCrary	1933-1934
S.H. Mingus	1935
A.W. Laxton	1936-1937
John Malcome Laxton	1938-1943
J. Cornette	
L.E. Cagle	
Ray Hilton[31]	
Donald Chadwick	1948-1949
James Barnett	1949-1959

Wilburn Parker	1959-1962
W.J. Tolbert	1962-1966
Mary Fagerstrom	1966-1969
Charles Camp	1967-1970 and 1973-1974
Danny Wallace	1974-1975
Woodrow Tucker	
J. Ted Watson	1975-1976 and 1981-1982[32]

Ann Austin, who served as postmaster in Rhodhiss, had two sons, Chris and Fritz, who went to Rhodhiss Elementary School in the 1960s and 1970s. Ann commented on the school:

What did I think about Rhodhiss School? I thought that it was great. My boys loved Rhodhiss School. They really did. Chris had really good teachers there. Well, Fritz did, too. I never had any problems with the school. They loved going to Rhodhiss School. In fact, when Fritz was away at school, I told him 'Your little red schoolhouse is going to be closing.' He said, 'No! My schoolhouse. Oh, no! They can't do that to my little red schoolhouse.' I took him up there one day when all the construction was done to it, and that furniture plant left. We went in there, and Fritz was just torn to pieces. He said, 'I can't believe this.'[33]

Not only was it sad when the school was turned into a furniture plant, but when it burned, many former students shed tears. The school closed in June 1982, and it was sold to various people after that. The land now belongs to the Town of Rhodhiss. The former school building burned in 1992. In an article in the *Lenoir News-Topic* on January 20, 1992, Brit Nelson, a reporter, wrote, "The alarm sounded at 4:30 AM and volunteer firefighters were there immediately. The structure was engulfed in flames when they arrived. Granite Falls firefighters aided the Rhodhiss Fire Department."[34]

Rhodhiss School had a special place in the hearts of many people, whether they were principals, teachers, students, staff members, or town citizens. That school was the hub of activity for the village. We went to school with friends who shared commonalities. The school was filled with love, laughter, learning, and loyalty.

Former elementary teacher, Mary Laws, wrote a brilliant and heartfelt editorial for the *Lenoir News Topic*. Mary penned:

TO THE EDITOR:
Viewing the charred ruins of Rhodhiss School in the January 20 paper evoked a sadness in me. As a young, inexperienced teacher, I was hired by Charles Camp in 1971 as the fourth-grade teacher in Rhodhiss. Through the years I have reflected many times on the dear people of Rhodhiss who made such lasting impressions upon me. I can still visualize Mr. Boyd Hollar leaning against the auditorium door surveying his spotless floors and manicured grounds. 'Mr. Boyd' also shared his boyhood memories

of Rhodhiss and bits of history with the students. Mrs. Martha Yount's ever-smiling face greeted us in the office. Her baked treats were often brought for us to enjoy. Everyone in the school and community loved Martha. She endured with patience as disease ravaged her body. What a beautiful life! Mr. Joe Fowler taught seventh-graders practical lessons in self-respect and an awareness of their environment. He was beloved by his students. Mrs. Boyd Brown and the two Rubys nurtured us with their delicious meals. The list could go on. Many children passed through Rhodhiss School. They were taught by devoted educators, several of whom are still in Caldwell County Schools. I treasure the memories I have of the children I taught and the friendships I developed at Rhodhiss. Mary T. Laws from Lenoir.[35]

Mary Laws was a teacher at Rhodhiss when I was there. I never had the privilege of her teaching, but my brother Tim did, and he loved her as did many others. Ironically, Mary's presence would come back into my life in the middle 1990s when I taught in Statesville. Mary went to Kings Creek Elementary School after Rhodhiss. At West Iredell during Teacher Appreciation Week, I always had my students write a letter to their favorite teachers thanking them, and I mailed the letters. One of my seniors Micah said, "You will never find my teacher. She is in Caldwell County." I told Micah that I was from Caldwell County, and I would try. I asked him which school in Caldwell County, and he responded, "She's at Kings Creek." I then said, "Mary Laws. Is she your favorite teacher?" Micah was floored, and it was with great joy that I mailed his letter. In her editorial Mary was able to express the feelings of many people who still feel that way today. This letter to the local paper shows why Mary Laws was deemed a favorite for many. The love for Rhodhiss School was also shown in September 2010 when there was a school reunion for all of those that attended or taught there. It was held on the old school grounds.

ZENO CRUMP'S PERFECT ATTENDANCE
CERTIFICATE. ZENO CRUMP COPY.

Education was of the utmost importance to the Rhodhiss community. In 1900 John Rhodes convinced Mrs. Wilson to serve as a teacher at a subscription school. Then in 1903 he provided the first free public education for the town's children. He made sure that the children's needs were met regarding school. Mr. Rhodes was the first to provide these services, but fortunately for the town many others followed in his footsteps and gave of their time, talents, hard work, and themselves for the little red schoolhouse to prosper.

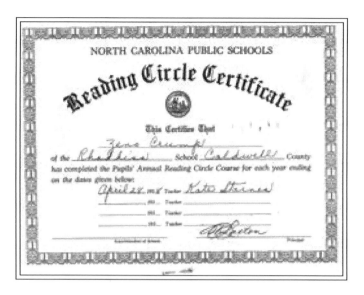

ZENO CRUMP'S READING CIRCLE CERTIFICATE.
ZENO CRUMP COPY.

RHODHISS ELEMENTARY SCHOOL, 1939.
LENOIR NEWS-TOPIC PHOTO.

1939 FACULTY AT RHODHISS. NOTE THAT THE MEN ARE CALLED "PROFESSORS."
LENOIR NEWS-TOPIC PHOTO.

MAE HILTON'S PERFECT ATTENDANCE
CERTIFICATE. SUSAN YOUNT COPY.

MAE HILTON'S READING CIRCLE CERTIFICATE.
SUSAN YOUNT COPY.

MAE HILTON'S CERTIFICATE OF PROMOTION. SUSAN YOUNT COPY.

RHODHISS SCHOOL 1945/8TH GRADE WITH PEGGY COBB, RUTH WALSH, VIVIAN FRANKLIN, RUTH POPE, LOUISE PHILLIPS, ILA MAE MINTON, LOIS WALKER, LAWRENCE HOLMAN, BURGESS CHURCH; ANNIE HIGH AS TEACHER AND MR. CAGLE AS PRINCIPAL. RUTH WALSH PHOTO.

MR. JAMES BARNETT, Principal

RHODHISS' PRINCIPAL JIM BARNETT. CARL HOLLAR PHOTO.

RHODHISS ELEMENTARY SCHOOL GLEE CLUB 1952. PACIFIC TRUTHS MAGAZINE PHOTO.

RHODHISS SCHOOL EIGHTH GRADE 1954. CARY ROSS, CHARLES LANEY, JERRY TOWNSEND, NORMA TUCKER, LINDA CLINE, BETTY ANNAS, LINDA BOWMAN, LANNY ELMORE, AND OTHERS. CARY ROSS PHOTO.

RHODHISS ELEMENTARY SCHOOL 1961.

RHODHISS ELEMENTARY SCHOOL 1963
AND 1964.

SEPTEMBER 12, 1963, GRANITE FALLS PRESS
ARTICLE WITH FACULTY PICTURE.

RHODHISS SCHOOL KINGS AND
QUEENS: JIM RHEA, COY WILSON,
KIM RHEA, AND JULIE SIGMON,
1964. TOMMIE RHEA PHOTO.

CIRCA 1965 ACTIVITY IN SCHOOL'S AUDITORIUM WITH
CROWD. SHERRIE HARTSOE SIGMON PHOTO.

RHODHISS SCHOOL'S SECRETARY, FRANCES ROSS AND PRINCIPAL PARKER IN THE 1960S.

1960S RHODHISS SCHOOL ACTIVITY IN THE PARKING LOT WITH CROWD.
SHERRIE HARTSOE SIGMON PHOTO.

1960S RHODHISS SCHOOL ACTIVITY. SHERRIE HARTSOE SIGMON PHOTO.

1960S RHODHISS SCHOOL ENTRANCE FROM CALDWELL STREET.
SHERRIE HARTSOE SIGMON PHOTO.

RHODHISS BASKETBALL TEAM, MIDDLE TO LATE 1960S: MR. EDWIN BARTON, COACH; WAYNE
HODGES, CURTIS HOOKS, BARRY SIGMON, TERRY HENDRIX, RANDY BUMGARNER, ?, ____
WORKMAN, REX MCKEE, ___WORKMAN, RANDY CHURCH, COY WILSON. WORKMAN BOYS ARE
GARY AND LARRY. CARL HOLLAR PHOTO.

RHODHISS SCHOOL FIRST GRADE 1965-1966, CLARA MANCHESTER, TEACHER; TAMMY BURNS, DALE MCLEAN, TERRIE HARTLEY, JANICE PENDERGRAST, WILL KELLY, ROGER BUFF, JACKIE POWELL, JAMES HENTSCHEL, BEVERLY MITCHUM, PAULA BROWN, CAROLYN MORETZ, ROGER BUFF. CARL HOLLAR PHOTO.

RHODHISS SCHOOL SECOND GRADE 1965-1966, NELL ROBERTS, TEACHER; HERBIE DULA, DEBRA CHURCH, DALE BUFF, KATHY MCKEE, JAMES HERRING, TERRY COFFEY, MICHAEL PRICE, EDDIE CANNON, KAREN ANNAS, JOHN GRAGG, DAVID CHESTER, SHARON CHURCH, SHARON MCLEAN, ROBIN CURTIS, PAM LUNSFORD, PATSY CARVER, GARY MCDANIELS, SHERRIE HARTSOE, RANDY ANNAS, MARTHA KELLY, ROBERT GIBSON. SHERRIE HARTSOE SIGMON PHOTO.

RHODHISS SCHOOL THIRD GRADE 1965-1966, KATHERINE YOUNT, TEACHER; GARY RASH, LORETTA STILWELL, DANNY BRYANT, TOMMY JOHNSON, ELESA MCKINNEY, SHERRY HARRISON, JAMES CANNON, JOYCE BUFF, NICHOLAS HUSKEY, ALFREDA DAMERON, MICHAEL HENTSCHEL, RANDY LOCKE, REGGIE SETTLEMYRE, DOROTHY HERRING, DWAYNE PENDERGRAST, JEFF ROBERTS, KEITH CHURCH, DANIEL CLONTZ, RANDY COOK, TIM BROWNING, VERNON COOK, DARLENE MORETZ.

RHODHISS SCHOOL FOURTH GRADE 1965-1966, CONNIE KIRBY, TEACHER, RAY KIRBY, ROBIN YODER, PAM HAMBY, JULIE SIGMON, YVONNE BUMGARNER, ?, DEBRA WALSH, BRENDA WILSON, BARRY GOODMAN, DANIEL CARVER, VICKIE MORRISON, DORAN DAMERON, JERRY MCKEE, PAT EDWARDS, ?, SKIPPER HOLLAR, TONY MINTON, RICKY BUCKNER, DEBORAH MASSAGEE. PAUL AND HELEN BUMGARNER PHOTO.

RHODHISS SCHOOL SIXTH GRADE 1965-1966, CLARENCE COOK, TEACHER, BARRY SIGMON, TERRY HENDRIX, ?, COY WILSON, DAVID HOLLAR, WAYNE HODGES, ?, ?, RANDY BUMGARNER, ?, DONNA DULA, JAMES ANNAS, SHARON LUNSFORD, ROBIN HARRIS, ?, ROBERT FLEMING, REX MCKEE, TRUDY COWICK, GARY WORKMAN, ?, RAMONA ANNAS, KATHY ESTES, LARRY WORKMAN. CARL HOLLAR PHOTO.

RHODHISS SCHOOL SEVENTH GRADE 1965-1966, CHARLES LANEY, TEACHER, DONNIE MCDANIELS, BOBBIE CARVER, PATRICIA CHURCH, PATSY SETTLEMYRE, DEBBIE RYDER, KAREN DEAL, JERRY ECKARD, PAM EDWARDS, WAYNE BROWN, JAY WILLIAMS, NITA EDWARDS, EUGENE GIBSON, DOUG ELMORE, JUDY JOHNSON, JERRY CHILDERS, BRUCE HARTSOE, RANDY BOWMAN, WANDA LUNSFORD, DIANE MCKEE, THEDA PRICE. BRUCE HARTSOE PHOTO.

RHODHISS SCHOOL EIGHTH GRADE 1965-1966, NAOMI CRUMPLER, TEACHER, PAM HUSKEY, KENNETH YOUNT, LIBBY DEAL, BARRY BOWMAN, BRENDA HELTON, MITZI DULA, GLENDA HENDRIX, SUZANNE HAMBY, ?, KENNETH CHURCH, CHRIS AUSTIN, ?, DANNY KELLER, NEIL MORRISON, MIKE HARRISON, WILLIAM SETTLEMYRE, JACKIE WILLIAMS, KAY COWICK, ANNAS, ?, ?, BROWN, DENNIS GRAGG, ?, BOBBY MCKEE, TOMMY PRICE, ?, ?. ANN AUSTIN PHOTO

APRIL 1970 GRANITE FALLS PRESS ARTICLE.
DANIEL CARVER, TONY MINTON, BOYD
HOLLAR, BILL STONE, JOE FOWLER, AND
CHARLES WARD. GRANITE FALLS PRESS
PHOTO.

APRIL 16, 1970, GRANITE FALLS PRESS
ARTICLE. BOYD HOLLAR, DEBORAH
MASSAGEE, CINDY KIRBY, WAYNE ROUSE,
CHARLES WARD, NORMA KIRBY, MARY
SIMPSON, AND JOE FOWLER. GRANITE FALLS
PRESS PHOTO.

TOM ROSS AS RHODHISS' REPRESENTATIVE TO SCHOOL BOARD. HUITT KEENER, MR. MOORE, E. M.
WHITE, MR. CAGLE, ?, MR. FORLINES, AND TOM ROSS, 1960S OR EARLY 1970S. SHERRIE HARTSOE
SIGMON PHOTO.

RHODHISS ELEMENTARY 4-H CLUB 1962-1963

JOHNNY BIDDIX, JAMES HERRING, TERRY ELMORE, GEORGE BRYANT, GREG ESTES, MIKE CURTIS, KEITH CHURCH, CHRIS ESTES, MIKE PRICE, JACKIE POWELL, HERBIE DULA, DANNY GREENE, TERRY COFFEY, DALE MCLEAN, JOHN GRAGG, JAMES HENTSCHEL, GLENN BIDDIX, EDDIE CANNON, KEITH BUCKNER, JEFF HARRIS. GRANITE FALLS PRESS PHOTO.

1970S FOOTBALL TEAM: BRENT HELTON AND GREGG TRAVIS, COACHES; KEVIN LEDBETTER, RANDY CRUMP, GEORGE BRYANT, JAMES HENTSCHEL, WILL KELLY, DAN GREENE, KEITH BUCKNER, SCOTT LEDBETTER, JEFF HARRIS, JOHN GRAGG, GREG ESTES, DALE MCLEAN. CARL HOLLAR PHOTO.

1972 EIGHTH GRADE CLASS, WILLIAM STONE, THE TEACHER; RANDY ANNAS, MIKE CURTIS, GLENN BIDDIX, CHRIS ESTES, EDDIE CANNON, KEITH CHURCH, TERRY COFFEY, JAMES HERRING, LARRY NICHOLS, CINDY KIRBY, MIKE PRICE, KAREN ANNAS, PATSY CARVER, PAM LUNSFORD, TERESA COX, HERBIE DULA, SHERRIE HARTSOE, DONNA TEAGUE, MICHAEL HENTSCHEL, DEBRA CHURCH. GRANITE FALLS PRESS PHOTO.

1973 EIGHTH GRADE CLASS, JOE FOWLER AND BRENT HELTON, THE TEACHERS; PRINCIPAL CHARLES CAMP; DALE MCLEAN, GEORGE BRYANT, RANDY CRUMP, PAULA BROWN, TAMMY BURNS, CAROLYN MORETZ, JANICE PENDERGRAST, DIANE TEAGUE, SHEILA BALL, WILL KELLY, JAMES HENTSCHEL, KEITH BUCKNER, JOHNNY BIDDIX, SCOTT LEDBETTER, JACKIE POWELL, DANNY GREENE, JOHN GRAGG, RICKY TRAMBLE. CARL HOLLAR PHOTO.

1974 RHODHISS SCHOOL EIGHTH GRADE CLASS, (NOT IN ORDER) BRENT HELTON AND SYLVIA DEAL, TEACHERS; CAROL POWELL, PAM PRICE, RITA MORETZ, ANN MARIE LONGSHORE, SHERRY TRAMBLE, GREG ESTES, RITA MORETZ, TAMMY DAMERON, SUSIE PRICE, ALLISON FORTENBERRY, BECKY HENTSCHEL, CRICKET LUNSFORD, GREG ESTES, AND OTHERS. CARL HOLLAR PHOTO.

RHODHISS SCHOOL PLAYGROUND WITH MONKEY BARS IN THE FRONT.
LOOKING DOWN THE STREET TO JOE CHURCH'S STORE.

1970S WALTER BIDDIX AND DEBBIE MCLEAN
IN FRONT OF RHODHISS SCHOOL.
CARL HOLLAR PHOTO.

1974 JOE FOWLER, DONNA ABERNETHY,
AND VICKIE DAMERON ON BEAUTIFICATION
COMMITTEE. GRANITE FALLS PRESS PHOTO.

1976 BICENTENNIAL PICTURE OF RHODHISS SCHOOL'S STAFF, RUBY DECKER, RUBY EDWARDS, DAPHNE WEAVER, CORA BROWN, AND RUBY ELLER. CARL HOLLAR PHOTO.

THE LAST DAY OF SCHOOL AT RHODHISS FOREVER. CHIEF JACK HENDRIX, TIM BOWMAN, MICHELLE BOLICK, LORI HOUCK, STACEY BENFIELD, JAMIE NICHOLS, MELINDA MANN, BRIAN CAPPS, MELENA BROWN, TINA COLLINS, AND OTHERS. GRANITE FALLS PRESS PHOTO.

RHODHISS SCHOOL BURNS. HICKORY
DAILY RECORD PHOTO.

JANUARY 1992 THE RHODHISS SCHOOL BURNED.
RHODHISS FIRE DEPARTMENT PICTURES.

NOTES

1   Laxton, J. M.

2   Laxton. J. M.

3   "Two Teachers, Six-Month School Term: Rhodhiss Opened Doors in 1900." *The Communicator of the Caldwell County Schools*. June 1975. Vol. 1 No. 2. Lenoir, NC.

4   Herman, Willard and Tom Ross.

5   Crump, Zeno.

6   Rhodhiss Town Minutes. 24 October 1938 and 13 February 1939.

7   Elmore, Fred and Martha and Tom Ross.

8   Kiziah, Ruth Walsh. Personal Videotaped Interview with Sherrie Hartsoe Sigmon. Granite Falls, NC. 20 April 2012.

9   Rhodhiss Town Minutes. 15 May 1941.

10   Rhodhiss Town Minutes. 22 January 1945.

11   Laney, Charles. Personal Videotaped Interview with Sherrie Hartsoe Sigmon. Hickory, NC. 20 April 2012.

12   Compton, Carl. Email Interview with Sherrie Hartsoe Sigmon. 22 June 2017.

13   Barker, Gladys.

14   Bean, Ned and Elvie and Tom Ross.

15   Brown, Boyd and Cora.

16   Jones, Calvin and Tom Ross.

17   Rhodhiss Town Minutes. 17 March 1953.

18   Herman, Willard and Tom Ross.

19   "Rhodhiss School Graduates 28." *Pacific Truths*. 1953.

20   *Caldwell County Schools 1952-1953. Directory and Suggestive Materials*. Caldwell County Board of Education, Lenoir, NC. Pamphlet.

21   *Caldwell County Schools 1956-1957. Directory and Suggestive Materials*. Caldwell County Board of Education, Lenoir, NC. Pamphlet, p. 14.

22   "Rhodhiss United Fund Gift for Additional Teacher." *Granite Falls Press*. 3 October 1963.

23   Bean, Ned and Elvie and Tom Ross.

24   Bean.

25   Brown, Boyd and Cora.

26   Craven, Bill. Personal Interview with Sherrie Hartsoe. Rhodhiss, NC. 28 March 1988.

27   Fagerstrom, Mary. Personal Interview with Sherrie Hartsoe. Granite Falls, NC. 27 April 1988.

28   Laney, Charles.

29   Bumgarner, Paul and Helen.

30   Camp, Charles. Personal Email Interview with Sherrie Hartsoe Sigmon. 30 July 2010.

31   Laxton, J. M.

32   Hawkins, John O. *The Most American Thing: A History of Education in Caldwell County, North Carolina*. Lenoir, N.C: Education Foundation of Caldwell, 2001.

33   Austin, Ann, Thad Martin, Shelley Teague.

34   Nelson, Britt. "Rhodhiss Landmark Burns; Arson Suspected." *Lenoir News-Topic*. 20 January 1992, pp. 1&2.

35   Laws, Mary T. "Treasured Memories of Rhodhiss School." *Lenoir News-Topic*. 27 January 1992.

CHAPTER 12
CHURCHES

T he Rhodhiss community from the beginning had two strong foundations: education and religion. When John Rhodes came to town, he quickly organized a school and a church. Within the village a Lutheran Church began in either 1901 or 1903. The Baptist Church's origins date to 1906, and a Methodist Church started in 1913. Thus, three churches were available within the small village, and another church, Friendship Methodist, was on the outskirts. In addition, the Granite-Rhodhiss Church of God originated in 1931, and it was in No Man's Land. Several other churches came as time progressed. Rhodhiss had many houses of worship.

John Rhodes, a Lutheran, had a son-in-law who was a Lutheran pastor. In either 1901, 1902, or 1903 Pastor Joseph Cromer arrived to minister to the community. A magazine entitled *Lutheran Church Visitor* indicated that Pastor Cromer came in 1901. A 1906 magazine article states, "The church property in this charge is now worth eight times what it was when Pastor Cromer took charge five years ago."[1] Thus his arrival would have been in 1901. An article in the *Lenoir News-Topic* in 1902 indicated that he was starting to service the Granite Falls Lutheran Church. Pastor Cromer was to start preaching at Philadelphia Lutheran according to the article. It states, "Rev. J. L. Cromer, the new pastor of the Lutheran church has moved to Rhodhiss. He will preach here (Granite Falls) twice a month, the second and fourth Sundays."[2] Pastor Cromer most probably started in 1902; however, the archival records at the Crumley Library at the Lutheran Theological Seminary in Columbia, South Carolina indicate that Bethany Lutheran Church in Rhodhiss started in 1903 with Cromer as the pastor.[3] In a 1904 article in the *Lutheran Church Visitor* Bethany was mentioned. "The new Lutheran church at Rhodhiss, N. C., Rev. J. L. Cromer, pastor, has been completed, and as soon as the bell shall have been placed in the tower and the carpet put down, it will be dedicated."[4] The congregation gave him a young horse, buggy with a top, and harnesses, all valued at $225 per the Rev. Cromer.[5] In addition, Timothy Scott Reeves, Archival Assistant at Crumley Library gave the following information on Bethany Lutheran in Rhodhiss: In 1903 and 1904 the membership was 28 people. In 1905 the church had 41 adult members and 34 children. Membership fell to 30 adults in 1906 and 21 children. In 1907 only 13 people were included in the total membership. In 1908 adult membership was 15 with 18 children. The years 1909 and 1910 saw membership at 14 and 15, respectively. The Reverend Joseph Cromer was pastor from 1903 to 1906, and Pastor J. P. Price served from 1907-1910. Their church assignments varied from year to year. In 1903 Cromer was a pastor to Bethany (Rhodhiss), Philadelphia (Granite Falls), and Mt. Zion (Hickory). In 1904 Cromer served Bethany (Rhodhiss) and Mt. Zion (Hickory). The year 1905 found Cromer at Bethany (Rhodhiss), Mt. Hebron (Hildebran), and Mt. Zion (Hickory). Cromer's last year was 1906, and he was assigned to Bethany (Rhodhiss), Salem (Lincolnton), St. John's (Hudson), and St. Martin (Maiden). The Reverend J. P. Price came in 1907 and served Bethany (Rhodhiss), Shiloh (Hickory), Trinity (Vale), Mt. Hebron (Hildebran), Philadelphia (Granite Falls), and Mt. Zion (Hickory). In 1908 Price attended to the needs of Bethany (Rhodhiss), Mt. Zion (Hickory), Philadelphia (Granite Falls), St. John's (Hudson), and Mt. Hebron (Hildebran). Lastly, in 1909 & 1910 Pastor Price was at Bethany (Rhodhiss), Shiloh (Hickory), Trinity (Vale), Mt. Hebron (Hildebran), and Philadelphia (Granite Falls).[6] Bethany's minister in Rhodhiss had a difficult job because he had to serve several congregations. In 1906 according to the *Lutheran Church Visitor*, "J. L. Cromer, of Rhodhiss… having received a call from Maiden…has resigned his pastorate…The Rhodhiss pastorate have unanimously refused to accept his resignation and have offered him an increase in his salary of $150 if he will withdraw his resignation and remain with them. Pastor Cromer has not yet announced his decision in the matter."[7] The Reverend Joseph Cromer left Rhodhiss in 1906, shortly after his son Voigt was born on July 31, 1906. In 1905 the Rhodhiss Manufacturing Company sold several parcels of land to the Lutherans for $100.[8] Then in 1907 the mill company sold more property to the Lutherans for $600.[9] The Lutheran Church stayed in Rhodhiss till 1910, and in 1911 the church building was sold to the Baptists for $1,200 as per the Caldwell County records.[10]

With the Baptists' purchase of the old Lutheran space, they were able to strengthen their membership. The following information is taken from a pamphlet detailing the history of Rhodhiss Baptist. On February 16, 1906, twenty-nine Baptists met and organized a church, which was named Rhodhiss Baptist Church. W. P. Southern, a member, was elected pastor. The Rhodhiss Baptist Church became a member of the Caldwell Baptist Association on September 16, 1906. They have continued to support the Association as well as the Southern Baptist Convention. The church held its first services in the homes of members and in the conference room in the upstairs of the mill company offices. On July 11, 1911, the church voted to purchase the Lutheran church building. Through the years the church has continually engaged in a building program. In 1922, under the leadership of Rev. J. G. Benfield, additional Sunday School rooms and auditorium space were constructed. Other additions were made to the Sunday School department over the next fifteen years. Under the pastorate of Rev. C. B. Bobbitt, the congregation realized that a new building was needed, and renewed emphasis was placed upon the building fund for a new church to be located on the land donated by Pacific Mills.[11]

RHODHISS BAPTIST CHURCH WHICH WAS ORIGINALLY BETHANY LUTHERAN CHURCH. NORA AND
DEWEY ANNAS AND FLORA ANNAS, AROUND 1920S. JOANNE PROPST PHOTO.

RHODHISS BAPTIST CHURCH. *LENOIR NEWS-TOPIC* PHOTO FROM CENTENNIAL EDITION 1941.

MEN AND WOMEN WHO ATTENDED RHODHISS BAPTIST. 1939
CALDWELL COUNTY PHOTO NEWS. MARCH 30, 1939.

FIRST ROW, left to right: Mr. Short, Pauline Short, Thelma Church, Theresa Foxx, Sherrill Hyder. Second row: Joan Annas, Mrs. Annas, Gail Annas, Mrs. Williams, J. F. Foxx, J. J. Foxx. Third row: Mrs. Hollar, Inez Hollar, Mrs. Hope, Flossie Mullinax, Naomi Kirby. Fourth row: Paul Bowman, Louise Triplett, Mrs. Pawnee Simmons, Mrs. U. D. Brady, Sadie Church and Pearl Munday. Fifth row: Roy Corsica, J. D. Walker, Harry Wilson, G. C. Church, C. L. Barker and W. A. Wood.

ANOTHER GROUP OF RHODHISS BAPTIST MEMBERS. 1939 *CALDWELL COUNTY PHOTO NEWS.*
MARCH 30,1939.

THE RHODHISS BAPTIST CHURCH OFFICIALS. 1939
CALDWELL COUNTY PHOTO NEWS. MARCH 30, 1939.

RHODHISS BAPTIST TRAINING UNION AT THE CHURCH STREET LOCATION DURING THE 1950S.
DWIGHT KIRBY, PAUL BUMGARNER, TYNCE MUNDAY, HELEN BUMGARNER, VANCE AND NORMA
KIRBY, THE DULA GIRLS, AND OTHERS. PAUL AND HELEN BUMGARNER PHOTO.

1958 GROUNDBREAKING FOR NEW BAPTIST CHURCH. VIRGINIA JONES HOLLAR, JOANNE PROPST, TYNCE MUNDAY, AND OTHERS. GLADYS BARKER PHOTO.

On Sunday morning, May 11,1958, the church voted to build a new edifice. Ground was broken that afternoon, and construction began the next Tuesday morning. The first worship service was held in the new building on December 21, 1958. As the members of Rhodhiss Baptist Church left the old beloved building looking forward to reaching more for Christ, they marched up the hill to the new facility singing "Onward Christian Soldiers." On January 12, 1958, the name of Rhodhiss Baptist was changed to the First Baptist Church of Rhodhiss. The church built a pastorium in 1963 located at 205 Park Avenue, Rhodhiss. At the morning worship on May 2, 1971, the congregation observed the liquidation of debts on the church property in a note burning ceremony. The church was not to be debt free for very long. One year later, in May 1972, the church voted to begin a Bus Evangelism Ministry and purchased two buses. On January 7, 1973, the church voted to finish the third floor of the educational building and air condition the building. In 1978 the library opened, and a tape fund was established to be used for those people who were not able to attend the worship services. New choir robes were purchased in 1979. The loan for the extension of the church building was paid in full on December 9, 1980. All properties have been debt free since that time.[12]

THE CORNERSTONE AT THE PRESENT FIRST BAPTIST CHURCH OF RHODHISS.
SHERRIE HARTSOE SIGMON PHOTO.

RHODHISS BAPTIST CHURCH IN THE 1960S. SHERRIE HARTSOE SIGMON PHOTO.

1963 BUILDING THE CHURCH SIGN. JOHN BOLAN, DWIGHT HELTON, CHARLIE KIRBY, AND
PREACHER HAROLD BROWN. SHERRIE HARTSOE SIGMON PHOTO.

The First Baptist Church of Rhodhiss is active in the Southern Baptist Convention programs at the national, state, and associational levels, and they contribute to missions through the Cooperative Program. Missions and evangelism are a very important part of the First Baptist Church of Rhodhiss. The church began a Women's Missionary Union in 1931. Realizing how important this organization was to the church, the members have continued to be active through the years by meeting the needs in the community and beyond. In 1958 the Brotherhood began, making mission education available to all members of the church as they studied about missionaries and prayed for them and their work. Many members have volunteered for mission trips beginning with the church sending its pastor, the Reverend. E. Guy Longshore, Jr. to be a part of a crusade in Uganda, Africa and to work with the Reverend Lanny Elmore, missionary to Uganda and former member of First Baptist Church Rhodhiss. The first youth mission trip was to Ohio with four youths and two adults participating. The 1980s, 1990s, and 2000s continued to be exciting years as youth and adults shared Christ in West Virginia, Ohio, South Carolina, New York, Texas, Mississippi, Missouri through Backyard Bible Clubs, Vacation Bible Schools, revivals, musicals, survey work, and one-on-one witnessing. The second international mission trip involved two adults working with missionary kids in Honduras during Mission Meeting, a time when all missionaries and their families came together for evaluation and planning. Three youth and two adults were involved in the North Carolina partnerships with Brazil and South Africa. Following the crisis of Hurricane Floyd in eastern North Carolina, six members of Rhodhiss First Baptist Church joined the Disaster Services of Caldwell Baptist Association on eight trips to feed the hungry. One member helped the association with construction at Caswell, a North Carolina Baptist

Assembly. In the years ahead First Baptist Church of Rhodhiss looks forward to greater involvement for the cause of Christ and reaching the world for Him.[13]

The twenty-nine charter members of the Rhodhiss Baptist Church included: Mrs. Nola Jay, Miss Ollie Munday, Rev. J. F. Crisp, Mrs. Leah Crisp, Miss Mary Crisp, Miss Fannie Crisp, Miss Addie Crisp, Miss Pearl Crisp, Mrs. M. R. Wilson, Miss Ollie Crouse, Mrs. Martha Holsclaw, Miss Myrtle Wilson, Mr. and Mrs. Phillip Crouse, Mr. and Mrs. Thomas Crouse, Mr. James Ferguson, Miss Hattie Morrison, Miss Hettie Crouse, Mr. and Mrs. R. P. Scruggs, Mr. Marvin Scruggs, Miss Lether Holsclaw, Mr. G. F. Smith, Mr. Haskell Dryman, Miss Eulola Dryman, Mr. Robert Branch, Mrs. E. R. Mull, and Mrs. L. G. Holsclaw. The first full-time minister was the Rev. O. C. Abee. The church voted to pay him $4,000 a year. The Rev. H. B. Chronister died while a minister at Rhodhiss on February 20, 1930.[14] The first baptism was on July 4, 1906. In 1941, the church had 400 members under the ministry of the Reverend R. F. Mayberry.[15]

A 1983 pamphlet of the church's history includes these facts: The Reverend W. L. Pitts conducted the first service in the new church on December 21, 1958. In 1983 the oldest in membership by letter and baptism were Mrs. Dovie Jones on November 26, 1914, and Mrs. Will Byars on September 10, 1911. Mr. Joe Sydney Church and Mr. Boyd Hollar were baptized on April 27, 1919. Larry Grindstaff served as the first bus pastor/director on March 4, 1973. A library opened in memory of L. A. "Shorty" Elmore with donations from the Elmores. The Bible-on-Tape Ministry was given in memory of Mr. John Hyatt by Stella Hyatt. A tape ministry for shut-ins was started in August 1978. On December 9, 1980, a note burning was held to pay off the mortgage. The service included Pastor Cool; Roger Kirby, Chairman of Trustees; Reggie Propst, Chairman of the Deacons; and Tynce Munday, original committee building member.[16]

The 2006 Rhodhiss Baptist Church pamphlet indicated that several members felt the call to be pastors: The first was S. A. Stroup who was ordained on September 9, 1911. Others include Q. T. Curtis, Guthrie Curtis, Grant Miller, John Haas, Jeta Porch, Joe Bill Church, Lanny Elmore, Dan Greene, Chris Hefner, Robert Hefner, Ashley Crouse, and Danny Townsend.[17] Some of the interviewees in 1988 gave more names. Violet Curtis added Bane Poarch.[18] Willard Herman added Guy Haas.[19] In addition, Willard Herman and Martha Elmore named Grady Hamby.[20] Thelma Church was the first to mention all the people who were called into the ministry. Her son Joe Bill was one of those. She stated, "All of these have really made good. Take Q. T. He's had a church in Alabama, Sage Avenue Baptist Church. He's been there for 25 years or more. Joe Billy's been in Valdese at one church for almost 21 years. Like everybody says, 'Rhodhiss has a lot to be proud of.' There are good people that are from Rhodhiss, and they did good."[21] Violet Curtis and Willard Herman were also proud of this accomplishment of the Rhodhiss Baptist Church. Willard was the uncle to Q. T. and Guthrie Curtis, and Violet was their mother. Willard said, "No other church in the area can say that they produced that many ministers."[22] Fred and Martha Elmore whose son Lanny became a minister, were interviewed, too. Martha stated, "The Rhodhiss Baptist Church members are to be commended. You don't ever hear of that many going into the ministry."[23] Lanny served several churches in North Carolina, and then he felt the call to be a missionary to Uganda, East Africa. He and his wife, Brenda Clay Elmore, were there for five years. Upon his return he was a supervisor for the North Carolina

Department of Corrections. From there they went to Hartsville, South Carolina. His last call was to First Baptist Church of Dallas, Texas where he served as the Minister of Missions for 25 years. At the age of 60, Lanny obtained his doctorate degree. Lanny died in Texas in 2021. His contributions to society are indicative of the love and hard work that surrounded him in his hometown of Rhodhiss.[24] At the end of this chapter is a full list of the ministers serving First Baptist Church Rhodhiss.

JOE BILL CHURCH WHO GREW UP AT RHODHISS BAPTIST RECEIVED HIS DEGREE. *GRANITE FALLS PRESS* PHOTO.

Willard Herman explained the difficulty that churches had in paying their pastors, so the mill company offered supplements. Willard stated to Tom Ross and me:

> WH: During the Depression they started cutting wages at Rhodhiss, and I believe that they were paying Preacher Thomas $11 a week. The company was paying him that much, and maybe the church was giving him what they could, $3 or $4 a week. Anyway, they had put up notices every week that they were going to cut wages by 5%. They keep doing that. I think that they cut his till it got to about $7 a week. I don't remember, but Pacific Mills continued to pay after they came in. They paid some.
> TR: Yes, they paid for a while.[25]

Mill companies often supplemented the salaries of the pastors within the mill village.[26] Mill owners had a lot of control over the lives of their millhands. In some villages, "the church was usually built on land owned by the mill which also provided its financial support. Thus, sermons frequently followed the theme of hard work, deprivation, and suffering as the path to salvation…The mill village system was meant to control all aspects of the workers' lives--from church to education to the welfare system."[27] The people whom I interviewed did not feel that the mill company was controlling their lives, but in some villages millhands felt this way. Doughton Beshears did, however, say that one superintendent, Mr. Edwards, made it known that if workers weren't in church on Sunday, then they faced the chance of being fired on Monday.[28] Thelma Church also mentioned the supplements that the company paid the pastors. She stated, "I think that it was before Pacific, the old Rhodhiss Mills used to pay our (Baptist) pastor and the Methodist pastor so much a week because the churches weren't able to pay them. They gave the pastors a supplement every month. Each church, the Methodist and the Baptist, and they gave them the same amount. It wasn't much, but it was a supplement."[29] Edna Edwards Laney Stilwell and her brothers Arthur and Jack Edwards mentioned the supplements. They said that before Pacific came, the mill company gave the churches $11 a week to help with expenses. The company gave preachers jobs in the mill because the churches could not support a pastor completely, and he had to support his family.[30] Lastly, Butler Monteith, Shelley Teague, Doughton Beshears, and Tom Ross discussed the pastors' supplements. They declared:

> BM: The mill company paid the preachers so much. Doughton, wasn't it something like $400 a year?
>
> DB: I think that's what they paid the Methodist preacher.
>
> BM: I am thinking that it was $400 a year. When Pacific came, they stopped that.
>
> TR: After a while. They paid for a while.
>
> ST: My granddaddy preached at Rutherford College and Friendship Church. He was a circuit preacher. He would preach one week here and one week there. They gave him $400 a year, but mama said that he would come in with chickens, pigs, pumpkins, and watermelons. That's the way they paid part of their tithe.[31]

The mill company provided parsonages for the pastors of the Methodist and Baptist churches. Most probably, the house for the Lutheran Pastor Joseph Cromer was provided, too, since his son was born in the village. Butler Monteith stated that he and his wife, Hazel Knox Monteith, were married in the house that served as the first parsonage for the Rhodhiss Baptist Church.[32] This house at 301 Church Street is directly beside the present-day Church Street Baptist Church, which was the former site of the Lutheran and Baptist churches. Another parsonage for the Baptist congregation was on Birch Street. Arthur Edwards said that he purchased the old Baptist pastorage when he heard that the church wanted to sell it in the early 1960s.[33]

Tommy Elmore, whose dad was L. A. "Shorty" Elmore, said that he attended Rhodhiss Baptist Church. Tommy also mentioned that his dad was first a Lutheran, but when the building was sold to the Baptists, he stayed at the church. Tommy said, "Dad would say, 'Get in the car. It's time to go to church.' When he said that, you knew to do it."[34] Ned Bean also mentioned that Shorty Elmore was his Sunday school teacher, and Shorty had told his class that he was a Lutheran first in the old building, and he chose to stay with the church building.[35] In addition, Willard Herman stated, "Shorty Elmore was my Sunday school teacher. He was a former Lutheran," and Tom Ross' response to that was "This community owes a lot to Luther Elmore. He did a lot of things for the community."[36] Mr. L. A. Elmore "Shorty" was a man that many people admired.

Thelma Church and Paul Bumgarner discussed their baptisms at Rhodhiss Beach. Thelma stated, "But when I married Joe, he was a Baptist, and I was a Methodist, so I joined the Baptist and was baptized. Mary and I both were baptized over there in the river, over there up from the beach. Preacher Thomas baptized us."[37] Mary was Thelma's sister; similarly, Paul Bumgarner, who was the son of Mary, and the nephew of Thelma discussed his own baptism. Paul said, "Rhodhiss Beach is where I was baptized." His wife Helen added, "Yeah, they used to baptize down there at the beach. The

Sunday that I was baptized, Kurt Smith was baptized."[38] Kurt Smith lived and worked at Rhodhiss in the cloth room. In addition to discussing baptisms, Paul and Helen elaborated on the condition of the old Baptist Church on Church Street. They stated:

> PB: At the old church we built a wing on the right side, and then we built one on
> the left side. I don't know how much there was to the original building.
> HB: About thirty years ago, we started the nursery at the church. We had to get mattresses
> and rocking chairs. Mrs. Compton's small children's class had to meet in a dirt area of the old
> church. She had an old plank bench back in there.
> PB: One time in the old church our furnace fell in and wouldn't work. We called Mr. Barnett
> (the school's principal) and asked him if we could use the school, and he agreed. Our church
> met there that Sunday.
> HB: That was up here in the new church.
> PB: No, it wasn't. We walked from the old church up there to the school. You know how the
> preacher usually gets up and says, 'It's a pleasure to be here with you today.' Well, that day the
> preacher got up and said, 'It is not a pleasure to be here with you today because you people are
> going to let that church down there fall in.'[39]

PREACHER OSCAR TUCKER FROM LINCOLNTON BAPTIZING HIS CHURCH MEMBERS AT RHODHISS
BEACH IN THE 1950S. EILEEN COOL PHOTO.

PREACHER OSCAR TUCKER FROM LINCOLNTON BAPTIZING PEOPLE AT RHODHISS BEACH IN THE 1950S. EILEEN COOL PHOTO.

The Baptists were happy to move into their new sanctuary in 1958. The First Baptist Church Rhodhiss celebrated its 100th anniversary in 2006 with four services. The dates and speakers follow:

February 19, 2006	Speaker, the Rev. Dale Fisher
March 19, 2006	Speaker, the Rev. Lanny Elmore
April 23, 2006	Speaker, the Rev. James Cool
May 21, 2006	Speaker, the Rev. David Philbeck[40]

During the March 19, 2006 service the members tried to reunite the 1970s "Singing Inspirations." This group included: Tammy Burns, Drenda Burns, Beth Kirby, Cindy Kirby, Anne Marie Longshore, Gwen Longshore, Tina Weaver, Lorrie Lowman, Dana Lowman, Cindy Jordan, Vickie Browning, Vanessa Tramble, Sue Evans, Rita Moretz, Jewel Philyaw, Sandra Aldridge, Cathy Herring, Beth Brady, Danny Greene, Rick Jordan, Mike Kirby, Terry Lowman, Dwayne Tramble, Jackie Powell, James Wiles, Steve Moretz, and Carl Dewey.[41] Rhodhiss First Baptist Church has served the community for over 100 years, and their concern for the citizens is evident by their many kind deeds, love, and pride within the village. Many fine people still attend the church where their family members served as saints before them.

The First Baptist Church of Rhodhiss offered the old church for sale to several Caldwell County investors in 1959. In 1971, these owners sold the building to Church Street Baptist Church.[42] The edifice burned in 1973, and the church built back at the same location soon thereafter. The Church Street Baptist Church still sits at the same location and continues to spread the word of God, and they serve the community through their charitable kindnesses.

CHURCH STREET BAPTIST CHURCH ROSE OUT OF THE ASHES OF THE FIRE IN 1973 AND REBUILT.
2022 CARL COMPTON PHOTO.

Rhodhiss Methodist Church came into existence in 1913 according to numerous sources; however, the *Lenoir News-Topic*'s Centennial Edition in 1941 was the only source to indicate that the date was 1912. According to the article, Rhodhiss Methodist started on December 29, 1912, and they immediately planned to build. Planners were E. A. Rockett, Astor Peeler, W. R. Icard, J. P. Cline, A. E. Ritch, A. H. Mauney, W. D. Whisnant, Walter Green, E. R. Fisher, William Walker Branch, and others.[43] The Rev. G. W. Fink was an organizer and builder according to Pam Edwards Triplett, the church's historian.[44] In 1941 the Methodists moved to the old school building. By remodeling, the Methodists' auditorium could seat 500; they added eight classrooms and a complete heating system. "The Methodists of Rhodhiss are loud in their praise for Mr. R. C. Moore, president and Mr. Clarkson Jones, general manager and superintendent of the Rhodhiss mills (sic) for the gift of the building and the heating system. In addition, with the aid of the Duke Foundation, and with contributions, they transformed the building into a $10,000 structure."[45] The building committee was Chairman J. B. Hemphill, Treasurer R. D. Beshears, Clarkson Jones, J. P. Cline, M. P. Benfield, and Pastor Max Brandon. The church was dedicated on the second Sunday of September 1941 by the Bishop Clare Purcell of Charlotte. Their membership was 121. Others involved in service to the church included: Mrs. J. B. Hemphill, President of Christian Service; Cecil Perkinson, President of YP organization; J. P. Cline, Sunday school superintendent; Stewards: M. P. Barfield, J. P. Cline, Clyde Keller, and Paul Costner.[46]

The first building that housed the Rhodhiss Methodist Church was located on Marion Avenue in Burke County. This structure later comprised apartments, and then those were converted into a club house in the 1970s. Precious Kelley said that in the summertime the building was hot, so they held Sunday school underneath the church because it was not underpinned.[47] The first minister was

Pastor Fink, and according to Fletcher Lutz, "Preacher Fink lived on River Street."[48] Several people recalled the church's being at this site in Burke County. Helen Hemphill who was the postmaster for years stated, "I lived in Rhodhiss a long time, in Duke Power village. I went to church there across the river. I had to walk across that icy bridge to get to the Methodist church."[49] The bridge was a nightmare during the 1960s by car, but it was worse by foot. Arthur and Jack Edwards along with their sister Edna Stilwell talked about the bridge. They said that they crossed the old plank bridge to get to the church.[50] Thelma Branch Church also talked about going to the old church in Burke County. Her dad, William Walker Branch, is mentioned as one of the original planners of the church. Thelma explained, "It was a church building. They finally made an apartment out of it. It was an old wooden church. We went over there until my father died. We were always Methodist. My father was raised a Methodist."[51] Lastly, Ned Bean who was born in 1926 remembered the old clapboard building, too. He explained, "I can remember going there to church when it was the Methodist church. I remember going over there on Sunday night trying to pick up a girl."[52] The first site evoked many memories amongst the interviewees.

THE ORIGINAL METHODIST CHURCH BUILDING ON MARION AVENUE IN BURKE COUNTY DURING THE 1920S. PRECIOUS KELLER KELLEY PHOTO.

THE SUNDAY SCHOOL CLASS OF THE METHODIST CHURCH DURING THE 1920S OR 1930S.
PRECIOUS KELLER KELLEY PHOTO.

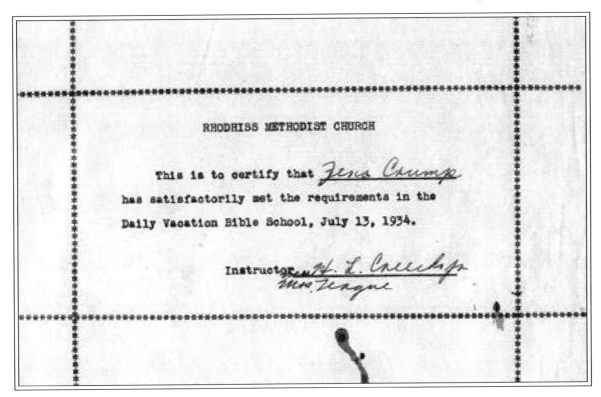

ZENO CRUMP ATTENDED BIBLE SCHOOL AT THE OLD SITE IN BURKE COUNTY. ZENO CRUMP COPY.

The Methodist members tried to relocate during the 1930s in a location off Dogwood Drive across the street from Calvin Jones' old house. Calvin stated:

> Well, since I retired, I was roaming around in the woods down below my house. I ran across a foundation down there. It had a basement dug in it. I couldn't figure out what it was. It had been grown up down in there so long. Up above Ab Story's house and down below my house down in the woods. I started questioning around. Somebody said, 'That's where they started to build the Methodist church.' The people in the church had a disagreement, and they never did get it built. They got the foundation built and stopped right there. This is what I was told. I don't know how true it is, and I forgot who told me. Some of these old timers should remember.[53]

Calvin's home was on Dogwood Drive. His information was confirmed by Willard Herman who gave further information to Tom Ross and me:

> WH: Right down below Calvin Jones' house, Tom, you will probably remember this. Mr. Keller and his family were Methodists. They poured the footings for a foundation there at Calvin's across the street. They were going to build a Methodist church down there. Somehow, they stopped and converted the school into a church.
> TR: I didn't know about that.
> SH: Calvin told us about that the night that we talked to him. Calvin said that he was down there one day messing around and found the foundation. He started checking around and found out what it was.
> WH: That's what it was. They started to build the Methodist church there, but some were opposed to it.[54]

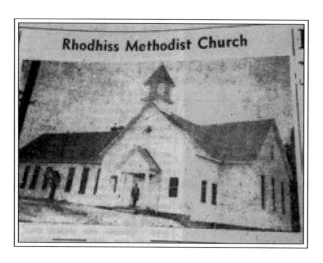

Rhodhiss Methodist Church

The church members could not come to an agreement about the building of another church in Burke County, but they did agree on taking the old school building and renovating it as their church.

AROUND 1941. THE METHODIST CHURCH MOVED TO THE OLD SCHOOL BUILDING ON CHURCH STREET. *LENOIR NEWS-TOPIC* PHOTO.

ANOTHER PICTURE OF THE METHODIST CHURCH AFTER MOVING TO CALDWELL COUNTY AROUND 1941. THIS BUILDING BURNED. PRECIOUS KELLER KELLEY PHOTO.

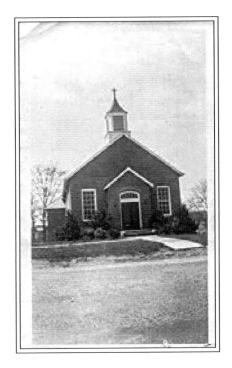

RHODHISS METHODIST CHURCH: THIS CHURCH WAS BUILT IN 1944 AFTER THE OLD WOODEN STRUCTURE BURNED. SUSAN YOUNT PHOTO.

THE CORNERSTONE OF THE RHODHISS METHODIST CHURCH ON CHURCH STREET. SHERRIE HARTSOE SIGMON PHOTO.

1940S RHODHISS METHODIST CHURCH SUNDAY SCHOOL CLASS. PRECIOUS KELLER (KELLEY), JACK
HEMPHILL, GARNIE MCDANIEL, LEVI BROWN, MARGIE HAND (COWICK), AND OTHERS.
PRECIOUS KELLER KELLEY PHOTO.

1960S RHODHISS METHODIST CHURCH ON CHURCH
STREET. SHERRIE HARTSOE SIGMON PHOTO.

1960S RHODHISS METHODIST
CHURCH SIGN. SHERRIE HARTSOE
SIGMON PHOTO.

As Willard Herman stated earlier, the church decided to convert the old school building into a church. As indicated in a previous paragraph, R. C. Moore and Clarkson Jones were instrumental in giving the old school building to the Methodists along with a new heating system. The old school building was in Caldwell County on present-day Church Street, where the Boy Scout hut is now. The Methodists worshiped in this facility in the early 1940s till it burned a short while later. As per Ned Bean, "The Methodist Church started having services in the old school building. Then it burned. Then they built the new building."[55] Doughton Beshears, Butler Monteith, and Shelley Teague elaborated on several aspects of their church:

> DB: We got the old school building from the company and made a church out of it. Then it burned, and we had church down there in the hall.
>
> SH: The old schoolhouse burned?
>
> DB: Yeah, I guess that we met in the hall for over a year.
>
> ST: I used to walk. Me, and Mama, and Seth, and Bob from home up there all the way across the river to that Methodist church over there on Sundays. In the summertime we would have to wear shoes, and I couldn't wait to get home to take off my shoes because I went barefooted all the time. My shoes just killed my feet, and we had to dress up. Buddy, we had to dress. The women then in church all wore hats.
>
> BM: As quick as I walked in the door, I had to take off the clothes that I wore to church.
>
> ST: Yes, sir.
>
> BM: That was the unpardonable sin to leave your church clothes on.[56]

Shelley Teague explained his family's Sunday voyage on foot to the first site of the church. From Shelley's house on lower Duke Street to Marion Avenue, the distance is approximately 1.5 miles. Butler also added that it was a must to remove good church clothes once children arrived home. These gentlemen also said that the Methodists worshiped in the old Company Store building in the lodge hall while their third building was being constructed. Precious Keller Kelley also agreed. She said, "See when our church burned, we had our services there in the lodge hall."[57] Jack Edwards discussed the fire. He stated, "We put a piano through that downstairs window during the fire to save it, and it is still in our church."[58] Thad Martin added, "Yeah, I helped carry benches out the Sunday that it burned."[59] Buzz Winkler went to the Methodist church when she was younger because "'they had the best youth group around. This was a lot of fun to be around and a part of.'" She recalled the old church burning while family and friends raced to save whatever they could out of the church. She believes that the fire brought them even closer as family.[60] Billie Sue Laney said that to build the brick church after the fire, various people in the mill bought bricks for the Methodist church.[61] The new church was completed, and the cornerstone reads 1944. A few years after that, Rebecca Church Sigmon played the piano there. Her dad was Joe Church, and he approached the Methodist minister and asked if they needed a pianist. The Methodist minister explained that they needed one, but they didn't have the money to pay her. Joe told the pastor to leave that to him. Unbeknownst to Rebecca, her dad got her the job and paid her salary, too. She held this job for a short time while she was in high school.[62]

Several people discussed the Methodist parsonage. As stated earlier, the first preacher, Reverend Fink, lived in a mill house on what was referred to then as "River Street." Butler Monteith, Doughton Beshears, Shelley Teague, and Tom Ross, who are all Methodists, discussed the parsonage. They explained:

ST: The first parsonage was across the river.

TR: Lula Harris lived in that house at one time.

BM: Didn't they give that house up on top the hill to the church first.

TR: Yes, afterwards they gave them the one beside Doug Cowick's.

ST: Which house up on top of the hill?

TR: Where Paul Elmore lived.

DB & BM: Yeah, yeah.

DB: The company just furnished that house. They never gave it to the church.

ST: Which house did Paul Elmore live in? Beside of me? Paul Elmore moved in that house beside me when it was new. I moved in mine when it was new. He moved to be near Ruth Herman and them because his wife wanted to be over there.

TR: Doughton, I guess that the church must have sold this house over here on Magnolia.

DB: Yeah, they did.

TR: But the preacher lived in the house rent free.

BM: That's right.

DB: Yeah, he lived rent free across the river, too.

TR: Preacher Lay lived in that house over yonder across the river.

BM: He lived there all the time, the whole time that he was here.[63]

The first parsonage according to these men was on Carolina Avenue in Burke County. Then it moved to Magnolia Street in Caldwell County. Ned and Elvie Bean along with Tom Ross discussed the issue further:

SH: Do you remember where the Methodist church parsonage was?

NB: The one for the new church? We didn't have a Methodist church parsonage until later. The first one was across the river. McFarland lived in it. Then they traded. The first one was on Burke side. Paul Elmore lived in the corner house; then somebody else lived in one; then the next one was the Methodist parsonage.

EB: I thought the Methodist parsonage was on the corner.

TR: I thought that it was where Paul Elmore lived.

EB: It was on the corner, Honey.

NB: Was it on the corner?

EB & TR: Yes.

NB: Well, okay. I am wrong then. It was on the corner.

SH: Then in '55 it moved to Caldwell?

NB: Yeah, they traded with the company, and got the one beside Margie Cowick.[64]

This house at 302 Magnolia belonged to the Methodists until they sold it in 1980.[65]

The Rhodhiss Methodist Church administered to the needs of the community until 2017. At this time the church closed. During their 100th birthday celebration in 2013, an article in the *Hickory Daily Record* explained that the members' ages ranged from 5 to 93. Judy Tucker played the piano at the church and started when she was 12 years old. Judy stated, "'Back then I only knew how to play two hymns. The pastor used to joke with me when I would learn a few more…Playing the piano in church keeps you faithful. You don't have to wake up on Sunday morning and wonder what you're going to do today.'" Judy saw over 20 pastors come and go over a 60-year period.[66] According to Pastor Joyce Reynolds each Sunday morning was like a family reunion. She added, "'…this congregation has worked hard over the last 100 years to keep a Methodist presence in Rhodhiss.'"[67] In addition, Leona Brown painted a mural of Jesus praying in the Garden of Gethsemane on the church wall. Brown raised her children in the church. Leona voiced, "'We love each other. That's what has kept us together.'"[68] Unfortunately, almost four years after celebrating their 100th anniversary, the church closed. The Reverend Joyce R. Reynolds was the pastor during their anniversary celebration on Sunday, December 29, 2013. The last service was held on Sunday, June 18, 2017, and the minister was the Reverend Jennifer Hege. Rhodhiss Methodist Church members abounded in talent. They had so many members who had beautiful voices, and their singings always had great attendance. Also, several members had their artwork or handiwork displayed within the church. These people shared their God-given talents with the church and community. Today the old Methodist church building on Church Street houses the Boy Scouts.

SIGN ANNOUNCING THE METHODIST CHURCH'S CLOSING IN 2017.
PHOTO FROM METHODIST CHURCH MEMORY BOOK.

LEONA BROWN'S BEAUTIFUL ARTWORK THAT HUNG IN THE METHODIST CHURCH.
PHOTO FROM METHODIST CHURCH MEMORY BOOK.

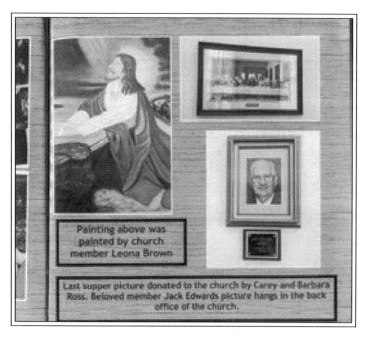

ANOTHER PAINTING BY LEONA BROWN, A PICTURE OF
JACK EDWARDS, AND THE LAST SUPPER DONATED BY
CARY AND BARBARA ROSS. PHOTO FROM METHODIST
CHURCH MEMORY.

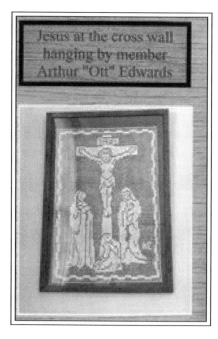

ARTHUR "OTT" EDWARDS'
HANDICRAFT OF JESUS'
RESURRECTION WHICH HUNG IN THE
CHURCH. PHOTO FROM METHODIST
CHURCH MEMORY BOOK.

AFTER THE CLOSING OF THE RHODHISS METHODIST CHURCH THE GRANITE FALLS/RHODHISS
BOY SCOUTS WERE GIVEN THE BUILDING. CARL COMPTON PHOTO.

Another Methodist church lies outside the actual village, but within the city limits. Its address is 703 Burke Street. Friendship Methodist Church's has origins before 1800. The exact founding date is unknown, and no records are available. It is thought that Friendship was organized as the result of a Methodist camp meeting on the present site in Burke County. The church was rebuilt in 1800, and again in 1880 when it was moved to its present location. Again in 1938 it was rebuilt. An educational building and fellowship hall were added in 1968.[69] According to *Friendship Methodist Church-A Brief History* the church started sometime in the 1790s. Their history states:

No exact date is known nor are records available of the number of members at the time of its organization. Its origin was the result of a meeting camp or a brush arbor meeting. Initially called the Methodist Episcopal Church South, it began as a log church on land donated by Elijah Paige. It was made into a permanent structure in 1800 and was rebuilt in 1880 with lumber donated by Thomas Hildebran who owned and operated a sawmill. Inside was a raised pulpit in a half circle with steps at each end which led down into the congregation. Long pews were located in the center of the room to accommodate large families. Smaller pews sat on each side-those on the left for single men and those on the right for single women. Kerosene lamps hung on the walls and lanterns were suspended from the ceiling. Three windows were on each side of the early church and two were located behind the pulpit. A black wood stove sat upon blocks and had a deep wooden basin around its bottom filled with dirt. Circuit riders provided sermons one Sunday each month; however, Sunday School was held each week. According to Ms. Daisy, Friendship was on the same circuit as Big Hill. Separate rooms were not available, so different age groups gathered in certain locations in the structure. Since winters were harsh, meetings were discontinued after Christmas but resumed at Easter. About 1920 the church building was moved to its present location from a spot approximately 300 yards to the south by a homemade winch pulled by a small black mule owned by Milas Paige. The land on which the building now resides was given by the Hudson family of Connelly Springs. After the church was moved, the old cemetery gravestones were straightened into rows for easier maintenance. The church building underwent extensive renovations in 1938 when the frame structure was brick veneered. The parsonage was built in 1953 and the fellowship hall was added in 1968. Friendship's most recent renovation occurred in 1984 when the two buildings were connected, and the sanctuary was reversed. In 1997 a wing was added to the rear of the parsonage and the inside was refurbished.[70]

Friendship Methodist Church still provides weekly worship opportunities for its parishioners and others within the community. Their long history of serving Rhodhiss began a century before there was a mill village.

THE CORNERSTONE OF FRIENDSHIP
METHODIST CHURCH INDICATES ITS HISTORY.
SHERRIE HARTSOE SIGMON PHOTO.

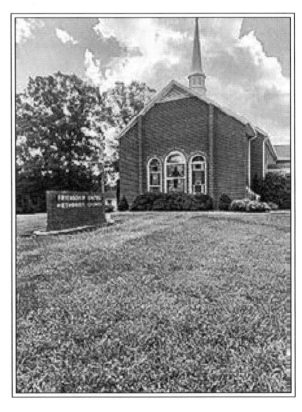

FRIENDSHIP METHODIST CHURCH TODAY.
SHERRIE HARTSOE SIGMON PHOTO.

FRIENDSHIP METHODIST CHURCH 2022.
SHERRIE HARTSOE SIGMON PHOTO.

FRIENDSHIP METHODIST CHURCH 2022.
SHERRIE HARTSOE SIGMON PHOTO.

Another church in the area was located at 158 Duke Street, Granite Falls, and many Rhodhiss citizens attended this parish. The Granite-Rhodhiss Church of God was organized in 1931 per its cornerstone. According to James Hamby to the best of his recollection, the wooden building burned when he was a young lad.[71] A brick structure was placed on the original site in 1955 according to the cornerstone. In the 2000s Granite-Rhodhiss Church of God united with a Church of God on the Cedar Valley Road in the Hudson area. Another church has started at the old location of Granite-Rhodhiss Church of God, and it is Anchor Church of God.

Another church within the town limits is TGIF Ministry at 300 Burke Street. This church has come into existence over the last decade, and it is located beside the former town office in Burke County. The original purpose of this building was Glass' Supermarket. TGIF Ministry offers their love and compassion to the community, and their doors are opened to all.

THE CORNERSTONE OF GRANITE FALLS-
RHODHISS CHURCH OF GOD TELLS ITS HISTORY.
SHERRIE HARTSOE SIGMON PHOTO.

TGIF MINISTRY IS IN BURKE COUNTY. CARL COMPTON PHOTO.

TGIF MINISTRY IN 2022.
CARL COMPTON PHOTO.

Rhodhiss was full of opportunities to worship. Today within the city limits the First Baptist Church Rhodhiss, Church Street Baptist, Friendship Methodist, and TGIF Ministry are open to serve all. Rhodhiss Methodist contributed to the success of the community and aided the citizens for over 100 years. The Church of God gave assistance to the town's people for over 80 years. Rhodhiss has been fortunate to have so many churches serve the community with such fervor and love.

RHODHISS FIRST BAPTIST CHURCH PASTORS
Beginning February 18, 1906

Pastors	Years Stayed	Years
Rev. W. P. Southern	2 years	1906-1908
Rev. G. C.Ivey	1 year	1908-1909
Rev. C. M. Ervin	3.5 years	1909-1912
Rev. C. A. Rhyne	4 years	1912-1917
Rev. W. A. Stephenson	1 year	1917-1918
Rev. O. C. Abee	6 months	1918
Rev. J. G. Benfield	8 years	1918-1926
Rev. T. A. Payne	9 months	1927
Rev. H. B. Chronister	3 years	1927-1930
Rev. W. D. Early	4.5 years	1930-1935
Rev. Leroy Thomas	5 years	1935-1940
Rev. L. W. Teague	6 months	1940
Rev. R. F. Mayberry	4 years	1940-1945
Rev. Jeta Baker	3 years	1945-1948
Rev. Frank Colburn	2 years	1948-1949
Rev. Vernon Connell	2 years	1949-1951
Rev. C. B. Bobbitt	5 years	1952-1957
Rev. W. L. Pitts	2 years	1957-1959
Rev. Harold Brown,Sr.	4.5years	1959-1964
Rev. Millard Crumpler	4.5years	1964-1969
Rev. E. Guy Longshore, Jr.	7.5years	1969-1977
Rev. James D. Cool, Sr.	8.5years	1978-1986
Rev. David Philbeck	3years	1986-1989
Rev. Bob Wiggins	2years	1990-1992
Rev. Conrad Hefner	9.5years	1993-2003
Rev. Bill Harrison	1year	2005-2006
Rev. John Coffey	3years	2007-2010
Rev. Rick Miller		2011 to present[72]

NOTES

1   "Rhodhiss, N. C." *Lutheran Church Visitor.* Vol. II, No 46. Columbia, SC. 2 August 1906, p. 12.

2   "Chips From Granite." *Lenoir News-Topic.* 28 February 1902, p. 3.
        https://newspapers.digitalnc.org/lccn/sn97064560/1902-02-28/ed-1/seq-3/#words=Rhodhiss.

3   Reeves, Timothy Scott, Archival Assistant at Crumley Library at Southern Theological Seminary, Columbia, SC.
        Emails: 6 July 2022.

4   "New Church Completed." *Lutheran Church Visitor.* Vol. 1, No. 8. Columbia, SC Thursday, 29 September 1904,
        p.12.

5   Sipes, Edward, Sr. Personal Email Interview with Sherrie Hartsoe Sigmon. 2 May 2012.

6   Reeves, Timothy Scott.

7   "Rhodhiss, N. C." *Lutheran Church Visitor.* Vol. II, No 46. Columbia, SC. 2 August 1906, p. 12.

8   Caldwell County Online Records. http://72.15.246.185/CaldwellNC/. Date 01/01/1905. DocNo. 90185173.
        Book: 40. Page: 308.

9   Caldwell County Online Records. http://72.15.246.185/CaldwellNC/. Date 01/01/1907. DocNo. 90187042.
        Book: 44. Page: 490.

10   Caldwell County Online Records. Date 01/01/1911. DocNo. 90167300. Book: 50. Page: 460.

11   "Rhodhiss First Baptist 100th Anniversary: 1906-2006." 19 March 2006.

12   "Rhodhiss First Baptist 100th Anniversary: 1906-2006." 19 March 2006.

13   "Rhodhiss First Baptist 100th Anniversary: 1906-2006." 19 March 2006.

14   "Rhodhiss First Baptist 100th Anniversary: 1906-2006."19 March 2006.

15   "Rhodiss (sic) Baptist Started in 1906 with 29 Members." *Lenoir News-Topic.* Reprinted 12 September 1941.

16   "History 1906-1983: First Baptist Church At the Corner of Park and Magnolia Streets."

17   "Rhodhiss First Baptist 100th Anniversary: 1906-2006." 19 March 2006.

18   "Curtis, Violet, Willard Herman, and Tom Ross.

19   "Curtis, Violet, Willard Herman, and Tom Ross.

20   "Curtis, Violet, Willard Herman, and Tom Ross and Elmore, Fred and Martha and Tom Ross.

21   Church, Thelma.

22   Curtis, Violet, Willard Herman, and Tom Ross.

23   Elmore, Fred and Martha and Tom Ross.

24   "Lanny Elmore: Our Missionary." Pamphlet by Rhodhiss Baptist Church, 2006.

25   Herman, Willard and Tom Ross.

26   Hall, p. 125.

27   Byerly, Victoria. *Hard Times Cotton Mill Girls.* New York: New York State School of Industrial and Labor Relations,
        Cornell University Press, 1986, p. 12 & p. 14.

28   Beshears, Monteith, Ross, and Teague.

29   Church, Thelma.

30   Edwards, Arthur and Jack and Edna Edwards Laney Stilwell.

31   Beshears, Monteith, Ross, and Teague.

32   Beshears, Monteith, Ross, Teague.

33   Edwards, Arthur, Jack, and Edith Stilwell.

34   Elmore, Tommy.

35   Bean, Ned and Elvie and Tom Ross.

36   Herman, Willard and Tom Ross.

37   Church, Thelma.

38   Bumgarner, Paul and Helen.

39   Bumgarner, Paul and Helen.

40   "Rhodhiss First Baptist 100th Anniversary: 1906-2006." 19 March 2006.

41   "Rhodhiss First Baptist 100th Anniversary: 1906-2006." 19 March 2006.

42   Caldwell County Online Records. Date 01/01/1971. DocNo. 90006916. Book: 620. Page: 814.

43   "Methodist Church of Rhodhiss Was Organized in 1912." *Lenoir News-Topic*. Reprinted 12 September 1941.

44   Triplett, Pam Edwards. Phone Interview with Sherrie Hartsoe Sigmon. 20 July 2008.

45   "Methodist Church of Rhodhiss Was Organized in 1912."

46   "Methodist Church of Rhodhiss Was Organized 1912."

47   Kelley, Alvis and Precious.

48   Lutz, Fletcher and Tom Ross.

49   Hemphill, Helen.

50   Arthur and Jack Edwards and Edna Edwards Stilwell and Tom Ross.

51   Church, Thelma.

52   Bean, Ned.

53   Jones, Calvin and Tom Ross.

54   Herman, Willard and Tom Ross.

55   Bean, Ned.

56   Beshears, Monteith, Teague, and Ross.

57   Kelley, Alvis and Precious.

58   Edwards, Arthur and Jack and Edna Edwards Stilwell.

59   Austin, Ann, Thad Martin, and Shelley Teague.

60   Stout, Al. "Church Congregation To Celebrate 100 Years." *Hickory Daily Record*. 21 December 2013. Pages 7A and 9A.

61   Laney, Billie Sue. Telephone Interview. 28 December 2021.

62   Sigmon, Rebecca. 21 May 2022.

63   Beshears, Monteith, Ross, Teague.

64   Bean, Ned and Elvie and Tom Ross.

65   Caldwell County Online Records. Date 09/16/1980. DocNo: 00198920. Book: 753. Page 148.

66   Stout.

67   Stout.

68   Stout.

69   Anderson, pp. 181-182.

70   "Friendship Methodist Church-A Brief History." Friendship Methodist Church print out.

71   Hamby, James. Personal Interview with Sherrie Hartsoe Sigmon. Lenoir, NC. 27 July 2022.

72   "Rhodhiss First Baptist 100th Anniversary: 1906-2006." 19 March 2006.

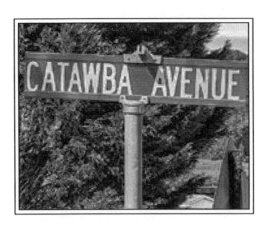

CHAPTER 13
THE 1916 FLOOD

In 1916 one of the state's worst natural disasters hit the mountains and piedmont of North Carolina. Destruction was widespread causing damage to crops, bridges, dams, trestles, and businesses. The front pages of the *Lenoir News-Topic* and the *Hickory Daily Record* detailed this disaster, which was big news for the time. Rhodhiss suffered immense damage, and it is a wonder that the village was able to recoup its losses.

The *Lenoir News-Topic* stated, "Today Lenoir is marooned, isolated from the outside world with no chance of outside communication for several days, and no possibility of train or freight service within thirty days, or even longer. Everything on the Catawba River, railroad bridges, county road bridges and every avenue of transfer has been swept away. The property loss is staggering--inestimable. Loss in life may also be great."[1] Citizens felt great despair and uncertainty as to when their lives would return to normal. The article added, "The smaller streams, swollen to great rivers by thirty-six hours of torrential rain at times reaching cloud burst magnitude, have been the feeders of the Catawba River and with the rainfall in the Catawba bottoms raised it forty-five feet higher than normal and sixteen feet higher than it has ever been before."[2] The rain started late Friday and continued through Saturday night. The Carolina and Northwestern trains were rendered inoperable and estimated to be out of service for thirty to sixty days. "At the river the big railroad bridge is washed away and it is thought that the several miles of track between the bridge and Cliffs station is washed away. On this side of the river the Rhodhiss depot, several box cars loaded with cotton and about a half a mile of track were washed away."[3] Rhodhiss' plight looked bleak for the citizens and the mill owners.

In this same article Rhodhiss was described as "desolate and destitute." The water reached forty-two feet higher than normal Sunday at 1:00, and water was on the second and third stories of the mills on both sides. Two houses, the bridge, and a warehouse washed down the river. Four hundred bales of cotton also floated down the river. A future shipment of $50,000 worth of finished cotton was in the warehouse as it drifted away. A train car of flour which was ready for shipment was also washed away. People came from all areas to see the destruction in Rhodhiss. An estimated several thousand people saw the Catawba River at its highest recorded water mark. The spectators observed homes, bridges, lumber, and automobiles glide with the current. One person saw more than fifty stacks of wheat float by. Cows, horses, and hogs bobbed about in the water. Spectators pulled a live hog out of the river.[4] The turmoil was massive in the village of Rhodhiss.

Mill company owners at Rhodhiss assessed the damage to see when workers could return. The auxiliary steam power plant and machine shop caved in. The owners said that repairs would begin as soon as the water subsided; thus over 300 millhands were out of work. Rhodhiss fared much better than Mortimer where thirty houses floated away, and in Collettsville one child was knocked from his mother's arms and never seen again.[5] Later, the *Hickory Daily Record* stated that Collettsville suffered four drownings because of the flood. This same article confirmed that thirty houses washed away in Mortimer. "It was feared that pestilence might break out. The conditions at both places are critical, the stench is terrible, and aid is imperative. The Carolina and Northwestern is working great forces of men in an effort to repair the road to Lenoir, so that supplies can be received for that section, but there is said to be a shortage of provisions at Lenoir."[6] Times were very difficult during this catastrophe. Crops were flooded, so no food was available, and stores had limited supplies because transportation was halted with bridges being obliterated.

The *Hickory Daily Record* reported that damage was done to both telephone and telegraph lines. The paper stated:

> The rainfall from Friday afternoon to Monday morning was 13.39 inches, the greatest for that length of time ever recorded here. The Rhodhiss Manufacturing Company and the Smith Manufacturing Company sustained damage estimated at more than $100,000. The plants were flooded to a depth of several feet and over 400 looms covered with sand. The sand was three and a half feet deep in the mills. Mail is being sent from Hickory to Granite Falls and Lenoir, it's going by way of Rhodhiss, where boats are operating on the river.[7]

All communication, transportation, and work came to a halt because of the flood. The clean-up would take days, and reconstruction would take several years. Decades after the 1916 flood a *Hickory Daily Record* reporter, Charles Pegram wrote, "Hundreds of fish trapped in shallows were caught by hand. An accumulation of sand at the Cliffs on the C&N-W tracks northwest of Hickory took 40 men and 15 teams of mules to remove in a week's-long process. Later it was to be learned that rainfall in the Globe section of northwestern Caldwell County totaled 36 inches in 36 hours."[8] The mills at Rhodhiss had to be plowed to get the dirt, mud, and sand out of the mill according to the stories that have circulated in town. Two category 4 hurricanes came together in July 1916 making the Catawba River 47 feet above flood stage. Every bridge in Catawba County except one was washed away, and survivors were rescued from treetops. It was the worst flood ever experienced in the Catawba River Valley. From July 14-16 the heaviest rains ever were recorded. People flocked to the riverbanks of the Catawba to observe. "Bales of cotton, the property of the Rhodhiss Manufacturing Company, swept by, and scores of haystacks, chicken coops, sheds, and a few houses were borne down the current. The Hickory Brick Company and Bud Poovey's brickyard were destroyed, entailing considerable loss."[9] Business owners continued to experience destruction and despair for employees and themselves.

Our State magazine did a story on the 1916 flood in 2002. Ken Blackwell, the author, gave many details in his story. Mr. Blackwell explained that rain from two systems saturated the ground. People were sinking in the mud. Crops were ruined, and this was the winter's supply. During the second storm, rivers flooded. "More than half a year's normal rainfall was dumped on the region in a 24-hour period." Estimates indicated that 90 percent of the moisture from this storm flooded the mountains' rivers and streams causing flooding in the piedmont. Property damage was estimated at $22.5 million and 80 people died in the flood. Hickory merchants started rationing their supplies for fear of a shortage.[10] In Rhodhiss most of the town purchased their goods from the Company Store, so the mill owners had the option to ration merchandise, too.

Matthew Bumgarner detailed the damage to the railroad in his book, *Carolina & NW: The Legacy of the Carolina and North-Western Railway.* The railroad company assessed that almost 47 percent of the C&NW was eliminated or damaged. Caldwell County suffered severe damage. "The huge 600-foot trestle across the Catawba River had plunged into the raging torrents and immediately isolated Lenoir and the rest of Caldwell County from the world."[11] The Pennsylvania Railroad Company pledged support with men and supplies. Contracts were quickly negotiated for a temporary trestle for the Catawba River between Hickory and Lenoir. "Meanwhile, work on the temporary Catawba River bridge from Hickory was completed on August 21. Construction of the 600-foot trestle took several thousand men 12 days to complete, working around the clock. Thirty-three days after having been cut off from the world, the first Carolina & North-Western train pulled into Lenoir."[12] It is amazing that the trestle was repaired in twelve days, but hard work was the ethic then. During those times transporting people to the worksite would have taken much longer than it would today, let alone moving the necessary equipment and supplies. Another author, Jay Barnes, wrote that "The flood divided the state, as nine railroad bridges and all highway bridges across the Catawba River were destroyed."[13] The people in the piedmont of North Carolina saw destruction. *The Heritage of Caldwell County, North Carolina* added that the Rhodhiss millhands had to remove dead animals from the floors after the dam burst during the flood. A ferry that ran by cables and ropes was dispersed to haul equipment, animals, and people across the river until a new bridge could be built. Carl Winkler was the operator of the ferry.[14] Moving from mill to mill would have been hard without the ferry. Supplies were always being transported between the two. That is why it was necessary for the company to have the livery stable. Horses and mules were used to transport equipment and commodities from the Caldwell plant to the Burke plant; however, with the livery stable washing away, the ferry became the mode of transportation.

Violet Curtis was able to tell of her firsthand experience during the flood to Tom Ross, Willard Herman, and me. She was a young child and had lived in Rhodhiss only a few years, but her vivid description gave a colorful account. Violet explained:

WH: Now, she can tell you, Sherrie, a little bit about the flood in 1916. She can remember because she was like 10 years old.

VC: Yeah, Ruth was the baby. I remember us a going, and the limbs were in the water. They had a pole with a nail on it. We'd go down, and they'd pull lumber out of the water with that pole. Way up there on the hill it backed up in that island in Rhodhiss. It was on up where that curve is. You'd go up Strawberry, and it was up to that curve. Now, remember Ruth was just a baby, and she was getting close. She ran up, and some of them got scared. Mama said, 'I'm not going down there again. I got so scared when Ruth ran up there. It could have jerked her in there.' It rained and rained. We had to go down there in the rain because it rained so many days. I forget how many days.

TR: The lumber that you were talking about. It was just floating down the river?

VC: Yeah. Logs, pigs, and everything came down that river. You know that they found a pig in the old mill in the quill room there. I remember my daddy coming home, and he had boots on from wading to get the cloth out of the weave shop. You know it came up into the weave room. I remember us going down there and walking around talking after the flood. That was a pitiful time.

TR: It is a wonder that they hadn't given up after that mess.

VC: The boiler room was going off. That opening room down there was going. Some of them across the river told about seeing where the cloth room used to be. It never did get to the Company Store. It was a pitiful time back then. I was about 9 years old; I reckon. The dam just broke over. They had a livery stable where they had horses and buggies.

SH: Didn't the livery stable wash away with the flood?

VC: Yeah.

SH: That is where Hazel Monteith's daddy worked.

VC: Yeah. It washed away, and they built another one back. Mr. Knox (Hazel's dad) used to work there. I can remember that. Way back yonder.

WH: Yeah, he ran the livery stable at one time.

VC: Mabel's daddy.

WH: She's talking about Hazel's older sister who married her brother. We are all tied up in that Knox family. An older sister married one of the boys. Several of our family married into it. There were about fourteen of those children. Matt, John, Frank, Jock.

VC: Mabel, Hazel, and Marie are the only girls living.[15]

A personal account of seeing the aftermath of the flood adds depth to the story. Violet's mother was so afraid of baby Ruth getting caught in the flood waters that she vowed not to go back to the scene. Butler Monteith, who was the son-in-law of Mr. James "Jim" Knox who ran the livery stable in 1916 said, "Well, the last time they had any mules to look after down there, my daddy-in-law looked after them."[16] Mr. Jim Knox was mentioned several times as the livery stable controller; however, Exie Hand said that her dad ran it in 1903 when they were building the first bridge.[17] Hans Townsend, a longtime citizen, talked about the livery stable and its purpose: "They had a livery stable down in there. You could rent a horse and buggy. People told me about it. The mill company used horses, too, to go back and forth across the river. They used to haul their cotton back and forth between the mills. Over there in the back of the mill, of course, there has been more built over there now. Water used to run this way around in front of the mill and then go across the road."[18] The livery stable served the town well, but it was washed away.

Gladys Kirby Barker, a longtime resident of Rhodhiss, was able to detail her family's experience with the flood. Her dad, Eli Kirby, worked for the mill company, and Gladys and her family endured the experience at home while her dad worked. Gladys stated:

> It rained all day on Saturday; the bridge washed away along with three houses. Employees were moving cloth to the top floor of the plants in order to save it. They worked until midnight. My dad was one of these men. He worked on the Burke side; that's the new mill, because the first mill became known as the old mill. The bridge washed away on Saturday afternoon late. The bridge and depot were gone. The warehouse that had cloth in it washed away. My dad needed to get to Caldwell side, so he and the others went to the trestle and crossed there with water coming over. My siblings and I didn't know until the next morning when we awoke how dangerous it had been for Papa. He had arrived home at midnight. We had simply gone to bed, but my older sister fixed a leak in the house where water was pouring through. Water was as high as the first and second floors of the plants. Houses, hogs, and cattle came down the river. Claude and his family walked to Rhodhiss from Sawmills to see all of the flood devastation.[19]

Gladys' dad's daring feat of going to the trestle to cross the river during the raving flood must have scared him and his family after finding out what he had done. The trestle did wash away.

Mattie Munday was a young lass when the 1916 flood happened. She recalled quite a few details regarding going to see its aftermath. Mattie noted:

> I had the flood song. I don't know where it is. I might have loaned it to somebody, but I know part of it. I remember some of it: 'Lonnie, Lily, and Julius was found, and Mary laid beneath the ground in a pillar of mud and a head of clay, and there they would lay to the last great day.' Now that was in it. Well anyway, my daddy walked from where we lived in Sawmills to help clean out the mills and took the fever. After he got a little better, they moved him down here on a one-horse wagon filled full of straw and a bed tick on it. Well anyway, when they did that, we moved to Rhodhiss. And I remember that just as good. Yeah, I remember going down there and Dwight Helton's aunt and her son went with us. There was water all up in the mill, you know. Along there about where the old warehouse is, there was little fish that had washed up in there in the water. And that little ole boy, Dwight Helton's aunt's little boy and girl, caught some of those little ole fish. I can remember that, and I wasn't but 8 years old, about 8. My

brother that is a little older than me, was so anxious about moving here that he said that the first thing that he wanted was for us to get life insurance so we wouldn't ever die. That's what he had planned, you know. Well, I had two brothers and a sister that was old enough to work, but they let you work then at any age in the mill.[20]

Mattie's brother had fears of Rhodhiss' flooding again. He was afraid to live there without life insurance. Earl Lutz, who lived in Rhodhiss, noted what his family told him about the flood. Earl said, "I heard dad tell about the flood. They said that you could stand out in the yard and see people's cattle going down the river, and buildings and everything else, but I don't remember that part of it. I do remember we moved from there up on the hill close to where the school and the First Baptist Church were. I remember the old bridge, or the one that replaced the bridge that was washed away in 1916."[21] Old timers were able to give their perspective of the 1916 flood or from that of their family. Shelley Teague is another one who said that his family came from lower Duke Street in Granite Falls to see the destruction. Shelley said, "I was just a baby when they brought me down here in a horse and buggy after the flood to look at it. Of course, I was only a month or two old, and we came down here."[22]

The 1916 flood brought people from all over the state to Rhodhiss to view or assess the damage. Their trip did not disappoint when they saw all the debris floating down the river along with cars, animals, bridges, houses, chicken coops, pig pens, and lumber. Rhodhiss suffered immense damage from the 1916 flood. The broken dam would not be replaced until 1925, and the bridge was replaced as quickly as they could erect a new one. The mills continued to operate after they were cleared of sand, mud, and animals. For years a mark on the Burke Mill showed how high the water came; however, that mark was no longer visible when the mill was painted. Rhodhiss survived another difficult time. Following are both the poem and the song written about the 1916 flood.

THE FLOOD ATTRACTED VISITORS.
PRECIOUS KELLER KELLEY PHOTO.

THE WAREHOUSE WASHED DOWN THE RIVER. THE PICTURE IS MARKED WH SHUFORD (WADE HAMPTON SHUFORD) SUPPLY. MR. SHUFORD RAN THE COMPANY STORE. PRECIOUS KELLER KELLEY PHOTO.

BURKE PLANT IN THE FLOOD. CALDWELL
COUNTY HERITAGE MUSEUM PHOTO.

1924 THE HORSESHOE DAM THAT BROKE.
DUKE POWER PHOTO WITH PERMISSION.

FRONT PAGE OF *HICKORY DAILY RECORD* ON JULY 18, 1916.

The 1916 Flood (poem)

It was on one Sunday eve
Many hearts were made to grieve
By the Story I shall tell.
'Twas the sixteenth of July
And Catawba's floods were high
From the awful rain that fell.

Long and constant poured the rain
Till each brooklet, creek, and drain
Made a torrent deep and wide.
Then, Catawba, from her head,
By these dashing torrents fed
Roughly rolled and undefied. (sic)

Bridge and trestle swept away,
Dams and houses, too, they say
Till they reach the Southern Main
There the railroad called a crew
To Save its trains and trestle too.
But their efforts were in vain.

Few if any tears were shed
When their parting words were said
As the workmen left their home.
Naught, or little, did they dream
That Catawba's maddened stream
Should engulf them in their gloom.

In an instant all was crashed,
As the heaps of rubbish clashed
'Gainst the trestle's massive piers.
Twenty men in all went down.
Chances were to swim or drown
Then came sobs and screams and tears.

When this tragic message spread
Of the missing and the dead.
Swiftly night was coming on.

Hands were wrung and hair was torn
Men must work and women mourn
For their loved ones lost and gone.

Thanks to God not all were drowned,
Some could swim and reach the ground
Others lodged and still were brave
But when dams above were crushed,
Afterwhile their pleadings hushed
For they found a watery grave.

While your Lord and loved ones plead
Now my sinner friend take heed,
Cleanse yourself from sin and crime.
You are but a workman, too,
On life's road and trestle crew,
Moving o'er the River Time.
--E. L. Fant (possible author).[23]

The Land Slide (song, author unknown)

In the month of July, the year sixteenth
The worst tropical storm that ever was seen
As it made its way from the ocean wide
Struck full force on the mountain side.
At the head of the Jackson branch
There were a father and a mother and children five all alive,
They stood in the door and watched the rain come down,
They saw how quick it covered the ground.
The pleading voice of little Perry was heard to the Pine,
Let us all go together
The words of the boy was just spoken
The windows of heaven thrown wide open.
The downpour come with a terrific roar.
It struck the house they were all thrown to the floor.
The newborn babe in the cradle at rest,
The mother snatched up and pressed to her breast.
As the house went down it struck a tree
They were all thrown out except the three

As the house went down and the horses too,
The neighbors said 'there's work to do.'
Julius and Wilson in their haste
Turned their steps toward the Wilson place.
They had to take a higher ground
When they reached the place not home was found.
Down in the house which Williams built
Lonas and Lillie and children knelt
Said Julius to Lonas and Lillie too
Are your children all safe I see only two.
Oh no said she I fear they are drowned.
They have not been seen since the house went down.
But down in the bottom by the St. Clair Pond
The babies of Lewis and Jennie were found.
As the neighbors come and walked around
Their teardrops fell fast on the ground
But poor little Perry has not been found,
He sleeps somewhere beneath the ground.
With a bed of mud and pillow of clay
He may not be found till the last great day
When the angels come with a trumpet sound
To wake the dead that are under the ground.
As he awakes in the morning and upward flies
To meet his loved ones beneath the sky
Our God in mercy and thy great love
Prepare them all to meet above.
That when their trials are past
They may all find a home in heaven at last.
Through eternity to sing his praise
For dying love and saving grace.[24]

The 1916 flood brought destruction all over western North Carolina. Rhodhiss was hit hard, but the employees and owners managed to overcome the turmoil and rise out of despair. The hard work of the community after the flood allowed them to return to the company. Rhodhiss had at this point survived a cyclone and a flood. More natural disasters awaited.

NOTES

1   "Lenoir Isolated from Outer World." *Lenoir News-Topic*. 18 July 1916. Volume XVIII. No. 12, p. 1.

2   "Lenoir Isolated."

3   "Lenoir Isolated."

4   "Lenoir Isolated."

5   "Lenoir Isolated."

6   "Collettsville Visited by Terrible Disaster." *Hickory Daily Record*. 21 July 1916. Vol. 1, No. 265, p. 1.

7   "Late Reports Indicate Great Damage By Flood." *Hickory Daily Record*. 18 July 1916. Vol. 1. No. 265, p. 1.

8   Pegram, Charles B. "Worst Flood In Unifour History: July 1916." *Hickory Daily Record*. 1 August 1993, p. 7C.

9   "Great Flood of 1916." Catawba County, North Carolina. http://ncgenweb.us/catawba/flood. Accessed 22 October 2021.

10   Blackwell, Ken. "The Flood of 1916." *Our State*. September 2002. Pp. 24-27.

11   Bumgarner, Matthew, pp. 57-58

12   Bumgarner, Matthew, pp. 57-58.

13   Barnes, Jay. *North Carolina's Hurricane History*. University of North Carolina Press, Chapel Hill, NC, 2013, p. 60.

14   Anderson, pp. 181-182.

15   Curtis, Violet, Willard Herman, Tom Ross.

16   Beshears, Monteith, Ross, Teague.

17   Hand, Arthur and Exie.

18   Townsend, Hans and Katherine and Tom Ross.

19   Barker, Gladys.

20   Munday, Mattie and Louise Keller.

21   Lutz, Earl.

22   Beshears, Monteith, Ross, Teague.

23   "The 1916 Flood." *Hickory Daily Record*. 1 August 1993, p. 8C.

24   "Song Recounts 1916 Tragedy." *Hickory Daily Record*. 1 August 1993, p. 7C.

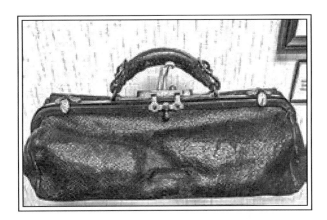

CHAPTER 14
DOCTORS, SMALLPOX, TYPHOID, 1918 FLU EPIDEMIC, MEDICAL CHARGES, AND WWI LIST

Rhodhiss was not immune to disease and sickness. For that reason, doctors were frequently called to town, or the citizens went to nearby Granite Falls or Hickory to be treated. The mill company did not provide health insurance for the employees in the early years. It was not until after 1945 that workers were offered this benefit from Pacific Mills. Prior to that if millhands had coverage it was through a private group called Mutual Aid. When smallpox hit the town in 1910, the mill company helped in many ways. Later the 1918 flu epidemic claimed the lives of many citizens, and typhoid kept recurring throughout the first part of the twentieth century. The village survived these medical perils with the help of doctors, the company, and the community.

Dr. George Flowers is one of the first doctors mentioned in the Rhodhiss Town Minutes. In December 1908 he completed medical exams for the mill company. He was paid $5.95 for this service.[1] It is unclear who received these examinations, but Dr. Flowers' office was in Granite Falls, and he started practice in 1889.[2] A health issue during this time was smallpox. Gladys Barker was still living in Hudson when smallpox hit the area. She did not move to Rhodhiss until after the smallpox epidemic. Gladys said, "Dr. C. L. Wilson from Lenoir came to my house to give me the vaccine while I stood on the front porch. If you had smallpox, you had to go live in a 'pest' house. Food was taken to the people in this house. Rhodhiss was under quarantine."[3] Dr. Wilson was the Caldwell County Superintendent of Health. Fletcher Lutz also mentioned the pest house. He explained, "I forget where the old pest house used to be over there. Somewhere on the other side of the river (meaning Burke County). The pest house is what they called it. They had places for people to go who were infected with diseases. The community was in danger. That's why they had pest houses."[4] No one knew where the pest house was in Rhodhiss, but two people suggested that there was such a place.

According to the town minutes, the first time that smallpox was noted was in 1909. A special meeting was held on March 12, 1909, and Mayor C. E. Nabors, Councilmen G. F. Smith, L. W. Kirkman, and J. W. Espey were present, in addition to W. S. Taylor and F. S. Mosher, the Secretary and the General Manager of Rhodhiss Manufacturing respectively. The meeting's purpose was to stop the spread of smallpox into Rhodhiss. Since Hudson, North Carolina had reported cases of smallpox, the men voted to quarantine against the Town of Hudson and to place guards at roads to hinder these citizens from entering Rhodhiss. Notices were also placed in conspicuous places, and everything possible was done to prevent the spread of smallpox.[5] Although the town and the mill company tried to prevent the disease from ravaging the village, in less than a year the first case was announced. At a February 1, 1910, meeting Mayor F. S. Mosher reported that W. L. Spencer had contracted smallpox as reported to him from Dr. O. J. Corpening. The mayor "authorized Dr. Corpening to make all necessary quarantine arrangements and also post the yellow flag which is required by law."[6] On February 25, 1910, the Mayor and Council held a meeting with George B. Hiss, the President and Treasurer of Rhodhiss Manufacturing; W. S. Taylor; Dr. C. L. Wilson, County Superintendent of Health; and Dr. O. J. Corpening, Town Physician. The resolutions on smallpox were unanimously adopted and ordered.[7] Dr. Oscar J. Corpening practiced medicine for 65 years in Caldwell County. He was from the North Catawba area. He was described as a versatile man who had "a sausage cannery, a hosiery mill, a cotton mill, furniture and radio manufacturing, a mica mine, timberlands, farms, a laundry, a pharmacy, orchards, a clothing store, and a vineyard." He first traveled through the area in a horse and buggy and later purchased one of the first cars in Caldwell County.[8] Dr. Corpening served the town of Rhodhiss during the smallpox epidemic. Vaccinations were administered, and five months later in July the town voted to pay $275.00 to Dr. Corpening, the Company Store, and Granite Falls Drug Company for the goods or services that they provided during the smallpox epidemic.[9]

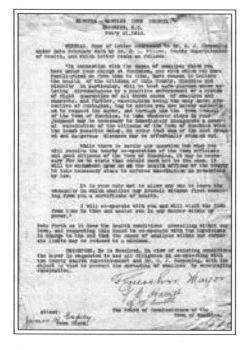

SMALLPOX RESOLUTIONS FROM THE
RHODHISS TOWN MINUTES.

Smallpox would return to town on various occasions. Violet Curtis explained that she had smallpox a few years after moving to Rhodhiss, which was after the 1910 epidemic. Violet and her brother-in-law, Willard Herman, explained:

WH: Did anybody tell you how dirty the water was at the school? And children shared the same dipper.
SH: No.
WH: We had to carry it from the well. It was dirty.
VC: Yes, it was. They said that is how I got smallpox by sharing the dipper. I was about the second in Rhodhiss that got smallpox. Mama told the doctor, 'No, I kept her out of school. It's not smallpox because she hasn't been in that well.'

We had to go down to that well below the school to draw our water. That's where I got the germ of smallpox.

SH: When did you have smallpox?

VC: Oh, I must have been about 11 years old something like that.

WH: A lot of people in Rhodhiss came from Rutherford County back in the early days when the mill first started up. The Carroleen Mill and the Henrietta Mill were mills that they left to come here.

VC: My daddy came to Rhodhiss, and I believe it was for $8 a week. The Heralds came from down in there.

SH: There was another smallpox epidemic when you were about 11?

VC: Yeah.[10]

Violet must have had smallpox around 1916 or 1917. She was not happy about contracting the disease, and neither was her mother. Pawnee Simmons told about another outbreak around 1926. Pawnee explained:

PS: My dad really did love his work. I am telling you. I was about eight years old, I guess when daddy took the smallpox. My sister got smallpox at school, the first year that she went to school. Then daddy got it.

SH: This was in Rhodhiss?

PS: Yeah. We lived up there where Hub Eller lives now. We lived in that house. Of course, it was in the wintertime. It was right after Christmas when he got sick. You could see straight across from his bedroom window the number two mill because there weren't any leaves on the trees. They were doing something. I don't know what they were doing at the mill, but he was pretty sick there for a couple of days. He'd get up at night and go stand at the window, and as the workers would go from place to place, they'd have a light, you know. I could see the light. He knew where every window was. He would go watch them. I would be so tired standing there at that window.

SH: That wasn't an epidemic in town, was it?

PS: I don't know.

SH: About 1910 there was a smallpox epidemic, and it closed the town.

PS: Well, we weren't here then. It was later. It didn't make my sister too sick. We had all been vaccinated for it, but Flossie and daddy got it. He really loved his work, and he was upset that he couldn't be there. He knew everything about the mill and town. He made all those materials. He knew every pipe and where the cut off was. He knew everything about the water and electricity. He used to make blueprints at night.[11]

Smallpox kept showing its ugliness throughout the village for years. Mattie Munday said, "I remember when Louise was a baby a lot of people had smallpox. They wouldn't let anybody go anywhere."[12] Louise was born in 1926, so this outbreak would have been about the same time that smallpox hit the

Mullinax household.

Exie Hand, who grew up in the Henry River area before moving to Rhodhiss when she was 18 years old, told me that the people of that area forded the river to get to Caldwell County doctors. Exie explained:

> EH: I don't remember too much about daddy fording the river. It was back when I was really young. He'd tell us about fording the river. Well, everybody over in there did. When they came to the doctor, they had to ford the river.
>
> SH: They did it because they went to Granite to the doctor?
>
> EH: Yeah.
>
> SH: Was Doctor Corpening living then?
>
> EH: Oh, yeah. Doctor Copening (Corpening), ain't been dead too many years. Dr. Copening, Dr. Russell, Dr. Kent, Dr. Bill Copening (Corpening), Dr. Copening's son.
>
> SH: But the Henry River people forded the river?
>
> EH: If they came over here, they did. Or they had to go around by Hickory.
>
> SH: That was a long route.

Exie mentioned several doctors in the Granite Falls area. Dr. Charles Russell practiced in Connelly Springs and Granite Falls for 50 years. He, too, first traveled by horse and buggy and then purchased a car. He delivered over 5,000 babies.[13] Alvis Kelley said that "Dr. Russell could really sew you up. He done a wonderful job on Poker Man (not his real name) because I saw it before he ever saw it. Ole Poker Man was pretty bad to fight."[14] Several others mentioned Dr. Russell and his attire. Fred Elmore stated, "Well, he was a dude. He wore those spats day and night. Oh, yes! He was a good doctor."[15] Fortunately, for the people in Rhodhiss and Granite Falls, many good doctors were available in the area. Exie also mentioned Dr. Kent and Dr. Bill Corpening. Dr. Alfred Kent, Jr. had an office in Granite, and he followed in his father's footsteps by becoming a doctor. His father was also a state senator. Dr. Kent, Jr. started his practice in Granite on February 1, 1934, after attending UNC, Duke, and Jefferson Medical College. He died in 1975.[16] Dr. Bill Corpening, who was the son of Dr. O. J. and Alice Corpening, was also mentioned by Exie. Dr. Bill attended UNC and then the University of Maryland School of Medicine. In 1947 he returned home to practice with his father. Dr. Bill practiced medicine until his retirement in the early 1980s.[17]

Calvin Jones and Tom Ross discussed Dr. Martin Jones along with Dr. Russell. Calvin and Tom came to Rhodhiss in 1946 to work for Pacific Mills. They elaborated:

> TR: I've been telling her about Dr. Russell. You remember him?
>
> CJ: Oh, yeah. He wore spats all the time. He drove around in a convertible automobile with a dirty hat. He was some more doctor. They say that he was a good doctor. I never did go to him.
>
> TR: I didn't either. We kept Jones up back then.
>
> CJ: I don't know what we would have done without Jones.
>
> TR: He came about the time we came here.[18]

Dr. Russell must have been quite a character with his spats. Calvin and Tom said that their families went to Dr. Martin Jones. Dr. Jones was a Granite Falls native, but his mother worked in Rhodhiss briefly as a teacher, and his dad built the first Rhodhiss bridge. Martin attended Duke University as an undergraduate and medical student. He returned to Granite Falls to practice in 1949 and retired in the late 1980s. Dr. Jones "focused on family medicine, and he was on call seven days and nights a week. He frequently made house calls and delivered babies."[19] Obviously, the doctors in Granite Falls were busy because of the large area that they served. In addition, the average life expectancy was 45 years in 1900, and in 1980 it increased to 75 years.[20] People in the early part of the twentieth century suffered from medical issues for which no medicines were available. Thankfully, life expectancy has increased since 1900.

The last doctor was Dr. A. D. Jones whose practice was in Granite Falls. Dr. Jones was not related to Dr. Martin Jones who arrived in the late 1940s. Dr. A. D. Jones started his practice in 1876 after graduating from the University of Louisville and had an active practice for fifty years.[21] Willard Herman discussed him to Tom Ross and me:

> TR: Was he related to Dr. Jones?
>
> WH: No, I don't think that they were any relation, but his home, Tom, sat just about where the Fresh Air Market sits up here, right about where Boyd Poovey's house is. He had a great big two-story gray weatherboard house, and he had a little weatherboard office built right almost at the railroad. Just a walk between it and the railroad. That was his office.
>
> TR: Was he the only doctor around?
>
> WH: No, Dr. Corpening. He was here at that time, but he was a young doctor. Dr. Jones was a fairly old man, and he had an awfully large family of children.
>
> TR: I hadn't heard about him.
>
> SH: I hadn't either.
>
> WH: Dr. A. D. Jones. I can remember having to go to his little ole office up there, sat up by the railroad track. Well, not too far from the old Granite Falls depot.[22]

Dr. A. D. Jones' office was on Main Street in Granite Falls near the post office and the present-day insurance company. Fred Elmore also remembered Jones while talking to Tom Ross and me.

> FE: Yeah, Dr. Jones lived near the Main Food Market just this side of it in that big white house. His office was where the old wood building is now beside it. That's in Granite Falls.
>
> FE: We had Dr. Russell and Dr. Corpening.
>
> TR: I well remember Dr. Russell. He was still practicing when we moved here. They said that he was a good doctor.
>
> SH: Willard told us about Dr. Russell's driving across the bridge and a little boy got knocked off into the water. He jumped out of his car and went and rescued him. Willard said that the

child's last name was Dale.[23]

Earl Lutz verified this same story. Earl said, "I remember one time my mother telling me Dr. Russell came down there to see somebody because they made house calls then. She told who it was, but I forgot. They said that there was a kid going across the bridge, and Dr. Russell came across there in a car and scared the little boy. The boy backed off and fell on a sandbar. It didn't hurt him or anything, but it scared the dickens out of him."[24] Dr. Russell rescued a lad who fell into the river. Effie Kirby had told me that same story in 1969 when I interviewed her. Fletcher Lutz also verified the services of Dr. Jones, Dr. Russell, and Dr. Corpening. Fletcher said, "We only had two doctors during that time, too, and Granite Falls shared with us. The two doctors were Russell and Copening (Corpening). Oh, yes, A. D. Jones was a doctor, so there were three."[25] Earl Lutz, the brother of Fletcher, added more when he talked to me:

> EL: I remember that Rhodhiss and Granite together had two doctors. Dr. Corpening and Dr. Russell. Did you ever hear their names mentioned?
> SH: Yes, sir. Old Dr. Corpening.
> EL: Yeah. Young Dr. Corpening is still doctoring over there, but this was his old man. I remember back then after we moved to Hickory, our family doctor was Dr. Russell, and he'd drive all the way to Hickory if some of us got sick.
> SH: I heard that he was a good doctor.
> EL: I've heard my dad talk about the 1918 flu epidemic. They just died faster than they could bury 'em during that time. But there wasn't much they could do for you back then.[26]

Earl discussed doctors and the arrival of the flu epidemic in 1918. Earl's father sold coffins at the Company Store during this time. All over the world a pandemic hit that caused the loss of more lives than people killed during World War I. This event hit Rhodhiss and the surrounding area hard. Earl Lutz's sentiment was shared by Thelma Church, who lost her father, her half-brother, her half-sister, and her aunt within weeks. Thelma told me:

> TC: When my father died out there, he died in November, but they didn't have his funeral till March because people wouldn't go to the churches, afraid that everybody was sick.
> SH: Because of the flu? They waited that long?
> TC: His funeral was in March.
> SH: Was he buried before that?
> TC: Oh, yeah. They buried him. They did them at home. They did the bodies at home. They would come and take them to the cemetery. They would dig the graves.[27]

Thelma, too, had the flu along with her siblings. Thelma survived, but she had to be transported to Statesville on the train because that was the only hospital in the area that had an available bed. Mattie Munday was able to elaborate on the Branch family's plight:

SH: Do you remember the flu epidemic?

MM: A little bit. Thelma Church's people died.

SH: She said several people in her family died.

MM: At that time, we lived up there where that trailer is now, and her family lived up there in that big house. They had Mary and Kathleen, and Thelma was a baby, and a girl named, I believe, Jennie. Mr. Branch had other children.

SH: She said that her dad, half-brother, and half-sister died.

MM: Yea, Jennie, Eben, and Mr. Branch. But my oldest sister would go up there and stay a lot at night. Well, after they died, they would come about every night to get her to spend the night. They had John and Pee Wee as they called him. If she didn't go, they would come after her. She would go up there and stay. I remember when Thelma was bad, and they had to put a tube in her. She was about to die. I remember when the flu was because I had typhoid fever, and I was just getting over the fever.[28]

Mattie said that her sister would go to the Branch house to stay with some of the children because of the vast suffering that the survivors experienced. Mattie herself had typhoid during this time. Gladys Barker discussed the flu epidemic, too. Gladys said, "Some families lost up to three people, and one to two in other families died. The mill closed, and it is a sad time when the community is sick. Everybody in my family was sick except for Charlie and Papa, who took care of all of us. Papa waited on us, and he got sick later after we were all well."[29] The 1918 flu really wreaked havoc in Rhodhiss, and many families felt the burden of sickness and death.

THE RED CROSS ARRIVED IN RHODHISS TO HELP WITH THE FLU EPIDEMIC.

MOST LIKELY THIS PICTURE WAS TAKEN THE SAME DAY AS THE RED CROSS PICTURE BECAUSE THE
PEOPLE ON THE BRIDGE ARE BARELY VISIBLE IN THE RED CROSS PICTURE. JOHN EDGAR HAAS
PHOTO WITH PERMISSION FROM HIS GRANDDAUGHTER, ANITA M. HAAS.

According to the town minutes on October 11, 1935, more typhoid cases were reported within the town. The council voted to offer vaccinations to all villagers. This vaccine was paid for by the state, and the town paid the attending physician.[30] These vaccines were administered most likely at the Company Store as was discussed earlier by Jack Edwards in Chapter 4. The Edwards family also discussed a drug store that was in the location of the old Van Foxx shop on the lower end of Duke Street, and it was run by Jack Cline during the 1940s.[31] This store operated for a brief period. Mattie Munday also confirmed the Edwards' assertion. Mattie said, "Where Van Foxx had his old building was a drug store. Cline's Drug Store, I think. I used to walk up there."[32] Mattie, the Edwards siblings, and others mentioned this drug store. Leona Hunsucker talked to Tom Ross and me further about this establishment:

> LH: That's where Van Foxx's store was. The Clines. It was Jack Cline. He run it.
>
> TR: Well, Jack Cline's family lived in that corner house.
>
> LH: Yeah, they lived right there on Cline Street. Ed Cline and his wife. They were nice people. Jack and there was another boy that died.
>
> TR: Jack worked in the drug store uptown.
>
> LH: Yeah.
>
> TR: Then he decided that he wanted to come down here and start a drug store, which was a good drug store there at one time.
>
> LH: Yeah, it was busy.[33]

Lena Cline who worked for Jack Cline, her brother-in-law, spoke to me briefly. Lena said that she recalled Calvin Jones' visiting the drug store.[34] I asked Calvin about this, and he reflected:

> SH: Please tell me about the drugstore. Lena Cline told me to ask you about it.
>
> CJ: You mean the one in Granite?
>
> SH: No, the one in Rhodhiss.
>
> CJ: Oh, yes. The one that Lena's husband's brother ran.
>
> SH: Yes, her first husband that was killed.
>
> CJ: Yeah. Jack Cline was the owner.
>
> SH: Lena said that you would remember because she could remember your coming into the store. She worked there for Jack, her brother-in-law.
>
> CJ: Yeah, I used to go up there on the weekends or on Friday afternoons to get Cokes. It didn't stay there too long.
>
> SH: Lena said that she couldn't remember too much about it, so it must not have been there too long.
>
> CJ: No, it wasn't there too long. I remember Lena more at the drugstore in Granite Falls. She and Mabel Teague both worked there. Then Jack worked up there a while; then he came down here and opened this place. I don't remember exactly how long it lasted, but it didn't last too long. I don't know what it was next. Van Foxx has his store out there now. Of course, Jack died just a month or so ago.
>
> SH: That is what Lena said. He has not been dead too long, and she said that when he closed up the store here, he moved to Salisbury.
>
> CJ: Yeah, I saw it in the paper. He lived down around Salisbury.[35]

The Cline Drug Store in Rhodhiss had a short existence, but it was there for a while during the late 1940s. It had a good business and reputation while it operated.

Medical care in Rhodhiss was adequate during the twentieth century. Many capable doctors were available for various crises, such as typhoid, a flu pandemic, and smallpox outbreaks. To be such a small town, Rhodhiss' medical needs were attended to by doctors who practiced in nearby Granite Falls, which is approximately two miles away. Lastly, a list of the agreed upon costs in 1907 of certain medical conditions is attached.

1907 Fees adopted by Caldwell Medical Society

The undersigned, agreed to be governed by these fees on December 15, 1907:

Doctors: A. A. Kent, C. B. McNairy, J. C. Moore, G. J. Mattocks, G. E. Flowers, A. D. Jones, O. J. Corpening, C. M. White, L. F. Coffey, P. G. Flowers, Dr. C. L. Wilson, G. H. Carter, J. G. Storie.

Ordinary prescription or advice $.50

Examination and prescription $1.00 to $2.00

Town visit in daytime $1.50

Town visit between 9 p.m. and 7 a.m. $2.00

Country visit over 1 mile and under 2 miles $2.00

Country visit over 4 miles and up to 5 miles $3.00

Country visit over 5 miles, 50 cents per mile one was and $1.00

Country visit at night double the day rate

Visit in extremely bad weather, 50 per cent additional

Consultation visit, 50 cents per mile and $2.00

Visit to smallpox cases, mileage and $5.00

Writing certificate of health, burial, etc. $1.00

Giving opinion involving legal issues $5.00

Attendance on court as expert, per day $5.00

Examination for life insurance $5.00

Vaccination, single $1.00

Vaccination for family, each person $.50

Unusual detension in ordinary practice, per day or night $5.00

Post mortem examination $10.00

Ordinary case of labor in town $10.00

Ordinary case of labor in country, 50 cents per mile and $10.00

Delivery twins, additional $2.50 to $5.00

Visit when too late for delivery, mileage only

Craniotomy or evisceration $20.00 to $50.00

Removal of uterine fibroid $10 to $100.00

Removal of ovarian tumors $5.00

Minor operations without anesthetic $1.00 to $5.00

Minor operations with anesthetic $5.00 to $10.00

Removing foreign body, nose, ear, eye, etc. $1.00 to $3.00

Removing ingrowing nail, tonsils, polypus, hemorrhoids, small tumors, etc. $5.00 to $10.00

Reducing hernia by taxis $5.00 to $10.00

Reducing hernia by operation $25.00 to $100.00

Reducing dislocation of hip joint $10.00 to $20.00

Reducing other dislocations $2.00 to $20.00

Reducing fractures $5.00 to $20.00

Sewing incised wounds $1.00 to $5.00

Dressing wounds after operations $1.00 to $3.00

Amputation hip joint or shoulder $100.00

Amputation of thigh $50.00 to $100.00

Amputation leg, arm, hand, foot or breast $25.00 to $50.00

Operation for appendicitis $50.00 to $100.00

Operation for empyema $10.00 to $25.00

Assistant at operation 10 to 50 per cent of fee

When surgical cases are out of town mileage is to be added.[36]

Men who served from Rhodhiss in World War I-1917.

Aiken, Russell

Armstrong, Jas E.

Childers, Fred N.

Church, Walter G.

Church, Midus

Church, Cub

Cooper, Horace

Gilliland, Nelson

Hartsoe, Phillip

Helton, John

Hoyle, Julius

Lail, Elleck

Munday, Len M.

Munday, Worth

Monk, Alonzo

Smith, Joe

Teague, E. A.

Teague, John R.

Triplett, Chas C.

Whisnant, Stephen (Officer)

Killed in Action from Rhodhiss:

Laney, John C.

Melton, William Baxter

Died of Diseases-Domestic from Rhodhiss:

Link, George P.

Wounded in Action from Rhodhiss:

Bentley, Jack

Munday, Morgan O.[37]

NOTES

1   Rhodhiss Town Minutes. 21 December 1908.

2   Alexander, Nancy. A Medical History of Caldwell County. 1981, p. 7.

3   Barker, Gladys.

4   Lutz, Fletcher.

5   Rhodhiss Town Minutes. 12 March 1909.

6   Rhodhiss Town Minutes. 1 February 1910.

7   Rhodhiss Town Minutes. 25 February 1910.

8   Alexander, Nancy. A Medical History of Caldwell County, 1981, pp. 11-12.

9   Rhodhiss Town Minutes. 2 July 1910.

10   Curtis, Violet, Willard Herman, and Tom Ross.

11   Simmons, Finn and Pawnee, and Tom Ross.

12   Munday, Mattie and Louise Keller.

13   Alexander, Nancy. A Medical History of Caldwell County, 1981, p. 17.

14   Kelley, Alvis and Precious and Tom Ross.

15   Elmore, Fred and Martha and Tom Ross.

16   Alexander, Nancy. A Medical History of Caldwell County, 1981, p. 11.

17   "Corpening, William."
     https://www.legacy.com/us/obituaries/charlotte/name/william-corpening-obituary?id=15221658.

18   Jones, Calvin and Tom Ross.

19   Jones, Martin Evans. https://www.findagrave.com/memorial/195820893/martin-evans-jones.

20   Alexander, Nancy. A Medical History of Caldwell County, 1981, p. 34.

21   Alexander, Nancy, p. 8.

22   Herman, Willard and Tom Ross.

23   Elmore, Fred and Martha and Tom Ross.

24   Lutz, Earl.

25   Lutz, Fletcher and Tom Ross.

26   Lutz, Earl.

27   Church, Thelma.

28   Munday, Mattie and Louise Keller.

29   Barker, Gladys.

30   Rhodhiss Town Minutes, 11 October 1935.

31   Edwards, Arthur, Jack, and Edna Edwards Laney Stilwell and Tom Ross.

32   Munday, Mattie and Louise Keller.

33   Hunsucker, Leona and Tom Ross.

34   Cline, Lena. Personal Interview with Sherrie Hartsoe. Granite Falls, NC. 15 May 1988.

35   Jones, Calvin and Tom Ross.

36   Alexander, Nancy. These Eternal Hills: A Collection of Columns Which Have Appeared In The Lenoir News Topic, pp. 90-91.

37   "Caldwell County Boys of the First World War-1917." Lenoir News-Topic. September 1941 Centennial Edition.

CHAPTER 15
DUKE POWER

R hodhiss Manufacturing and E. A. Smith Manufacturing operated in Rhodhiss from 1902 and
1914 respectively to 1919. George Hiss had controlling interest in both mills. In 1919 Duke
Power, which previously had been called Southern Power, wanted the water rights, so they purchased
the land, the mills, the houses, the Company Store, the office building, and the school; thus, Duke
basically bought the town for the water rights. They were not interested in running the mills, so they
leased them back to various stockholders. Ned Bean said that the mills operated under the name
Rhodhiss Cotton Mills when they were run by the stockholders.[1] R. C. Moore from Charlotte was the
primary shareholder. He operated both mills from 1919 to 1945, and the town continued to thrive.

In the magazine *Women's Wear* an article detailed the purchase of the mills. It stated:

> One of the largest textile deals made in this section in recent months has been
> consummated under the terms of which the J. B. Duke interests have acquired the
> Rhodhiss Mills, embracing the Rhodhiss Manufacturing Co. and the E. A. Smith
> Manufacturing Co. both at Rhodhiss, N. C. Although the price was not divulged
> it is understood to have been $2,400,000 for the Rhodhiss Manufacturing Co. and
> $1,800,000 for the E. A. Smith Manufacturing Co. The first mentioned has 15,000
> spindles and 466 looms, while the latter has 30,000 spindles and 456 looms. Both
> plants manufacture heavy sheetings and drills. The properties are considered unusual
> value, because they are both operated by waterpower. They are located on opposite
> banks of the Catawba River, and together constitute the town of Rhodhiss. George B.
> Hiss, who lives in Charlotte, owns a controlling interest in both mills.[2]

E. A. Smith and George Hiss agreed to this purchase in 1919, and the agreement was made public in 1920. According to *The Charlotte News*, "The properties are considered of exceptional value as mill property because of the fact that they are operated by water. Both are regarded as among the most satisfactory mill properties in the state."[3] *The Heritage of Burke County* noted, "Both water powered mills were sold to Duke Power Company in 1919 and were converted to electric power in 1924."[4] *The Lenoir News-Topic* suggested that the plants were still owned by Rhodes and Hiss;[5] however, Rhodes left town in the early 1900s as stated in Chapter 2, but he could have been a stockholder. The article further stated, "Then in 1919, working together, Rhodes and Hiss and Smith sold the plants and the entire village to Duke Power Company who wanted the site for water rights. Duke Power stockholders operated the plants… when four men, three of them were Clarkson Jones, Walter Moore, and R. C. Moore, operated the plants until 1945 when they sold to Pacific Mill Industry."[6] Another source added the name of Harvey Moore to this list of stockholders.[7] Duke Power built the dam and powerhouse in Rhodhiss to produce electricity. The *Lenoir News-Topic* provided further information: "In 1924, the dam was completed and electrical power was put into the houses in 1926. The first power was furnished free of charge, but only from dusk to daylight. However, to appease the women, on Thursday the power was turned on at 1:00 p.m. so that the ironing chores could be completed. Later when meters were installed, each family was allowed a certain amount of power without cost."[8] As a matter of fact, meters were not installed on the houses till years later in 1955.

Finn Simmons and Tom Ross discussed the mills' being run by stockholders.

FS: It was R. C. Moore. You never did know him.

TR: No.

FS: He owned and ran those two mills.

TR: Right.

FS: Then he brought Clarkson Jones up here. That was his relative.

TR: That was after Duke Power bought the plants.

SH: Clarkson pretty much took over.

FS: He did take over. R. C. Moore came back up here as long as it was Rhodhiss Mills.

SH: R. C. owned it with a couple of others, didn't he?

FS: That's right. There were stockholders. Cobb worked down there. Dewey Milstead worked there. There was a Hefner that worked down there then.[9]

Finn confirmed that R. C. Moore was the primary stockholder and that he lived in Charlotte.

Doughton Beshears, Butler Monteith, Tom Ross and Shelley Teague discussed Duke's buying the mill for the water rights and leasing them to stockholders:

ST: Now, I remember when they built the dam. My mother was the postmaster then.

SH: Your mother was the postmaster?

ST: Yeah, when they built the dam in 1920 something. How long did it take?

BM: Oh, they started the powerhouse in the 20s.

ST: 1923, 1924, 1925 they built it.

TR: Now, Duke bought the mills.

ST: They basically gave the mills back to them, I think, to run.

TR: Yeah, Duke bought for the water rights.

SH: Is that the only reason that they bought the mills?

TR: Yeah, yeah.

ST: Somebody said that they just gave the mills back. I don't know.

DB: They practically gave the mills back, or they at least got the mills back cheap.

TR: Who ran the mills? Walker or Walter Moore, Clarkson Jones, and who?

BM: Dewey Milstead

TR: He was the supply room man.

ST: Dewey Milstead was in the office.

DB: R. C. Moore and Clarkson Jones owned the mills. Walter Moore was just the cashier. He was more or less the payoff man.

ST: The first superintendent that I remember was McIntyre.

TR: That must have been the man that lived in the big house.

ST: He did.

SH: That's who lived in Charlie Kirby's house. Thelma Church said that they used to go down there for ice cream socials.

ST: That's right. He did. After McIntyre, an Edwards man took over. He lived in that big house, too.

DB: That is right. I came to work here when Joe Edwards was there.

ST: Well, McIntyre was before him.

TR: Who had the big family of children?

ST: McIntyre had Grady, Carl, Jeff, Mack (four boys)

BM: There were two girls.

ST: Virginia, and what was the other girl's name?

BM: I can't remember.

ST: Well, I know that McIntyre had four boys.

TR: Now, what was his job?

ST: He was the superintendent or general manager.

BM: He was the superintendent.

ST: He was under Clarkson Jones and Moore, wasn't he?

BM: Yeah, I don't believe when he was here, Clarkson Jones was here.

ST: Yeah, Moore was the big boss, wasn't he? Well, who lived in that big house when McIntyre was here? Moore lived in Charlotte, didn't he?

BM: R. C. Moore lived in Charlotte, yeah.

ST: Well, who lived in the big house on Burke side that Richard Deal lives in now?

BM: They built that one when Clarkson Jones came up here.

ST: Did they? Well, I didn't know.

DB: Clarkson Jones was R. C. Moore's nephew.

ST: That's right. That's the way he got that job, I reckon.

SH: Clarkson Jones was whose nephew?

ST: R. C. Moore's.

TR: R. C. Moore was part owner instead of Walter Moore?

DB: Yeah, Walter Moore was the paymaster.

BM: R. C. Moore and Walter Moore's mother owned the mill.

SH: Now, this was after Mr. Rhodes and Mr. Hiss had already left?

ST: Yeah.

TR: Duke Power gave it back to them.

ST: Somebody said that they gave it back. I don't know. That's before my time.

BM: I don't know that they gave them back.

ST: It might have been in the deal. I will tell you who built the dam. Reinhardt and Dennis built that dam up there. It was Southern Power Company then before Duke got it. Southern Power.

BM: Well, it was still Duke Power. They just hadn't changed the name.

TR: Now who all worked in the office? R. C. Moore

ST & BM: No, no. R. C. Moore didn't.

TR: Excuse me.

ST & BM: Walt Moore

TR: Walt Moore, Dewey Milstead.

DB & ST: Dewey didn't come till later.

BM: H. C. Cobb

TR: H. C. Cobb, Sudie Anderson

ST: H. C. Cobb was over the outside bunch, wasn't he?

BM: No, no.

ST: That was Gus Poovey. Gus Poovey was over the outside.

DB: H. C. Cobb worked in the office all the time.

BM: He was shipping and receiving.

DB & ST: Yeah [10]

Although these men tended to argue during the interview, they were able to provide interesting information. Clarkson Jones was the nephew of R. C. Moore who was the principal shareholder. A large house on Jones Drive was built solely for him and his wife. The three men who were controllers of the mills were R. C. Moore, Clarkson Jones, and Walter Moore. Mr. McIntyre was a superintendent for a while, and Sudie Anderson and H. C. Cobb worked in the office. Shelley was even able to name the construction company that built the dam, Reinhardt and Dennis. Willard Herman confirmed that Reinhardt and Dennis Company came to Rhodhiss to build the dam. Willard noted:

WH: Were you two aware that the mill on Burke side was the E. A. Smith Plant?

SH: Yes, E. A. Smith Manufacturing.

WH: It went by that name for a while. Then it was sold to Duke Power Company. Then R. C. Moore and a group, I don't know who all was in it with him, they leased them from Duke Power Company and named them Rhodhiss Cotton Mills. Before Duke Power built that dam suckers and catfish were about all that was in that water. Sucker is good eating fish, but there's bone in there. Reinhardt and Dennis built shacks for the black workers over at Rhodhiss Beach when they were building the dam.[11]

Willard added information about the housing for the black workers. They lived in less than adequate facilities at the Rhodhiss Beach area.

Shelley Teague and Butler Monteith were also able to describe the living conditions of the black people who were the laborers for the dam construction. They elaborated to Tom Ross, Doughton Beshears, and me:

ST: I was 8 years old when they built that dam, and Paul Costner was running dinghies up there. I would slip off and go up there and ride in the dinghy with him. They would go to blasting down in there making the tail rigs, and they would blast in there, and they would toot the whistles, and I would crawl under the little ole cars.

BM: Hazel's (his wife) brother drove one of those things, too. They would grind the stone over here, and the dinghies would come by and pick up the stone. The cars weren't very long or wide.

SH: Well, is there any truth to the story that a man is buried in the dam?

ST: Ah, they have told that. That's just a 'dam' lie. The ones that worked on that were blacks that lived over there in tar paper shacks over there at the Rhodhiss Beach. That is where they lived. The boss man over there was called 'Cadillac Sam.' He drove a Cadillac touring car.

BM: They lived in shanties.

ST: He drove the boss man of the dam. He was his chauffeur. Cadillac Sam.

BM: Big Bones was the boss man down here.

ST: Wonsir was a boss man down here, too. He lived up there in the Rocket house. Wonsir was a boss man, too.

BM: Well, there were several.

ST: Cadillac Sam didn't haul Wonsir.

TR: The dam was finished when you got here, Doughton?

DB: Yeah.

TR: That dam must have really been something for the community.

BM: Oh, man I am telling you. On Sundays after they built that road down there by the house down there, well, there was an old road. It wasn't as far as the Triplett house where Kizer lived. You couldn't get up and down that road on the weekends. When they first came in here, they brought an old steam shovel. Everybody around the country came to see that thing operate.

That was something else.

TR: How about that?

ST: I used to keep a king pole and some worms in the post office so that I could go fish.[12]

Shelley and Butler were able to enlighten us that the black people had less than ideal housing, and their job was very difficult, especially for the era. One of the boss men lived in the Rocket house which was on lower Duke Street in Granite Falls. A local newspaper announced the start of construction: "Southern Power Company engineers are seeking for rock bottom on the Catawba river (sic) above the present dam at Rhodhiss. By building the dam several hundred feet above the present site, the company will not be compelled to dismantle the two cotton mills there or remove other buildings near the river."[13]

Violet Curtis and Willard Herman were able to discuss the hard labor put in by the blacks that lived in the makeshift camp. They told Tom Ross and me their memories because both were living in Rhodhiss when the dam was constructed:

WH: That was something else to see that being built. They didn't have trucks and things to do that. They had little dinghies. They put some of them on

the railroad. They sat there for years.

TR: I heard that, but I never did see them.

WH: Reinhardt and Dennis never did move them out. I don't know who moved them out. They were still there when I left town. Reinhardt and Dennis Company was out of West Virginia.

SH: Smokey mentioned Paul Costner, and so did Finn Simmons. They said that he helped build that dam. Do you know him?

WH: Lawd, yeah.

VC: I guess that he did.

WH: There were hundreds and hundreds that worked on it, but the black labor was the largest part. Of all of those eight houses that sit out from the dam that whole area out there was full of tar paper shacks. They were little shack houses. The black people lived in them. The same thing over here where there were Duke Power houses. They were all down through there. That was shacks on that side. They had a shack roister. They had a big robust fella by the name of Dick Bowles. He was the one that woke the black people up, and he made sure that they were up. He's the one that married Tex Munday. That's Raym Munday's sister.[14]

The beach area had eight mill houses according to Willard, and Duke Power constructed small shacks for the black laborers near the beach and near the Duke Power area. They were the work force that built the dam.

Ned Bean was the first person to tell Tom Ross, Elvie Bean, and me that the rock from the rock quarry area was used to build the dam. Ned's information noted:

NB: The old Rhodhiss Mill Company was leased to. I forgot who.

SH: The Moores

NB: Yes, the Moores. R. C. Moore and those people from Charlotte.

SH: Clarkson Jones.

NB: Yes, Clarkson Jones. Several people leased them back from Duke Power Company and ran them. During the War or in 1945 that was the end of the Rhodhiss Mill Company. Now, there's a rock quarry. Do you know where that is?

SH: Yes, that's up from the beach.

NB: Did you ever see the blood spot on the rock quarry where they said that the guy was blasted off? I haven't been up by there in years but going up the river by the rock quarry in a boat there is one of the rocks that came out at the bottom. There was a real dark spot there. I can remember from being a kid hearing that was a man's blood who got blasted off that rock quarry. I don't know if that's true. I always looked at that dark spot and thought of that story.

SH: I have never heard that.

TR: I had never thought about the rock quarry being where they got their rock for the dam. Someone told us about the little tram rail to carry the stone down to the dam site to dump it in. Then it was mixed with cement, I guess.

EB: I will tell you that those Rhodhiss boys were all over those hills and valleys, and riverbanks.[15]

This story makes for mysterious conversation among school-aged children as they were roaming the hills, valleys, and riverbanks of Rhodhiss. No confirmation exists to its truth. Earl Lingle was able to talk more about the rock quarry. Earl told Tom Ross and me:

EL: We used to slip off and go over there to the dam. We'd get on the back of the dam, and it really made a good slide. They finally put an old barge up there.

SH: Now, the old barge, what did it do?

EL: Well, I guess they did some work on the powerhouse with it, didn't they? They'd go out there on the wheels and that thing had, well, we could dive down and go under it. We didn't have much room.

TR: Did you ever swim in the old quarry up there?

EL: Oh, yes. That used to be our regular diving at the rock quarry.

TR: They got the rock out of that for the dam, I understood. They used the train to haul it. I had never associated those two together.

EL: You can still see some holes drilled in those rocks.[16]

Earl and Ned were not around when the dam was being built, but both would have grown up during the 1930s, and the stories from the dam's construction would have been shared by their families.

Finn and Pawnee Simmons talked about the construction of the Duke Power Dam, too. Pawnee lived in Rhodhiss, and she discussed dynamiting. They told Tom Ross and me:

PS: I came here in 1923. My mother was afraid of all the woods because she thought that bears lived there.

FS: Pawnee's family came the year that they started building the dam.

PS: They wanted to convert from waterpower to electricity. That's why daddy came here.

SH: How many people were there to build that dam?

FS: There were a lot of blacks over there. Just a few white people who set the dynamite.

PS: Yeah, we would be out in the yard, and we'd hear the blasts.

FS: They'd pour concrete.

SH: Would they let you know that they were going to blast?

PS: Yeah. Boy if we were in the yard, you knew it. I don't think that any rocks ever came down to us. They dynamited a lot of places. I would fly in the house.

FS: Paul Costner could tell you because he run a dinghy down there. He's got to be 84 or 85 years old.[17]

Pawnee grew up in Rhodhiss, and she was able to witness the dynamite blasts.

Fred Elmore said that one of his first memories was their building the Duke Power dam. He also discussed the poor quality of housing for the black laborers. Fred told me:

FE: When they were building the dam, over there at the beach area is where the black people lived who worked on the dam. I heard that a man was buried in that dam, and they didn't try to get him out. He fell off the scaffold, but that isn't confirmed. My daddy was the mayor for a while.

SH: We heard that a man was buried in the dam, but we have not found that to be true. We have no real facts.

FE: They had some sort of shelter for the blacks at the beach when building the dam. I don't know exactly what they were. Tents or what.

FE: I walked across that dam down there when it was running over. It still scares me to think about it.

SH: Why did you do that?

FE: Ted and I did it the first time. Ted said, 'Let's walk the dam.' I said, 'Yeah, we will walk the dam.' We walked across, and it was pouring over. Such things as the lake freezing over. A bunch of us boys went down to get on the ice. We got a boat, and one of us walked the ice, and the others rode in the boat behind the guy walking. If it ever broke, we had a boat and could get them out. You never see that anymore.[18]

During the building of the dam and power plant, a storm caused flood damage. The *Lenoir News-Topic* elaborated:

A loss of not over $10,000 is the estimate placed on the damage caused by flood waters at the power plant of the Southern Power Company under construction at Rhodhiss. The greatest damage was in washing out two cofferdams and a trestle across the river. These are being replaced and repaired this week. One derrick was undermined and washed down. No equipment was lost, however. When the water began falling, pumps started to pump the water out of the excavations made for the tail race. This was completed last night, and today work is being resumed on the excavations. Within a week work on all parts of the big development will be under way again.[19]

Rhodhiss experienced a cyclone in 1904, a massive flood in 1916, and another smaller flood in 1924. These forces of nature caused stress for the mill company, citizens, and Duke Power.

Leona Hunsucker confirmed that R. C. Moore and Clarkson Jones were over the mills during the time that her dad worked there. That would have been in the early 1920s and beyond. Leona stated:

> Well, you remember that Clarkson Jones and R. C. Moore from Charlotte, owned those mills. Well, they managed. Well, Clarkson managed the office, and Mr. Moore would just come occasionally. He would go through the mill, you know, and check. He was really nice. He would talk to the people. Clarkson was a nice man, too, but they had been going over some records somehow, and he went out there and told my daddy, 'Mr. Kirby, you go home, and stay today with pay. I never saw such a record in my life.' I forget how many years he had worked and hadn't missed a day. He never did say anything about it. He just liked to work. We children were in school, and he needed to work. We didn't have any money, but we didn't know it. Nobody else had any. We were just like everybody else. You know what I mean. We were just poor people, but we were just all together. Everybody worked together. I don't remember any real needy people, but if somebody got sick, people went in and helped and did things for them. We were the average person.[20]

Leona's father was certainly a good worker, and she talked about their lifestyle during this period. She later worked in the mill herself for a short while.

Tom Ross was the first person to discuss the fact that Duke Power had its own village on Duke Power Road (Powerhouse Road). Mr. Ross noted:

> Sudie Anderson was good. She did payroll when I was office manager. Sudie had help from Polly Starnes Moore and Faye Smith. She had several people in the payroll department. Sudie lived over here in Duke Power village. Her husband worked for Duke Power, and they lived in one of the Duke Power houses. Duke Power owned all the houses over on Duke Power Road. There were several. Mr. & Mrs. Hemphill lived in one. The Hefners lived in one. The Andersons lived in one. Mr. Kizer was in one. On down below Doughton Beshears' house in the flatland, there was a house

down in there. That is where Mr. Kizer lived. I believe that he was the superintendent of the power plant, Duke Power. Just a little further on around up on the hill is where the Hemphills lived. Now on this side were the Andersons, the Hefners, and it seems like there was another house over there. That was a nice village. It was small. Those folks could walk to work with no problem.[21]

Rhodhiss had the mill village and the Duke Power village. As Mr. Ross said, the Duke employees could walk to work easily as was the case for the millhands from their houses. Leona Hunsucker mentioned Mr. Massie Mullinax who came to town from Gastonia to help wire the mill and houses with electricity. Leona and Tom Ross discussed the Duke Power village further:

LH: Mr. Mullinax was a mechanic.

TR: He was ahead of everybody else. He was a genius for his time. He was a self-made good mechanic.

LH: Oh, building the dam was a big thing. The dam, it was big. People would come and look. Just the traffic, well there was a lot of traffic on that road. Now they built a village out here. It was a real nice village, houses, but you can't envision it now. It was where that new powerhouse thing is now. There were four or five houses in there, where Doughton lives. It was woods, and then you go around the curve out beyond the dam; you go down to the bottom of the hill and then you turn right over on that hill were four houses. They were nice houses that belonged to Duke Power. The employees when they got it finished, they hired these employees and they lived there. Then a good many years ago they decided that they weren't going to keep the houses, and they sold them and moved about all of them. Nora and Dewey Annas live in one now, and the Ogles live in one.

SH: Leo and Judy Tucker told me that the Ogle house is not where it was originally.

LH: They moved it. It was out there beyond Doughton's, about where that new powerhouse metal stuff is. That was woods, and they just cleared places out for the houses, but it was a real nice village. The superintendent lived down at the bottom of the hill on the right. There must have been at least ten houses out there. Mr. Kizer was superintendent. Then when he retired Dewey Annas was superintendent.

TR: What about J. R. Hefner's dad?

LH: Yeah, Mr. Hefner worked down there. Hemphill, too. Mrs. Hemphill stayed in the post office for a long time.[22]

BERNICE, BEATRICE, AND BETTY HEFNER IN 1930S DUKE POWER VILLAGE. BERNICE MILLER PHOTO.

A Duke Power village home in the 1930s. Bernice Miller photo.

A Duke Power village home in the snow, 1930s. Bernice Miller photo.

Leona was able to describe the location of many of the houses in this village. Precious Keller Kelley also described the houses since she lived on that street. Precious and Tom Ross commented:

> TR: Let's see. Helen Hemphill lived over here.
>
> PK: Oh, yes. There were five houses right here, and one down in the flat.
>
> SH: They tore them down?
>
> PK: What they didn't move. There were four on the other hill over there. The first one that was moved was the one that Fritz Annas lived in. It was moved over here back behind where Flora lives now. That was the first one that was moved. I don't exactly remember how the others were moved or torn down. But the house out here that Nora Annas lives in it right here opposite me, they moved it whole out there. The house that the Ogles live in was the Kizer house down in the flat. It was moved whole out there where the Ogles live.
>
> TR: Now, Mrs. Hemphill and her family lived up on the hill.
>
> PK: She lived in the first house.
>
> TR: Behind the Kizers.[23]

Many of the houses were moved. One was relocated to 163 Duke Street, Granite Falls. Several remain on Duke Power Road. One was purchased by Jack Moretz, and he moved it to Deep Gap.[24] Lastly, Jim Hemphill grew up in Duke Power Village. He commented on the houses to his wife Mae and me:

> JH: Yes, Duke leased the mills.
>
> SH: Jim, I didn't know that Duke Power had its own little village over there, too.
>
> JH: Yes, and those houses were torn down, and they are better houses than what's being built today.
>
> SH: Several of them were moved, weren't they? Then the others were torn down.
>
> MH: One of those houses is still standing, and they moved it.
>
> JH: They were nice houses. Had bathrooms. I never lived in a house without a bathroom in it.[25]

Jim Hemphill's dad, James "Jay" Hemphill worked at the Duke Power Plant. Mrs. Helen Hemphill said, "We came from near Camden, South Carolina, the Wateree Plant. We came here in 1925. I think that it was in February. It was as cold as a whiz."[26] Mrs. Hemphill was not happy with the living accommodations since she left a nice house in South Carolina. She added, "That house was sitting up there on that hill. I saw it, and I cried. I had a two-story house down there in Wateree, you know. It was on Duke Power Road. Yes, my husband was a Duke Power man."[27] Mrs. Hemphill lived in Duke Power village for many years until her husband died, and like mill housing at least one person living in the household had to be employed by the company. With his death she was forced to seek housing elsewhere.

Mattie Munday had a different perspective on the building of the Duke Power dam. She was interested in "courtin" because various newcomers came to town to help with the construction. Mattie stated to me:

> SH: Do you remember their building the dam?
> MM: Oh, yeah. I had some boyfriends then. Yeah, I was old enough to court then. I would go up there on Sunday evening with my boyfriend and walk around, and it wasn't Raym. Well, I don't really know what to tell you. I remember on a Sunday evening they were bringing in their equipment to start working on the dam. We stood up on the bank and watched them. Like I said when they were building the dam, we would walk up there with our fellas on Sunday evening. I wasn't going with Raym then, and I was dating a boy named Farris Mobley. He was from South Carolina, and he was a painter in the powerhouse painting it and all. I knew Raym, but he went with Lucy Church. She's dead now, but one day Farris was going to have to leave and be transferred back to South Carolina or somewhere. We went a walking on the railroad up here. We got along down near the mill, and we sat down on the railroad track. He said, 'You know that I wouldn't mind leaving so bad, but I know when I get gone, you'll be dating Raym Munday inside of a week.' I said, 'What makes you think that?' He said, 'I know because we sit up there at the store on the steps and talk. I know that you will be going with him within a week because he loves you.' I don't know how long it was after that. Raym bought Lucy a comb and brought it to work to give it to her. He brought it, and she didn't come in that day. He said, 'I bought this for Lucy, but don't tell her, and I will give it to you.' I didn't have enough sense not to take it. Then about the next day he brought me an apple. This went from there.[28]

Mattie was able to give the entertaining side of Duke's construction. She jilted the Duke worker for the man that would become her husband, Raymond Munday.

Surprisingly, when Duke built the power plant and started electricity for the mill company, they did not own the power lines within the town. They were under the ownership of the mill company. One story indicated that Rhodhiss was the first small town within the state to be completely electrified. Tom Ross discussed with Hans Townsend the mill company's ownership of the power lines.

> HT: The houses were wired, but they turned the power off in the daytime. Every Thursday afternoon they turned it on so you could iron.
> TR: Pacific sold out the lines to Duke eventually. I don't know how or when that was. Duke came in and changed all the wiring. Rhodhiss had the old wires. They sold electricity to the people in the houses. I don't know how much the power was. Do you remember, Hans?
> HT: It wasn't much. I don't remember now, Tom.[29]

Tom said that Duke came in and changed the wiring in the houses. People did not purchase electricity from Duke Power; instead, the mill company furnished the electricity to the houses, which was included in the rent. Calvin Jones and Tom Ross discussed the power lines further:

SH: When did people start buying power from Duke Power instead of the mill company?

CJ: When was that? 1955?

TR: Yes, it was when the houses were sold, I believe.

CJ: Yes, when they sold the houses.

TR: Duke bought the lines.

SH: Oh, that is interesting. Duke Power purchased the lines from the mill company.

TR: Yes, Calvin, you kept it up pretty good, but it was

CJ: In need of updating.

TR: For Duke standards, yes.

CJ: With all the electrical appliances coming into the homes and people wanting them, we needed to put in larger transformers all over the whole village. This is what Duke did.

TR: Yeah, yeah. Duke really did us a good job.[30]

Rhodhiss owned the power lines, and in 1955 Duke purchased the lines from Pacific Mills.[31] The town minutes also indicate that Calvin Jones and Junior Starnes were appointed electrical inspectors to check on electrical installations and rewiring of buildings within the town limits.[32] The Duke plant bought the lines from the mill company and updated them, and the company maintained all their equipment. A retired 33-year worker at the Rhodhiss Hydroelectric Plant, Jim Teague, discussed many aspects of the plant's history and operation. Upon observing the pictures that Duke gave the town for use in this book, Jim pointed out the water lines that were used for the steam jack hammers. The boiler for these lines was on top of the hill, often called Reservoir Hill. Jim also explained the inspection gallery that is used to inspect the three generators. The lake water is drained once the government inspectors announce their forthcoming visit, thus ensuring their entry.[33] The government and Duke work hard to maintain the safety of the plant.

Christy Churchill wrote an interesting online article for Duke Energy in 2018. She gave detailed specifics about the Rhodhiss Hydroelectric Plant. Churchill stated:

> The Rhodhiss station on the Catawba River was one of three Duke stations that met a commitment by James B. Duke, one of Duke Energy's founders, to bring electricity to the rapidly growing textile industry. Because Rhodhiss Hydro Station retains its original function and much of its original equipment, and it played a significant role in the development of the region, the dam and powerhouse are eligible for listing in the National Register of Historic Places. Duke Energy manages Rhodhiss Hydro Station to maintain its historic characteristics while ensuring the facility continues to provide reliable, renewable energy for its customers. Lake Rhodhiss provides water for Granite Falls, Lenoir, Morganton, and Valdese. The powerhouse contains three generating units each capable of producing 8.5 megawatts of power. While some equipment upgrades have occurred over the years, much of the generating equipment is original and dates

to the mid-1920s. The concrete gravity Rhodhiss Dam and overflow spillage is 1,517 feet long and 72-feet high. Other than normal generation and transmission upgrades, the dam and powerhouse have undergone minimal alterations since the plant began operating in 1925. In 2001, anchors were drilled in the spillway and flood walls were added to the north and south abutments of the dam to meet new feral flood standards. Rhodhiss Hydroelectric Plant in Caldwell County, N. C., can generate 26 megawatts of electricity.[34]

The hydroelectric plant at Rhodhiss supplies various cities with their power. This plant has been in existence for almost 100 years. Dr. Edward W. Phifer, Jr. wrote about Lake Rhodhiss in his Burke County history, and he gave information prior to 2000. Phifer stated:

Before the impounding of their waters by the hydroelectric developments at Lake James and Lake Rhodhiss, the Catawba River and its tributaries were noted for the fertile bottom lands adjacent to their banks. Rhodhiss Lake, created by damming the Catawba at the eastern boundary of the county, is a small, relatively narrow, lake with a surface area at full pond of 3,515 acres with 90 miles of shoreline. The project was built in 1925-1926 and generates 25,500 KW. The powerhouse is located on the Caldwell County side of the lake. Thus, the Catawba is bottled up at both the western and eastern boundaries of the county by the power company dams. In 1925, the Bridgewater plant was valued for tax purposes at three million dollars and the Rhodhiss plant at $250,000. Transmission lines in the county were valued at $291,710. Duke Power was estimated to own 30,500 of the county's 323,840 acres in 1974, second only to the Federal government which owned approximately 50,000 acres. In 1968, 18 species of fish were found in Lake James by scientific sampling, and two years later 15 species were found in Lake Rhodhiss.[35]

The town of Rhodhiss has always served the community, the state, and surrounding cities. Even today the hydroelectric plant powers many nearby areas. Although the company has expanded its sources of power and now calls itself Duke Energy, it continues to provide many North Carolinians with electricity.

THE MILL VILLAGE BEFORE DUKE'S DAM WAS BUILT. CALDWELL COUNTY LOOKING INTO BURKE.
IN THE FAR DISTANCE SOME SHANTIES ARE VISIBLE. THESE WERE USED FOR THE HARD-WORKING
PEOPLE WHO RESIDED AT THE BEACH AREA. DUKE POWER PHOTO.

THE ROCK FROM THE ROCK QUARRY HAULED TO THE SITE. DUKE POWER PHOTO.

CONSTRUCTION MATERIALS. DUKE POWER PHOTO.

THE TRAIN HAULING ROCK. DUKE POWER PHOTO.

NEARBY ROCK USED IN THE DAM'S CONSTRUCTION. DUKE POWER PHOTO.

STEAM JACKHAMMER USED TO BREAK UP THE ROCK. DUKE POWER PHOTO.

STEAM JACKHAMMER WATER LINES VISIBLE. THE BOILER WAS ON TOP OF RESERVOIR HILL.
DUKE POWER PHOTO.

CONSTRUCTION SITE 1924. DUKE POWER PHOTO.

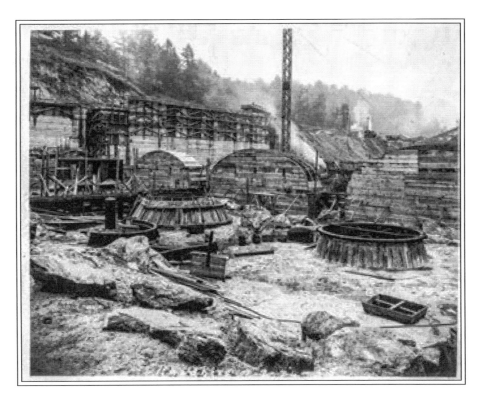

CONSTRUCTION 1924. DUKE POWER PHOTO.

CONSTRUCTION CONTINUED. 1924. DUKE POWER PHOTO.

A WATER LINE IS VISIBLE BECAUSE THEY WATERED THE SITE NIGHTLY TO SETTLE THE DIRT AS PER JIM TEAGUE. DUKE POWER PHOTO.

JACKHAMMERING ROCK. DUKE POWER PHOTO.

JUNE 1924. DUKE POWER PHOTO.

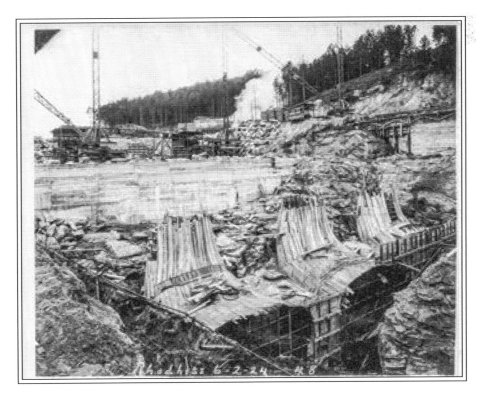

POURING THE FOUNDATION FOR THE POWERHOUSE. DUKE POWER PHOTO.

COMPLETING THE DAM. A COUPLE POSES FOR THE PHOTO. DUKE POWER PHOTO.

DAM CONSTRUCTION: CLOSER VIEW OF DAM. DUKE POWER PHOTO.

DAM CONSTRUCTION. DUKE POWER PHOTO.

THE THREE GENERATORS ARE HOUSED HERE. DUKE POWER PHOTO.

MORE ROCK WAS NEEDED. DUKE POWER PHOTO.

NOTICE THE INTRICATE WORK WITH THE BRICK ON THE POWERHOUSE. MANY HOURS WERE SPENT
ON THIS. JIM TEAGUE BROUGHT THIS TO MY ATTENTION. DUKE POWER PHOTO.

THE STEAM JACKHAMMER AT WORK AGAIN. DUKE POWER PHOTO.

A WELL-DRESSED MAN VIEWING THE DAM'S COMPLETION. DUKE POWER PHOTO.

THE THREE GENERATORS AT WORK. 1928. DUKE POWER PHOTO.

DUKE POWER AT WORK. JUNE 1928. DUKE POWER PHOTO.

DUKE POWER IN THE SNOW. A SIMILAR PICTURE IS ON THE COVER. DUKE POWER PHOTO.

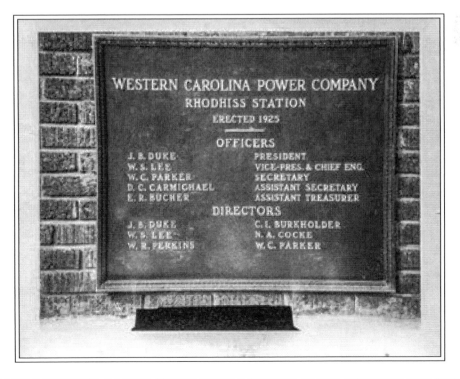

THE DAM WAS FINISHED IN 1925. THESE PEOPLE SERVED AS THE OFFICERS AND DIRECTORS. DUKE POWER PHOTO.

DUKE POWER STATION. DUKE POWER PHOTO.

A 1939 PHOTO OF THE POWERHOUSE. DUKE POWER PHOTO.

1958, HUGH BROWN, DEWEY D. ANNAS, FRITZ ANNAS, AND T. L. KIZER, WHO SERVED AS SUPERINTENDENT. DEWEY ANNAS REPLACED KIZER UPON HIS RETIREMENT. DUKE POWER PHOTO.

POWER PLANT WORKERS EARLY 1970S. JACK MORETZ, KEN DULA, BUD DULA, BEN THOMPSON, CLAY HOYLE, WINFORD WILSON, BROOKS MOSS, NORMAN HILMER, HARRY POOVEY. JACK MORETZ BECAME SUPERINTENDENT WHEN DEWEY ANNAS RETIRED. DUKE POWER PHOTO.

POWER PLANT WORKERS IN 1973. BEN THOMPSON, CLAY HOYLE, JIM TEAGUE, DEAN KIRBY, HARRY POOVEY, JACK MORETZ, BROOKS MOSS, WINFORD WILSON, AND BOBBY THOMPSON. WHEN JACK MORETZ RETIRED, HARRY POOVEY BECAME THE SUPERINTENDENT. JACK MORETZ PHOTO.

1981 MAINTAINING THE DAM. DUKE POWER PHOTO.

A NICE SHOT OF THE DUKE POWER FACILITY IN RHODHISS. DUKE POWER PHOTO.

ANOTHER DUKE POWER PICTURE WITH LAKE DRIVE VISIBLE. DUKE POWER PHOTO.

A PICTURE OF RHODHISS. THIS WAS TAKEN AFTER 1972 WHEN THE NEW BRIDGE WAS BUILT AND BEFORE 1995 WHEN THE CALDWELL PLANT BURNED. DUKE POWER PHOTO.

DUKE POWER PLANT 1990. *HICKORY DAILY RECORD* PHOTO.

NOTES

1   Bean, Ned and Elvie and Tom Ross.

2   "Duke Interests Get Rhodhiss Mills." *Women's Wear*. 6 January 1920, p. 50.

3   "Duke Interests Buy Two Mills." *The Charlotte News*. 5 January 1920, Edition 1, p. 1.
      https://newspapers.digitalnc.org/lccn/sn91068256/1920-01-05/ed-1/seq-1/#words=Rhodhiss.

4   Hildebrand, Abbie Seals, p. 50/section 27.

5   "Rhodhiss Shows Much Progress." Lenoir News-Topic. 26 February 1969, p. B13.

6   "Rhodhiss Shows Much Progress." p. B13.

7   Pegram, Charles B. "Burlington Mills Begins To Close 1 Rhodhiss Plant." *Hickory Daily Record*. Spring 1975.

8   "Rhodhiss Shows Much Progress."

9   Simmons, Finn and Pawnee and Tom Ross.

10   Beshears, Doughton, Butler Monteith, Tom Ross, and Shelley Teague.

11   Herman, Willard and Tom Ross.

12   Beshears, Monteith, Ross, Teague.

13   "Power Co. Begins Work At Rhodhiss." *Lenoir News Topic*. 1 May 1923. Vol. XLVIII. No. 51, p. 1. https://
      newspapers.digitalnc.org/lccn/sn92073196/1923-05-01/ed-1/seq-1/#words=RHODHISS+Rhodhiss.

14   Curtis, Violet, Willard Herman, and Tom Ross.

15   Bean, Ned and Elvie and Tom Ross.

16   Lingle, Earl and Tom Ross.

17   Simmons, Finn and Pawnee and Tom Ross.

18   Elmore, Fred and Martha and Tom Ross.

19   "Estimate Loss at Rhodhiss $10,000." *Lenoir News-Topic*. Vol. I. 2 October 1924, p. 1. https://newspapers.digitalnc.
      org/lccn/sn92073196/1924-10-02/ed-1/seq-1/#words=Rhodhiss.

20   Hunsucker, Leona and Tom Ross.

21   Ross, Tom. Personal Interview with Sherrie Sigmon. Rhodhiss, NC. 20 April 1988.

22   Hunsucker, Leona and Tom Ross.

23   Kelley, Alvis and Precious and Tom Ross.

24   Teague, Jim. Personal Interview with Sherrie Hartsoe Sigmon. Hudson, NC. 17 August 2022.

25   Hemphill, Helen, Jim, and Mae.

26   Hemphill, Helen, Jim, and Mae.

27   Hemphill, Helen, Jim, and Mae.

28   Munday, Mattie and Louise Keller.

29   Townsend, Hans and Katherine and Tom Ross.

30   Jones, Calvin and Tom Ross.

31   Caldwell County Online Records. http://72.15.246.185/CaldwellNC/. Date: 01/01/1955. DocNo: 90066629.
      Book: 304 Page: 502. Accessed 20 May 2022.

32   Rhodhiss Town Minutes. 24 August 1955.

33   Teague, Jim.

34   Churchill, Christy. "Breathtaking Scenery Surrounds Hydro Plant in NC." http://illumination.duke-energy.com/
      articles/breathtaking-scenery. 5 January 2018. Accessed 30 December 2018.

35   Phifer, Pp ix, 24-26.

CHAPTER 16
ENTERTAINMENT

L ife in a mill company involved a lot of hard work, but the millhands knew how to enjoy themselves. They were heavily involved in church activities that provided a chance for people to enjoy fellowship with one another. They went to Sunday school picnics, revivals, and church singings. People savored the opportunities to congregate. The townspeople in Rhodhiss found enjoyment in pulling pranks like overturning outhouses. They had cake walks, box suppers, and dances. The fraternal organizations were very popular during the early days of Rhodhiss. Because transportation was an issue, most people stayed in town to enjoy themselves in whatever way that they could; however, Rhodhiss people were good at making their own entertainment.

The mill company provided the children a Christmas party. Fred Elmore, whose dad, Luther "Shorty" Elmore was plant superintendent for several years, discussed some of his favorite times in Rhodhiss with his wife Martha, Tom Ross, and me:

FE: Oh, yeah. They gave treats to the kids at the Christmas parties. We had company parties in the spring or summer, too. They would have a greased pig and a greased pole. All that stuff. At Christmas they always gave fruit: oranges, raisins. The church did it, too, but not as big as a scale as the mill company. Everybody got a grocery bag full of treats.

SH: What was it like to live in Rhodhiss as a child?

FE: Well, I had the time of my life.

SH: What did you do to have the time of your life?

FE: I couldn't tell you. We had a good time as kids. We made our own toys. We played mumble pegs and did a little courtin. What kids do. We raised cows.

ME: How long did you live in Rhodhiss before you moved out on the farm?

FE: First time I remember living in Rhodhiss was over in the woods near the ball park. There was one house over there.

SH: The one that burned a few years ago?

FE: Yeah, and then we moved to the house at Red Frazier's. That's the old Cobb house.[1]

Fred lived off Park Avenue in Rhodhiss on Maple Street. He moved to the lower end of Church Street beside the Church Street Baptist Church. He enjoyed his childhood and teen years in Rhodhiss. Beatrice Branch also discussed the mill company's giving a treat at Christmas with my mother, Mildred Hartsoe, Betty Branch Terry, and me. Bea said:

BB: My mama married a Fowler. We lived in Tennessee. We lived with her sister while he went job hunting, and Rhodhiss is where he landed. We moved here about two weeks before Christmas in time to get a treat from the mill.

MH: That is the one of the only treats that I had when I was growing up. The oranges were so good.

BB: That was a good treat, too. Wasn't it?

MH: Yes, it was. The oranges came all the way from Florida!

BBT: How old were you then, mother?

BB: Well, that was December, and I was 9 in January.[2]

Beatrice, Fred, and my mom enjoyed those treats from the mill company, and at that time Florida seemed as if it were a million miles away. Fred also talked about the church's giving treat bags at Christmas. Leona Hunsucker discussed this event:

At Christmas they had a great big ole Christmas tree up in the church. Nobody had trees in your house then. Down at the Baptist church that is. I mean it was as tall as the church. Gorgeous tree like the Lutherans have, those great big ole trees. Somebody in the congregation would bring it. They would get it out in the woods because you could find them. They would put it up there and decorate it. Gorgeous. Then people would bring their children's gifts a lot of them and put them under the tree. We never did. Each class treated their class with a bag of fruit and candy. They would call out the teacher and get up and call out all their names. They would go up and get their treat.[3]

Leona said that people did not have trees in their homes, so the church provided a tree for all to admire and share.

A person who spent almost her entire life in Rhodhiss was Gladys Barker. She said that sometimes they might have a party at various people's houses on Saturday night. There was no dating during the week unless people saw each other at church. They might also see each other at revivals. There were hayrides over to South Mountain, but that wasn't often. This was in a wagon pulled by mules. People just stayed at home, or they might visit each other. Gladys concluded by saying that people went to work and church, and that was about it.[4] Mattie Munday, who was born in Rhodhiss said that sometimes boys might walk girls home from church. She stated:

> Like I said when they were building the dam, we would walk up there with our fellas
> on Sunday evening. We always went to church. The funny thing you know was a crowd
> of girls would go to church, and the boys would stand in the vestibule, and when we
> came out, they would say, 'Can I see you home?' If you didn't want to go with them, you
> would just turn around. They had a depot over here near the railroad. You could get a
> ticket to ride the train. I think that it was a dime or a quarter, or something like that.
> The Kizers lived on down from Duke Power area. Ben Church lived over there. We
> would go over there, and a black man and his family lived over there. He would pick
> his guitar, and we would sing. One time that man invited us to his house to sing. I have
> had many a good time over there playing and singing.[5]

Mattie was not the only one that had an escort home from church. Gladys Barker said that one day she was walking to the Methodist Church on the Burke side. Claude (whom she later married) stopped her and asked if he could walk her home after church. She said yes; another guy was at the church waiting on her, and he thought that he was walking her home.[6] The church certainly played a role in the lives of the millhands. Arthur and Jack Edwards said that they also went to the Baptist Church and waited for girls to come out.[7] Pawnee Simmons discussed going to church. She stated, "We didn't have too much social activity as far as going out of town or doing things. It was all right there. The church was the big thing. I went to the Baptist Church. They also had a Methodist Church. We intertwined. When the Methodists had revivals, we'd go to that. When we had revivals, they'd come, you know."[8] Church was the biggest non-work activity in the village. Frank Byars said in the early days of Rhodhiss, "Yes, we were almost in complete isolation. A trip to Hickory was like a safari."[9] However, there was a bus that people could take to Granite Falls. The Edwards family, Arthur, Edna, and Jack, talked about riding the bus to Granite a couple of times.[10] Tommie Rhea also said that she took the bus to Granite for a ten-cent fare.[11] Fletcher Lutz also agreed that a bus ride to Granite Falls was a dime.[12]

Lawrence and Nancy Brady mentioned that fishing gave them great joy. He would sometimes fish till 12:30 AM to 2:00 AM and come home with fish. Nancy and her sister would get up and fry fish, and they would eat about 4:00 AM. Sometimes he would set his bait baskets out before work. He would come home to get Nancy, and they would get the boat and go to Castle Bridge at 11:00 PM to collect his baskets of fish.[13] Leona Hunsucker said that fishing was not her idea of fun. She stated, "Some people fished. I never did go fishing, but one time with my grandchildren. I don't like to fish. Clete liked to fish. I can't be still." Then she added, "Another thing that young people did, they walked the railroad track from the Company Store to down almost to the Hickory bridge. That was just like walking now to town to get some exercise. Young people would walk down there and back on Sunday afternoon or when you would have a lot of time when the train didn't run. That was something unusual."[14] Pawnee Simmons agreed that walking the railroad track was something that young people did. She said, "Yeah, just simple things. On Sunday afternoons when I was a kid, there used to be a track that came up to the plant. I spent a many a Sunday afternoon trying to walk the rails."[15] Casual walks gave the townspeople a chance to talk, exercise, and see the area.

Several older citizens discussed going to box suppers. Mattie Munday, Pawnee Simmons, and Gladys Barker mentioned this event. Mattie stated:

> You know they would have suppers, and they would vote for the prettiest girl. Sometimes they would raffle off a cake. They also had cake walks. When they stopped off, they got to kiss her and then get the cake. They had box suppers. The girls would fix a box of food, and we would go to the schoolhouse or somewhere and people would bid on that box. The highest bidder got to eat with that girl. That's one thing that we did. I don't know, just things like that. We had socials once in a while and ice cream socials. We would have BYPU (Baptist Young People Union). Sometimes we would give a little money, and the leader would have a social for us. Sometimes it was down here in the office.[16]

Gladys Barker said that social time was a box supper at the schoolhouse. She did not date a lot, but she said that she was dating one young man. He and Claude (her husband later) were having a bidding war for her box supper. The price got to $4. Claude added fifty cents and won it.[17] Four dollars had to be a huge amount then because wages were around that for a week in 1910. Pawnee Simmons also elaborated on box suppers. She noted, "I guess that you know down at the offices and general store there was the big meeting room. Oh, that was the social center. Then it was heated all the time in the winter and cooled in the summer because the mills owned it. They had box suppers, a lot of church socials. The whole church would go down there. They had tables and they had chairs. They had plenty of room."[18] Later, Pawnee married Finn Simmons. Finn said, "Ahhh. Rhodhiss had some pretty girls. From up above Joe Rockett's house all the way to the river, the girls were beautiful. Gosh, there wasn't any need to go anywhere else to look for girls. Plenty of them in Rhodhiss. In Granite, too."[19] It sounded as if Finn was smitten with Pawnee. His range of beautiful women went from lower Duke Street in Granite Falls to the Rhodhiss bridge.

One couple that met in Rhodhiss was Arthur and Edith Edwards. They were in school together in the third grade. They were married on the railroad track at the mill by Luther Haas, the third shift supervisor.[20] Another couple that met in Rhodhiss was Hans and Katherine Townsend. They said that they went to the movies in Granite when they would double date with Bill and Mildred Keller because Bill had a car. Hans said that Mr. Sherrill owned the movie when he went, and the admission was ten cents.[21] Lawrence and Nancy Brady also went to the movies for fun on Saturday nights. They bought grapes to eat at a nearby store.[22] Thelma Church discussed the Granite Falls movie experience:

> SH: Who owned the theatre in Granite when you went to the movie?
> TC: Tallie Sharp. He owned everything. He's the one that somebody said came to town barefoot and riding a bicycle and ended up being the richest man in Granite Falls. His wife did, too; he died later. She was Mrs. Maxey. Well, I don't know if he was the first one that owned that theatre, but he's the only one that I can remember.

SH: Is that the theatre that Dr. Jones owned later?

TC: This one was on Main Street about right there where Suzanne's Florist is today. They just opened on Saturday. That's about the only time that anybody had any money. Nobody had money during the week. There weren't any streetlights. Lord, they would burn old candles and had lamps burning in these places and you couldn't half see.[23]

Thelma Church was not the first person to tell me that Tallie Sharp came to town barefoot and riding a bicycle, and then later owned Granite Falls. Bonnie Poovey told me that in the early 1980s. Ned Bean also agreed with Thelma Church. Ned told his wife Elvie, Tom Ross, and me:

NB: We went to the movies in Granite for entertainment. That's what everybody did. We walked back and forth.

EB: How much was the movie?

NB: Ten cents.

TR: Was the movie where I know that it is?

NB: Old Man Sharp owned the building. It was where the City Café and Suzanne's Florist is.

SH: Yes, Mrs. Church said the same thing. She told me that Tallie Sharp owned it. She laughed and said that he came to town barefoot and riding a bicycle, and he ended up owning all downtown.

NB: He did. That is true.

EB: Didn't you say that they had a potbelly stove in there, and you would be frozen by the time that you got to Granite?

NB: Oh, yeah. They had one stove way down in the corner. We would all walk up there and buy our tickets. Then we would all go down to that stove to get warm before we sat down to watch the movie. There was a gas pump at the service station right near there. There wasn't a whole lot to Granite Falls besides Dr. Corpening's office. There was a cemetery behind it. We used to go out there and look at tombstones. Then they tore all of it out and moved it.

TR: That was right in town then.

NB: Yeah, right behind Doc Corpening's. You know where Dr. Corpening's office was. On the other street.

SH: Who owned the gas station?

NB: Tallie Sharp.

EB: Is that a relative of the lady that you always called 'Old Lady Sharp?'

NB: Yes, he was her husband. Miss Maxey.[24]

Everybody in Rhodhiss apparently knew Miss Maxey and Tallie Sharp, and Ned's and Thelma's descriptions of the movie theater's location was verified at Sanborn maps.[25]

Several other people went to see the movie. Mattie Munday said, "You could go to the movie for a dime. Buy a box of candy or drink for a nickel. We would go to the movie once in a while. We walked to Granite."[26] Pawnee Simmons said, "Oh, yeah when I got old enough, I went to the movie. I grew up old school. Girls weren't allowed to do certain things, you know. There wasn't a Women's Lib, yet. My parents were very strict. Well, I was way up in high school before I went to the movie."[27] Gladys Barker said that she and Claude went to the movie in Granite one time.[28] Paul and Helen Bumgarner also mentioned attending the movie.

> PB: There wasn't a lot to do around here to have much fun.
> HB: We had corn shuckings and square dances.
> PB: Ten cent movies and corn shuckings. That's about all that you had to do.
> HB: There were a lot of movies on Saturday in Granite.
> PB: Yeah, ten cents.
> HB: And Paul still watches them on TV on Saturday. You can hear him popping that popcorn. I don't know how he can stand those black and white things.[29]

Helen did not live in Rhodhiss when she and Paul dated. She lived in Grace Chapel (near Granite Falls). Helen mentioned that Paul rode his bike to date her. They stated:

> HB: He rode his bicycle to court me, you know.
> SH: You rode your bike to Granite Falls to court her, Paul?
> PB: Granite Falls?
> SH: I mean Grace Chapel.
> PB: That's when you had to go around the old road. It wasn't tar and gravel. Dad said, 'Why don't you stay away from her once in a while to see if she really likes you.' On the 16th of this month, I will be married 46 years.
> HB: Sherrie, one night he couldn't get home because of the rain, so he spent the night over there on the couch. Back then, you know that was terrible. It worried his mama and daddy to death. The next morning his daddy came over there in the car. Paul had to go then.[30]

Paul Bright also talked about riding bikes when he was growing up. Paul was born in 1926, so he, Ned Bean, and Paul Bumgarner were contemporaries. Paul Bright said that he, Ned, Ernest "Gooney" Church, and Zeno Crump were good friends. They used to ride their bikes to the airport every Sunday to see the planes coming in. When Zeno moved to Icard, his dad dammed up the creek and made a swimming pond for them to swim in, so they quit going to the airport. Paul talked about Rhodhiss boys as being rough and tough, and they were not afraid of hard work. The boys also liked to play fight at school. He and Ernest Church were professionals at this. Paul added that "Gooney" Church's slogan was "Rhodhissians don't back down."[31]

Ned Bean talked about having a hoop which was better than a bike. He discussed this object with Elvie, Tom, and me:

> NB: Oh, when I was a little boy, we lived in the house right below the house that
> Boyd Yount lived in. There used to be a pump in that yard where everybody on that street

went to get their water. Mel Paige had an A model with a canvas top. I was rolling my hook up through there, and he came by and got too close to me. I cut out on him with my guide, and I hit him on the back of the head. He turned around and came back down there to the house.

TR: Did you have one of the wire hooks?

NB: Yes, wire hooks.

EB: Everything was homemade.

NB: With bottlecaps.

SH: Please explain this to me. I don't understand.

EB: It was before your time, honey.

TR: Better than a bicycle. I had one of those in South Carolina.

NB: You took the hook, you know. You had a rim off the top of a draw can. You would take a wire and bring it down and bend it over. You rolled that hook. You would take a harness strap and take a Prince Albert can and bend it to make a guide for a hook.

EB: The trick was to get the hook to stand up and roll.

NB: Did you ever make rubber guns when you were a kid?

TR: No, oh are you talking about rubber band guns?

NB: Take an old harness slap and a clothes pin and make a gun. Take an old innertube and cut out a strip and stretch it out over the pin. You could burn a blister with it.

EB: That's the same way that you made a slingshot, isn't it?

NB: Yeah.

TR: We would take a spindle and play with it. It's a wonder that we didn't kill somebody with it.

NB: I was telling Elvie that when we played pegs, the one that hit the shortest distance had to root the peg. The one that hit the longest distance had to drive it down in the ground, and you had to pull it out with your teeth.

TR: Oh, my goodness.

NB: You would drive that thing down in the ground and get over there in the dirt and try to pull it up with your teeth. That was one of our favorite games.[32]

Ned lived on the present-day Church Street near the post office. Some of those homemade toys sound dangerous, but Ned seemed to have enjoyed them.

Another activity that was popular in some homes was dancing. Paul Bumgarner and Mattie Munday both discussed this. Mattie stated to me:

SH: Pearl Cooper told my mama that before there were phones to call people that she and her friends used a red handkerchief on a pole to let others know that they could go to the movie on Saturday. You had to look outside to see who had a red handkerchief flying.

MM: I can't remember that, but I can remember mighty well going to her daddy's house to a dance. They lived up there about where, you know where you used to live in that house. I believe they lived in the next house there. Somebody came that could play a fiddle. Daddy let us go. Pearl was there, and Marie and Louise and me and Mit's older sister, Jake Curtis, Pearl's daddy, and Oz Munday. There would just be a whole crowd. They would take everything out of that big room. You know how those four room houses are, and they have a big room. They would take and pour cornmeal on the floor to make them slick. We would go and dance till about 1:00 in the night, and we got up the next morning to go to work at 6:00.[33]

They danced till the wee hours and still went to work the next day. The Jake Curtis' house was on present day Church Street across from the post office. The cornmeal feature was an interesting idea, and Paul Bumgarner agreed that cornmeal was used to get the floor slick for square dancing on Saturday night.[34] Arthur and Jack Edwards and Edna Edwards Stilwell said that they listened to a battery-powered radio at night, and weekly programs drew hordes of listeners.[35]

An activity that became quite popular in Rhodhiss was overturning outhouses, especially on Halloween. Hans Townsend was the first person to discuss this with Tom Ross and me:

HT: I was going to tell you about that hotel that they had up there. Mrs. Sims and her husband ran that. He was really old and couldn't get around.

SH: Now, which one was that? Where the Deckers live today?

HT: Yeah, one Halloween night a bunch of boys, you know we had outhouses. A bunch of boys saw him go in that outhouse. They turned it over, and it rolled all the way down the hill and liked to have killed him.

TR: Goodness gracious. It would have been on the edge of the hill.

HT: Yeah, that was a favorite sport at Halloween.

TR: People would put outhouses up in trees and things like that.

HT: They turned over all the outhouses at Clarkson Jones' house. Clarkson would get awful mad about that.

TR: I guess so. I heard that they also put buggies up in trees.

HT: Oh, yeah. Some fella down there, and I don't remember his name, he was always telling those boys about killing bears with his bare hands, and he wasn't scared of anything. One night they went down at the railroad and there was an old crosstie. They took it down there and set it up against the door of this fella's house. They knocked on the door, and he opened the door, and that crosstie fell in the room. The next day he went and bought chicken wire to wire his door shut. It wouldn't do to tell the boys stuff like that, you know.[36]

Hans' recollection of the hotel outhouse was located on the present-day Oak Street in Rhodhiss. He also mentioned Clarkson Jones' house, which was on Jones Drive. Mary Starnes Bolick who worked at Rhodhiss for 49 years recalled the outhouses' being turned over. Mary said, "Yeah, I remember those johns. You know they turned them over at Halloween. Back then you could go up and down the road, and they were all turned over. We'd come along in there, and the outhouses would be turned over."[37] Hans Townsend's sister, Exie Hand, recalled pranksters' turning outhouses over, too. Exie noted:

SH: I have certainly enjoyed talking to Hans. He told me about people turning
over outhouses.

EH: Oh, Lord yeah. When Halloween night would come, they'd get out and turn them over.

SH: Hans said that Mr. Sims had a rough night one time. Hans said that he knew the boys
that turned it over. When they pushed it over, it went all the way down that bank where Hotel
Hill is.

EH: I didn't know about that. Well, I'll tell you just about everybody's outhouse was turned
over. You had to take your chairs off the porch, or they would take them over there on the
highway and tie them in trees.

SH: Your chairs?

EH: Yeah, you would never know who did it. Everybody cleaned up everything but the
outhouses. I think about it, and it's funny.[38]

Exie thought that the Halloween joke was funny, but Earl Lingle had an experience that wasn't too
pleasant. Earl said, "Yeah. I liked to fell in an outhouse one time. We'd turn that thing over, and I
almost fell in."[39] Lastly, Fred Elmore said that he was involved in some Halloween shenanigans. Fred
explained:

Yes, we used to turn over outhouses. Every Halloween. We put wagons in trees, too, on
Halloween. We would take a bucket and put it up on the barn roof over in Pumpkin
Center. Yeah, me and Junior and that bunch put the buckets up on barns. We turned
outhouses over. We used to steal a case knife and stick the knife handle down in the
weatherboarding. We would tie a string to it. We would play it like a banjo. People
would come out of their houses to see what the noise was, and they never could find
it. If we got caught doing something like that, we would always run and call someone's
name like we were leaving him behind. 'Hey, Victor, wait on me.' That person wouldn't
even be there.[40]

Fred, Hans, Earl, and Exie were witnesses to the outhouse adventures in Rhodhiss.

Earl Lingle talked about making his own fireworks from the leftover mill scrapes. Earl
commented, "My mother and daddy worked down there. We used to slip in there and get bobbins.
We'd take them and soak them in kerosene oil. We'd get out on the weekend of a night and set those
things afire and throw them over the houses."[41] Fred Elmore was able to verify that the boys would
make their own pyrotechnics. Fred discussed this with his wife Martha, Tom Ross, and me:

SH: I was told that some guys would take bobbins and dip them in kerosene in
order to have fireworks.

ME: They really must have had a fun time. Great day. You all must have had a lot of fun, or
you were mean one.

FE: Yeah, bobbins with thread on it. We weren't mean, just mischievous. We would go to the trash piles at the plants and fish out those old rubber belts. We used those to half-sole our shoes.[42]

Fred described the boyhood pranks as mischievous and not cruel.

Calvin Jones described a comical production that the mill company officials performed at the local elementary school in the 1950s. Calvin stated to Tom Ross and me:

CJ: I'll tell you another interesting thing that happened. Do you remember when we had the womanless wedding? Piney Randall was the groom and Superintendent Elmore was the bride. Do you remember that, Tom?

TR: No. I think that I was in the hospital then.

CJ: That was something. Doing that dress rehearsal that night was fun. Sudie Anderson is the one that put this thing on. She was the director, but I never laughed so much in all my life at that dress rehearsal that we had up here at the schoolhouse. It was just the supervisors down here putting it on. We put it on twice to make money. I don't know what we used the money for.

TR: We started the Preacher Lay Educational Fund for scholarships and loans.

CJ: After we did the womanless wedding, they wanted us to put it on again. Then Granite asked us to put it on up there. Word got around, and they just wanted us to keep putting on that.

SH: Did you do it again?

CJ: No, no. We did it two times. I was the grandma in the thing. I blacked out one of my front teeth and looked snaggle toothed. Everybody was in it. Scooter Willard was in it, and Feaster Newton. It was a good thing that we had a dress rehearsal because we never would have gotten through the thing if we hadn't. Everybody looked so funny dressed up like a woman.

SH: The Ruritan did that later, and I saw that one. I went to the Ruritan one because Kenneth Yount was the flower girl. Boyd Yount was in Ruritan.[43]

Rhodhiss did not have many entertainment options, but when the people in the town staged a performance, it was stellar. The school was often the venue for these activities. The fall festivals at the school were well attended and provided fun for the entire family.

In the early years of Rhodhiss the fraternal organizations met at the hall which was above the mill company offices, Company Store, and the post office. Doughton Beshears, Butler Monteith, and Shelley Teague were the first to tell Tom Ross and me about these groups:

TR: What else did they have in the way of entertainment?

DB: All of the lodge events were down there.

SH: What were the lodges?

DB: Woodmen, The Junior Order. They met in the hall. The other lodge met in the top of Joe

Church's old store.

TR: The Woodmen and The Junior Order were strong down here.

DB: Oh, yeah.

SH: I haven't heard of The Junior Order.

DB: I belonged to it at one time. It's still going.

ST: The Woodmen. They still have that, don't they?

DB: Oh, yeah.

ST: My wife belongs to the Woodmen.

TR: Auxiliary?

ST: No, it's just the Woodmen. They don't have an auxiliary.

BM: I know that they have a Junior Order in Morganton.

ST: My daddy used to belong to that Junior Order.

DB: I believe that he belonged to the Red Men group up here in Joe Church's store.

ST: I don't know, but I do know that he belonged to The Junior Order because he had a ring.

TR: Were the Masons involved in this area?

DB & ST: No.

DB: Talking about having a ball. When you went to The Junior Order meetings if you took someone to a meeting, they really put on a show for them. It took about an hour and a half to have the ceremony for the various degrees. The next week you got the second degree. Then the third week you got the third degree.

ST: Let me tell you how big that lodge area was. When you went upstairs, that whole area was for the hall.

TR: Were there steps at the back so that you could come up the back?

BM: Yeah, that is how you mainly got up to the hall. Some of that area is where they kept supplies.

TR: Oh, they did?

TR: They didn't have them out next to the cloth room?

BM: No.

TR: Milstead ran the supply room.

DB: The supply room was upstairs in the back of the hall. Yeah, they gave a drink to fella down there one time, and he tried to jump out the window. They just caught him in time. He was about to go out.

TR: That must have been your entertainment.

DB: That it was.

ST: They used to vote there, too.

BM: They had suppers, too down there in that hall. It was about every two months.

SH: Who had the suppers?

BM: Woodmen, The Junior Order.

DB: They had something down there all the time.

TR: Upstairs down there it sounds like there was a lot of entertainment and activity going on.

DB: Oh, yeah.

ST: That's the only place that they had activity.

TR: That was good. You guys didn't go to Hickory or Lenoir?

DB: No, it was all right there.

ST: Well, people walked everywhere that they went then. There were just a few cars. They used to talk about hard times. That Willard and Ruth Herman used to live right over there on Strawberry. They used to joke and say that when they decided to go anywhere that one of them had to stay at home because they just had one pair of shoes. They said that they took turns wearing that one pair.[44]

The Woodmen of the World (WOW) and The Improved Order of Red Men are both still in existence today, but they are not as popular as they were in the early part of the twentieth century. In 1918 *The News-Herald* detailed a meeting of the district Junior Order. According to the article, Rhodhiss was represented by R. L. Herman, Lewis Hollar, William Walker Branch, and Astor Peeler. The report indicated that Rhodhiss paid $500 to the Red Cross and $12 in sick benefits. Minutes cited that 22 new members were acquired; 6 members were suspended; 75 members were in good standing; 6 were awaiting initiation; 6 members were in the military service with council paying their dues. Astor Peeler and William Walker Branch gave brief talks. The next district meeting was scheduled to be held in Rhodhiss.[45] The Rhodhiss Junior Order had a large following, successful projects, and great leadership.

THIS PICTURE IS TAKEN IN FRONT OF RHODHISS ELEMENTARY IN THE 1920S. THE JUNIOR ORDER WAS ESTABLISHED IN THE EARLY DAYS OF RHODHISS. TOWN OF RHODHISS PICTURE.

IN FRONT OF RHODHISS ELEMENTARY SCHOOL IN THE 1920S. TOWN OF RHODHISS PICTURE.

Leona Hunsucker also detailed the fraternal orders and other activities in Rhodhiss. She discussed these events with Tom Ross and me:

LH: Yeah, they had the secret orders, Woodmen of the World, Daughters of America. Those things were active at one time and met down there. A lot of other things.

TR: It just sounded like there was always something going on up there.

LH: All the time. Yeah, it was just a public place. It was orderly and nice. That was your recreation, social life. Oh, oh. A town hall they called it. Everything met. They used to have oyster suppers. That's what I can remember as a teenager. Different people, you know, and organizations would have oyster suppers. Oh, I couldn't stand oysters. You could smell that stew, but I went because that was the entertainment. I would have to go out on that porch. They had banisters all around, and I had to get some air to keep from upchucking from smelling that oyster stew. I went every time anyway. I didn't tell anybody that I was so sick. I just went outside. We had a happy life growing up, but it was really quiet to what it is now. They would have singings, gatherings where people would sing. There was a man who went around and taught singing at what they called singing schools at different churches in the whole area because he knew music. Churches would ask him to come. You didn't get any money. You just went, so people could read music and sing in the choir. Then he led the singing as they called it. Effie Kirby was the one that played. I can't remember the ones before then. They just had a plain organ. You know one that you pedaled. That's where I learned to play the organ. Our family, my daddy and my brother and me, we sang in the choir. My brother could play banjo, mandolin, and guitar, several other instruments. My daddy could play the violin. What is so sad, not any know what went with his violin. Well, they called it a fiddle. I played the organ. I could play any hymn that you put up there. Then other people would come and teach singing schools, you know to get people interested. Everybody would go that loved music. Then we had little social hours sometimes like for your choirs, Sunday school class, your missionary society, and Sunbeams, and all that. You just had all those things growing up.[46]

Leona mentioned oyster stew suppers and singings that took place during the 1920s and 1930s. Precious Keller Kelley also discussed her family's part in the fraternal orders, and she alluded to the Daughters of America, as did Leona. Precious said:

PK: Back before you came here, Tom, we had the hall down there, the
Daughters of America and the Woodmen of the World used to meet there.
TR: Doughton mentioned that, and he said The Junior Order.
PK: My daddy was a Junior and a Woodman. He and Uncle Pink were more of Woodmen than anything. I've got his belt buckle and a thing that they wore when they went to funerals. I have a tie clasp that said WW on it. Just a whole bunch of stuff of my daddy's. Here is a group picture of the Woodmen of the World. Back before you came and we had the hall down there, the Daughters of America and the Woodmen of the World used to meet there.[47]

Precious was describing the late 1920s and 1930s. Pawnee Simmons, too, discussed the Daughters of America, and she said that it was part of the Junior Order. Pawnee explained:

All the fraternal orders, they would have oyster stews there. They had the Junior Order. They had the Woodmen of the World. They had the Daughters of America which was part of the Junior Order. They had the Woodmen Women. Anything in the community that wanted to meet met there. It was just a gathering place if they wanted to have any kind of town meetings or social meetings. I know that my mother and daddy were very enthusiastic about the meetings. They met there at election time, too. They just called it the Meeting Hall.

1928 JUNIOR ORDER. PRECIOUS KELLER KELLEY PICTURE.

Everybody down there knew where it was. We all had our own little individual parties. Sundays we went for walks.[48]

WOODMEN OF THE WORLD, 1928. PRECIOUS KELLER KELLEY PICTURE.

Rhodhiss was a happening place. People found entertainment in many forms. The fraternal orders though offered many activities for all to enjoy.

On a couple of occasions brothels were closed in Rhodhiss. Frank Byars, who was born in 1910, explained that as a lad, he saw a man trying to enter one of these establishments. Frank explained to his wife Jo, Tom Ross, and me:

FB: My dad was a mayor. They went up the river. They were having a cookout or general melee up there, and the sheriff's department went up there and arrested them. That was a long time ago.

TR: We haven't heard that.

SH: We heard that there was a house of ill repute in Rhodhiss once, too.

FB: Yeah, the house down over the road.

JB: How do you know about it, Frank? Were you peeking in windows or something?

FB: A man that I know was the one . . . Dad had a T-model. The man used to borrow Dad's T-model to furnish everybody with the white lightning. That's the reason that I knew where it was. The house where it was is the house on the main road that the roof was about even with the road. Well, it was one of those houses and this man was drunk. He was down there banging on the door, 'Let me in, let me in.' You could hear him for half a mile, and I had no trouble recognizing him. I didn't stay long to see if he got in or not.

JB: He tells of all these experiences every time we come up here.

FB: Well, I don't think about it unless I come up here.

SH: There was a lot of gambling that took place in Rhodhiss, too.

FB: That is why they arrested Dad and all the rest of them that night. Gambling and drinking.[49]

Frank's dad was mayor in 1913-1914, and he may have served longer, but the records are not available from 1914 to 1919. Later in the 1940s there was another brothel that was shut down. Tom Ross explained to Hans Townsend and me:

TR: In the late 1940s there was a house above the old barbershop that some of the girls were rounders. There were two girls. It was right behind the office.

HT: The house that you are talking about was on the left, the last one down there. They tore it down.

TR: It was a red-light district.

SH: Really? In Rhodhiss? I certainly never knew that.

TR: Well, you weren't supposed to know that.

HT: There are a lot of things that happened down there that you don't want to know.[50]

Recently, I interviewed Paul Bright who was born in 1926. I told Paul that women were selling sex in Rhodhiss, and their business was closed. I asked if he knew about it. Paul jokingly responded, "Well, that's what I was looking for, but I couldn't find it."[51]

Gambling was also a vice of several people within the town. Finn Simmons said, "Then right down there below the city limit sign behind Grandma Winn's restaurant. They played poker there in the woods and right there behind Annas' Store on Duke Power Road off down in the woods at Grandma Teague's creek they played. You could go down in there and knock a stump over and find a half a gallon of liquor. There were people within a stone's throw of my house that sold liquor.[52] Several others confirmed the poker location near the railroad tracks. Paul and Helen Bumgarner and I talked about that location:

SH: Finn told me that where he lived on Duke Street people sold liquor within a stone's throw of his house.

PB: I wouldn't doubt that.

HB: Bootlegging was common.

SH: I heard that there was a lot of gambling going on.

PB: Well, down there next to the railroad track there were big old trees and grassy areas. It was just as slick as a whistle, and we sat down there and played poker. There was a lot of that at the Tater Hole, too.[53]

Mattie Munday mentioned the Tater Hole. She said, "Then up above that there was a place that they called the Tater Hole in that bank. People would keep their potatoes there for the winter."[54] Hans Townsend, too, talked about this location. Hans and Tom Ross stated:

SH: The gambling? Was it poker, dice, or whatever?

HT: Cards.

TR: They said that they used to go to where Smokey (Shelley) said was Lover's Lane over there. It was down where Clarkson Jones lived, down in there. I think that they played poker down in there, didn't they? And behind the schoolhouse, too.

HT: Yeah, behind the schoolhouse. There used to be an old service station down there in front of Joe Church's old store. They tore it down after it burned. They would go back down in there near the railroad. They sold booze there. They sold booze at the pool room, too.

TR: Kids when they were walking through the woods could find spots where they knew that they had played cards.[55]

Gambling happened in the village, and most people knew about the location behind the old gas station.

Alvis Kelley told about the gambling at this location, and he added further details about a stabbing that was mentioned in Chapter 14 that discussed Dr. Russell. Alvis stated:

TR: She's interested in some of the outside sports, you know. Like playing poker in the woods.

AK: Oh, my Lord! That's the reason that I don't play poker. Before I ever got married, they paid off on Friday. I would go over there, and I always liked to see what was going on. They played out down there behind the filling station down in the woods. It's burnt down now.

TR: The old filling station.

AK: It was on that side of the road.

TR: In front of Joe Church's Store.

AK: They would go down there and start playing poker. I would stand and I saw people with hundreds of dollars in their pockets. I wasn't playing myself. People never minded me walking around because I never told what they had in their hands.

TR: You didn't give anything away.

AK: No sir. I would stand over there, and I watched people lose the last penny that they had. They hadn't been home or paid the grocery bill or anything. They would borrow $5 to play. I made up my mind, I just told myself that will never happen to me. But I've played poker, and I was pretty good at it. I had three or four decks, and each deck feels different. I had every kind of deck that was sold around here. Down at my sister's I spent hours at a time, dealing cards. See if we were playing five-card stud, blackjack, and all that, I was really good at it. I played, and I would always say how much I was going to lose. I would say, 'Now, that's all that I am going to lose.' The last that I ever played was on Sunday morning along in August before we got married in December. The law came along, and I finished about 6:00 that morning. Earlier someone said, 'Do you want to play some poker?' I said, 'Yeah, it doesn't make any difference to me.' We played for a penny back then, you know. You didn't play for a dollar. It might add up to a dollar, but you didn't play for a dollar. I won $1.65 in money. My opponent sold me his pocketknife for a dollar, and I won that. Then he had a five-cent box of matches. I won that. He didn't have anything. He had the awfullest look on his face. I had been thinking about quitting anyway because I was planning on getting married. I told him, 'If you never let me see you play another hand of poker, I will give you back your knife, your matches, and a dollar of your money.' He said, 'All right.' Well, I gave it back to him. He's probably played poker since then, but I haven't seen him play poker. That's the last time that I ever played in my life.

TR: You say that they played over near Henry Smith's, too?

AK: Oh, yes! Poker Man played, too. (Not his real name).

TR: That's a name that I was trying to think about. He was a big poker player, wasn't he?

AK: One Sunday I decided to go up to the filling station. I went up there, and it was hot. Here come Poker Man out of the woods down there from behind the filling station. He had blood all over him. I am not lying when I say that I could have stuck my hand in that gash. Smith had cut him.[56]

This story was well known in Rhodhiss because Earl Lingle confirmed the stabbing. Earl explained to Tom Ross and me:

TR: We finally humored some people to tell us about the gambling.

EL: Oh, good gracious. Yeah, right across behind the filling station down there in the woods.

TR: Somebody told us about Poker Man.

EL: Oh, yeah. Yeah, I remember when Smith really whacked Poker Man good.

SH: So, there was a lot of gambling behind that store?

EL: It was on down at the railroad track. There was a creek down there, and if you got thirsty, you could get you some water. They used to gamble in the old Tater Hole, too. They used to have a big game in the big hole, you know. They had a little hole over there, too. We boys would go down there and play in the little hole.

TR: You know where the Tater Hole was, right?

SH: Down near where the second depot was.

TR: No, no, no. In Granite and go down.

SH: Well, they told me that it was behind the old café.

EL: It was down behind Van Foxx's place.

SH: Yeah, there was a Tater Hole in Rhodhiss.

TR: Oh, oh, oh. I see.

SH: They stored their potatoes in there.

EL: Yeah, the Potato Hole.

TR: I was thinking about the one in Granite.

SH: That's what I thought originally until someone told me where it was in Rhodhiss. I was told that the first Tater Hole was in Rhodhiss.[57]

Gambling took place within the town, and it was most probably down in the woods because the mill company would not have allowed it within the confines of their company-owned housing.

Another place where people would congregate was the pool hall. Several people mentioned its location, which was at the intersection of Duke Street and Duke Power Road. Hans Townsend said, "They sold booze at the pool room, too. It was right over there beside that store there, and a pool room was on the other side. They were playing cards out here one time and two men got into an argument, and one shot the other in the stomach. He lived. It was a narrow, long building. It got burned up a few years ago."[58] Willard Herman told of another incident at the pool room, and it was a different set of men from Hans' story. Both men told the names, but those will not be revealed. Willard said, "One man shot another fella in the pool room and killed him. The shooter served time."[59] Lastly, Leona Hunsucker lived in that area, and she talked about the pool room. She stated:

> SH: Now who ran the pool room?
>
> LH: A Triplett.
>
> SH: Who owned it, do you know?
>
> LH: Finn Simmons owned the building later. He didn't own it when it was a pool room. I can't remember who owned it then. Later, Finn ended up with the building, and they quit having the pool room, and they made a duplex, two apartments, and he rented that. Then when they remodeled, they pulled that building back to the back and used it as storage. Then it burned one night. Nobody ever knew how it burned, but it burned from the inside. It was in the summer. It was burning big. I happened to think of Finn, so I ran in here and called him and told him, and he came down here. The people that ran that building had an unlisted number, so I couldn't get them. It was Green Valley Garden Center. That building burned. The man was sick that ran the business.[60]

Leona was able to discuss the building's catching fire. Green Valley Garden was there in this location when it burned in the 1980s.

Another type of entertainment was drinking. Rhodhiss had access to quite a bit of moonshine as per the people interviewed. Butler Monteith said, "You could go over and get you a $1 liquor; that's when you come back and divide it up."[61] When discussing gambling, Finn Simmons and Paul Bumgarner talked about bootlegging. I questioned Finn further about the drinking. Finn and Pawnee stated:

> SH: So, was there much drinking down there?
>
> FS: Some.
>
> SH: I find that amazing because I keep being told that if you drank and got caught, you lost your job.
>
> FS: Noooo!
>
> PS: Naw.
>
> FS: No such a thing.
>
> PS: If you didn't come to work, they'd come and get you.
>
> FS: No, they didn't stop you from drinking. If they had, there wouldn't have been anybody to

run the mill. There were all those boys close to 20 years old. You take a boy about 20 years old then, they were pretty much on their own. They just drank. Anytime that whiskey is involved somebody might get drunk before the day is over.[62]

The mill company wanted workers, so if people did not show up to work, they sent someone to get the employees. Alvis Kelley also discussed bootlegging. Alvis told us:

TR: You say that they played poker over near Henry Smith's, too?

AK: Ohhhhh, yeah. They sold liquor over there.

SH: Where's that?

AK: You go down there on the Airport Road.

SH: Was that bootleg whiskey?

AK: Oh, yeah. That's all that there was.

SH: Was it made around here?

AK: Oh, yeah. Oh, there were a lot of places that it was made close around here. Over in South Mountains. Over towards Dudley Shoals. Down here near Poovey's Grove Church. There were a lot of places. Might have been some closer than that around. I just didn't know it. I was over in Wilkes County one time, and I walked up on a still. They were pretty bad over there. I walked around this tree, and there they were making that liquor, and boy I was expecting a bullet at any time. I was hunting, but I wasn't shot.

TR: There wasn't anybody around the village that sold, was there?

AK: Oh, yeah. There have been several around here.

TR: Really? I had never heard it mentioned.

AK: Poker Man did, but not in a big way.[63]

Unbonded liquor was available all over the area as these people have indicated. Paul Bright said that moonshine was also sold on the Cedar Valley Road in Granite Falls.[64] Lastly, Fred Elmore told me about another area where alcohol could be purchased:

FE: An awful lot of people in Rhodhiss used to bootleg or make unbonded alcohol. One Saturday morning early about 7:30, Daddy and I were walking across the bridge and ran into a man. Daddy said, 'Where you been so early this morning?' He said, 'I been over in the country to see about getting some chickens.' He walked on and his bottle was coming out of his back pocket. Daddy said, 'You better put your coat over that chicken that is getting ready to come out of your pocket.' Everybody would go toward Pumpkin Center every weekend.

SH: Where is that?

FE: That's the place in Burke County where they bought alcohol. That store where there is a fork in the road (presently The Cape Hickory Road and Cape Hickory Cut off). Well, you could get it at that old house on down by the creek or Pumpkin Center. Alcohol was sold there.

SH: We were told that if you were a nuisance and a drunk, then you wouldn't have your job.

FE: Oh no, they wouldn't put up with that. They considered it their business if you came in drunk on the job. Some people did slip around and drink in the mills occasionally, but very little of it. They had to have that white liquor over the weekend.[65]

Moonshine was available in several nearby areas. Paul Bright and Alvis Kelley both discussed people's going to Ed's Beach which was on Lake Hickory at the Hickory bridge. Both said that they had gone there one time.[66]

Finn Simmons talked about the large number of children in two families (over 10 in each). Finn said that the two women were running a race having babies. One would holler down the hill, "I'm having another baby." The other woman would holler back up the hill, "I'm right behind you."[67] Gladys Barker talked about women needing an escort if they were to be in public. She said that Dewey Cook hired her daughter, Mary Frances, to work in the office at the mill company. Mary Frances worked with and was good friends with Helen Poovey Spencer. Pacific gave a Christmas party for the office staff and overseers at the Hickory Hotel in the late 1940s. She said that Helen and Mary Frances were not able to attend because they did not have an escort.[68] Women needed an escort for a public event according to Gladys.

The Rhodhiss community had many forms of entertainment. Some of these were attending box dinners or fraternal organization meetings, pulling pranks, gambling, dancing, singing, drinking, and seeing movies. Entertainment allowed the millhands to escape the hard work that faced them at their jobs. Although the village was small, the villagers never lacked for entertainment, but most of the time they had to make their own.

NOTES

1   Elmore, Fred and Martha and Tom Ross.
2   Branch, Bea, Betty Branch Terry, and Mildred Hartsoe.
3   Hunsucker, Leona and Tom Ross.
4   Barker, Gladys.
5   Munday, Mattie and Louise Keller.
6   Barker, Gladys.
7   Edwards, Arthur and Jack and Edna Edwards Laney Stilwell and Tom Ross.
8   Simmons, Finn and Pawnee and Tom Ross.
9   Byars, Frank and Joe, Fred and Martha Elmore, Tom Ross.
10   Edwards.
11   Rhea, Tommie.
12   Lutz, Fletcher.
13   Brady, Lawrence and Nancy and Tom Ross.
14   Hunsucker, Leona and Tom Ross.
15   Simmons, Finn and Pawnee and Tom Ross.
16   Munday, Mattie and Louise Keller.
17   Barker, Gladys.
18   Simmons, Finn and Pawnee and Tom Ross.
19   Simmons, Finn and Pawnee and Tom Ross.
20   Edwards.
21   Townsend, Hans and Katherine and Tom Ross.
22   Brady, Lawrence and Nancy and Tom Ross.
23   Church, Thelma.
24   Bean, Ned and Elvie and Tom Ross.
25   Sandborn Fire Insurance Maps 1925. https://www.loc.gov/resource/g3904hm.g3904hm_ g064261925/?sp= 25&st=image&r=0.405,0.423,0.208,0.087,0.
26   Munday, Mattie and Louise Keller.
27   Simmons, Finn and Pawnee and Tom Ross.
28   Barker, Gladys.
29   Bumgarner, Paul and Helen.
30   Bumgarner, Paul and Helen.
31   Bright, Paul.
32   Bean, Ned and Elvie and Tom Ross.
33   Munday, Mattie and Louise Keller.
34   Bumgarner, Paul and Helen.
35   Edwards.
36   Townsend.
37   Bolick, Mary and Tom Ross.
38   Hand, Arthur and Exie.
39   Lingle, Earl.
40   Elmore, Fred and Martha and Tom Ross.
41   Lingle, Earl.
42   Elmore, Fred and Martha and Tom Ross.
43   Jones, Calvin and Tom Ross.
44   Beshears, Monteith, Ross, and Teague.

45   "District Meeting Of The Junior Order." *The News-Herald*. 22 August 1918, p. 1.https://newspapers.digitalnc.org/ lccn/sn84001806/1918-08-22/ed-1/seq-6/#words=Rhodhiss.

46   Hunsucker, Leona and Tom Ross.

47   Kelley, Alvis and Precious and Tom Ross.

48   Simmons, Finn and Pawnee and Tom Ross.

49   Byars, Frank and Joe, Fred and Martha Elmore, Tom Ross.

50   Townsend and Ross.

51   Bright, Paul.

52   Simmons, Finn and Pawnee.

53   Bumgarner, Paul and Helen.

54   Munday, Mattie and Louise Keller.

55   Townsend, Hans and Katherine and Tom Ross.

56   Kelley, Alvis and Precious and Tom Ross.

57   Lingle, Earl and Tom Ross.

58   Townsend and Ross.

59   Herman and Ross.

60   Hunsucker and Ross.

61   Beshears, Monteith, Ross, Teague.

62   Simmons and Ross.

63   Kelley and Ross.

64   Bright.

65   Elmore, Fred and Martha and Tom Ross.

66   Bright, Paul and Alvis Kelley.

67   Simmons.

68   Barker.

CHAPTER 17

SPORTS ENTERTAINMENT: BASEBALL, SWIMMING, AND BOXING

From the early days of Rhodhiss people were interested in sports. Baseball was very popular in the twentieth century. Since Rhodhiss is located on the Catawba River, swimming was a favored pastime. During the first half of the twentieth century boxing and wrestling were welcomed sports within the confines of the mill community. Rhodhiss citizens enjoyed baseball, swimming, and boxing as forms of entertainment.

Leona Hunsucker was the first to talk about a man's getting killed by a loose bat at the Rhodhiss baseball field. Leona explained:

LH: Baseball was really popular back then. They had big crowds go. It seems like they had some bleachers out there, just crude things. Anyway, they were playing ball, and a bunch of men were standing over in the corner away from the game. I don't remember who hit the ball, but the bat got out of his hand and flew right over there and hit him in the head and killed him. He was a Hartsoe, but it was so long ago that I can't remember his first name.

SH: That was here in town?

LH: Right there in Rhodhiss.

SH: Do you know what year that was?

LH: No, but I was at the ballgame, and I'll never forget it. That just scared us to death. I was young. That's been a long time ago. Everybody was so upset. That boy didn't mean to let his bat go. It just got away from him, but it just hit him right in the head.

SH: So, you went to the ballgames?

LH: There were just a few men that ganged up way out off the field. It was just an unusual accident.

TR: You see that happen now some in the big leagues.

LH: Yeah.

TR: They use pine rosin, and they use batting gloves and everything else, but sometimes the bat slips out of their hands.

LH: But people went. They patronized the ball team. They had a good ball team. People went to the ballgames.

SH: Were they sponsored by the plants?

LH: I guess they were. I can't remember, but I have an idea that they were.

SH: Alvis said that at first, they just went out and found their own company to sponsor them. Then later the mill company sponsored them.

LH: They might, but they had uniforms. I guess with just business names. Maybe later. I believe that the company sponsored it just to get it started.

SH: That ball field was company land, wasn't it?

TR & LH: Yeah.[1]

Leona mentioned that the man that was killed was a Hartsoe. Findagrave.com located Phillip Govan Hartsoe's grave in Granite Falls, North Carolina. The short obituary noted, "Phillip Govan Hartsoe died tragically at the age of 22 after being 'struck in head with bat--accidental.'"[2] Leona would have been quite young then, but she could recall some details of the accident. Several others mentioned his death in 1922. Willard Herman knew Phil Hartsoe, and he told the story to Tom Ross and me. Willard also indicated where the accident happened:

WH: Right across in front of the Methodist Church in Rhodhiss in the old school building that used to be there, used to be the baseball diamond.

SH: There was one there at the old school?

WH: Yeah, it was across the road from the old weatherboard schoolhouse. I'm going to take you back. There was a fella, and I don't know if he was any relation to you or not, I don't know. Phil Hartsoe.

SH: Daddy said that he's not any relation. See, I have never heard that story until I started doing this.

WH: Anyway, he was killed with a baseball bat at a ball game one Saturday afternoon. I don't know who, but the mill used to have a team. They played ball there on Saturday afternoon. I can remember Mitch Church, Spider Killian, and a lot of those fellas that were baseball players. He was sitting on the porch of the old schoolhouse. People sat on the steps. Somebody turned a baseball bat loose, and it wasn't done intentionally.

TR: Oh, I see, an accident.

WH: Yes.

SH: Daddy said that when he started to work down there in '46, everybody asked him if he was related to that Hartsoe man that was killed.

WH: Phil Hartsoe.[3]

Willard said that the first ball field was located across the street from the present-day Scout Hut (old Methodist Church) on what now accommodates the Rhodhiss Town Office. This field served as the elementary school's ball field for years.

Children of all ages played ball in Rhodhiss. Thelma Church said that she used to play in the area called Pee Ridge which would now be lower Hickory Street. Thelma said, "Most of what I can remember is after I started to school, but I played with everybody in Rhodhiss. Down there in the flat where Matt Munday lives, that is where we all gathered. We played hopscotch, and we played ball from daylight to dark."[4] Paul Bumgarner agreed with Thelma's sentiment. Paul stated, "We would get out and pitch horseshoes. We played ball till dark."[5] Ned Bean concurred that ball was the favorite among everyone. He said, "Yeah. The big thing was baseball when I was growing up in Rhodhiss. They had ball games over at the ball park over where I used to live. Back then they had loudspeakers. People would gather in there on Saturday afternoon. They would fill the whole thing up. Rhodhiss had a really good mill team. Granite had one. Highland had one. Maiden. Baseball was the big thing."[6] Ned talked about the ball field near where he lived. That would have been on Park Avenue in Rhodhiss. Ned and Elvie Bean continued the conversation with Tom Ross and me:

NB: If they could play baseball, the company would give them a job. We had a
pretty good baseball team. Kurt Smith was the baseball team manager, so he took in players.
EB: I guess the baseball field is there because they were big in baseball.
TR: Oh, they had a good baseball team.
NB: I remember back when I was a boy and went out there, there were a lot of ball players.
Some went on to the majors.
SH: Tommie Rhea told me about going to the ball field to watch games.[7]

Ned stated that the mill company hired baseball players who also worked in the plant. Jacquelyn Hall states in *Like a Family*: "Mills also financed workers' baseball teams and organized factory leagues in an effort to transform sandlot games into a sport sponsored by and identified with the company."[8] The town minutes indicate that a committee representing the ball team approached the town board to ask if they could play on Sundays. The council voted unanimously "no."[9] Numerous people commented on watching baseball games and the star players. Shelley Teague, Butler Monteith, Tom Ross, and Doughton Beshears discussed these athletes:

TR: Who was the guy in the weave room number two that was a good baseball pitcher?
BM: Grady Reece.
TR: That name I couldn't think of.
DB: Yeah, Grady was good.
TR: He could have played professional ball, I understand, if he wanted to.
DB: Well, he threw his arm out.
ST: I'll tell you somebody else that used to work down here that could throw a baseball, Dock

Simmons, Finn Simmons' daddy.

TR: Yeah, I heard about him.

BM: Connie Mack sent the scouts down here, and they scouted three players over here at this ballpark.

TR: Is that right?

BM: Yeah.

SH: Who were they?

BM: Grady Reece, Bedford Teague, and Lindsay Deal. They offered to send Grady to Duke for his arm, but he never would go. He was a major league ball player all the way.

ST: Lindsay Deal played triple A for years. He played with Indianapolis.

TR: Everybody was interested in baseball back then.

ST: We had a good team, too.

SH: Who paid the team or sponsored it? Who paid for the uniforms?

DB: The mill company.

ST: Yeah, they used to hire, give them jobs.

TR: They brought players down here from Appalachian after I came here. The catcher from Lenoir, what was his name? He's scouting the big leagues right now.

ST: Walker, Rube Walker?

DB: Yeah, Rube Walker.

TR: Yeah, he had a brother who used to catch for Rhodhiss. I can't remember his name.

ST: We used to have a catcher who would drink a half a pint of liquor before he would catch. He caught for that old Carolina league. Perky. He was a catcher for the old outlaw league. He came over here, and they said that he wasn't worth a dern unless he drank a half a pint of liquor. He was a good ball player.

TR: Tell her some of the names: Johnny Hyatt, J. D. Gaston.

ST: There are so many of them.

TR: Q. T. Curtis.

BM: Roy Tramble

SH: Roy Tramble played?

ST: Yeah.

DB: Ernest Church.

SH: Roy Tramble was Santa Claus when I knew him.

DB: Ernest Church played out there.

BM: He was a pretty good ball player.

ST: I was thinking back before Ernest and them.

TR: Guthrie Curtis, Paul Bumgarner.

DB: Paul broke his ankle out there.

ST: That was in Granite.

DB: Was it Granite where he broke his ankle?

SH: He told me he broke it in Granite and that he didn't play for Rhodhiss much, but he did play for Rhodhiss.

BM: When they had a really good team is when they had Cec Bowman, Grady Reece, Mack Mathis.

ST: Mack Mathis played second.

BM: John Hoffman on first, and I don't remember who played third.

ST: Who played shortstop?

BM: Hetchman.

DB: I will tell you who can give you all the history on the ball teams, Alvis Kelley.

BM: Anything that you want to know about baseball Alvis Kelley can tell you. He was the manager at one time.

ST: Kurt Smith was a manager longer.[10]

Dock Simmons was mentioned as an exceptional ball player in Rhodhiss. Finn Simmons discussed his dad and baseball:

> Well, back when I was growing up, I'd spend time over there at Grady Reece's. They used to get the professional baseball players from the mill villages in South Carolina and in North Carolina. They'd take them and put them in the majors. Some of them went pro. Some of them came back because they couldn't stand the pressure. I've seen scouts lined up to look at them down there. There used to be a line of plum trees in the back of that center field over there, way out there. Lindsay Deal was a good ball player. Now Bedford Teague played down there. They had a good baseball team. My daddy played down there. They played Lenoir Rhyne. They went to Brookford and played them. That was good baseball back then. I heard Mitch Church talk about my daddy throwing a ball all the way across the river from one plant to another. He was as quick as a cat, too.[11]

Finn's dad was a player for quite a while in the village, and he also worked in the mill. Paul and Helen Bumgarner talked about Dock Simmons and his ability to pitch:

> PB: When our catcher for the ball team used to catch, he would put a beef steak in his glove. A raw steak.
>
> SH: Okay, explain what they would do.
>
> HB: It took the sting out of the ball.
>
> SH: So, Dock Simmons was that good?
>
> PB: Yeah, Dock threw his arm out throwing rocks across the river down here.[12]

Many people knew Dock Simmons' reputation as a phenomenal ball player, and Finn said that his dad was the overseer of the weave room.

Doughton Beshears, Shelley Teague, Butler Monteith, and Tom Ross mentioned Alvis Kelley's role as the team manager for the mill company. Alvis held this job for many years. He was able to recall team members and their positions. He gave these to Precious, his wife, Tom Ross, and me:

AK: You just want their name? Or do you want the position that they played, too?

SH: You know the positions?

AK: Oh, yeah!

SH: Well, go ahead and tell us the position, too.

AK: I was personally acquainted with them, and I gave a few of them cussings, too.

TR: What year are you starting with now, Alvis?

AK: Well, it's all mixed up, but the first one that I am going to give you is the first ball team that they had after I came here.

SH: Was that a Pacific team?

AK: No, Rhodhiss Manufacturing Company.

SH: Okay, and did they buy their uniforms? Did Rhodhiss Manufacturing buy their uniforms?

AK: No, they didn't because back in those days each company sponsored a uniform and had their slogan on the back of it. Like Killian's' in Granite. I believe that we even had some from Lenoir. Everybody was sponsored by some store. I don't believe that Rhodhiss Manufacturing ever bought uniforms. I believe that Pacific was the first to do that. John Rosten, outfielder and was one time manager. Will Carter, outfielder. Jim Whisnant, third baseman. Oscar Bumgarner, outfielder. Grady Reece, pitcher. Hugh Fields, pitcher. Lannie Knox, catcher. Harvey Winn, pitcher and first baseman. Lindsay Deal, outfielder, and he went to the major league, Philadelphia Athletics.

TR: Connie Mack scouted him, right?

AK: Yeah. Mack Mathis, second baseman. Fred Starnes, outfielder. Ab Corpening, second baseman. Bill Corpening, shortstop. Red Teague.

TR: The doctor?

SH: That's what I was going to ask, Dr. Bill Corpening?

AK & PK: Yes!

SH: Well, I never knew that.

TR: I didn't either.

AK: Ab was a doctor, too. He played here.

SH: Was he related to Bill?

AK: Yeah, his older brother.

PK: He got killed in a car accident.

SH: And this was the first team that you are still talking about? He played on it?

AK: Oh, yeah. Bill was a really good shortstop, and a really good runner. Absolutely, Bill Corpening was. Now when Bill and Ab got out of high school, they played down here. Some of these others that I am going to mention went to Granite Falls High School, but they played ball in Rhodhiss. Let's see the last that I mentioned was Red Teague; he was catcher. Bedford Teague was shortstop. Red Gray, he was catcher, and he was from Marion. Muck McCoy, he was a pitcher from High Shoals. Bill Gardener, he was pitcher. Windy Poovey, outfield. Guy Warlick, he was first baseman. Pert Warlick, he was outfielder. They were both from Granite. Spider Killian, he was outfielder, and he was from Granite. Woodrow Triplett, he was shortstop. Corky Triplett, he was shortstop. Wade Johnson, he was outfielder. Q. T. Curtis, he was shortstop. Guthrie Curtis, he was third baseman. Max Smith, he was catcher. Horace Ramsey, he was pitcher. Hailey Brock, shortstop. Perky, that was Kurt Smith's catcher. Roy Tramble, pitcher. P. Hammer, he was from Alexander County. He played with us. L. Jolly and P. Hammer were outfield. Paul Hartley, a second baseman. John Hyatt, outfielder. Paul Bumgarner, outfielder. Ernest Church, outfielder. Mitch Church, catcher. Dock Simmons, pitcher. Hub Eller, pitcher and handyman. Russ Capps, pitcher. Reed Linebarger, pitcher. Cecil Fleming, pitcher. Albert Barnette, outfielder. E. B. Barnette, catcher. Louie Starnes, shortstop. Ab Turnmyre, pitcher. Bill Cozart, pitcher. Now this here, C. McRary, we always called him 'Screwball.' I think that the C is for Clyde. He was a pitcher. Jim Terrell, he was shortstop. Wayne Owens, he just had one arm. He was outfielder. Cut Cozart, he was a pitcher. He went to the Boston Braves, Major League.

SH: Boston Braves?

AK: Yeah, they were the Boston Braves at that time.

SH: Then they went to Atlanta?

AK: Yeah. No, they went to Milwaukee, and then they went to Atlanta.

TR: Jack Curtis was with them when they were in Milwaukee.

AK: J.D. Gaston, second base, third base, or infield.

SH: I didn't know that J. D. Gaston played baseball.

AK: I guess that's all of them.

TR: J.D.'s brother never played down here, did he?

AK: No.

PK: Edwin Gaston?

AK: Edwin, that was his name.

TR: He lives in Australia now. The musician.

SH: Are those all the names?

AK: Yeah, I gave you 52, I believe that it was.

TR: Isn't that Jim Barnett over there, Alvis, in this picture?

AK: Yeah, I forgot about him. I should have had him down. He was the best ball player that I ever had because he did it like I wanted it done. He did whatever I wanted. Yeah, I forgot Jim Barnett. Be sure that he's on there.

TR: He's the one that was the school principal. Don Davis hired him.

AK: Now, the year that picture was made, I didn't mess with them. I took over the next year. I might have taken over that same year, but anyway, at the time that picture was made, I was not messing with them. Now, that picture there may have been made when I was gone.

TR: Who was handling it with your being gone?

AK: Roy Tramble.

TR: Oh, okay.

SH: I understand that Rhodhiss had quite a good ball team.

AK: Ohhhhh! At one time we had the best baseball team around here. We won the first championship in the Catawba Valley League.

TR: Tell her who was in the Catawba Valley League. Hickory Spinners

AK: Hickory Spinners, Rhodhiss, Brookford, Newton-Conover, Taylorsville

TR: Did Granite have a team?

AK: No, they weren't in it.

SH: What year did you win that?

AK: I don't recall. It would have been back in the '30s.

TR: There again that was mill-sponsored, recreational type activities. He named some names that I have heard about.

AK: There was a crowd every time that we played.

TR: How many hundreds are we talking about?

AK: It was a big crowd. The grandstand would be full, and people were standing down first baseline and third baseline.

TR: There were easily a thousand people.

SH: Did they charge admission?

AK: Yeah.

SH: How much did it cost to get in?

AK: I don't remember any more because I never had anything to do with it. I was on the field. I might have known at that time. I don't know what they charged. I never had anything to do with that at all.

TR: Would they drink at the ball games?

AK: Oh, yeah.[13]

Alvis served as manager for several years. He was able to give a lot of details about his former players. When this interview took place, the time lapse from the interview to his coaching days would have been 30 to 50 years. His memory was unbelievable. He discussed three players who were major league material. Earlier several other interviewees alluded to Connie Mack scouting at the Rhodhiss ball field.

Violet Curtis and Willard Herman talked about another major league baseball player from Rhodhiss, Jack Curtis, who was Violet's son and Willard's nephew. Violet and Willard told Tom Ross and me:

WH: Her youngest son was born at Rhodhiss. He grew up and went to school there. He graduated from high school over here in Granite. He went straight from high school to the Chicago Cubs. That is Jack. He was in the major leagues for years.

VC: I have eight children. Six boys and two girls. Six boys, now!

TR: They were raised in Rhodhiss, too. All of them good ball players.

VC: I'm proud of them. Two of them preachers.

TR: Yeah. You should be.

VC: I have to say that I have fine boys and girls. Jack was a ball player. Joe, he works at the GE plant. Charles worked at Rhodhiss, and he works at Valdese now. Jones works down at the station.[14]

Jack Curtis played professionally in the late 1950s and the 1960s. His family was very proud of his accomplishments as were the citizens of Rhodhiss. The Edwards family also mentioned Jack Curtis and another professional ball player, Babe Munday. Arthur, Edna, and Jack stated:

AE: Edith's daddy, while we were going together, he burnt wood. We would go on his boat over on the river and paddle up the river to what they called the swimming hole, and pile that wood up. We would hire old man Joe Munday to go over there to haul it to his house.

SH: Who was old man Joe Munday?

JE: Was that Joe's grandpa?

ES: No, he came from Alexander County.

AE: No, he was Coline Laney's daddy. He wasn't related to Raym.

SH: Coline was a Munday?

ES: Yes.

AE: Don't you remember that he kept a team of horses over there all the time.

ES: He had one son that turned out to be a professional ball player, Babe Munday.

JE: The Curtises had a son to be a professional ball player, Jack Curtis.[15]

The mill village provided an opportunity for many young men to play baseball on an amateur level, and some advanced to the professionals.

Tommy Elmore said that he grew up in Rhodhiss, and his favorite pastime was watching baseball because being a spectator was so much fun.[16] Carl Compton said that he watched baseball, and he liked to play, too. He added that he participated in a lot of baseball and softball games with the school and church teams along with "make-up teams" in the summer. Carl detailed a humiliating and embarrassing experience playing ball:

We were playing a team from Oak Hill, and there was a good crowd in the bleachers, and I was catching that game. No one wore uniforms then, and I was wearing a pair of threadbare Wranglers. I reached out hard to catch a pitch that was coming in on the outside of the plate. There was a BIG ripping sound, and I felt fresh air. My pants had ripped all the way from the front to the back. I mean I was standing there with both legs separated. Of course, there was a big roar from the crowd in the bleachers. While everyone was laughing, some of the players helped me tie a shirt around my waist, and we continued the game.[17]

Carl also attended the mill team games, and he said that was a "big" deal back then. He knew a few players, mostly those who were his dad's friends. "I always enjoyed watching Roy Tramble when he was umping. I could see him now, pumping his fist and hollering 'Strike' with authority."[18] Cary Ross, who is a contemporary of Carl's also enjoyed playing baseball and watching the game. Cary stated:

> I certainly remember playing on the ball field and remember fondly watching the mill team play. John Hyatt was still an active player. We could chase foul balls behind the bleachers during games and were given broken bats as payment. We fixed the bats and used them. I could always find balls past the outfield fence after games. I played on teams (baseball and softball) that Jim Barnett formed. I don't know who we played against. It was not in a formal league. We certainly never had uniforms. This was during my elementary school days. I did not play in high school.[19]

Rhodhiss provided many opportunities to play baseball and softball. Pick-up games were common in the area throughout the twentieth century. Church leagues had baseball teams, too. In June 1980 baseball was played again at the ballpark on Park Avenue. The town voted to allow Hoyle Ryder to arrange games with the understanding that no games start after 10:15 PM, and any game in progress would stop at 11:00 PM.[20] Many Rhodhiss children grew up playing the all-American game of baseball.

Another sports activity that was prominent within the town during the 1930s and 1940s was boxing. Paul Bright mentioned a well-known boxer from Icard named Big Bill Wilson. He said that Big Bill had been beaten only one time, and that opponent was a well-known boxer. Paul said, "Tommy Elmore wanted me to attest to the fact that I saw Thad Elmore box Big Bill Wilson from Icard. Thad did well in this fight although he lost. Big Bill Wilson's only loss was to Rocky Marciano." Paul added that Roy Tramble was also a good boxer and a good baseball player, and Red Bean boxed, too.[21] Doughton Beshears, Shelley Teague, Tom Ross, and Butler Monteith also discussed boxing in Rhodhiss. Weekly events were held in the lodge hall which was over the Company Store and post office. These men stated:

> SH: Mr. Ross was telling me that for entertainment they used to have boxing matches on the top floor.
> BM: Yeah, it was on the top floor of the Company Store.
> DB: They called that the 'hall' then.
> ST: Yeah, Earl Bumgarner used to box.
> TR: Who sponsored them? The mill didn't do it, did they?
> ST: No, they did it on their own.
> DB: Yeah, they did it on their own.
> BM: They used to box over the top of the old store there.
> ST: They had wrestling over the old store.
> BM: They had boxing up there, too.
> ST: Ole Luke Price wrestled all the time. He was pretty good they tell me.[22]

Several men within the town were contenders. Paul Bumgarner also added a few names to the list of boxers. Paul stated:

PB: We were down there for boxing about every Saturday night.
SH: You were. I heard that Luke Price was a boxer.
PB: Oh, yeah. You should have seen John Laney in there fighting.
SH: I hadn't heard that.
PB: They were about 250 pounds apiece. They would hit each other in the stomach. It was something to watch. They just got in there to slug it out. June Bumgarner and a Childers man fought there, too. It was just for fun. I don't think that there was a charge. They would get in there to fight, just to be fighting. That was our entertainment.[23]

Lastly, Mattie Munday talked about going to the lodge hall for boxing and political speeches. Mattie noted:

They used to wrestle down here, too. Boxing. They would have political speaking for people running for something. I remember one that I went to. I never will forget it. There was an old bald-headed man talking, and I went to sleep. He was talking really slow, and I got tired, you know, and I dozed. Directly, he started beating on the desk and started hollering, 'The end's a coming. The end's a coming.' I jumped up and started to run. Raym's sister was with me, and she saw me. It woke me up when he was hollering.[24]

Many people recalled the boxing events that took place above the Company Store. Saturday nights were full of excitement at the hall.

Another favorite sports pastime was swimming. Earl Lingle was a very good swimmer who had a reputation for long distances. Earl told Tom Ross and me about his wintertime swimming adventure:

EL: That summer in '47 Ray Parker and I jumped in the river at the bridge and swam down to the big trestle and walked back up the railroad, so that conversation started there, and these fellas didn't believe that we could swim that far. When the wheels were on, you know that you could just float. The current would carry you on down. So, one thing led to another, and I didn't want them to put me down, you know. This one fella said as he pointed down between the mills, 'Well, that's a long way right there. I bet you can't swim that.' I said, 'Well, what do you bet?' It just happened to be payday. My check was for $24 and some few cents. I think his was about the same. He threw his check on the floor, and I threw mine on top of it. Winny Icard took the money. I went home and put on my bathing suit and waded through the December snow and jumped in the river and came out on the other side. It was shift-changing time, and both banks were full of people watching it. I went up into the waste house and covered up with some cotton and got pretty warm.

TR: Did you ever swim in the old quarry up there?

EL: Oh, yes. That used to be our regular diving at the Rock Quarry.

SH: Well, I like the story about winning the wager. So, the man gave you, his check?

EL: Yes, I won it.

SH: Who was the man?

EL: Bud. I came an ace of getting Dude's check, too. He threw his check down, and then he reached down there and grabbed it when he saw that Winny was going to take it.[25]

The cold weather would have caused many people to wager against Earl, but he was able to win the bet. Tommy Elmore attested to Earl's victory. Tommy stated, "I saw Earl Lingle win a paycheck because he bet people that he could swim across the river in December."[26] Several other people took the plunge and went swimming in the wintertime. Arthur and Jack Edwards mentioned this to Tom Ross and me:

AE: I swam in the river several times. I swam from up above Doughton's house to over to the beach.

SH: Earl said that this was in December when he swam the river.

AE: Oh yeah, a lot of people swam the river in the winter.

TR: The winters were colder then than they are now, right?

JE: Didn't the lake freeze over one time?

AE: Oh, yeah.[27]

The Catawba River was so enticing that several young people ventured into its depths in the cold of the winter. Louise Keller talked about her sister Sharon swimming the river. Louise said, "I never did do it, but Sharon used to slip off and go swim in that Ferguson Lake, with Boney Edwards. Sharon was a little younger than I was, but we used to love to go up there to that river."[28]

Rhodhiss offered many chances for an active lifestyle. People chose to play baseball and softball, swim, or box. The townspeople worked hard and played hard. They enjoyed the company of their fellow athletes and relished the fact that they were having fellowship with people that shared a common interest in the sport and the town. They savored these moments as a respite from mill work.

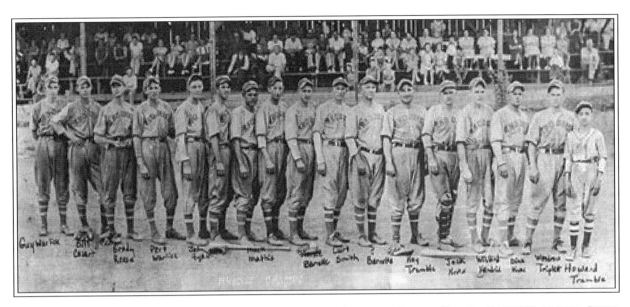

1930S BASEBALL TEAM: L TO R: GUY WARLICK, BILL COZART, GRADY REESE, PERT WARLICK, JOHN HYATT, MACK MATHIS, HORACE BARNETTE, CURT SMITH, _____ BARNETTE, ROY TRAMBLE, JOCK KNOX, WILLARD HENDRIX, DINK KNOX, WOODROW TRIPLETT, HOWARD TRAMBLE.
BUTLER MONTEITH PHOTO.

1950S BALL TEAM. DENNIS KINCAID, JOHN HYATT, LEONARD HARRIS, CORKY TRIPLETT, TOMMY WRIGHT, HYATT, WAYNE HARRISON, GARY HENSON, ? , JOE KINCAID, ERNEST CHURCH, JOHN RHEA, ROY TRAMBLE, JOE KELLEY, MR. MASSAGEE, ?, WAYNE HOLLAR, JOHNNY SIMMONS, MAYBE GRADY REECE, CHARLIE HAYES, JIM BARNETT, PAUL BUMGARNER. TOMMIE HAAS RHEA PHOTO.
ALVIS KELLEY IDENTIFIED THE TEAM.

1950 Rhodhiss Champions, Jim Barnett, Burgess Smith, Sam Travis, Tommy Wycoff, Ernest Church, Paul Bumgarner, Grady Reese, Gene Miller, Duck Pons, Q. T. Curtis, Les Bowman, Roy Tramble, John Hyatt, Johnny Simmons, T. Roberts, Jay Hurst, Pete Berry, Wade Johnson. Granite Falls Press Photo via Yvonne Hentschel.

Rhodhiss Baseball Field on Park Avenue, 1960s. Sherrie Hartsoe Sigmon photo.

1962 RURITAN-SPONSORED BASEBALL TEAM: JOHNNY ALDRIDGE, JOHNNY ELROD, IVEY WALSH, NEIL MORRISON, PAUL LUNSFORD, BARRY ROBERTS, BILLY ELMORE, GEORGE KELLER, JERRY GILBERT, TERRY WILLIAMS, BILLY WILLIAMS, JACKIE SIMMONS. *GRANITE FALLS PRESS* PHOTO.

RURITAN-SPONSORED BASEBALL TEAM IN 1962: BARRY BOWMAN, RICK BROWN, JACKIE WILLIAMS, RANDY BOWMAN, DENNIS CHURCH, DONNIE CHILDERS, JAMES CHURCH, MIKE POPE, STEVE SIMMONS, STEVE LUNSFORD. *GRANITE FALLS PRESS* PHOTO.

1970S RHODHISS BASEBALL TEAM: RANDY BUMGARNER, STEVE LUNSFORD, __CLARK, __CLARK, BUSTER CHURCH, COTTON LINGERFELT, BUD WINKLER, TERRY EDWARDS. CARL HOLLAR PHOTO.

TERRY EDWARDS, JERRY CHILDERS, AND OTHERS. CARL HOLLAR PHOTO.

JACK CURTIS FROM RHODHISS INDUCTED INTO THE CALDWELL COUNTY SPORTS HALL OF FAME.
EDDIE SIPES PHOTO.

NOTES

1   Hunsucker, Leona and Tom Ross.
2   "Hartsoe, Phillip." Find a Grave. https://www.findagrave.com/memorial/95862105/philip-govan-hartsoe.
3   Herman, Willard and Tom Ross.
4   Church, Thelma.
5   Bumgarner, Paul and Helen.
6   Bean, Ned and Elvie and Tom Ross.
7   Bean, Ned and Elvie and Tom Ross.
8   Hall, p 135.
9   Rhodhiss Town Minutes. 5 July 1933.
10   Beshears, Monteith, Ross, Teague.
11   Simmons, Finn and Pawnee and Tom Ross.
12   Bumgarner, Paul and Helen.
13   Kelley, Alvis and Precious and Tom Ross.
14   Curtis, Herman, and Ross.
15   Edwards, Arthur and Jack and Edna Edwards Laney Stilwell and Tom Ross.
16   Elmore, Tommy.
17   Compton, Carl. Email Interview. 22 June 2017.
18   Compton, Carl.
19   Ross, Cary. Email Interview. 21 June 2017.
20   Rhodhiss Town Minutes. 10 June 1980.
21   Bright, Paul.
22   Beshears, Monteith, Ross, and Teague.
23   Bumgarner, Paul and Helen.
24   Munday, Mattie and Louise Keller.
25   Lingle, Earl and Tom Ross.
26   Elmore, Tommy.
27   Edwards, Arthur and Jack and Edna Edwards Laney Stilwell and Tom Ross.
28   Munday, Mattie and Louise Keller.

CHAPTER 18
UNIONS AND THE GREAT DEPRESSION

T he Great Depression hit the United States hard in the late 1920s and the early 1930s. Rhodhiss was spared the brunt of this economic crisis, but people were still affected. Along this same time and continuing into the 1940s several attempts were made to unionize textile facilities throughout the Carolinas. Rhodhiss citizens saw union organizers among their midst. The union was never able to mobilize the Rhodhiss employees enough to obtain a union; however, efforts came close in the 1940s. Rhodhiss experienced the Depression setbacks and the unions' flying squadrons.

Jacquelyn Hall states in her book, *Like a Family*, that Francis Gorman, the vice president of the United Textile Workers encouraged "'flying squadrons' of cars and trucks to speed through the countryside."[1] They flocked to textile villages throughout the South trying to find people who were sympathetic to the union's cause. Some millhands found solace in their literature because they felt that they were not being treated fairly by management; however, the majority in Rhodhiss found unions to be distasteful. Hall stated that oppressed mill workers "were like any other factor of production--a commodity to be purchased as cheaply and used as efficiently as possible."[2] Several people who worked at the Rhodhiss Manufacturing Company discussed the flying squadrons' appearances in Rhodhiss. Mattie Munday said, "They shut the mill down one time when they thought that the union was coming. They sent everybody home."[3] Mill company executives sent employees home to avoid the encounter with the unionizers. This was either for the millhands' safety, or it could have been to keep them ill-informed. Fred Elmore talked about going with his dad, Luther "Shorty" Elmore, on one occasion when the flying squadron roared through town. Fred noted to Tom Ross and me:

SH: Were you there when the flying squadrons came through?
FE: Oh, I was working the night they came through. Well, Clarkson Jones heard that they were coming. He owned most of it at that time. So, he went and got Dad, and I went with them. They thought about closing the plants. When they came, Clarkson Jones talked to them.

Clarkson was high on the steps of the second floor. He told them that they didn't want any trouble. People didn't want anything to do with the union. Clarkson told them that if they wanted trouble, that is what they would have to get. They were outnumbered, so they finally left.

TR: They didn't go in the plants, then?

FE: Oh, no. Back then people held the plant together. They came around dark; I would guess. Back then about 99% of the people in the plant were armed. So, they didn't go in.

SH: I bet that was a tense situation.

FE: Yes, it was. One wrong move from either side, and it would have been trouble.

TR: What kind of guy was Clarkson Jones?

FE: One of the finest men you ever saw. He would give you the shirt off his back. He lived where Richard Deal lives now.[4]

Clarkson Jones lived on present-day Jones Drive. Fred stated that they thought about closing the plant. If Fred's estimate of 99% of the employees' being armed is accurate, then the situation could have gotten bloody. The flying squadrons came through Rhodhiss on several occasions, and one time according to Mattie Munday, Doughton Beshears, Shelley Teague, Butler Monteith and Hans Townsend, the plant was closed. Beshears, Teague, and Monteith discussed this with Tom Ross and me:

TR: Well, I remember one time we were afraid that the union was coming in.

DB: Yeah, they came around up there around Horseshoe Curve up there, yelling and going on.

ST: During the Depression when Rhodhiss had it, they came in here in a truck. You remember it. They came in and were the darnedest looking things that you've ever seen.

DB: I talked to the sheriff. We called Clarkson Jones down here. A sheriff and a deputy came. Clarkson Jones reared back and said, 'You, SOBs better get away from here.' They left. The sheriff was there. They ran them off.

TR: What year was that?

BM: That was back in the 30s.

TR: That's the same time that they hit Lyman, South Carolina. Flying squadrons.

ST: Yeah, that's it, flying squadrons.

TR: They went from one mill to another.

BM: They knew that they were coming. Clarkson was ready for them. He was standing up at the mill on the hill. He already had everybody notified.

DB: They shut the mills down, too.

BM: Yeah, when they saw them coming, Clarkson gave a signal, and the people went flying out of there. Before they could get to the mill, everybody had gone home.

ST: They tried several times, but they didn't have the gang coming around like in the 30s.

BM: It was a fleet of cars that came in here in the 30s.

ST: I remember the truck.

BM: They were not a good bunch.

ST: Yeah, yeah.

TR: We used to go to work, and there were machine guns on top of the mill in case anything happened in South Carolina.

ST: In Lyman? Where are you originally from?

TR: Close to Lyman. Greer. Seven miles. I worked 13 years down there before I came here. I remember the union tried to line us up a preacher to preach. He was for the union. He was in a boxcar outside the gate. He would preach all day.

ST: Did Pacific own Lyman when you were there?

TR: Oh, yeah. Pacific started in Lyman in the 1920s.

ST: You were with Pacific when you came up here.

TR: Right, right. They built Lyman way back in 1922.[5]

Mr. Ross discussed the National Guard's presence at the mill company in South Carolina when the flying squadrons came through. In Rhodhiss Doughton Beshears who was involved in policing at the time said that the sheriff's office came to assist. Doughton also said that they came around Horseshoe Curve. That would be behind the Burke County plant at the park on Carolina Avenue.

Hans Townsend talked to Tom Ross and me about the flying squadrons' coming to Rhodhiss. Hans noted:

TR: She's trying to accumulate the history. Hans, this was a good place.

HT: It was.

TR: It had to be.

HT: Yeah, it had to be. Well, there was one or two every now and then that didn't want to work, but not often. Most people wanted to work.

TR: And the union didn't have a chance of coming in here, did they?

HT: They tried one time, but they didn't get anywhere. I know back there when we worked 12 hours, they came through here, a bunch of them one time, and Clarkson Jones came over to the mill and shut it down. He sent us home. They were over there at the mill. Clarkson opened it back up the next morning.

TR: Is that when the flying squadron came around?

HT: Yeah, they started back up the next morning though. They didn't come back for years. They couldn't organize a union down here.

TR: That's when Mr. Elmore, they thought that it was going to be in the Burke plant where you were at, and they went over to the other mill.

HT: Way back then in the 30s they came through here though.

TR: Yeah, that bunch tried to shut down a lot of mills.

HT: I heard that they were having a lot of trouble in Gastonia back then.

TR: That is where they started.

HT: I think that they shot someone down there. Two or three, or something. Down there about Firestone or something.[6]

Hans alluded to the Firestone Mill strike in 1929. The Rhodhiss interviewees were against unionization; however, in Gaston County many people were for unions. Ella May Wiggins exposed the millhands' poor working conditions and low pay.[7] In 1924 Ella moved to Gaston County where she hoped that she could find a good job with decent pay. Unfortunately, this was a time of upheaval in North Carolina textiles. Women were being paid the lowest wages.[8] On September 14, 1929 "'in broad daylight, a caravan of gun thugs ambushed a truckload of unarmed Bessemer City strikers enroute to a union rally in South Gastonia, and shot Wiggins, then pregnant with her tenth child, in the chest.'"[9] Rhodhiss was fortunate that no one was hurt during the visits from the flying squadrons.

Calvin Jones and Tom Ross discussed union organizers coming to Rhodhiss in the late 1940s. They also discussed their experiences with flying squadrons during the 1930s in South Carolina where they lived prior to moving to Rhodhiss. They stated:

CJ: I don't know if Tom told you this. They tried to organize a union down here one time. They'd come around and stand at the gate and pass out these leaflets, you know, trying to get people to join the union. I had a watchman down there that fired boilers before we changed over. He was firing the boiler, and he did the watching. He came out one day, and this guy handed him a leaflet. He said, 'I don't want that thing.' He refused it and pushed it aside. He walked on. A day or so later they were passing out leaflets again. He told them, 'I told you not to give me one of those things.' He grabbed the fella by the back of the neck. Do you remember this, Tom?

TR: No, no.

CJ: He headed toward the river with him. He was going to throw him in the river. He was a little ole bitty fellow.

TR: Oh, my goodness.

CJ: He was my watchman. A fine boy. Anyhow, Joe Cobb got a letter from the union about that. So, Joe wrote a nice letter back and told them 'from now on, we will assure the guy has police protection.' We never did say anything to the night watchman about it.

TR: I am sure that guy was scared.

CJ: Yes, he was. That's how much the watchman felt for the company, and he felt for me. He just felt like I was doing the right thing. That's the type of employee that he was. I had another one just the same way. Ray Hart. He was one of my watchmen, too. He was just as faithful as he could be.

TR: Some people were interested in the union. There were always a few around.

CJ: We always had a few. They were holding meetings around back then.

TR: It was in the 30s that the flying squadrons came around. Was that '36 and '37? I was in Lyman.

CJ: Somewhere in that area. Sometime in the 30s, I was in high school in Greenville, South Carolina, and I was walking home, a bunch of us, from school one day. This gang of flying squadrons came by. I had never seen so many cars. I looked, and these people were driving down and pulled up to the mill and had parked. The mills knew that they were coming and had the National Guard there and the fence up and the gates locked. They had machine guns sitting down in front of the big gate. We kids were walking along there, and they had backed the truck up getting ready to knock the gate down. The lieutenant that oversaw the National Guard said, 'When I say fire, I mean fire to kill.'

TR: Shoooo!

CJ: Bud, you should have seen the people scatter, especially us kids. They didn't back that truck over that gate either.

TR: In Lyman the president of the union was in the National Guard.

CJ: Is that right?

TR: The Guard had gone out and lined the street in Lyman in front of the mill. He had to get in line just like everybody else. They were using bayonets and all.

CJ: He was going to fight against it even though he was president.

TR: That's right.

CJ: He had to do what he was told.[10]

Rhodhiss was spared from violence during the attempts for unionization, but the mill company came close to unionizing "in 1940, seventy-five percent of the employees in Mill No. 2 signed for the union, but the vote had to include Mill No. 1 so the overall election was canceled. Workers realized that the union would not materialize at this time."[11] Several other interviewees said that in the early 1960s, the union vote came close again, but it did not pass. Mary Starnes Bolick discussed the union with Tom Ross and me. She stated:

SH: Were you there when they were trying to bring in the union?

MB: Yeah.

SH: How was that taken by the employees?

MB: Well, some wanted it, and some didn't, but boy, I never did want to get involved in that mess.

TR: Well, it liked to have gone in in number two mill.

MB: A couple of times it did. That's all that you could hear them talking about. The union. The union.

SH: I didn't realize that it came that close.

TR: Oh, yeah.

MB: They'd stand outside the plant handing out these ole papers. Sometimes I'd take one to see what was going on, so I'd be aware of it.

TR: I remember they sent Mr. Elmore over there from number one. Thinking that Mr. Elmore could settle things, you know.

MB: Yeah.

TR: He knew everybody. It died down. I guess that they used to meet in people's houses and things like that.

MB: Yeah, I think they did.[12]

Mary said that she did not live in town, so she was not in the confines of the discussion of unions after the work hours. She appreciated that she was not a part of that conversation.

The flying squadrons came through Rhodhiss before, during, and after the Great Depression. People had a difficult time during this era. Thelma Church, who ran a grocery store with her husband Joe talked about the plight of millhands:

> Everybody knew everybody then, but now I don't know anybody since I've been out of the grocery business. There are so many new people. You get out of contact with people, but when you are in the grocery business you learn who everybody is. You know everybody and their problems because they bring them to you kinda like they do a preacher or somebody like that. Lord, when the Depression hit, Joe used to hear it. People were just out of work, and we just let people have groceries on credit. They were out of work and couldn't pay for it. When they went back, they couldn't pay for it. Joe would say, 'You gotta help people.' So, we owned land out here. At that time, we just owned the land, and we rented a house out here up the road. We got so indebted that the wholesalers came in and took judgment on this land. Joe built that house out there and sold it to Maude for a $1,000 for the land and house and paid off the bill. Then later we built our house here. We lost a lot of money, but we gained a lot. Everything that we sold back in those days was on credit. We also delivered it. Joe would go around and take orders three times a week on Mondays, Tuesdays, and Wednesdays. He would bring the book back to the store, and we would fill the orders. Then he would put them in the truck and deliver them. People did that in those days. Nobody had cars, so we would go get their stuff. Everybody had cows and hogs, and you had to have bales of hay. It was awful to deliver stuff in those days. Like I say, there were a lot of people out of work and didn't have money. You know that the government was giving this food and stuff away in Lenoir, like flour, beans, and oatmeal, all this. That old store building back then had a great big front porch. Joe would go up there and get all that he could get on his truck and give it out. Back then you got 50 pounds of flour. You didn't know what a 5- or 10-pound bag of flour looked like. They put it up in big bags. He would bring it back down there and put it in front of the store because they gave it away. People had to have papers that they were really in need. They would come up there and get it. Joe would haul it down here from Lenoir and put it there in the front, and they had to come to get it. Oh, it was horrible back in those days. It really was bad how some people had to live.[13]

With shortened days of work and fewer groceries, people had to sacrifice to live. Thelma mentioned the free food that was distributed by the government. The villagers were thankful for the assistance and for Joe's ability to transport it to town.

Hans and Katherine Townsend also mentioned the Depression while talking to Tom Ross and me. They stated:

HT: Yeah, times were so hard back then that the river only ran three days a week. You know. That's true because they cut the wheels off when the mill didn't run. When the mill would close for a few days, and they cut the wheels off, it would be dry up there all the way up to the dam.

SH: If you started to work at 14, you worked down here during the Depression.

HT: Oh, yeah.

TR: You weren't there when they had waterpower.

HT: No, I came later.

KT: We all never really got all the chicken that we wanted. Mama would make a lot of gravy. One day we were sitting at the table eating, and my sister said, 'I will be glad when I get married, and I will get all the chicken that I want to eat.' We worked hard for the food that we had.

TR: So many people did back then.

KT: We didn't know anything else, but work.

HT: Yeah, you were talking about the Depression. First time I ever got hurt was back during the Depression while eating breakfast.

TR: What happened?

HT: Fell out of a persimmon tree and broke my arm.

TR: That was right in the middle of the Depression, wasn't it?

SH: So, tell me about the work schedule during the Depression.

HT: Oh, we worked two or three days a week, something like that.

TR: They gave out odd jobs, too, didn't they?

HT: Yeah, you might unload coal that would come in. Dig out households. Half a dollar to do that.

TR: Did they clean off the banks of the river?

HT: Oh, yeah. All of that.

TR: That's the kind of thing that I heard.

SH: The mill company still paid them for this?

TR & HT: Yeah

KT: Fifty cents would go further than $5 now.

TR: Obviously, the mill company tried to help their help.

HT: Yeah, they tried to look after them, you know. It wasn't their fault that they weren't selling.

SH: Did they keep everybody on the payroll?

HT: Oh, yeah.

TR: People wouldn't leave either because there wasn't a reason to leave.

HT: I've seen at changing time; you know when the second shift came in. The way that you got a job then was you went in, and they hired you at the mill. I have seen fifteen standing there in line.[14]

Hans liked to joke about the persimmon tree, as did Butler Monteith about turnip greens. Butler, Shelley Teague, Tom Ross, and Doughton Beshears also discussed Rhodhiss during the Great Depression:

> BM: Times got so bad down there at the mill one time that they paid off in turnip greens.
> ST: I will tell you during this bad Depression, Rhodhiss worked, but they did close a few days a week.
> SH: So, they just closed a couple days a week during the Depression?
> ST: Yeah, they would close only a couple, two or three days. They didn't shut completely down.
> TR: Somebody told me that they paid the employees one time to clean off the riverbank.
> BM: I went in there once when the looms didn't have warps on them, and I went in there with kerosene and washed those old machines down.
> DB: I've done that, too.
> ST: Roy Tramble told me that there used to be blackberry vines all along the road banks, and back during the Depression they would pay them $1 a day to cut vines.
> BM: Well, if you did something wrong down here, and the town got ahold of it, they would sentence you to do community work, just like they do now, but it was forceable then.
> TR: Is that right?
> BM: Yes, sir.[15]

The mill company found odd jobs for the employees during this time of economic upheaval. The millhands made some money even though the company was not running at a steady pace.

Lawrence Brady also alluded to the hours being cut during the Depression. He said that his work week was cut to 36 hours instead of the 60 that he worked previously and that when he started work at Rhodhiss, he made ten cents an hour. Lawrence noted, "They were dedicated workers. A lot of people worked without missing days. They were very dedicated. People back then felt obligated to work. They felt like they needed to be there. People didn't go somewhere else looking for a job.[16] Shelley Teague would have started about the same time as Lawrence Brady. Shelley noted his beginnings with the mill company:

> Back then, I used to carry lunch for my aunt. I would bring it every day down here in an old basket. Back then, they didn't pay you to learn. While she was eating dinner, I would fill batteries for her. She was a weaver. They didn't pay you to learn. You had to go down there with your folks or your kin to learn. If you just went in there, someone would teach you, but you had to do it on your own. You didn't get paid until you went to work, and they gave you a job. I used to do that at dinnertime. Back then, they went

to work when they were 11, 12, 13.[17]

Shelley learned how to do the job while visiting his aunt at work and allowing her to take her supper break. Many people talked about learning the job and not getting paid until it was mastered.

Mary Starnes Bolick, who lived in Granite Falls but worked in Rhodhiss for 49 years, talked about changing from twelve-hour days to eight hours. Mary and Tom Ross discussed this with me:

SH: So, when you first started working there, you worked eleven hours a day?

MB: Yeah, eleven. I believe that was '33.

SH: Then later you changed to eight.

MB: When did that go into effect? Do you remember, Tom?

TR: That was in the 30s. I don't know if it was '33 or when it was. Right along in there.

MB: Well, I don't believe that it changed until I went back to finish school. I didn't work too long that summer.

TR: Well, see I went to work in '32. We were working long hours. I can't remember when it we went on the NRA (National Industrial Recovery Act). Roosevelt was in office. That's when they changed it and increased our pay and everything. Shortened our hours.

MB: Yeah, I know that I got $12 a week. Yeah, eight hours a day.

TR: You got more money, worked less time.

MB: Boy, we thought that we were something.

TR: Oh, man. We worked a while, Mary. They didn't cut our hours, but they were already on the new pay schedule. We did that for a while before they shortened the hours. I remember that I drew a big paycheck then.

MB: Well, I think when I made $12, everybody made $12 for any of the jobs. Then whenever I started smashing, I made $14. Then the more we made, the more they took. Then groceries and stuff would go up.[18]

Mary and Tom Ross discussed their working fewer hours during the Great Depression.

Finn and Pawnee Simmons also discussed Rhodhiss and how it was hit by the Great Depression. They noted to Mr. Ross and me:

PS: The Depression was so bad in other places. Maybe I wasn't old enough to realize, but I know that they did have work in Rhodhiss. Now my grandparents that lived in Greenville, South Carolina, it was awful. There were so many people, well more people were affected because everybody in Rhodhiss had a house. A lot of places in Greenville, they didn't. That helped a lot. Sometimes the farmers around worked here gave away food, so really, we weren't as bad as a lot of places.

FS: Well, it depends on how you look at it. The labor turnover wasn't as bad. That's for sure. At Falls Mills you had to wait for somebody to die to get a job. They paid money, but they didn't have too many jobs. That's like Rhodhiss down there. You were not going to get rich, and you were working all the time. When I got out of school, I could have gone right back down there and started to work because I had worked two summers. Old Man Oakley and Charlie Kirby were down there. Charlie did whatever Shorty Elmore told him to do. That's like Massie Mullinax, my father-in-law. He had all the boys there in the shop listening to him. He wouldn't give me a job because I'm too contrary. I went down there one night, courtin'.

TR: You were already courtin' Pawnee then?

FS: Yeah, I went down there, and he said that he'd give me a job. I was interested in that stuff. He offered me a job down there on the third shift oiling. I didn't want that. I wouldn't have it. He never did offer again.

PS: Well, you should have taken it and worked up.

FS: That's about the bottom. Anybody that has eyes and any sense at all can see when something needs oiling.

PS: That's what Mendel, my brother, had to do.

FS: Well, I finished school in '34. I guess that I might have worked about two years down there. I worked down there one year when I was a sophomore to a junior. Then junior to a senior. Two summers. Then when I got out of high school I went to Lenoir. I came back to Rhodhiss and stayed down there. I was there when the NRA went into effect, 12 hours a day to 8 hours a day. I worked on the second shift then.[19]

Finn liked to tease Pawnee about his not taking the job that her dad offered him. He did work at Rhodhiss for a brief while though. He alluded to the National Industrial Recovery Act that was enacted by President Franklin D. Roosevelt. Mary Bolick and Tom Ross had discussed it previously. Many millhands in North Carolina felt that President Roosevelt helped their plight. Victoria Byerly, who wrote *Hard Times Cotton Mill Girls* noted that one millhand said, "The best thing that ever happened to working people was when President Roosevelt got in. He was the only president I've ever known that helped the poor people….He cut our hours down from twelve hours a day to eight hours a day, and mill owners couldn't cut our pay."[20] Similarly, Jacquelyn Hall states in her book, *Like a Family*, "Piedmont millhands viewed Roosevelt as a 'God sent man,' an emancipator who could turn patterns of domination upside down."[21] With the National Industrial Recovery Act, few people saw the need for unionization.

Fred and Martha Elmore discussed difficult times in Rhodhiss and how Luther "Shorty" Elmore helped people. "Shorty" was the plant superintendent for many years. Fred and Martha told Tom Ross and me:

FE: People passing through during the Depression did try to steal. Everybody knew everybody. There was something going on all the time.

ME: And the people were responsible. They took care of people. You could depend on them.

TR: And I give your dad, Mr. Elmore, credit for that, Fred because I don't know what this community would have done without Mr. Elmore.

ME: I do, too. He was a great person.

TR: He gave to the community as well as the manufacturing aspect. He helped everybody, no question about it.

ME: People with children had a hard time, and I have known him to go buy shoes for kids, and nobody knew who did it. You know that farm raised a lot. He had two old farms. He would load the wagon with eggs, potatoes, watermelons, beans and take it to people he knew, not one time, but many, many times.[22]

There were several people who deserve credit for helping fellow citizens during difficult times, and Luther "Shorty" Elmore was certainly one of them.

Zeno Crump, who grew up in Rhodhiss, said that he had a pleasant memory from the Depression. Zeno noted:

> I was born in 1926, and I grew up during the Depression years when the cotton
> mills were going through it. Luckily, Rhodhiss seemed to have weathered that period
> pretty well because I don't remember my father having to come home from work except
> for a few times. I remember him coming home one day in the summertime because he
> didn't have enough work to do that day. He came home for the whole day. He came
> and got the old water bucket, and he said, 'Let's go across the lake.' He had borrowed
> my uncle's boat, and we paddled across the lake. We went to pick blackberries. He said,
> 'Let's go pick some blackberries today since I'm not working.' I have some very pleasant
> experiences growing up in Rhodhiss.[23]

Zeno was proud of his Rhodhiss days. He was a man who took pleasure in some of the simple things that life had to offer.

Alvis Kelley praised his wife with getting the family through some difficult times. He noted that he and Beulah were married 43 years and 8 months when she died. He stated, "She could make dresses and shirts. We didn't buy many clothes. She could do more with Irish potatoes than anybody that I've ever seen in my life. She could fix them so many ways. You had to at that time. Back when I had them all, I bought 50 lbs. of pinto beans at a time."[24] Families learned how to cope with difficult financial situations. Gladys Barker alluded to the fact that her family didn't go hungry, even during the Great Depression.[25]

Rhodhiss experienced difficult days during the Great Depression. People were able to mobilize and take care of each other to survive. Perhaps that is one of the reasons that the flying squadrons and the union agents could not make headway. The townspeople felt that they were already united as a family, and they were leery of outside forces trying to unite them.

1939 MILL WORKERS. FRED ELMORE PHOTO.

1939 MILL WORKERS. FRED ELMORE PHOTO.

1939 MILL WORKERS. FRED ELMORE PHOTO.

1938 MILL WORKERS. FRED ELMORE PHOTO.

1939 MILL WORKERS. FRED ELMORE PHOTO.

1939 MILL WORKERS. FRED ELMORE PHOTO.

1939 MILL WORKERS. FRED ELMORE PHOTO.

1939 MILL WORKERS. FRED ELMORE PHOTO.

1939 MILL WORKERS. FRED ELMORE PHOTO.

1939 MILL WORKERS. FRED ELMORE PHOTO.

1939 MILL WORKERS. FRED ELMORE PHOTO.

1939 MILL WORKERS. FRED ELMORE PHOTO.

1939 MILL WORKERS. FRED ELMORE PHOTO.

1939 MILL WORKERS. FRED ELMORE PHOTO.

1939 MILL WORKERS. FRED ELMORE PHOTO.

1939 MILL WORKERS. FRED ELMORE PHOTO.

1939 MILL WORKERS. FRED ELMORE PHOTO.

1939 MILL WORKERS. FRED ELMORE PHOTO.

NOTES

1   Hall, p. 329.
2   Hall, p. 53.
3   Munday, Mattie and Louise Keller.
4   Elmore, Fred and Martha and Tom Ross.
5   Beshears, Monteith, Ross, Teague.
6   Townsend, Hans and Katherine and Tom Ross.
7   Huber, Patrick. "Mill Mother's Lament: Ella May Wiggins and the Gastonia Textile Strike of 1929." *Southern Cultures*. 15.3 (2009): 81-110. p.102.
8   Huber, pp. 83 & 87.
9   Huber, p. 102.
10   Jones and Ross.
11   Kirby, Beth.
12   Bolick, Mary Starnes and Tom Ross.
13   Church, Thelma.
14   Townsend, Hans and Katherine and Tom Ross.
15   Beshears, Monteith, Ross, Teague.
16   Brady, Lawrence and Nancy and Tom Ross.
17   Beshears, Monteith, Ross, Teague.
18   Bolick, Mary Starnes and Tom Ross.
19   Simmons, Finn and Pawnee and Tom Ross.
20   Byerly, Victoria, p 165.
21   Hall, p. 323.
22   Elmore, Fred and Martha and Tom Ross.
23   Crump, Zeno.
24   Kelley, Alvis and Precious and Tom Ross.
25   Barker, Gladys.

CHAPTER 19

1940 FLOOD, 1941 PEARL HARBOR, WORLD WAR II

The year 1940 brought a new decade to the world and another flood to Rhodhiss. The 1940s would be a trying time for the world because of World War II. In 1941 the United States would join the war because of the bombing of Pearl Harbor. Rhodhiss played a large role in the effort, and the lives of many Rhodhiss people were affected.

Precious Keller Kelley recalled that the mill was closed during the 1940 flood. Precious noted, "There was a flood in 1940. It was '40 because I was dating. I think that Clyde came to see me one night during the week because the water got in the mill across the river (Burke) where he worked. They shut it down. I know that flood was before I got married."[1] The 1940 flood did not reach the magnitude of the 1916 flood, but the area did see high waters, the closing of the mill, and debris washing down the river. Earl Lingle also remembered this flood. Earl stated, "I remember that I was 10 in 1940, and I witnessed the flood. I was up at one of those houses on the back porch facing the bridge. My dad and Pee Wee and several of them. There was a

THE 1940 FLOOD. THE FIRST CHURCH WHERE THE METHODISTS WORSHIPED IN BURKE IS IN THE BACKGROUND. CALDWELL COUNTY HERITAGE MUSEUM PICTURE.

hog that came floating down that river. He was squealing, and the water was up pretty close to the bridge. They were down there trying to catch that hog, but they couldn't."[2] The 1916 flood, too, had pigs floating down the river. Rhodhiss was able to endure the hardships of the '40 flood.

Several people mentioned the town's place in history during World War II. The mill company produced material for the war effort. Fred and Martha Elmore detailed the bombing of Pearl Harbor to Tom Ross and me. They stated:

> ME: One of the scariest times for me is when they declared war. We listened to the radio because of no TV. It was the morning after the war was declared.
>
> FE: The Japanese attacked Pearl Harbor on December 7. The next morning, I got up to go to work and went out on the back porch, and the whole road was lined with soldiers. They had already deployed the Army. They set up camp in the yard of the power plant.
>
> ME: After Fred went to work, I went to the door, and two soldiers were there with rifles and everything. It scared the life out of me. They told me, 'Don't be afraid. We are looking for the power plant. How do we get there?' They had a camp out there.
>
> FE: The camp was at the power plant. They guarded both sides of the power plant. Guards were on the bridge.
>
> ME: Two or three boys from New Jersey would come out to see Fred and talk. It was so cold. Several times they came in to eat and get warm. The wind came off the lake, and they almost froze standing on that bridge while guarding it.
>
> FE: They camped a week to ten days, and they sent out word that anyone that had boats on the river near the Company Store to get them out if they wanted them. People had homemade boats, and they had to get them out before they busted them up. They did that, too.
>
> TR: They were really prepared to protect that dam. We hadn't heard that story.
>
> ME: They stayed a long time because they didn't want power crippled.[3]

Tom Ross and I listened to this story with great interest because no one had mentioned it. During the war Fred and Martha lived near the Rhodhiss Beach area on Lake Drive. Later, Jim and Mae Hemphill gave their account:

> SH: I didn't know until last night that when Pearl Harbor was attacked, they mobilized the Army down there to protect the dam.
>
> JH: Yeah, they had troops down there in tents near our house.
>
> SH: I have interviewed 38 people as of today, and the Elmores were the first ones to tell me that.
>
> MH: You know what, people know that, but they just take for granted that everyone else knows.[4]

Jim Hemphill lived in Duke Power village, and he said that the tents were near his house. The *Hickory Daily Record* reprinted an article on December 7, 2021, that explained the soldiers' protecting the

Rhodhiss dam. It is entitled "Trespassing Forbidden at Nearby Dams: Soldiers On Guard Have Orders To Open Fire." The article reads:

No hunting, fishing, or trespassing of any kind will be permitted within one mile of the Lake James, Catawba river (sic), and Broad river (sic) power dams now being guarded twenty-four hours a day by the Twenty-ninth Infantry, according to Captain C. P. Greyer, the commanding officer. Fire will be opened, he said, on any person seen within a mile of the dams, which are as follows: Oxford and Rhodhiss, of the Hickory area; Paddle's Creek, Catawba river (sic), and Linville river (sic) on Lake James; and Broad river (sic) near Cliffside in Rutherford county (sic). The Duke Power company (sic) has erected flood-lights around the Lake James dams, it is said. All roads across the dams or near the spillways at Lake James have been closed and only school buses and mail carriers will be permitted to pass, according to Captain Greyer, a native of Morganton. School buses will not be allowed to pass, he added when more than one male person is aboard. Captain Greyer declared that fire would be opened without questions being asked on persons seen within a mile of the dams and warned citizens, as a consequence, to strictly obey the warning. Neither will motorboating be permitted within a mile of the dams, he stated. These strict orders went into effect at four p.m. Tuesday, it was said. The infantry, composed of 280 men and six commissioned officers, will use the Morganton Armory for headquarters.[5]

HICKORY DAILY RECORD ARTICLE DETAILING THE PROTECTION OF THE DAM IN RHODHISS. *HICKORY DAILY RECORD* PHOTO.

The United States government did not want anyone to attack power sources; therefore, the power plant in Rhodhiss along with others was fortified.

Clarkson Jones received a letter in early 1941 from J. Edgar Hoover, the head of the FBI giving instructions for the mill company. Even before Pearl Harbor was attacked, the town had already taken precautions to guard the mill because the plants were producing war materials. The Town Minutes from May 12, 1941, stated, "The Town Clerk was authorized to hire 5 policemen at a salary of $100 per month for the privacy duty of guarding property within the town as war work. This was a request of the War Department."[6] Tom Ross and Hans Townsend explained some of the war materials:

HT: Well, there were over 400 looms in that one mill across the river, small looms. Some of them were 30 inches. They started making that material that had stripes on it. They started making that duck cloth for the Army for World War II on big looms.

TR: Osnaburg is glorified burlap. It is used for a lot of different purposes, but the yarn in it was coarse, and it didn't have to have as much twist as a better fabric would. That was the kind of fabric that they ran. Now during the war down here they ran a lot of tent material.[7]

Many Rhodhiss citizens talked about the mills' making tent material for use during World War II. The employees also made uniforms for the soldiers serving in the armed forces.

Government personnel were placed in various locales within the community, the powerhouse, the bridge, and the mills. Mattie Munday and Louise Keller discussed these soldiers:

MM: Yeah, they had soldiers down here. I remember that, but I don't remember what year it was. They had soldiers down here guarding.

LK: They brought the soldiers over here during the war to work, too.

MM: Yeah, they brought them in to guard. They thought that the enemies would come in.

LK: I know that they brought them in during the war to make stuff for the army, and they were pushing them to get it out, and they came in and worked, the soldiers did. We worked down there with them.

MM: They were tickled to death when people made them biscuits.

LK: I don't know where they slept.[8]

FIRST PAGE OF A SIX-PAGE LETTER RECEIVED BY CLARKSON JONES WHO WAS THE PLANT MANAGER AT RHODHISS FROM J. EDGAR HOOVER. 1941.

Soldiers were brought in to work and make war materials according to Louise. The mill company could not make the materials fast enough, and help was needed. The guards were at the mill on duty until at least January 1943 because the Rhodhiss Town Minutes stated, "The mill company advised the commissioners that the Army no longer required guards around the mill."[9]

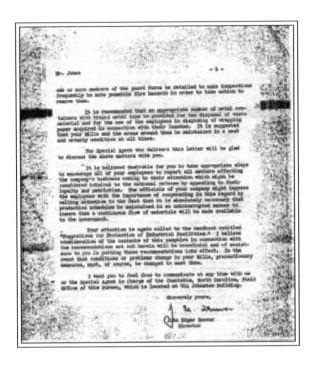

LAST PAGE OF A SIX-PAGE LETTER TO CLARKSON
JONES FROM J. EDGAR HOOVER IN 1941.

Another safety measure implemented during the war was blackouts. Thelma Church discussed this. The citizens would be told that lights were to be extinguished on certain nights to practice for possible air raids. Thelma stated:

> Right there during the war we had several old people that lived over the store in apartments. They had a blackout night, you know, turning all the lights out. Warning people in case there would be a war or something. Well, this old lady, Mrs. Hicks, she had an old coal heater up there. She took her ashes out to sit in the window seal in a pan. There were holes in the bottom of the pan. You know what? It set that thing on fire. That night because all the lights were out in Rhodhiss, somebody saw it and got them out, or they would have all been burned up. They sure would have.[10]

Thelma's store and apartments almost burned because of the ashes set in the window. Paul Bright discussed his working at the local Rhodhiss gas station, and he had to make sure that the gas was rationed.[11] Another war effort was to collect metal. Ned Bean said that some of the remains of the bridge that washed away in 1916 were used in this appeal. Ned said, "The old bridge that washed away in 1916 part of it is still down the river over there. I know where it is. They took most of it out during the war for the metal. There was one piece of it still left in there."[12] Billie Sue Laney added more information to Ned's story. She said, "During World War II there was a metal drive. The equipment that was left over from the completion of the Duke Power dam was used."[13] Reinhardt and Dennis had simply left large equipment near the dam because removing it was not cost effective, so the townspeople included this metal in the drive. Many sacrifices

RATION COUPON FROM THE WAR. RICK
JUSTICE COPY.

were made during the war. Whether it was rationing of gas, collecting metal, or extinguishing lights, people did what was necessary.

METAL WAS COLLECTED IN RHODHISS FOR THE WAR EFFORT. SHERRIE HARTSOE SIGMON PHOTO.

With so many of the men being called to serve in the armed forces, more women went to work. Martha Elmore had been staying home to raise her son Lanny while her husband Fred was at war, but the Rhodhiss Mill Company was short staffed. Martha and Fred noted to Tom Ross and me:

ME: I worked, but not all the time. I didn't work till Lanny went to school. My mother came and lived with me to take care of Lanny because Fred was in the service. There was a shortage of people to work. The mills couldn't run because of the shortage. I had not intended to go to work, but one day Mr. Elmore, my father-in-law, came, and he told me or asked me to go down to the mill and work a few hours a day cutting off yarn. They couldn't find anybody to take off yarn, so winders couldn't work. He said to just come a few hours a day so they could run winders. I told him that I would. I went back. Kurt Smith from the cloth room asked me to come down there and run the machine a few hours a day.

TR: Didn't they bring soldiers into the mill to work?

ME: Yeah, it got so bad that they did.

FE: They brought the Army in to help.[14]

Martha had grown accustomed to staying home, but she did return to work during the war. In addition, Mary Settlemyre Darty said that during war time, they worked long hours. When the National Industrial Recovery Act started, people began working eight-hour days instead of twelve. "We worked 40 hours a week; then in war time we worked 6 days a week. I first worked on the morning shift. Then I got on the second shift. My dad was working down there then. We had to work Saturday evenings. We went to work at 2:00 then and worked till 10:00. That was 6 days. Yeah, we worked all the time six days a week during war time."[15] Rhodhiss millhands worked hard to contribute to the country's success during the war. Alvis Kelley was proud to know a man who worked at the plant after the war. His name was Charlie Lee, and he had been a POW (Prisoner of War) and in the Bataan Death March. This was a 66-mile march with 66,000 Filipinos and 10,000 Americans which lasted five to ten days in 1942. "The captives were beaten, shot, bayoneted, and, in many cases, beheaded…. Only 54,000 prisoners reached the camp; though exact numbers are unknown; some 2,500 Filipinos and 500 Americans may have died during the march." Some of those who arrived at camp succumbed to starvation and disease with those numbers being an additional 26,000 Filipinos and over 1,500 Americans.[16] Alvis praised Charlie Lee for his leadership and bravery, and Mr. Lee was a weave room supervisor after the war.[17] People all over the country gave of themselves during World War II, and Rhodhiss was no exception.

RHODHISS MILLS COMPANY
Rhodhiss, N. C.
RHODHISS COTTON MILLS COMPANY

Statement of Wages Paid To:

Name ....

S. S. No. ....

FROM	TO	HOURS WORKED	TOTAL GROSS WAGES	DEDUCTED FOR S. S. TAX
JAN 1 1941	DEC 3 1 1941		222 34 43 68	2 24 43

Paid By—RHODHISS MILLS COMPANY—RHODHISS, N. C.

56 0876360   NCUCC No. 22-14-002

To Employee: This statement is required by Regulations of the Social Security Board. Keep this record as it may help you in determining your Old Age Benefits.

KEEP AND PRESERVE THIS STATEMENT

A W2 WITH WAGES FOR A RHODHISS EMPLOYEE IN 1941. NOTE THE SENTENCE AT THE BOTTOM, "KEEP THIS RECORD AS IT MAY HELP YOU IN DETERMINING YOUR OLD AGE BENEFITS." THE NAME AND SOCIAL SECURITY NUMBERS WERE REDACTED. PETE SETTLEMYRE PHOTO.

According to the "North Carolina Directory of Manufacturing Firms 1944," Burke County had many textile mills. Of the ones listed at this time, the Rhodhiss plant was the largest in Burke County. Rhodhiss Cotton Mills, Plant 2 employed 301 to 350 people. The second highest textile employer in Burke County was Alpine Cotton Mills in Morganton with 251 to 300 people. Nearby mills were Henry River which employed 101-150; Quaker Meadows in Hildebran utilized 151-200; Valdese Manufacturing had 201-250 workers; and Valdese Weavers worked 151-200.[18]

The Rhodhiss Mill Company was able to persevere during difficult times in the 1940s. A flood caused work to cease because of the high waters. Then employees and soldiers rose to the occasion to manufacture war materials for the United States government. People labored long hours to fulfill orders for the government and other companies. Metal was collected, gas was rationed, and people returned to work to help during World War II. The village united to serve the country with their traditional work ethic.

NOTES

1   Kelley, Alvis and Precious and Tom Ross.

2   Lingle, Earl and Tom Ross.

3   Elmore, Fred and Martha and Tom Ross.

4   Hemphill, Helen, Jim and Mae.

5   "Trespassing Forbidden at Nearby Dams: Soldiers On Guard Have Orders To Open Fire." *Hickory Daily Record.* 10 December 1941. Reprint on 7 December 2021.

6   Rhodhiss Town Minutes. 12 May 1941.

7   Townsend, Hans and Katherine and Tom Ross.

8   Munday, Mattie and Louise Keller.

9   Rhodhiss Town Minutes. 22 January 1943.

10   Church, Thelma.

11   Bright, Paul.

12   Bean, Ned and Elvie and Tom Ross.

13   Laney, Billie Sue.

14   Elmore, Fred and Martha and Tom Ross.

15   Darty, Mary Settlemyre and Tom Ross.

16   Norman, Elizabeth M. and Norman, Michael. "Bataan Death March". Encyclopedia Britannica, 10 Sep. 2022, https://www.britannica.com/event/Bataan-Death-March. Accessed 7 October 2022.

17   Kelley, Alvis and Precious and Tom Ross.

18   "North Carolina Directory of Manufacturing Firms 1944." *North Carolina Digital Collections.* https://digital.ncdcr.gov/digital/collection/p249901coll22/id/399338/rec/14. Accessed 8 February 2022.

CHAPTER 20
PACIFIC MILLS 1945

Pacific Mills approached the stockholders who were leasing the mills from Duke Power, and they offered a complete buyout of the company. The stockholders agreed, and the ownership was transferred to Pacific in 1945. This apparently was a welcomed change for the employees because they were given benefits for the first time, and the millhands were ready for a transformation. Pacific not only offered fringe benefits, but they also reformed the mills and the village.

One change that Pacific instituted was the addition of air conditioning. Calvin Jones said that it was added first in the weave rooms at both mills during the early 1950s. Calvin noted that it should have been implemented in the spinning departments first.[1] Another adjustment that Pacific made at the plant was removing some of the antiquated equipment and structures. Calvin Jones and Tom Ross discussed the removal of the water flume that was installed for water-powered machinery in the early 1900s. They explained:

TR: Didn't you have to do something with those shafts that were left over when the water line was used?

CJ: Well, that was the reason the line shafts were down through there. They had an old rope at the back end of the mill. Do you remember when we came here?

TR: Yeah, yeah.

CJ: And they had the old water flumes that the water came in to pull the water wheel. Had the pulleys that the ropes were pulled up on and went around by the line shaft and back down to the water wheel. All that was still in when we came here. I tore all that out. They weren't running it by waterpower. They had electric motors, but at one time they did run it with water lines. They put in large motors to pull each line shaft down through the mill. Then when we came with Pacific, we took all that down and put individual motors on each machine.

Each loom, each spinning frame, each card, each draw frame. We had individual motors on everything, which was a lot easier to maintain.[2]

When Duke Power came and electrified the mills in 1925, there was no longer a need for the waterpower. Willard Herman added to Calvin and Tom's discussion. Willard said, "I'd like to see over on the Burke side a picture of the road and the old waterway canal. That used to be a great big sight when the water went out front of the plant to the water wheel and back in the river. Pacific Mills filled that in and made a parking lot across the road. There used to be a little hill right there. They cut that hill down."[3] Ned Bean and Hans Townsend both alluded to the canal. Ned explained to Tom Ross and his wife Elvie:

> NB: What they did, they came in and put the mill here, and then they came around to the canal. I remember when there was a canal around that mill. The water came down run through the wheel, and followed the mill, and went out that canal. Do you remember that canal?
> TR: Yeah.
> EB: Back into the river?
> NB: Then it came back into the river.
> EB: That's on the Burke County side.
> NB: Yeah, when I used to deliver papers when I was a little boy, there was a foot log across that canal. You walked across that foot log down River Street.[4]

Ned had a paper route when he was a young lad which would have been in the late 1930s or early 1940s, and he had to cross the canal. Hans Townsend also discussed the canal with Tom Ross and me. Hans said, "Back when I came to work there, it wasn't fenced in either. On the other side of the mill all that was water. It came around and went under the road. They called it a canal."[5] Pacific saw the need to make a new parking lot and get rid of the canal and the old water wheel.

Finn and Pawnee Simmons and Tom Ross talked about Pacific's removal of other items within the mill, in addition to the water wheel. They noted:

> FS: I will tell you right now, Pacific Mills spent a world of money down there. They took those columns out of the mills.
> PS: Do you know what happened to that big old water wheel? For a long, long time it was just there. They didn't use it, but it was just there. It may still be there. I don't know. I was wondering if the wheel is still there.
> FS: It was in that old roadway when I was there.
> TR: I've never seen it. Was it in the back of number one mill?
> PS: I never did hear if it was still there.
> FS: It was in the back of number two. They had both the plants there when they built that dam in '23. We had to put water on the filling. They had warps on the loom. Put the battery in there. It would automatically change into the shuttle. Used to when my daddy worked down

there, when the shuttle run out of filling, you had to take it out of there, and put a new bobbin in, and start it again. That's why you couldn't run over ten or twelve looms each person.

TR: You're talking about putting water on the filling. Willard was talking about taking care of that at the back of the mill.

PS: If it was damp, it wouldn't break as easy. We'd bring that cloth out of that weave room, and it would sometimes still be damp.

FS: Yeah, I've poured many a bucket of water on them. That old roadway down in there was ideal for the conditions. You didn't have to worry about the water because it went on the concrete.[6]

The old columns were removed from the mill to allow more room for additional machines. Pacific was ready to add new equipment that would increase production and cut out personnel, and it would allow for the changeover to synthetics.

Pacific's intent from the onset was to cut the workforce in half to enhance productivity. Tom Ross came to Rhodhiss in 1946 when he agreed to a job transfer from Lyman, South Carolina's Pacific plant. Tom stated, "There were 900 employees in both mills when I came here. I know that some of the Pacific men said that they could run the mill with half that number of people. When they got the machinery changed, they wanted to go with half the people."[7] Tom added this sentiment again when he talked with Doughton Beshears, Butler Monteith, and Shelley Teague and me. The men attested:

TR: I think that there were over 900 employees at one time.

ST: That's when it was Rhodhiss Mills.

DB: Yeah, with two shifts at two plants.

BM: Lord have mercy. They kept cutting out, cutting out. Pacific wasn't as bad, but when Burlington took over.

ST: Well, they put in different machinery that didn't take

TR: As many people.

ST: That's right.

TR: They put in wider looms. They changed things around some. Well, I heard that they predicted to cut the workforce in half by adding new machinery.

BM: Well, I guess that they accomplished that.

ST: When Pacific took over, I went to work down there busting those old looms with a sledgehammer. We took what we busted up across the river. They sold the cast iron.

SH: It must have taken a while to get the old equipment out and the new in.

BM: You would be surprised. It didn't take too long. It took about eighteen months.

ST: Back then, people worked![8]

Shelley Teague mentioned "busting" up the old looms. Calvin Jones said that was the procedure. Calvin and Tom Ross elaborated:

CJ: We took sledgehammers and broke them up and rolled them out in wheelbarrows and dumped them in a cart off from the plant. That's the way that we did it. They were all to pieces.

TR: Not usable.

CJ: In fact, they were outdated, and I doubt whether there were any mills except Rhodhiss in this country that had line shafts down through the middle of the mill pulling looms. Now, I saw it in India when I was in service. I had never seen a line shaft until I went through a textile mill over there. They had line shafts there down through the middle of the mill with belts down toward the looms. The second that I saw was here at Rhodhiss.

TR: Mary Starnes Bolick told us about those looms. She said that people had to be careful because there was fear of being pulled into the looms.

SH: Unfinished material went to Lyman when it was Pacific?

CJ: Yeah. Pacific sent it to Lyman to finish it. Yeah, we came in here with line shafts. I never will forget getting up on a ladder and taking them down. You would think that you'd go up and unbolt this one and this one, take block and tackle. They had big shafts of steel about 20 feet long, coupled together down through the mill. The way that we took those things down, Will McGuire would get up on a ladder, 12 feet long, and take a sledgehammer and hit that bracket hanging down and break it because we were going to put it in the junk anyway. We'd make everybody get back, and when he'd break that heavy shaft, it dropped. It just snapped the other one. It snapped it all the way down till everything was lying in the floor. That's the way that we tore them down. When he first did that, it was lying down in five minutes, the length of that mill, all that weight. With three-line shafts on each floor.[9]

The equipment was destroyed because it was outdated and unsuitable for use.

Another reason for new equipment was because Rhodhiss was the innovator for converting from cotton to synthetics. The plants would continue their reputation as the first to step into the future with these new materials for years to come. In Rhodhiss the plants were ready to convert to blended rayon fabrics. Henry Bliss, the Pacific Mills President stated, "In the first full year of peacetime operations, the company has been operating at near capacity levels on the production of civilian goods which have been in such short supply." Mr. Bliss said that Pacific's success was because of consumer demand, good rapport within the company, and the benefit of new equipment.[10] Pacific started in Rhodhiss making wool blends; then they added synthetics. Mary Starnes Bolick and Tom Ross discussed this change over:

TR: Do you remember George?

MB: Yeah, boy he was something. He came there when they put these

TR: W4 looms.

MB: Now that was a big change. They were different type looms. They had two shuttles. Sometimes three. If you didn't watch how to do that, that's when they had all these big breakouts and fancy styles. Well, I mean fancy weave in it. You had to know that you had a certain harness to put that on for that to be right.

TR: That's when they started wool blends.

MB: Yes. That was about '46 or '47. Wasn't it?

TR: Yes, I believe that they did. They brought George in here to run those looms.

MB: He was good after you got to know him. Oh, he just cursed all the time.

TR: He was different than what we were used to down here.

MB: He was smart.

TR: Oh, Mary, you can tell her a little bit about when synthetics first came.

MB: Well, I mean I remember what a time we had with it. You'd put one warp on, and it wouldn't work. They'd have to cut that one off. They'd put another one. They had an awful problem with slashing it and getting it drawn in, too. They made this aerospace. I remember that.

TR: The yarn was so different.

MB: It was entirely different. We were used to cotton.

TR: Well, they tried to weave it on the same machines as cotton to start with.

MB: Now that was something. I can remember that they'd try. Dan Hartsoe and Boyce Hartsoe were both tying in, and they'd tie the knots, and they'd slip, and they'd have to redraw the thing again and start over because you couldn't pull it over. You couldn't do anything with it. Seems like they put kerosene on it or something one time. Something that could get them to tie the knot. I don't know finally what they had to do. I think it was getting a different machine to get it tied.

TR: This fiber was slick as opposed to cotton.

MB: Yeah, ask your daddy about it, Sherrie. He'll remember. He can tell you a whole a lot about it because he and Dan both tied those warps.

TR: I remember the accumulation of the waste down in the basement, too, Mary.

MB: Yeah, I remember that, too.

TR: We used to take inventory in that room down there. It would just be full of waste.

MB: Well, I think that they tried to hide it.[11]

Pacific had difficulty trying to run synthetic and blend materials on machinery that was designed for cotton; however, Rhodhiss' employees were successful after the proper equipment was installed. A *Women's Wear Daily* article quoted Henry Bliss, "'The Rhodhiss division, which was purchased as a coarse goods cotton mill in 1945, was converted by the installation of equipment to the manufacture of synthetics and blended fabrics. During 1949, this division has made good progress. . . it has given the company further diversification of product and significant stake in the growing field of synthetics.'"[12] Rhodhiss was the showcase plant for synthetics.

Hans Townsend and Tom Ross also discussed Pacific Mills' role in the textile industry's change from cotton to synthetic fiber. They explained:

TR: This was the first rayon plant here at Rhodhiss. Synthetics were first getting in the market.

HT: I know the first that we ran on slashers, I didn't get home, I think it was Friday, and I had to go back at 11:00 on Saturday night.

TR: They tried to run synthetics on cotton equipment. That's what they were trying to do. Do you remember how they used to store the waste down in the basement? Did you ever see it down there?

HT: Yeah.

TR: Oh, man. We used to try to take inventory. They made waste trying to process it, and they had that basement full. That's why slashers were so critical because the whole weave room depended on good warps.

HT: Yeah, and there were some of them that they had run them wet.

TR: The job was really skill.

HT: Yeah. It wasn't hard. You had to be on your toes. You couldn't leave that thing.

TR: The machine would run itself after it got started. Of course, the side mix was critical.

HT: If one end would break, and you weren't there, it wouldn't be a few seconds till there would be a dozen. That would be a mess. It would all wad up.

TR: If you can imagine all the warp ends. He ran the fabric. How wide was it, Hans?

HT: We had some 90 inches.

TR: They ran that through to size the yarn.

HT: You had to make that size right, too.

TR: I don't remember what the percentage was. Most everybody that came here tried to straighten the place out. They would work in the weave room on the looms and everything. They would change settings. I know that Estes must have changed every motion on it.[13]

Again, the men mentioned that Pacific tried to run synthetics on machinery modeled for cotton. Another article in *Women's Wear Daily* stated, "Pacific Mills has made a blended yarn which is 75% vicara protein fiber and 25% nylon. Only small quantities have been developed and sent out to hosiery mills in order to determine its future. After the mills access this material, the commercial use will be determined. The price has not been decided, but the yarn is manufactured in the Rhodhiss, North Carolina plant."[14] Again, Rhodhiss was the pilot program for Pacific's new venture. The Rhodhiss employees were known for their willingness to forge into the future. Pacific Mills started producing blends of rayon, dacron, and orlon at Rhodhiss.[15] Two more articles in *Women's Wear Daily* alluded to two men who were instrumental in Rhodhiss' success, Joe Cobb and H. C. Cobb. Joe Cobb was the plant manager, and he often gave speeches throughout the country highlighting the benefits of manmade fibers.[16] H. C. Cobb worked for Rhodhiss Mills and Pacific for 45 years.[17] The H. C. Cobb house was on the lower end of Church Street beside Church Street Baptist Church.

Another integral person to Pacific's and Rhodhiss Mills' success was Superintendent Luther "Shorty" Elmore. Tommy Elmore talked about his dad, Shorty. He said that Shorty worked hard for Rhodhiss, and he loved every minute of it. Tommy said that his mother, Linnie Bell Elmore was originally from just across the Virginia line, and she was the only one who called Shorty "Luther." Tommy noted that from the day that his dad was born Luther was called Shorty.[18] Luther worked at

Rhodhiss for many years. Tom Ross explained Luther's status to Luther's son, "Fred, your Daddy was personnel man, superintendent, and everything in between."[19] Doughton Beshears, Butler Monteith, Shelley Teague and Tom Ross had words of praise for Superintendent Elmore. They noted:

> TR: Talking about Super Elmore, he was a good man to work for.
>
> DB: Oh, Shorty was a good fella.
>
> ST: He was a superman to work for.
>
> TR: He did a lot of the hiring. Nobody has mentioned him. He was really Mr. Rhodhiss as far as I am concerned.
>
> ST: Luther is his real name.
>
> BM: We always knew him as Shorty.
>
> ST: He's Fred and Thad's daddy. L. A. Elmore. He was with Rhodhiss Mills, right?
>
> DB: Yeah.
>
> BM: He was here the whole time. He was superintendent.
>
> ST: He was over both weave rooms.
>
> BM: Shorty was the superintendent. He was never over the weave rooms.
>
> ST: I mean right before he retired with Burlington.
>
> TR: Shorty lived in the house that Clarkson Jones lived in.
>
> DB: Who Shorty?
>
> TR: Yes.
>
> DB: No, he lived in the house in the woods that burned down.
>
> ST: Shorty lived in Clarkson Jones' house.
>
> DB: Did he?
>
> BM & ST: Yes, sir.
>
> TR: He lived there until I guess he moved out in the country.
>
> ST: Till he retired, I guess.
>
> DB: Yeah, that's right. He moved from the woods here over to the Clarkson Jones house; then on out to the farm.[20]

The Elmore family lived on Maple Avenue near the old ball park on Park Avenue; then they moved to Jones Drive. Rhodhiss was fortunate to have good men who worked in management. Willard Herman also mentioned that Bernie Coleman was with Pacific, and he was a good weave room supervisor. Willard said, "I took over that weave room behind Bernie Coleman, and they made Bernie a superintendent, and I got the weave room."[21]

One of the benefits provided by Pacific Mills was a monthly magazine entitled, *Pacific Truths*. In a May 1949 article on Rhodhiss, Pacific boasted about Rhodhiss' success. The article mentioned the modernization of the mills with new machines which made fabrics for men's and women's clothing. Air conditioning and fluorescent lighting were added, and no dust was visible. Restrooms were made available in every building, and canteens were installed at each mill. Both plants were painted, and Number 2 mill had a new laboratory and experiment room. Number 1 mill had a new tower with a wide stairway that replaced narrow stairs. The offices were updated and remodeled, and the old wooden structure was bricked. An interoffice telephone service was installed as well as telephone communication between the two mills. Safeguards were implemented in each mill, and fencing was added for security. Esther Barrett served as the full-time nurse. Joe C. Cobb was the General Manager of Pacific Mills in Rhodhiss, and H. C. Estes and L. A. Elmore were superintendents. The paymaster was Mrs. Henry (Sudie) Anderson. Mrs. Leonard Lee was the president of the Woman's Club.[22] Rhodhiss was well accepted within the textile industry in the South.

Another benefit that was appreciated by the millhands was health insurance. Mary Starnes Bolick talked about the insurance that was solely paid by employees which was called Mutual Aid. This insurance was discontinued after Pacific started providing insurance for their employees.[23] Tom Ross and Calvin Jones discussed Mutual Aid and Pacific's employee group insurance program further:

> CJ: Pacific really had the influence. Another thing when we came here, there weren't a dozen cars down there at the mill. After Pacific had been here a few years, everybody had an automobile.
> TR: Everybody started taking vacations and going places.
> CJ: They sure did.
> TR: They started having operations.
> CJ: That's right.
> TR: I never will forget that. People didn't go to the hospital. There was no health insurance until Pacific came. If somebody had appendicitis or had something else, they knew insurance paid for it. It's amazing what all went on. Mutual Aid was obviously good, better than nothing.
> CJ: Well, when they got the insurance from Pacific, and they had the Mutual Aid, too, some people made money going to the hospital.
> TR: Yes, they did.
> CJ: Mutual Aid paid a little bit, and Pacific would pay almost all of it. This would pay you a little bit more.
> TR: Mutual Aid was developed by the people themselves. Somebody was smart setting that thing up.
> CJ: Yes, they were.
> TR: I don't know who.[24]

With health insurance the mill workers felt better able to care for their health. Previous health concerns were detrimental to employees and their families.

Another benefit added by Pacific Mills was paid vacation leave. Calvin Jones and Tom Ross noted this luxury:

> TR: Pacific started paying vacation pay. I guess industry in general started doing that, and Pacific followed. They initiated it here. People like Raym Munday and several people started traveling, you know. They'd come back and tell others. Raym Munday used to go to Baltimore.
> CJ: That's right, to Baltimore.

TR: Sherrie, they'd drive, and they said that Raym would get a car full, and they'd pay his expenses, and Raym wouldn't stop. He'd eat crackers and have a soft drink and keep driving.

CJ: Drive all night long to see a ballgame with no sleep.

TR: People had never been anywhere, and they had the money to travel. That was a vacation. The story that I used to hear told was that before Pacific people would put on overalls on a Sunday afternoon and go down and sit on the front porch of the office. That was their diversion to get out of the house.[25]

Tom Ross said that entertainment prior to vacation pay was to dress up and go down to the Company Store. Pacific allowed employees to venture out to other cities and states.

Jones and Ross also discussed bonuses that were given to the office staff during Pacific's tenure.

TR: Pacific paid us extra at the first of the year depending on whatever profit was made. I'm not sure how they did it.

CJ: It was a percentage of our salary. That's what it was.

TR: They determined whether they were going to pay you or not. They had to be successful.

CJ: They had to make money in order to pay us. There was one year that I got enough to buy a new automobile.

TR: I knew that there was a lot of money paid.

CJ: Yes, the extra was enough to buy a new car.

TR: Oh, man. New cars.

CJ: And as well as I remember, that was '53. No, '54, I believe. Because I bought a car. I had a '49. I wrecked it and bought a '50. Then I bought a '54. I believe that it was '54.[26]

Pacific allowed a working man to purchase cars, go on vacations, and have needed medical procedures.

Butler Monteith and Tom Ross discussed Pacific's providing a profit-sharing plan for their employees. Tom stated, "That was unheard of. Pacific Mills started it."[27] When Pacific Mills took over leadership of the plants, the eight-hour rule was already in vogue as per Roosevelt's National Industrial Recovery Act. Shelley Teague said that Pacific gave a bonus for overtime pay. Shelley said, "If you worked for Pacific over eight hours, it was time and a half. Burlington required it to be over forty hours. You didn't get time and a half unless you worked over forty hours.[28] Another benefit that was alluded to in the *Pacific Truths* article was the canteen. Willard Herman said that his wife, Ruth Earley Herman, ran the vending area. She worked mostly at Plant 1, but she also went over to Plant 2 when she was needed. She ran the canteen for Gene and Buddy Glass who operated the Company Store.[29] Employees benefited from an onsite canteen. Pacific brought many needed items to the mill workers to retain them and recruit others. Pacific Mills did hire people at the mills although initially they cut employees. Boyce Hartsoe and Dan Hartsoe came in 1946 and 1947 respectively. Joe Aldridge came in 1950. Joe stated, "I came here for the sole purpose of work because there was nothing in the mountains. Well, it was the 1950s, and there wasn't anything. Farming was all there was."[30] Pacific hired people that showed an interest in textiles and who were good workers. Boyd Brown determined that "Pacific was at the top for paying for textile workers."[31] Many people were interested in working for Pacific because of the pay, vacations, and health insurance.

Pacific Mills was instrumental in the success of the Rhodhiss community and the mill company. Prior to Pacific's coming to town, the mill company was lagging in new concepts and equipment. Working conditions were made better with the arrival of Pacific, and the hard-working employees relished the benefits that were offered for the first time. Rhodhiss' textile future was brighter with their arrival.

RHODHISS MILL VILLAGE LATE 1940S. PACIFIC MILLS PHOTO.

PACIFIC TRUTHS COVER MAY 1949, RHODHISS VILLAGE. PACIFIC MILLS PHOTO.

CALDWELL PLANT OF PACIFIC MILLS LATE 1940S WITH REFLECTION IN THE WATER.
PACIFIC MILLS PHOTO.

Miss Hendrix Honored

A Birthday Party was held in the honor of Miss Shirley Hendrix, daughter of Mr. and Mrs. Jack Hendrix of Rhodhiss at their home on Shelby Street, Saturday night, February 2, 1952. Games were played and refreshments were served to the following guests: Glenna Woods, Shirley Hendrix, Sue Kaylor, Patsy Craig, Mina Sherrill, Juanita Kirly, Loretta Hendrix, Peggy Teague, Gail Hendrix, Valerie Hendrix, Wayne Teague, Gary Hinson, Carol Wilson, Glenn Link, Raydee Parhams, Bud Dula, Jackie Bowman, and Johnny Perry.

ARTICLE IN *PACIFIC TRUTHS* 1952.

JUNE 1953 *PACIFIC TRUTHS* FATHER'S DAY COVER WITH CALVIN JONES, ROGER, GERALD, DAVID, AND RITA JONES. CALVIN'S SON HAROLD WAS ABSENT FROM THE PICTURE BECAUSE HE WAS VISITING GRANDPARENTS IN SOUTH CAROLINA

Jo Ann Childers, daughter of Mr. and Mrs. W. M. Childers, Rhodhiss Division, is an "A" student and will be in the 8th grade this fall. Mr. Childers is a Second Hand in the No. 2 Card Room.

and great grandson of the Henry Paynes.

Karen Leigh, six, is the daughter of Mr. and Mrs. Coleman Norman of the Rhodhiss Division. Mr. and Mrs. Norman are one of the numerous husband-wife teams working at Rhodhiss, both employed in No. 2 Spinning.

ARTICLE FROM *PACIFIC TRUTHS* 1953.

NOTES

1   Jones, Calvin and Tom Ross.

2   Jones, Calvin and Tom Ross.

3   Herman, Willard and Tom Ross.

4   Bean, Ned and Elvie and Tom Ross.

5   Townsend, Hans and Katherine and Tom Ross.

6   Simmons, Finn and Pawnee and Tom Ross.

7   Townsend, Hans and Katherine and Tom Ross.

8   Beshears, Monteith, Ross, Teague.

9   Jones, Calvin and Tom Ross.

10 "Pacific Mills Net Shows Big Rise over 1945." *Women's Wear Daily*. 19 February 1947. Vol. 74, Issue 35, page 7.

11 Bolick, Mary Starnes and Tom Ross.

12 "Pacific Mills 1949 Profit $3,806,194 on $99,807,948." *Women's Wear Daily*. 21 February 1950. Vol. 80, Issue 36, page 16.

13 Townsend, Hans and Katherine and Tom Ross.

14 "Pacific Develops Experimental Yarn of Vicara and Nylon." *Women's Wear Daily*. 15 May 1950, Vol. 80, Issue, 94, page 20.

15 Kirby, Beth.

16 "Cotton Spinners Cautioned on Handling Synthetics in Blends." *Women's Wear Daily*. 16 April 1952. Vol. 84, Issue 75, page 2B.

17 "H. C. Cobb." *Women's Wear Daily*. 9 May 1956. Vol. 92, Issue 91, page 15.

18 Elmore, Tommy.

19 Elmore, Fred and Martha and Tom Ross.

20 Beshears, Monteith, Ross, and Teague.

21 Herman, Willard and Tom Ross.

22 "Rhodhiss." *Pacific Truths*. May 1949. Pages 1 & 4.

23 Bolick, Mary Starnes and Tom Ross.

24 Jones, Calvin and Tom Ross.

25 Jones, Calvin and Tom Ross.

26 Jones, Calvin and Tom Ross.

27 Beshears, Monteith, Ross, and Teague.

28 Beshears, Monteith, Ross, and Teague.

29 Herman, Willard and Tom Ross.

30 Aldridge, Joe and Olive.

31 Brown, Boyd and Cora.

CHAPTER 21
PACIFIC MILLS: COMMUNITY IMPROVEMENTS

Pacific Mills not only improved the mills, but they also modernized the town. Within a few years of their arrival, they fixed the mill houses, built more homes, paved the roads, installed plumbing, and beautified the village. The millhands were still renting from the mill owners, but the homes needed repairs. Pacific saw the needs, and they were ready to make the village a community where inhabitants felt pride.

Tom Ross told Frank Byars about Pacific's acquisition of Rhodhiss. He stated, "Pacific Mills bought these mills for 18% of the book value, and that was nearly nothing. You would be surprised what they paid for the land: 500 and some odd acres. The mills were in bad shape when Pacific came in. They spent $2 million just on the village, and $5 million collectively. Pacific Mills saved this community."[1] Pacific took pride in their new community, and they were eager to make it the best that it could be. A 1946 *Women's Wear Daily* article entitled "Preliminary Net for Pacific Mills Put at $1,996,070," said, "In September of last year the company purchased Rhodhiss Cotton Mills Company in Rhodhiss, N. C. and is continuing its operation."[2] Obviously, Pacific Mills was a lucrative business with high aspirations for Rhodhiss.

Tom Ross and Calvin Jones both came to Rhodhiss from South Carolina. Tom had been working for Pacific in Lyman when he was given the opportunity to transfer to Rhodhiss. His wife Frances and their son Cary stayed in South Carolina until Tom decided he wanted to move permanently. Later, Frances and Cary made the move, too, and the family never regretted their decision.[3] Similarly, Calvin Jones came to Rhodhiss to run the shop and be the master mechanic, but he had not worked for Pacific before. He was working in Greenville at J. P. Stevens. He had gone to high school with Alan Dameron who worked at Rhodhiss, and later, another high school classmate would join them, Charlie Spencer. After visiting the mill company, Calvin and his wife Marguerite decided not to move, but Pacific called numerous times and increased the offer. The Joneses finally agreed to come in November

1946. When Alan Dameron left Rhodhiss, Calvin became the plant engineer. "I have been very well pleased with Rhodhiss. Pacific Mills was good to me. Burlington Mills was good to me. I couldn't ask for a company, well either company, to be any better than they were to me."[4] The Rhodhiss villagers knew Calvin Jones and Tom Ross well, and both were very fine men. They discussed how they were well received:

> TR: One other thing that I wanted to mention. We, coming in here from
> South Carolina, ordinarily you would think that when a company transfers people in, you'd have a hard time getting along. We were really received warmly, and we were treated just like we were kinfolk. It beat anything that I ever saw.
> CJ: We were. No doubt about it.
> TR: Yes. You would have thought that the villagers would have held grudges. If anybody bought a new car, nobody was jealous. Folks were just as happy for you as they could be.
> CJ: Yes, they were. They sure were.
> TR: That gets back to that same good community that was here that we've talked about. I mean, we from South Carolina came in and took this place over.
> CJ: Yes, we did. Because what they did, they moved everybody from those mills down there up here. They certainly did because they had people that they knew and depended on.
> TR: Well, the villagers knew that the mills were going to fall down.
> CJ: That's right. The mill company wasn't keeping up the machinery.
> TR: There were improvements needed in the village.
> CJ: Right. That helped a whole lot. It sure did.
> TR: That was a wise decision to do that quickly.
> CJ: If you remember, there wasn't anything but dirt roads here. That's all. Every street around here was dirt. The main road leading into the mill was paved.
> TR: The one across the river was dirt. (Burke).
> CJ: Yes, it was dirt.
> TR: The story I always heard was that you couldn't ride these streets on a bicycle because if you did, it would scratch your legs.
> CJ: Is that right?
> TR: Yes.
> CJ: I can believe that though because no one had cars.[5]

As Tom and Calvin stated, they were welcomed with opened arms by the villagers. The community was ready for better working and living conditions.

Pacific Truths magazine, which was published by Pacific Mills, did a feature story on Rhodhiss in May 1949. The article credited the Woman's Club for beautifying the town. Some of Pacific's improvements were blacktopped roads, houses being torn down to straighten the road, relocation of houses, and new home builds. The older houses had new roofs and brick underpinning (the old stilts were removed, and the houses were given foundations). After the water and sewer were completed, the mill company started the project of running water and indoor bathrooms. Grading was completed at the school, and the playground had superior new equipment. Two swamps were drained, and grass was planted while yards were raked and cleared. Many homes added front porches. The Methodist and Baptist churches had neat, green lawns and new shrubbery. Streetlights were updated. The school added a cafeteria, and there was a new community library. A boat dock was completed which made the personnel manager, J. W. Culclasure a happy man.[6] In 1949 Rhodhiss was one of the finest mill villages within the state.

When the roads were unpaved, they were not named. People referred to areas as hills or sections. Ned Bean described the main road in Caldwell County as Sand Clay Road in Chapter 9. This street was the first to be paved in the 1930s; none of the others were paved until after 1945 with the arrival of Pacific. Pawnee Simmons named some of the roads. She stated to Tom Ross and me:

PS: None of the streets were named. They were all dirt. There were sections that had names.

SH: Like Strawberry Hill?

PS: Strawberry Hill, Pee Ridge, Middle Hill, Riverside.

SH: Where was that? Beside the river?

PS: Yeah.

TR: I've never heard that.

PS: Hotel Hill. Church Hill, that's where the old Baptist Church was. Schoolhouse Hill. Everybody knew where the schoolhouse was. Barbershop Hill.

SH: You didn't have street names?

PS: No, just sections, you know. Superintendent Hill, Reservoir Hill.

SH: Reservoir, is that the Duke Power area?

PS: Yeah. Right before you go around the curve at the offices down there. That hill there. Now whether the reservoir was in operation or not, I don't know, but right on top of that hill there was the reservoir. So, they called that Reservoir Hill. Over there in that section where they built the last new houses that is where the ball park was. The name of it was Ball Park.

SH: The name of it now is Park Avenue.

PS: Is that right? Over there in back of the dam it was kindly remote like. It was called Lover's Lane. This picture is at part of the hill at Lover's Lane.

SH: Is this you and Finn?

PS: Yeah.[7]

FINN AND PAWNEE SIMMONS AT THE FOOT OF RESERVOIR HILL. PAWNEE SIMMONS PHOTO.

Pawnee lived in Rhodhiss when she was a young child after moving there in the early 1920s. She knew the neighborhoods and their names.

Tom Ross added information to Ned Bean about paving the roads. Tom said, "When they paved the streets, they had to rob everybody's yard and garden and everything else to get topsoil to go on those little ole hills."[8] Joe and Olive Aldridge were the first to mention GI Hill. They told me:

> OA: They started building houses on GI Hill.
> SH: GI, where's GI Hill?
> JA: Over here at Calvin Jones' house.
> SH: Why do they call it GI?
> JA: Well, a bunch of the houses were built for the GIs coming home from World War II. Well, some of them were for GIs. The more modern ones, up where Calvin lives on out that street.
> OA: We have Strawberry and Middle Hill. Then there's GI Hill.[9]

GI stands for Government Issue. The houses on GI Hill were designated for returning veterans because some of the materials were purchased from the government.

Calvin Jones as the plant engineer was very knowledgeable about the building of new homes and the modernization of the present ones. Calvin and Tom Ross spoke with me about Pacific's new builds:

> CJ: I think within three years here or at least the first three years that I was here, my understanding from the engineering department in Lyman was they spent $5,000,000 on the village and the mill. That's a lot of money. Back then, that was a lot of money!
> TR: Shoo!
> SH: $5 million. That is a lot of money.
> CJ: '46, '47, and '48.
> TR: Tell her about the troubles that we had getting it. We were trying to make it. We couldn't buy brick. Couldn't buy windows.
> SH: Because of war aftereffects?
> TR: Yeah.
> CJ: We built 40 houses as well as I remember.
> TR: You added up 42 the other day.
> CJ: Well, 42. Two were after houses burned down on Strawberry. We added two more over there. We had to saw the lumber and cut the trees at Henry Smith's. We had him saw the lumber up at his sawmill. They hauled to the site where we were building these houses. That's how we got the lumber. The government let us buy these old bathroom fixtures that they had stored somewhere. We couldn't let anyone move into the houses except a veteran, someone that had been in the service.
> SH: Is that why your area is referred to as 'GI Hill?'
> CJ: Exactly. That's one of the reasons. That was the first part that we built. That's the reason

that they call it GI because everybody that moved up there when they first opened it up after they built the houses were veterans. The company rented them, but they couldn't rent them except to veterans. That's how the government let us get this material. I was the first one that moved in because they were paying my room and board up here in Granite, and they were wanting to get that load off them and get me moved in. Of course, I was like Tom. I was going back and forth to Greenville every weekend. They wanted to stop that, too, because they wanted me here on the weekends to get a lot of work done. C. M. Guest, a building contractor from Anderson, South Carolina, was hired to build the houses, the last 42. Pacific had them working on a lot. Do you remember Clay Basinger?

TR: I was trying to think of that name.

CJ: He was the superintendent on the job for C. M. Guest.

TR: Is that right?

CJ: Tom, his brother, worked for him. Tom was a crackerjack carpenter himself. Of course, Tom married one of the Hendrix girls, and he lives over here in the country now.

TR: Tom Basinger?

CJ: Yes. He married Jack Hendrix's sister. You remember the Hendrix boys and girls.

TR: Yeah. I don't remember her per say. There were a lot of Hendrixes in the mill at one time.[10]

Pacific put five million dollars into the village and mills within three years. The town certainly flourished during this period.

Tom Ross, Shelley Teague, Doughton Beshears, and Butler Monteith discussed the building of the houses under Pacific, and the relocation of the main road in Burke County. They were able to add to Calvin's recollection:

ST: Yeah, they built those houses for returning veterans. They are newer houses. They built mine in '47.

TR: They built 40 houses or more.

ST: They sawed their own lumber to build them.

BM: Yeah, they cut down trees from here and back in there where Clarkson Jones' house was.

ST: Down in the holler, down in there.

BM: Old John Kirby

ST: He sold half of it.

BM: I believe that they brought somebody here to build them. Piney Randall would go over there and check the lumber.

SH: The constable, Piney Randall?

BM: Yeah, he would go over there and check it.

TR: Well, the sawmill was right down below the Baptist parsonage.

ST: There was one up about Perry Weaver's in the holler there. A sawmill up there.

DB & BM: Yeah

BM: You cut off there at the top of the hill.

DB: Right this side of the filter bed, right in there.

BM: Right there where Earl Bumgarner lived between those houses there was a wagon road that went down in there. I can remember the old road going around. Where the old Methodist Church was, it went around it. Then the next one went up by Kurt Smith's in that curve and went around. Just about like it is now to go up to GI Hill. Kurt Smith lived above the Rhodhiss Town Office (Burke Street).

ST: There were two houses sitting right in that curve. They moved the houses. Those two against the bank.

BM: They were facing this way.

ST: Yeah, they were facing this way as you go right up that curve to go to the Joneses. That's the way that the old road went.

ST: Those two houses, Kurt Smith lived in one and

BM: Fred Hendrickson

ST: I am talking about later. The carpenter boss, Willard Howell. He lived in the other one.

BM: Yeah, that was a long time ago.

ST: That was before they moved them.[11]

Calvin Jones lived on Dogwood Drive, and the lumber was cut above his house, closer to the Henry Smith area. In addition, the men noted that there were two other locations for sawmills within the town. The lumber was cut within the town and hauled to the worksite. The two houses above TGIF Ministry on Burke Street were moved to their present location. They were sitting in the present road area.

Willard Herman discussed the building of the mill houses when Pacific came in 1945. Willard declared, "Those houses were built out of green lumber to start with. They gapped them. They had big wide cracks in them. Estes said that he just wasn't aware of that. I believe that the way that they got permission to build the houses was that they had to move a veteran in. It was called GI Hill. Lew Hendrix had lived in one house, but when I went to work with them, it was vacant. They gave me that house."[12] The lumber used was still green when they built these houses. Finn Simmons also discussed the building of the houses on GI Hill. Finn stated, "That was a curve where you turn back down in there to go to Henry Smith's. They built those new houses up in there where Calvin lives when Pacific bought out. Go over here to John Kirby, right over here. He cut all that timber out in there for Pacific. Then going on up the hill there where J. R. Hefner or Perry Rice lived. There were only two houses there. Shortly Elmore lived in one of them, and Grover Church lived in the other. When they built the roads, they made that road in there by Calvin's."[13] Pacific built approximately 42 houses in Rhodhiss when they came. Some of those houses were on Dogwood, Park, Carolina, and Hillcrest.

In the early days of Rhodhiss near present-day Marion Avenue, the Methodists had a small church. Later, this became an apartment building. Then it became a clubhouse. Calvin Jones and Tom Ross detailed its remodeling. They said:

CJ: Yes. We remodeled it when

TR: We upgraded the village?

CJ: Well, we remodeled it to make apartments. Then we came back later and remodeled it for a clubhouse.

TR: I was thinking of the apartments.

CJ: Yeah, we made four apartments out of it.

TR: How did the building look before you started making the apartments? The construction.

CJ: Outside looked about like it did. We only changed the inside. It had two porches on each side and one on the front. That's the way it looked.[14]

The building was owned by the mill company, and it served various purposes. According to Joe Aldridge it was later burned by the volunteer fire department.[15] Another house that was built by Pacific was not in Rhodhiss. Land was purchased in Hickory to build a home for the plant manager. Tom Ross said, "They built the house in Hickory for Joe Cobb in the 1940s. Estes succeeded Cobb. Then Craven as plant manager lived there when he came with Burlington."[16] The era of the upper management living on Superintendent Hill had ended.

FORMER METHODIST CHURCH; LATER A CLUB HOUSE

Another huge luxury for the mill village was running water, which led to indoor plumbing. Doughton Beshears declared, "We didn't have water in the houses or inside toilets at one time. Pacific Mills came and took care of that."[17] Not having to carry water from a well or a spigot brought happiness and relief to the mill workers. Jack Edwards rejoiced, "Glory Days were when water was on the back porch."[18] The townspeople were thrilled to have water available on their back porch or within the house. Only a few houses had indoor plumbing prior to Pacific's arrival. Cora Brown said that when she moved to her house on Carolina Avenue in 1946, she liked to tell people that her home had "three rooms and a path."[19] Cora and Boyd liked to tease people about their outdoor toilet. She pointed to its former existence behind her house. Calvin Jones talked about Massie Mullinax, who was the mill's master mechanic. Calvin said, "Mr. Mullinax had plumbing packed into his house, and it was one of the few houses that had plumbing inside. He updated the water system within the village. Yeah, he was some more genius mechanic, Mr. Mullinax was."[20] Pacific installed plumbing in all the homes. Calvin and Tom Ross mulled over the bathrooms being installed. They said:

TR: I don't know how many carpenters you had back then.

CJ: Well, back when we were doing that, we had about five or six. We ended up though we only had two. Then we had Cary Johnson to come up and supervise. He was a crackerjack carpenter. He came up and kinda supervised and built all these bathrooms on all these houses. He just replumbed the whole house because they didn't have plumbing in the houses.

TR: They had to underpin them because they were so high off the ground.

CJ: Yeah, we had to underpin them to keep them from freezing, and it made them look better, too.[21]

Underpinning the houses allowed the homes to be warmer and safer. Some of the houses on those stilts looked as if they were ready to fall off.

Since the mill company and the town were one in the same until Burlington came, Pacific paid for the sewer system. The Rhodhiss Town minutes depict the story:

> December 12, 1947, the Town Council asked Pacific Mills (Mr. C. B. Hayes, VP) for funds to construct a sewer system and water line for Rhodhiss.
>
> December 20, 1947, the town was informed that Pacific Mills had contributed $200,000 for sewer and water lines. The town voted to employ Lockwood Greene Engineers, Inc. to draw plans, advertise for bids and supervise the installation of water and sewage systems.
>
> April 29, 1948, Lockwood Greene Engineers, Inc. announced that Elliott Building Company of Hickory, N. C. was the low bidder for the public sewer system and water system at a bid of $143,813, with 85% due when delivery takes place and 15% upon completion of the project. Secondly, the town will contract with R. E. Faw and Sons, Inc. of Hickory for the drilling of two wells, one in Caldwell County and one in Burke County.
>
> September 15, 1948, Contracted with Setzer Construction Company, Inc. of Hickory for approximately 7000 square yards of Bituminous Surface Treatment for the roads.
>
> January 10, 1948, Letter to Mr. C. B. Hayes, VP of Pacific Mills asking for more money for sewer and water.
>
> May 31, 1949, Pacific Mills sent another $100,000 for town improvement.
>
> September 27, 1949 Fifty cents will be levied on each household receiving water from the Town.[22]

Rhodhiss was well on its way to modernization with the help of Pacific Mills. An article in the *Lenoir News Topic* in February 1969 stated, "The sewer system was installed during 1949. One story has it that at this time Rhodhiss was the only village in North Carolina that was 100% on a sanitary sewer system."[23] Some sources suggested that Rhodhiss was the first town of its size to get electricity in 1926; then in 1949 it was possibly the first village in North Carolina to have water and sewer.

Calvin Jones and Tom Ross also discussed the filter beds that were installed during Pacific's ownership. They stated:

TR: You need to tell her about putting in the sand filter.

CJ: Well, we put in water and sewer. We dug trenches and laid pipe. We put in the new wells. Then we built a sand filter bed across the river, which Pacific Mills paid for. We had four sand filters over there. We had septic tanks that the sewer runs through. We had a septic tank on either side of the river. The sewer runs into it, and we had a pump station. I guess you've noticed that brick house to the left of the bridge. That's the pumping station. The solids stay in the septic tank and the fluid overflows into this pumping station. It pumps it across the river to the dossing tank. The dossing tank will kick off automatically when it gets full and dump 11,000 gallons of water over one sand filter. Then it will fill up again; then the second sand filter will dump and fill it up. The third one and the fourth one and start over again. By the time that the first one gets empty before it will start dumping again, it will be empty and be ready for another dump. It filters it out and goes through a chlorinator, and it's chlorinated and then sent back to the river, and it's 99% pure.

TR: You had to turn the sand over frequently.

CJ: Well, once a week I had to rake it to break the crust. If you don't, it will get waxy and seal off, and the water won't go through the filter. So, when I handled it, I had a man that would go over and take one day a week to rake the filter beds. He could do it in eight hours. That's the way it was when I left it. I don't know how it is now. The state was strict in their rules.

TR: Like they put that 20,000-gallon tank out there in front of number one mill.

CJ: You couldn't even dump the water in the river.

TR: He couldn't dump that water from the cleaning system into the river.

CJ: We used to dump the boiler water which is pure. I used to take the boiler water and put in my battery because it was purer than any water that you could get out of your faucet. It's kinda like distilled water. When it condenses, there are no impurities in it. That's what I put into batteries. They stopped us from dumping that into the river because they said that it was polluting the river. The only reason that it could pollute the river is if it had a leak in the boiler lines getting back to the steam. We had that to happen once, and I think that's the reason that they made us put that tank out there to put all this stuff in it. It went to the sand filters and filtered back.

TR: Oh man. These supervisors had hard jobs.[24]

As plant engineer Calvin oversaw many areas, sewer, plumbing, and electrical to name a few.

Calvin and Tom discussed an incident that happened after water and sewer were installed in the village. It was Thanksgiving, and when the plant closed for the holiday weekend, the weather was extremely nice and warm. Most of the management left town on vacation with Calvin and Tom returning to South Carolina. Over the holiday the temperature dropped drastically. Calvin and Tom described the problems to me:

CJ: Anyhow we got back here and couldn't get water on. When it began to thaw out, we began to have leaks. Water was running out all into the river, running off the bridge. We had a time. We just went to work on it, and we got fire hoses to get water across the river because we only had the well on this side of the river (Caldwell).

TR: It was up behind the schoolhouse.

CJ: Right.

SH: Did we have fire hoses, or did you have to get them from Granite?

CJ: The mill had them.

SH: Yes, I guess that the mill would have.

CJ: We were the fire department, day and night.

SH: Ohhh! So, until we got a fire department, was that the way that it was?

CJ: Yeah. Until Rhodhiss started a volunteer fire department.

TR: Sherrie, Calvin and his department were responsible for everything. Yeah. Calvin, I had forgotten about that fire department.

CJ: Yeah, when we had these three houses on fire. You know when you go up Strawberry, there's a road that you turn off to the right beside that little old Stevens house. It used to be a store. Back in that area three of those houses were on fire at one time. One of them burned down. We saved the other two.

TR: I didn't know that.

CJ: Yeah. It was the shop fire department that saved them. It happened while I was at lunch one day. When I returned, we had a telephone call that a house was on fire on Strawberry. So, I grabbed a bunch of the boys, and we jumped in the truck with the fire hose. We went up there.

SH: Were there hydrants?

CJ: Yeah. After we put in the water lines, we had hydrants. But the pressure wasn't enough to get the water on top of the houses. We did get up there and manage to save those other two houses that were on fire, too, but we lost the one.

TR: Yeah, if something happened at the house, commode stopped up, you called the shop. If a house caught on fire, you called the shop. If the mill stopped off, you called the shop.

CJ: That's right. We took care of the electrical, streetlights, and power lines on the streets.

SH: How many people did you have working in the shop under you?

CJ: When I first came to work, I was telling Tom the other day, I had on the shop payroll 130 some people.

TR: Shooo!

CJ: But we were doing a lot of work. We were doing work on the village.

TR: The village was being changed over.

CJ: We were building bathrooms on these houses, putting plumbing in these houses. We were changing the mill. We were taking out all the machinery in the mill. Putting in new machinery and rewiring. Of course, a lot of this was contract work, but they had to report to me. That's the way that we handled it.

SH: So, the new houses were contract labor?

CJ: They were contract labor, but I kinda supervised that. They'd come into the shop, and they would punch in at the shop. The shop when I came here was at the back end of this mill on this side (Caldwell), what we called the number 1 mill. It was on the second floor. Then later we cut a hole in the floor and built a place underneath that. It was a cement floor. We cut a hole in the floor and dropped the machinery down to the first floor. Then we stayed there for a while. We had a road right down beside the mill, if you remember that, Tom. It went into the shop. It was right beside the mill. I had some really good people in the shop. Really good people. Had people that knew their business: Will McGuire, Fred Elmore, Thad Elmore, Junior Starnes, Kelly Fulbright, Ellis Winkler, Floyd McRary.

TR: And they were all local people. You didn't have to go recruit.

CJ: That's right. I can just keep on naming good people: the Austin boys, Dude and Jim, and Jim was a crackerjack electrician; Dean Bowles; Claude Johnson; Ab Story; all were just good people. I mean that you didn't have to worry about them. You'd give them a job to do, and they'd go out and do it. Just really good employees. Mr. Mullinax was a crackerjack mechanic. Even his children were good mechanics. I had two of the boys on the second shift from time to time. I had one of them on the first shift. All of them were just good mechanics. Of course, rightly so because Mr. Mullinax was good himself because he did the training. He was the master mechanic down here for years. Of course, when Pacific bought, his health was bad, and Claude Carpenter was the master mechanic at that time.

TR: Who was the plumber that lived over in the Baton community, Calvin?

CJ: Charles Brooks. The police chief was on the company payroll. The mill company handled it. They told him what to do. He was on my payroll. The mill company owned the town.

SH: Mr. Ross, as office manager/town clerk, did you have to mail water bills?

TR: There weren't water bills then.

CJ: They didn't start sending water bills until the town took over from the mill company. They put the meters in.

SH: Were there taxes?

CJ: People didn't pay taxes.

SH: Can you believe that? That is interesting.

CJ: That is hard to believe, isn't it? It's true. The company owned the town. They took care of everything. I was telling Tom. People would call me at 3:00 AM or 4:00 AM because we had an electrical storm, and it would blow fuses. They'd call me, and I'd go put a fuse in. Just things like that. I'd get up, put my clothes on, go over, check it out, put the fuse in rather than have the boy go from the mill. I'd just go check it myself.

TR: He had one employee on third shift.

CJ: They'd call me day and night. I worked day and night for this mill, but they were still good to me. If they hadn't been good to me, I couldn't have done it.[25]

Calvin's and Tom's dialogue is so amazing. The mill company provided the fire department and the police department. The police salary was included in Calvin's shop budget. If there was a fire, the shop men had to fight it. The shop was responsible for changing fuses in the mill houses and all the upkeep. Employees were not billed for the water because a fifty-cent charge was added to their rent. Water meters were not installed on houses until they were sold. People did not pay taxes because they did not own property. As Calvin said, "the mill company owned the town." Tom Ross served as office manager for Pacific Mills and later Burlington. As stated in Chapter 7 when Pacific had the plants, the office manager also served as the town clerk and had to serve on the school board. That was part of the job description.[26]

At one point Tom Ross had discussed the shortage of materials in building the houses and in adding plumbing and underpinning. Appliances were also in demand. Calvin said that he and his wife could not secure a cook stove and refrigerator for their house that they rented from the mill company. Calvin stated:

> We couldn't buy refrigerators or ranges because there was just a shortage. We were buying a lot of Westinghouse equipment at the plant, and I went over to the Westinghouse dealer for Hickory, and they said, 'Goodness, we have forty people on the list wanting refrigerators and stoves. I can't tell you when we can get you a stove and refrigerator.' So, we were getting ready to put in a $100,000 switchgear here (Caldwell) and a $100,000 switchgear at the other mill (Burke) that Westinghouse was building. So, we told Westinghouse, and Westinghouse sent me a refrigerator and a stove with my name tagged to it to Hickory, and everybody else was still on the list. Of course, they would have gotten mad if they had known that they let me have it as a newcomer and people in Hickory were wanting appliances.[27]

Many items continued to be in short supply even after World War II. Bricks, appliances, lumber, electrical fixtures, and plumbing items were hard to find as the mill's shop employees found. Hans and Kat Townsend and Tom Ross discussed this shortage, too. They stated:

> HT: Yeah, we survived. It was a pretty good place.
>
> TR: Pacific was a Godsend to this place.
>
> HT: Yeah, Pacific was the best thing that ever happened here.
>
> TR: Pacific spent $2 million up here quick. They built more houses, underpinned the houses, paved the streets, put bathrooms in.
>
> HT: I will tell you. Pacific was fine people. They really changed this place. They paved the roads.
>
> TR: Back then, stuff was hard to get. They had trouble getting brick to underpin these houses. They got stuff from North Wilkesboro from Lowes up there. That was the only place that they could get it.
>
> KT: That was one of the best things that they ever did for the Town of Rhodhiss or the village. Underpinning helped a lot.[28]

Tom Ross and the Townsends were pleased with Pacific's ownership of the mills and the town.

Another addition to the town when Pacific came was the initiation of the Woman's Club. Many of the town's women were active in this club. As stated in Chapter 11, the Woman's Club raised the money for the school's cafeteria equipment. In *Pacific Truths* magazine an article detailed some of the events for the Woman's Club. The article stated:

> Installation of new officers and presentation of a club building by Superintendent H. C. Estes on behalf of Pacific Mills were highlights of the Rhodhiss Woman's Club held in May. Mr. Estes, in a surprise announcement, stated that a house across the street from the school was being presented the club as a Clubhouse and it is expected that this permanent headquarters will serve as an incentive for further fine work by this active club. Mrs. Paul Elmore, president, called the meeting to order with Mrs. D. D. Annas leading in prayer. Mrs. J. V. McKinney and Mrs. Hayden Hayes, delegates to the state convention, gave interesting reports of the meeting. Mrs. Gordon Starnes reported on the welfare work done by the club which gave the organization the state award for the second consecutive year for outstanding work. Mrs. Henry M. Anderson then introduced Mrs. Estes who presented the Woman of the Year, Mrs. Bernard Coleman, with a silver compote for her fine work in the community. Mrs. Linda Robinson installed the new officers, using a beautiful candlelighting ceremony. New officers are Mrs. Paul Elmore, president; Mrs. Bernard Coleman, vice president; Mrs. Tom Ross, secretary; Mrs. John Bolan, corresponding secretary and Mrs. J. V. McKinney, treasurer. The following guests were recognized by the President: Mrs. Worth Yount, President of the Granite Falls Woman's Club; Mrs. W. E. Yount of the *Granite Falls Press*; Mrs. Baine L. Smith, President Granite Falls Junior Woman's Club; Mrs. M. M. Barnett of Greenwood, S. C., mother of Mr. James Barnett; Mrs. Reid Thompson of Hickory, who was the former Mrs. Esther Barrett and a former member of the club; Mr. and Mrs. H. C. Estes of Hickory, Mrs. J. W. Bolan of Winterport, Maine, mother of Mr. John Bolan; and Mrs. Lina Robinson of Granite Falls.[29]

The house that was presented to the Woman's Club used to sit on the present-day Baptist Church property, but that house was moved to 208 Magnolia Street. Rhodhiss was fortunate to have women who gave to their community. They bettered the town by having beautification days, helping needy families, obtaining playground equipment, and providing a cafeteria for the elementary children.

According to the town minutes, in 1951 a taxi service was started in Rhodhiss. Ray Foxx, operator of the old Rhodhiss Shell Station made an application to the town to operate a taxi service with the headquarters to be a vacant lot between the town limits and the old Rhodhiss Shell Station. The fees follow: Shell Station to Granite Falls: 30 cents; E. S. Glass and Sons' Store and#1 Village to Granite Falls: 40 cents; #2 mill to Granite Falls: 40 cents; Strawberry to Granite Falls: 75 cents; Dogwood Drive and Hillcrest Avenue to Granite Falls: 75 cents; Shell Station to Hickory: $2.00;

Shell Station to Lenoir: $3; otherwise, 15 cents per mile. On December 3, 1951, Ray Foxx sold this service to O. G. Triplett.[30] Rhodhiss citizens were able to travel to Hickory, Lenoir, and Granite Falls easily with the taxi service if they had the fare.

Pacific Mills came to Rhodhiss as "a Godsend" in the words of Tom Ross. They put five million dollars into the town and company within three years. The villagers were able to live a life that allowed them happiness and luxuries for the first time. They had bathrooms in their homes, they were warm because of the underpinning of the houses, they had paved roads, they had health insurance, and they were able to go on vacations. Their children no longer had to return home from school for lunch because of the Woman's Club's providing a cafeteria. Yes, Pacific Mills really did affect the lives of the millhands in a positive way.

CAROLINA AVENUE, ALSO CALLED STRAWBERRY HILL. LATE 1940S. PACIFIC MILLS PHOTO

CAROLINA AVENUE, ALSO CALLED STRAWBERRY HILL. LATE 1940S. PACIFIC MILLS PHOTO

PARK AVENUE. LATE 1940S. UNPAVED ROADS. PACIFIC MILLS PHOTO.

PARK AVENUE. NEW HOUSES CONSTRUCTED. LATE 1940S. PACIFIC MILLS PHOTO.

MAGNOLIA STREET, ALSO CALLED BARBERSHOP HILL. LATE 1940S. PACIFIC MILLS PHOTO.

MAGNOLIA STREET, LATE 1940S, UNPAVED ROADS. PACIFIC MILLS PHOTO.

CHURCH STREET, LATE 1940S. PACIFIC MILLS PHOTO.

BIRCH STREET AREA, LATE 1940S. PACIFIC MILLS PHOTO.

CATAWBA AVENUE. LATE 1940S. PACIFIC MILLS PHOTO.

HICKORY STREET, ALSO CALLED PEE RIDGE. LATE 1940S, UNPAVED ROADS. PACIFIC MILLS PHOTO.

RHODHISS' WOMAN'S CLUB FEATURED IN
PACIFIC TRUTHS. 1953. PACIFIC MILLS PHOTO.

THIS SIGN WAS OUTSIDE THE CLUB HOUSE
ON MAGNOLIA STREET WHERE THE WOMAN'S
CLUB MET; HOWEVER, THE ORIGINAL SITE
WAS ON THE PRESENT-DAY BAPTIST CHURCH
PROPERTY, AND THE HOUSE WAS MOVED TO
208 MAGNOLIA STREET. SHERRIE HARTSOE
SIGMON PHOTO.

NOTES

1   Byars, Frank and Jo, Fred and Martha Elmore, and Tom Ross.
2   "Preliminary Net for Pacific Mills Put at $1,996,070." *Women's Wear Daily*. 12 February 1946. Vol. 72, Issue 31, page 15.
3   Ross, Tom.
4   Jones, Calvin and Tom Ross.
5   Jones, Calvin and Tom Ross.
6   "Rhodhiss." *Pacific Truths*. May 1949, pages 1 & 4.
7   Simmons, Finn and Pawnee and Tom Ross.
8   Bean, Ned and Elvie and Tom Ross.
9   Aldridge, Joe and Olive.
10   Jones and Ross.
11   Beshears, Monteith, Ross, and Teague.
12   Herman, Willard and Tom Ross.
13   Simmons, Finn and Pawnee and Tom Ross.
14   Jones and Ross.
15   Aldridge, Joe and Olive.
16   Elmore, Fred and Martha and Tom Ross.
17   Beshears, Monteith, Ross, Teague.
18   Edwards, Arthur and Jack, Edna Edwards Laney Stilwell and Tom Ross.
19   Brown, Boyd and Cora.
20   Jones and Ross.
21   Jones and Ross.
22   Rhodhiss Town Minutes, 12 December 1947; 20 December 1947; 29 April 1948; 15 September 1948; 10 January 1948; 31 May 1949; 27 September 1949.
23   "Rhodhiss History." *Lenoir News Topic*. 26 February 1969, p. B13.
24   Jones and Ross.
25   Jones and Ross.
26   Beshears, Monteith, Ross, and Teague.
27   Jones and Ross.
28   Townsend, Hans and Katherine and Tom Ross.
29   "Rhodhiss Woman's Club Holds Meet." *Pacific Truths*. June 1953, page 7.
30   Rhodhiss Town Minutes. 11 April 1951 and 3 December 1951.

CHAPTER 22

RECREATION: HILLSIDE BEACH, CAMPING, AND SCOUTING

Hillside Beach in Rhodhiss was a happening place in the 1950s, 1960s and 1970s. Most people called it "Rhodhiss Beach," but its appointed name was Hillside. This beach provided entertainment, swimming with lifeguards on duty, and a concession stand. It was located off Carolina Avenue on Lake Drive. In the early 1960s Burlington Industries held an event there for their employees and families. The beach continued to have success in the 1970s, and it was closed in 1980. The Boy Scouts and Girl Scouts were also organizations that brought the youngsters within the community together. These fellowships provided many opportunities for children. Camping out by the lake was also an activity that many citizens enjoyed. Camping, scouting, and Hillside Beach brought recreation to the people of Rhodhiss.

Fred and Martha Elmore discussed Hillside Beach with Tom Ross and me. They talked about how the youth during the 1950s really enjoyed their time there, and it was a good place for people to congregate. Pacific Mills was the first to get involved in the beach venue. Fred, Martha, and Tom Ross stated:

FE: The mill company helped a lot at the beach after we got it started. Smokey (Shelley) Teague is the one who pushed the beach development.

ME: You know that the people of Rhodhiss really enjoyed that beach. Outsiders took it over though.

TR: Mr. Hayes told me that you will regret the day you opened that beach.

FE: As long as it was watched after there, was no problem.

ME: When it was really going well, people enjoyed it. That is when Les Weaver was the policeman.

TR: It was nice over there.

ME: They really fixed it up with lunch and concession stands. When Lanny was about 16, he worked over there and helped take care of it. The money went to the town. All the youth had a good time when they went to the beach.

TR: Pat Harris called me the other night.

ME: She was a lifeguard at Rhodhiss Beach for some time. She was fantastic.[1]

Fred and Martha's son Lanny worked at the beach when he was a teenager. Pat Harris was the lifeguard at the beach for a time, and she later moved to Florida. They were both raised in Rhodhiss.

HILLSIDE BEACH CONCESSIONS. 1960S.
SHERRIE HARTSOE SIGMON PHOTO.

HILLSIDE BEACH ACTIVITY. 1970S.
GRANITE FALLS PRESS PHOTO.

HILLSIDE BEACH SIGN. SHERRIE HARTSOE
SIGMON PHOTO.

HILLSIDE BEACH, JULY 1973. *GRANITE
FALLS PRESS* PHOTO.

The Rhodhiss Town Minutes have several entries relating to Hillside Beach. The first description was on August 7, 1950. The town agreed with Duke Power on July 17, 1950, to lease an area of Rhodhiss Lake for public recreational purposes at a cost of $2.50 for the rest of 1950, and the cost would be $5.00 for subsequent years payable in advance each year thereafter.[2] The town minutes indicate that on July 19, 1951, the town leased the land from Duke and opened Hillside Beach to the public. A canteen was operated to cover the expenses of the lifeguard, canteen help, and upkeep.[3] There was a jukebox at the beach for the enjoyment of the patrons, but in 1958 the town minutes state: "On June 14, 1958, upon motion and seconded it was agreed that the 'Juke Box' be locked up until such time as it can be removed." Upon another motion by a commissioner and seconded, it was agreed that "no dancing be allowed at Hillside Beach and that signs to such effect be posted at Hillside Beach."[4] Burlington Industries had an employee appreciation event at the beach. According to the town minutes on August 10, 1964, Bill Eckard made a motion and Claude Barker seconded that Hillside Beach be sprayed on August 19 to prepare for Burlington's use of the beach on August 20, 1964.[5] This property was not mentioned again in the minutes for years except for the continued payment to Duke Power for its rental. In the summer of 1974, the minutes state that Mr. and Mrs. Jerry Bowman and Mr. and Mrs. Larry Yount asked to operate the beach. The couples agreed to open the concessions from noon till sundown. The town provided materials for maintenance. The Bowmans and Younts were contracted labor with profits to be split 50-50.[6] In 1976 the board voted to purchase a jukebox for $250 for use.[7] In 1977 David Hollar and Neal Morrison operated the beach for the months of June, July, and August, but mostly on weekends (Thursdays-Sundays). The gate was closed at 9:00 PM.[8] David Hollar operated this venue during the summer of 1979.[9] The summer of 1980 was the last season of Hillside Beach's operation. On August 11, 1980 "No Trespassing" and "Beach Area Closed" signs were posted.[10] The town did renew their lease with Crescent Land and Timber Corporation though.[11] Over the years many youngsters and adults enjoyed sun and fun at this beach. Many people have commented that they learned to swim there, they met their boyfriend or girlfriend there, they heard a song for the first time on the jukebox, or that they were even baptized at Rhodhiss Beach. Ellis "Pete" Settlemyre explained that Cephus Lunsford told him to go out to the right of the diving board, and in a certain area he could walk on the old road that used to come through there. Pete said that he indeed swam out to find the old road near the high dive.[12] The Rhodhiss Beach area intrigued many youngsters.

Billie Sue Laney voiced her experiences at Rhodhiss Beach. She said that it was "the place to be." She recalled going as a small child in the early 1950s. After church on Sundays, families would go over and place their blankets on the sand to enjoy their picnics and let the children swim or play in the water. Many women still had their church clothes on while sitting there. She and her sister Marlene walked over to Lake Drive from Hickory Street when she was 12 or 13 years old. One time they decided to walk home barefoot. As they approached the bridge, their feet were burning up from the asphalt, so they never did that again. The girls would wear their clothes over to the beach and change in the hut structures. Billie and Marlene would swim, and then they would put their clothes back on to walk home. Billie said that she and Marlene did not like changing clothes, so one day they started out the door at their home on Hickory Street in their swimsuits. Their mother stopped them and said,

"Over my dead body will you walk out that door with your swimsuit on." During this time a bathing suit was used only at a location where swimming would happen and was not acceptable in other public areas. Billie said that the entire beach area was so clean and neat. It was well maintained by the town. Later, in the 1960s the Rhodhiss Volunteer Fire Department took over the beach maintenance. The concession stand area had soft drinks and candy bars. The boys hung out at the concession stand, and the girls liked to visit that area to flirt. The jukebox was loud, but not too loud, and the swimmers could hear it when they were in the water. She mentioned that Thad and Ruby Martin were there when she had just turned 16 years old. They had recently purchased a brand-new car, and they let her drive it to Granite Falls. She said that they handed the keys to her as if it were nothing. Other activities at the beach included walking the path to the Boy Scout hut or going down behind Vercie Cline's house to go to the dam. While visiting the dam area, she and others walked across the dam on several occasions. Vercie lived in the first house on the left when leaving the beach. Up above the wing of the dam, the view was beautiful. One time Billie almost drowned because she could not swim. She wanted to jump off the rock like everyone else. Marlene was down below the rock because she had just jumped. Marlene yelled at Billie not to jump, but she did. She landed on Marlene and then got scared. Billie started struggling, and Marlene had great difficulty getting her ashore. This did not hinder her from returning. She, as an adult, took her boys over there in the 1970s for them to enjoy the beach, too. Billie believes that the people who lived in Rhodhiss were happy people, and they spread that joy to others. Billie said, "Rhodhiss is always in our blood."[13] Billie's memories of Rhodhiss and the beach are priceless.

At various times in Rhodhiss the Boy Scouts and the Girl Scouts were active. During the 1930s a Boy Scout troop was active. Paul Bright said that he was a member of the Rhodhiss pack when he was a young man. Boyd Kirby was his scoutmaster during the late 1930s and early 1940s.[14] Tommy Elmore was also a scout, and he said that he enjoyed scouting. The scout hut was on the river. His scoutmaster was Mr. Ramsey, who was really strict. They would have campouts at the hut, and Mr. Ramsey would tell them to go to bed and go to sleep. The guys would wait till Mr. Ramsey fell asleep, and they would sneak out and go play in the river all night long.[15]

Boyd and Cora Brown discussed the Boy Scout program in Rhodhiss during the 1950s. They stated to me:

CB: Yeah, Boyd worked with the Boy Scouts about five years, didn't you Boyd?

BB: Yeah. One boy all that he lacked making an Eagle was having his tooth fixed.

SH: I don't understand.

BB: He was trying to get his health badge, and he passed everything but that. Yeah. He did well. He left here and went to the Army, I think it was.

CB: A funny incident involving Preacher Lay who was working with the Scouts, when Boyd was. He got onto a boy and asked him to come to church, you know. He kept trying to get him interested, and finally Preacher Lay told him that he needed to find something that he was interested in. Well, the boy decided that he wanted to sing in the church choir. They said that he couldn't sing, and the other members got to complaining about his singing. They wanted

Reverend Lay to get him to quit singing in the choir. Pastor Lay kept sorta hinting. Finally, Preacher Lay told the boy, 'Well, I just have to tell you that they say that you can't sing.' The boy said, 'Well, that's all right, preacher. A lot of them say that you can't preach either.'

BB: Preacher Lay was the Scoutmaster. After he left here, we had to find another one.

CB: Yeah, Boyd, Ben Pearson helped you, too.

BB: Yeah, he did. We had one boy who said that he wanted to be a scout all his life.[16]

Many men gave their time in Rhodhiss to help with the scouting program. *Pacific Truths* magazine in June 1953 had a short article detailing the awards of a few scouts. It declared that James Austin received his first-class badge. Merit badges were given to Cordell Austin and Clyde Keller for firemanship, and Ney Austin received one for forestry. Fourteen scouts intended to go to camp in August at Lake Lanier, Tryon, North Carolina.[17] Rhodhiss' young men had the opportunity to join the scout program in the community, and they enjoyed this experience.

FROM FEBRUARY 1955 *PACIFIC TRUTHS* MAGAZINE; AT RHODHISS ELEMENTARY, A SALUTE TO BOY SCOUTS; TO THE LEFT, JOHN LESTER WEAVER, SON OF THE LATE LES WEAVER AND RUTH WEAVER. STANDING AT ATTENTION, JERRY BUMGARNER, SON OF MR. AND MRS. TED BUMGARNER. RUTH WEAVER WORKED IN THE TIMEKEEPER'S OFFICE. TED BUMGARNER WORKED IN NO. 2 CARDING AND MRS. BUMGARNER WORKED IN THE CLOTH ROOM. INFORMATION AND PHOTO FROM *PACIFIC TRUTHS*.

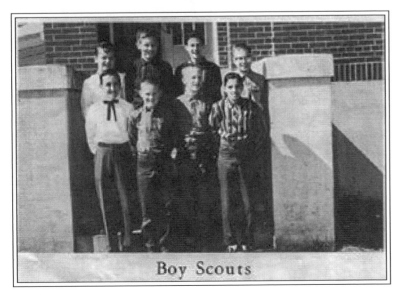

1962 BOY SCOUTS. R. L. SETTLEMYRE, DENNIS CHURCH, CHIPPER SMITH, DAVID JONES, PAUL BROWN, DONALD CHURCH, HAROLD JONES, REGGIE PROPST.

Gerald Jones shared a story involving camping out and using a Boy Scout tent for his adventure. Gerald wrote:

This was right after school had let out for the summer. A friend and I decided to camp out on the upper lake. We wanted to go to the side opposite the dam. At that time there was nothing but woods as was most of the Duke Power property around the lake. To camp out we would need a tent, sleeping bags, food, and a boat to get to the other side of the lake. We knew the scouts had sleeping bags and pup tents. Boyd Brown at the time was one of the scoutmasters, so we contacted him to see if he would let us use a pup tent and two sleeping bags for the one night. Being the nice guy that he was, he said yes. At this point we still needed a boat. At the cove where the scout cabin was located there was an old boat dock that the scouts used, and some of the fishermen in Rhodhiss would keep their homemade wooden boats there. The good boats were always locked and chained. There were always one or two of these wooden homemade boats that were no longer being used, and they had holes in them and were full of water. They would eventually rot. My friend and I pulled one of these hole-burdened boats out of the water, dumped the water, and decided it was worthy of transporting us to the other side. We would, however, need a cup to dip water out while paddling to the other side. There was an old worm can near the dock so we would use it to dip water. We now needed a paddle. We found an old wooden board behind the scout cabin that would work for paddling. We alternated paddling and dipping water from the boat, so we could get to the other side. It took us a while, but we made it safely to the bank opposite the dam. We decided we would pitch our pup tent about 30 ft. from the shoreline. We proceeded to gather some wood for a fire, so we could bake a couple of potatoes for our breakfast. We had heard that you could cover the potatoes with a thin layer of dirt and build a fire over that place and the next morning the potatoes would be cooked. We then checked out the area and walked the bank as far as we could before it got dark. We were just curious about what might be on that side of the lake. After returning to our campsite and eating our sandwiches, we set up the pup tent. We then built a fire a short distance from the opening of the tent with the wood we had gathered. We let the fire burn for a short time to get the embers glowing. At this point it was too dark to see well, so we decided to crawl into our sleeping bags and try to sleep. During the night the fire continued to smolder with the hot embers. The fire was on the sandy area of the riverbank and safely away from the woods behind us. What we didn't think about, and should have, was that Duke Power would draw the water down on the lake periodically to generate power. What that did was lower the level of the lake. This usually happened every day. After the drawdown stopped, the lake would fill back to a normal level overnight. When we pitched our tent, we didn't think anything about the water level. Close to morning we could hear the water lapping louder than when we went to sleep. We also started feeling water at the bottom of the sleeping bags. We were on a slant, so the water was just at the bottom of the sleeping bags and the opening of the pup tent. The water had completely covered the area where we had the fire. Our fire and potatoes were gone. The boat had a rope on it and was still tied to the root of a nearby tree. The lake had apparently been drawn down before we set up and filled back up during the night. So, there would be no breakfast. We decided to just dip and paddle back to the other side and head home. I can't remember how old I was at the time we did this, but it was around 8th or 9th grade. It was great growing up in Rhodhiss. We were always outdoors; we had the lake, the river below the dam, and the entire village for riding our bikes. The village was truly our playground. Too bad kids today don't have this luxury.[18]

Gerald Jones' account of his escapade on the river is representative of many other stories that have been shared by residents of their hometown, Rhodhiss. Children of all ages cherished their time spent with friends who were like family.

1955 GENE FREEMAN FISHING WITH HIS DOG BULLET IN RHODHISS. DALE HAWKINS PHOTO.

Gerald Jones confirmed that Boyd Brown worked with the Boy Scouts. Cora Brown directed the Girl Scouts at one time. She did such a wonderful job that she was given the title "Woman of the Year" by the Woman's Club. Cora declared:

> CB: Well, I had the Girl Scouts. I had the Bolin girl, Roy Tramble's daughter, and Teresa Munday.
> SH: When did you do Girl Scouts?
> CB: The same year that we had the Woman of the Year.
> SH: Who gave that award?
> CB: The Woman's Club. They selected one every year. That year I won it for my work with the Girl Scouts.
> SH: Was this during the 50s?
> CB: It was probably, yeah. It was before I went to work at the school. I remember because one

of the staff writers for the *Lenoir News-Topic* wanted information, and I told him that I worked with the Girl Scouts and the Juniors at the church. When it came out, it said that I was teaching! I couldn't believe that it said that I was teaching.[19]

Cora thought that her leadership of the scouts would have been during the 1950s. She was given the Woman's Club award for her excellence in scouting.

1953 GIRL SCOUT TROOP WITH LEADER CORA BROWN.
PACIFIC TRUTHS PHOTO.

The March 1952 *Pacific Truths* magazine discussed the success of the Girl Scouts in Rhodhiss. This article stated:

> Rhodhiss school cafeteria was the scene of a chicken dumpling supper for the benefit of the Girl Scouts on Saturday night, February 2, 1952. More than 200 people attended the supper served by the Rhodhiss Woman's Club from five o'clock until nine o'clock. Mrs. Leonard Lee was in charge of the supper. She was assisted by Mrs. Paul Elmore, Mrs. Dewey Annas, Mrs. Walter Cart, Mrs. Lester Weaver, Mrs. Bain Smith, Mrs. T. H. Ross, Mrs. Willard Herman and Mrs. J. C. Compton. Members of the club donated cakes and pies for the dessert. The Girl Scouts helped serve and wait on tables. The proceeds will cover the yearly expenses of the Girl Scouts. The sale of pot holders which were made by the Scouts was added to the total proceeds. Following the dinner, a square dance was held in the school auditorium with Grady Kincaid of Lenoir directing the dance.[20]

The Girl Scout program in the 1950s was very active and social. This organization ceased for a while in Rhodhiss, but it was resurrected in the late 1960s and early 1970s. Shanda Nichols was the Girl Scout leader during this time. The first meetings were held at the Club House on Magnolia Street. Later meetings were at the Club House in Burke County on Marion Avenue. The girls enjoyed a weekend at Myrtle Beach State Park camping. Later, Emily Ripley who worked at Rhodhiss Elementary School took over for Shanda Nichols. Emily lived in Hickory, and the girls enjoyed sleepovers and swimming at her house.

Rhodhiss' youth relished their time at Hillside Beach and at scouting events. The town provided the beach area for many years for the people of Rhodhiss and outsiders. All age groups delighted in the sun, fun, music, concessions, and water at the beach. The Boy Scouts also had their hut on the lake, so they, too, could appreciate their time there. The old Methodist Church on Church Street houses a Boy Scout troop that services the youth in Rhodhiss and other nearby towns. The Girl Scouts had fun whether it was going to Myrtle Beach, square dancing, having a sleepover, or selling cookies. Simply going to the river for a campout brought happiness to many people. Even though Rhodhiss was a small community, the citizens enjoyed organizations and amenities just like those who lived in a big city, but Rhodhiss' memories are filled with love!

BUTLER MONTEITH'S BIG CATCH WHILE FISHING AT RHODHISS.
SHERRIE HARTSOE SIGMON PHOTO.

NOTES

1   Elmore, Fred and Martha and Tom Ross.

2   Rhodhiss Town Minutes. 7 August 1950.

3   Rhodhiss Town Minutes. 19 July 1951.

4   Rhodhiss Town Minutes. 14 June 1958.

5   Rhodhiss Town Minutes. 10 August 1964.

6   Rhodhiss Town Minutes. 10 June 1974.

7   Rhodhiss Town Minutes. 12 July 1976.

8   Rhodhiss Town Minutes. 14 March 1977.

9   Rhodhiss Town Minutes. 14 May 1979.

10   Rhodhiss Town Minutes. 11 August 1980.

11   Rhodhiss Town Minutes. 10 November 1980.

12   Settlemyre, Ellis "Pete." Personal Interview with Sherrie Hartsoe Sigmon. Hickory, NC. 4 July 2021.

13   Laney, Billie Sue. Telephone Interview. 15 June 2022.

14   Bright, Paul.

15   Elmore, Tommy.

16   Brown, Boyd and Cora.

17   "Rhodhiss Boy Scouts Are Given Awards." *Pacific Truths*. June 1953, page 2.

18   Jones, Gerald. Email Interview with Sherrie Sigmon. 17 June 2022.

19   Brown, Boyd and Cora.

20   "Girl Scout Benefit." *Pacific Truths*. March 1952, p. 7.

CHAPTER 23
BURLINGTON INDUSTRIES 1954

Pacific Mills had great success while in Rhodhiss, but Burlington Mills arrived in 1954 to offer a buyout. Within any organization change is inevitable, and Burlington was no exception. Pacific had already started the process of selling the mill houses with the employees' being given first choice. For the first time ever the citizens of Rhodhiss were able to own their homes instead of renting. Changes were also implemented within the walls of the mills. Various plant managers came and left during Burlington's tenure. The employees continued to work hard for the new company as they had done with previous owners. Rhodhiss' employees were hard workers who completed their jobs with satisfaction and pride. That was one aspect that never changed throughout the life of the mill company in Rhodhiss.

Many of the employees were taken by surprise by Burlington's purchase of Pacific Mills. Tom Ross and Fred Elmore discussed this:

> TR: Pacific Mills did a lot for Rhodhiss.
> FE: Yeah, they came in the back door like Burlington and bought the mills out.
> TR: When we first heard that Burlington was trying to buy Pacific, we said, 'No, sir. Pacific was more apt to buy Burlington.' In the 1940s you never heard of Burlington.
> FE: I don't think Hayes and his outfit had enough stock in the company to make a difference. They just came in and got it.[1]

Tom Ross mentioned numerous times that Pacific never felt that Burlington was a company that had the ability to pursue a takeover of their company; however, Pacific did sell the Rhodhiss plants to Burlington Mills in 1954.

Pacific Mills had already started pursuing the sale of the mill houses to the occupants; then they offered the houses for purchase to any other interested people. Brent Glass, a textiles author, states that the upkeep of mill houses was too hard to maintain, and improved roads allowed outsiders to travel to the mills. The minimum wage law in 1938 prompted the mill owners to sell houses so they could recoup losses, and stopping child labor in the 1930s made the family unit of labor obsolete. J. Spencer Love, who was the head of Burlington Mills, was the lead in selling houses throughout the state.[2] According to the town minutes in 1955 Pacific started selling all the houses on July 18, 1955 except for 21 units; thus, water meters were installed on houses that were sold, and the board voted to increase the water rate from fifty cents a month to one dollar.[3] With rental housing the water was in their monthly rent as was electricity. Several weeks later Duke Power proposed a permit to build power lines and sell electricity within Rhodhiss. The board agreed.[4] An article in the *Granite Falls Press* explained that Burlington Mills gave two houses and land to two churches. The article stated:

> Final deeds were signed on August 10 by those who bought the houses and it was then that a deed for four lots, consisting of approximately 1.5 acres, was deeded to the Rhodhiss Baptist Church. These lots were on Magnolia Street and Park Avenue. The company also gave the church a six-room house for a parsonage. This is the same house that the church has been using for this purpose. To Rhodhiss Methodist Church, the mill gave the land surrounding it's (sic) present building and a six-room house on Magnolia Street for a parsonage. This house has been occupied by the Ed Nelsons. The Rhodhiss Womans (sic) Club will still continue to use the same building that Pacific Mills made available to it several years ago, but it will be moved to another location on Magnolia Street. This building was not sold by the mill since it was being used by this club for a meeting place. Most of the other houses were sold with Pacific Mill's employees getting first choice at the sales.[5]

Previous mill owners had provided the Methodist and the Baptist churches a house for their pastors to reside. Now with the sale of the mill houses the new company decided to give a house to each church. The Woman's Club's meeting place was moved to 208 Magnolia Street. Both Pacific and Burlington were eager to get rid of the rental program and the houses.

PACIFIC STARTED TO SELL THE MILL HOUSES IN 1955. *GRANITE FALLS PRESS* PHOTO.

THE HOUSE THAT WAS GIVEN TO THE
METHODIST CHURCH WHEN THE MILL HOUSES
WERE SOLD. THIS IS 302 MAGNOLIA STREET.
SHERRIE HARTSOE SIGMON PHOTO.

THE NEW BAPTIST PARSONAGE IN 1963.
GRANITE FALLS PRESS PHOTO.

THIS HOUSE WAS SOLD IN THE 1950S. IT SITS
AT 307 MAGNOLIA STREET. THE HELTONS
LIVED THERE AT ONE TIME. SHERRIE HARTSOE
SIGMON PHOTO.

A HOUSE AT 209 CHURCH STREET THAT WAS
SOLD IN THE 1950S. THE YOUNTS LIVED THERE
AT ONE TIME. SHERRIE HARTSOE SIGMON
PHOTO.

THE TUCKER CHILDREN, RONNIE IN FRONT;
BEHIND HIM ARE STEVE, SYLVIA, AND LEO
TUCKER. THEY ARE AT 209 CHURCH STREET
AT THE HOUSE OWNED BY MARTHA AND
BOYD YOUNT. THE HOUSE BEHIND THEM IS
THE HOUSE WHERE THE HARTSOES LIVED.
THE SCHOOLHOUSE IS IN THE BACKGROUND.
STEVE AND JANIS TUCKER PHOTO.

THE HARTSOE HOMEPLACE, 207 CHURCH
STREET, IN 2016. SUSAN YOUNT PHOTO.

Tom Ross and Calvin Jones discussed the upkeep and the sale of the houses. They stated:

SH: After Pacific came in and invested $5 million initially, did they spend
more money yearly?

TR: Yes. A tremendous amount.

CJ: Yeah, I was telling Tom, the last year that we had these houses, we spent $30,000 on just
the houses. Can you imagine that?

SH: So that was what, about '54?

TR: Yeah.

CJ: Yeah, '54. Cause '55 is when they sold them. So, we spent $30,000 that last year, and that's
$30,000 made. They could have given them to people, and they practically did, cause some of
the little three-room houses went for less than $1,000. I think it was $900.

TR: $700.

CJ: So, they just practically gave the houses to them to get this off their back. Really! They
sure did.

TR: It wasn't only here that it was happening. It was happening at other places, too. Pacific
was starting the sale of the houses, and Burlington came on the scene right at the time that it
happened. There was a Greenville real estate agent who came. Was that Alice Furman?

CJ: It could have been. I believe that it was.

TR: Yeah, Carlyle from Pacific. He had a problem with that thing. What they had to do,
Sherrie, they had to get the people to buy the houses and get the financing from the building

and loan. Pacific stood good for that loan. I don't know how they did that, whether they put money in there or what, but if that person hadn't paid that loan off, Pacific would. They underwrote it.

SH: Like a second mortgage?

TR: Really, it was the mortgage. So that influenced the building and loan to do it.[6]

Mill companies throughout the South were starting to sell their mill houses. For the first time millhands were homeowners, and they felt that owning their homes gave them more independence.

Many people discussed the sale of the houses. My parents bought their home on Church Street for $1,500 in 1955. Hans and Katherine Townsend voiced their thoughts with Tom Ross and me. They stated:

> SH: We were talking about the sale of the mill houses. Thelma Church said that
> the cheapest she heard was that one sold for $700. Did you ever hear that or even lower?
> HT: I heard that one went for $600.
> TR: I was thinking that mine was one of the lowest, but then I heard that.
> KT: A lot of them went for $600.
> HT: Yeah, I heard that some of them went for $600.[7]

Hans and Kat said that some houses were sold for only $600, but no confirmation was obtained. In addition, Butler Monteith, Doughton Beshears, Shelley Teague, and Tom Ross gave their thoughts. They noted:

> TR: You found out that one house went for $700.
> SH: I heard that one house went for $700. Now, I just heard that. I heard that it was the cheapest one sold.
> ST: I heard that one went for $400.
> DB: I don't think that any went for less than $700. A lot of them went for $1,200.
> TR: And $1,500.
> DB: I guess that they had to be better houses to go for $1,500.[8]

Lastly, Billie Sue Laney was able to give information about her mother's purchase of her home on Hickory Street. Billie said that Edna could not get a loan because she was a woman. Edna had maintained a job in the mill company for many years, yet she was denied a loan because of her gender. Billie's Pappy Laney had to secure the loan for her because the bank would not loan to a woman.[9]

One interesting fact about the town's history surfaced. "Prior to the 1968 Congressional elections, the town was in two districts; thus the residents, in a sense, had two Congressmen in Washington."[10] For the townspeople, this was a benefit. Similarly, Burlington liked to provide benefits and incentives for their employees. They frequently fed them whether it was hamburgers and hotdogs or steak. Doughton Beshears, Shelley Teague, Tom Ross, and Butler Monteith elaborated:

BM: If you had a good record for so long, they would feed you.

ST: Before we left there though every year we had steak, and the boss men would do the cooking. They fed everybody.

BM: I got some pictures of that. It was down here at the old warehouse.

ST: They took to cooking across the river outside the mill.

TR: That was about once a year, wasn't it?

ST: Yeah.

DB: Burlington gave you steak about once a year.

BM: If you had a good safety record every three months, they might feed you again.

TR: Safety was a big thing.[11]

Tom Ross mentioned that safety was an important issue for Burlington. Because of a poor safety record in 1963, Burlington held a training for employees provided by the Industrial Commission of North Carolina. Chosen employees attended four hours of safety training and two hours of first aid. After this workshop 1,253,755-man hours were logged without a disabling injury. Burlington also gave bonuses for the employees' suggestions that would enhance safety.[12] Obviously, a safe work environment enhanced productivity.

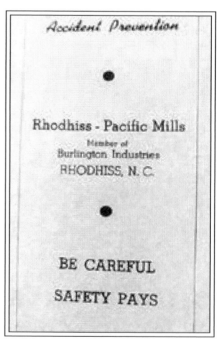

BURLINGTON TRIED TO ENSURE SAFETY. THIS SIGN CITED THEIR RECORD. SHERRIE HARTSOE SIGMON PHOTO.

SAFETY BOOKLET FOR EMPLOYEES. RICK JUSTICE COPY.

Joe Aldridge discussed Burlington's willingness to feed their employees for their stellar work. Joe and Olive noted to me:

JA: Oh, good night. They fed us often. Burlington is the only one that ever did that. But if things were going good, Burlington fed us about every three months.

SH: I know that they had those Christmas parties.

JA: Oh, they had some of the greatest Christmas parties. It was just so much to enjoy.

SH: I remember a big carnival. Do you remember that? They invited both plants. They had a little circus down there. There was a picnic. Daddy does not remember it.

JA: Yeah, yeah. It hasn't been that long.

SH: Well, it was the late 1960s.

JA: Yeah.[13]

Butler Monteith recalled this carnival and added that a band was present and that silver dollars were given away.[14] Another town event was documented in the the Rhodhiss town minutes. The board gave permission to the Ruritan to have a circus on a ball field in Burke County.[15] Burlington also celebrated with their employees at Rhodhiss Beach as stated in the previous chapter. Shelley Teague and Butler Monteith remembered that beach party, and they said that the company provided a big meal for the employees and their families.[16]

CARNIVAL HELD BY BURLINGTON. JIM KELLER, LUTHER SIGMON, LENNIS FOWLER, WILLIE FOWLER, BRENDA, CARL, AND RENITA COMPTON, AND OTHERS. SHERRIE HARTSOE SIGMON PHOTO.

THIS PICTURE IS DATED SEPTEMBER 14, 1961. THE OFFICE STAFF IS STANDING IN THE PARKING LOT OUTSIDE THE BUILDING THAT HOUSED THE POST OFFICE. MARTHA YOUNT, SUDIE ANDERSON, PRECIOUS KELLER KELLEY, AND BETTY CHURCH WRIGHT IN THIS PICTURE WITH OTHERS. SHERRIE HARTSOE SIGMON PHOTO.

BURLINGTON'S RECOGNITION OF EMPLOYEES
DURING 1960S. MARY DARTY, EDNA STILWELL,
SHORTY HELMS, MR. HELTON, HARLEY BROWN,
BOYCE HARTSOE, DAN HARTSOE, PLEZ RASH,
AND OTHERS. BOYCE HARTSOE PHOTO.

RICHARD DEAL, AL LOWDERMILK, ARLEY
CHURCH, ?, TOM ROSS, J. R. HEFNER, AND
PERRY RICE. SHERRIE HARTSOE SIGMON
PHOTO (? COULD BE WILLIE ANNAS, BUT NO
ONE WAS SURE).

HANS TOWNSEND AND NED BEAN IN THIS
PICTURE. OTHER MAN IS NOT KNOWN.
SHERRIE HARTSOE SIGMON PHOTO.

YVONNE HENTSCHEL, RUTH JACKSON, AND
NADINE DULA WITH OTHERS. *GRANITE FALLS
PRESS* PHOTO VIA YVONNE HENTSCHEL.

C. B. SPERRY, MARY BOLICK, LUTHER SIGMON,
AND ?. SHERRIE HARTSOE SIGMON PHOTO.

MACK HENTSCHEL AND TRUETTE CRUMP.
1970S. YVONNE HENTSCHEL PHOTO.

MACK HENTSCHEL AND MURPHY HEFNER,
1960S. YVONNE HENTSCHEL PHOTO.

MARY DARTY, MARY BOLICK, OTT EDWARDS,
WALTER STARNES, FRED BROWN, AND HANS
TOWNSEND. JUNE 28, 1973. GRANITE FALLS
PRESS PHOTO.

JUNE 28, 1973, HONORING BURLINGTON'S EMPLOYEES. *GRANITE FALLS PRESS* PHOTO.

VERCIE CLINE'S RETIREMENT. *GRANITE FALLS PRESS* PHOTO VIA YVONNE HENTSCHEL.

PERFECT ATTENDANCE AWARDS, EDNA STILWELL, MARY DARTY, SHELLEY TEAGUE, CARL COMPTON, DAN HARTSOE, TED HARTLEY, GLENN PRICE, LEWIS ALDRIDGE, MARVIN BUCHANAN, PAUL BUMGARNER, DONALD BALL, JACK EDWARDS, SLIM BROWN, JOHN AGNER, EDDIE LUNSFORD, CLYDE WINKLER, EVA WINKLER, RICHARD "BOLO" WHISNANT, AND OTHERS. SHERRIE HARTSOE SIGMON PHOTO.

BUCK TEAGUE, BOYCE HARTSOE, BUTLER MONTEITH, JOE ALDRIDGE, TOM RHEA, EDDIE
LUNSFORD, AND OTHERS. BOYCE HARTSOE PHOTO.

Mary Starnes Bolick explained that Burlington gave their employees a ham or turkey at Christmas. They also continued the traditional Christmas party that Rhodhiss Mills and Pacific had given. Mary elaborated to Tom Ross and me:

SH: Were there any other benefits? I know that they fed you a lot.

MB: Yeah, we always had an appreciation day. They were always having something like that. I always enjoyed that. Then when they had their 50th year, I believe they had a whole family day. I know that I had a 50-year magazine.

SH: When I was a child, I always looked forward to the Christmas parties.

MB: Yeah, they had Christmas parties, and they always gave treats out to the children, and they used to give them to the adults, too. Right toward the last, they stopped. They would give you a gift certificate.

SH: There for a while, didn't they give you a free turkey or a free ham?

MB: Yeah. I believe most times I chose a ham. Then one year I think that they gave turkeys. Then when I was there for 40 years, they gave me a television.

SH: They did. My daddy missed that because they closed.

TR: I didn't know about that one.

SH: Daddy got to pick something out of a catalog when he was there 35 years.

MB: I got something else, too. They gave me this plaque for how long I had worked when they closed the plant.[17]

The Burlington Christmas parties were the absolute best. As a child of an employee, I looked forward to those Sunday afternoon parties. The treat bags lined up in neat rows always got children excited. When I was young, Roy Tramble made the BEST Santa ever. Burlington gave gifts to their employees for their excellent safety records, good attendance, and hard work.

ROY TRAMBLE AS SANTA WITH UNIDENTIFIED BOY. SHERRIE HARTSOE SIGMON PHOTO.

BECKY HENTSCHEL AND DONNA HEFNER AT BURLINGTON'S CHRISTMAS PARTY. YVONNE HENTSCHEL PHOTO.

Bill Craven was plant manager from 1959 to 1970 at the two Rhodhiss Burlington plants. He and I talked briefly in 1988. He said that he enjoyed his years in Rhodhiss. Many interviewees called him an asset to the company. An article from the *Hickory Daily Record* in 1963 alludes to Mr. Craven and the Rhodhiss employees. The article stated:

Burlington plant manager, Bill Craven, recognized 240 employees for having 10 years with the plant. Mr. Craven noted that Burlington is proud of all of its employees, 'especially the 10-year group for the fine spirit of loyalty and cooperation shown during the days and years of change. Through efforts of its employes (sic), progress has been made in quality and efficiency currently placing the No. 1 and No. 2 mills in reality in first and second position in the 'Menswear Area.' Mr. Craven further pointed out that improved group insurance benefits were effected in 1962, and in 1963 the 'Profit Sharing Retirement Plan' for all eligible wage employes (sic) became effective. Mr. Craven introduced the speaker, R. A. Gilliam, area manager of Greensboro. Mr. Gilliam said, 'All changes have been necessary and Rhodhiss Mills has been a major contributing factor to the overall progress and success of the division. The understanding and cooperation by all employes (sic) is greatly appreciated.' Burlington's Personnel Executive from Greensboro, T. B. French, also attended. Each table had three-tier birthday cakes decorated with 10 candles. The employees were fed fried chicken and country ham. The oldest employee on each shift was asked to extinguish the candles. These employees were: 1st shift, Luther Lail, employed since 1912; 2nd shift, Arvin Crump, employed since 1927; 3rd shift, Calloway Austin, employed since 1923. Guests for this event were employees, the Town of Rhodhiss, ministers, and recently retired employees. Tommy Laney, who heads the summer recreation program for Rhodhiss, and Doug Tolbert, Rhodhiss School Principal, were in attendance.[18]

BILL CRAVEN, PLANT MANAGER 1959-1970. SHERRIE HARTSOE SIGMON PHOTO.

LUTHER SIGMON WHO WAS A MEMBER OF BURLINGTON'S MANAGEMENT TEAM. SHERRIE HARTSOE SIGMON PHOTO.

LACY HODGES, A MEMBER OF BURLINGTON'S MANAGEMENT TEAM. SHERRIE HARTSOE SIGMON PHOTO.

Burlington's profit sharing was instituted in 1963, and the employees were grateful to have a retirement plan.

BURLINGTON 1963 PROFIT SHARING. HUGH LYLERY, BETTY LYNN, VERCIE CLINE, JOE ALDRIDGE, LEWIS ALDRIDGE, BOYCE HARTSOE, MRS. LOWDERMILK, MRS. JOHNSON, DON JOHNSON, MR. FRANKLIN, AND OTHERS. SHERRIE HARTSOE SIGMON PHOTO.

Another plant manager was Mr. Cleon Estes.[19] Mary Starnes Bolick and Tom Ross said that Mr. Estes came in and got the plant "straightened out." He was liked and did a good job. Mr. Bill Craven replaced him.[20] Mr. Craven's changes helped the output of the company. Tom Ross and Hans Townsend discussed this. They stated:

> TR: I remember when Bill Craven came here. They would change settings. I
> know that Estes must have changed every motion on it. Craven went all the way back to the warp room. He said that if you can't make it right back there, you can't weave it. It wasn't long, and it was about 3⅝ seconds. It had been 15⅝ seconds when Craven first came.
> HT: Yeah, you got to make it right from the start.
> TR: Yeah, that was Craven's theory. It worked, and Craven got everybody thinking 100% quality, 100% quality. That's all that they talked about, isn't it Hans?
> HT: Yeah.[21]

Bill Craven preached 100% quality of the products that Rhodhiss produced. Carl Compton added that Rhodhiss' quality did improve. Towards the end of the Burke plant's existence, Carl stated that Burlington's goal was 1.5% seconds, but Rhodhiss ultimately had .05%. Burlington's efficiency goal was 95.6% per quarter, but Rhodhiss averaged 98 to 99%.[22] Rhodhiss' workers were serious about their production. I talked with my Uncle Dan Hartsoe about Rhodhiss' operation when I visited him in 2015. Uncle Dan said that one of the reasons that the Burke plant was so productive and successful is that they had good leaders and representation. He alluded to Burlington's policy of shift representation within each department at the executive meetings. Particularly, Uncle Dan mentioned that John Agner was the best representative that the fixers could have had. He said that John was willing to voice the concerns of the loom fixers to management without fear or trepidation. Dan said that many hourly employees benefitted from the representation within their departments, and his words of praise for a fellow employee, John Agner, showed the love and trust within the plant.[23]

Bill Craven was one of the many men who made a difference in Rhodhiss. In Chapter 8 Tom Ross and Mary Starnes Bolick discussed better lighting in the plant. Tom said that Bill Craven was the one who increased the lighting, and Mary added, "Yeah, he did. There was real light in there. You could see so much better."[24] In addition, Mary and Tom discussed Bill Craven's tenure at Rhodhiss. They declared:

MB: Ernie Skillman. Now he was good. Well, I told them that when Mr. Craven left that Rhodhiss would close.

SH: Is that what you said?

MB: Yeah, and it did. Number one closed first. I said that when Craven leaves or retires, we'll close.

TR: Do you remember when he first came there?

MB: Yeah, I remember when he first came there.

TR: Do you remember him coming through the mill? Do you remember his little black book that he had?

MB: Yeah.

TR: The first thing that he did when he came here was start talking to people finding out who they were and things like that. He wanted facts about people. He would write down in his little book. Then when he went through the mill again, he would come to talk to you about your child, your family.

MB: I know this guy, Carl Compton, was wanting to learn how to fix. Well, like some of the bosses, I don't remember who because they changed off to different ones. One day Mr. Craven come through. He stopped and talked to me and asked me what I thought about Carl Compton. I told him, I said, 'I think that he's one of the finest persons that they've got in here, and works, too. He's a good worker. He doesn't run his mouth all the time.' You know it wasn't long till they put him on learning to fix.

TR: And he did, too. Didn't he?

SH: Yeah, he was a fixer when they closed the plant.

MB: Because Craven knew that I was telling the truth. He'd always come along and talk to me about different things. If you had a problem, all you had to do was

TR: Talk to him.

MB: Talk to him, and he would help.

TR: Mary, there's not another person in the world like him.

MB: I don't think there was. I'll tell you. I hated that so bad when he left. Well, I'll tell you there's not another person like him. It's just all there is to it. But he always spoke to you. It didn't matter where you were at or anything. That was something that he spoke to everybody.

He was nice. I mean when he came in there, he would talk to everybody. It wasn't just one or two. If he wanted any information, he knew a lot of times where to get it.

TR: A lot of plant managers had their special ones that they'd go to. Bill wasn't like that.[25]

In addition to getting to know his employees on a personal level to relate to them, Bill Craven started the Ruritan Club in Rhodhiss. Calvin Jones commented, "Mr. Craven started the Ruritan Club. Then they started cleaning up the old apartment building."[26] One of the service activities for the Ruritan was to sponsor the Boy Scout Troop 261. As stated in Chapter 11 the Ruritan also supported the Rhodhiss Ruritan Teachers' Fund, which allowed one teacher's salary to be paid from Ruritan, PTA, and United Way Funds.[27] The Woman's Club was started during Pacific's tenure, and a club for the men was implemented with Burlington. This organization served the community well for many years, and they met at the club house that was on Magnolia Street and then the club house on Marion Avenue. Also, while Craven was in Rhodhiss several sports teams were started. The company's softball team had fifteen members who were runners up in the Tri County League playoffs. Thirty-one people played golf with the mill company. Over ninety people bowled from time to time with the mill's bowling team. Lastly, a basketball team played from 1964-1967, and they won the Caldwell County League championship in 1965-1966.[28] Many new groups were organized during Bill Craven's tenure as plant manager.

BOB GREGORY, VERCIE CLINE, JIM MULL, ?, OTT EDWARDS.
SHERRIE HARTSOE SIGMON PHOTO.

Rhodhiss' position in the hierarchy of Burlington was not at the top, but upper management knew about the two plants in Rhodhiss. As a matter of fact, the top brass from New York came to the area to get acquainted with the mills' procedures and management. An event was held at the Green Park Inn in Blowing Rock. Calvin Jones and Tom Ross discussed this with me:

CJ: We had a big meeting in Blowing Rock with the New York executives.

TR: Calvin, I haven't told her about that.

CJ: This Eli Calloway out of the New York office was president of the company. So, he came down, and we had a meeting at the Green Park Inn. We had a bunch of the rooms rented out. A bunch of the fellas from New York came down.

TR: Oh, everybody came.

CJ: Yeah, and we entertained people. All the supervisors from Rhodhiss went up there, and we entertained. Instead of having the people from Rhodhiss staying together, they mixed us up with the New York people.

TR: Sherrie, Hugh Lylery and I were in charge of the entertainment for that event that time. Hugh and I took a half a day trying to figure out what all to buy and everything. We tried to figure out how much liquor to buy.

SH: I would say that was coming from two men who didn't drink.

TR: Hugh might have tasted, but he never really drank. Anyway, we were trying to figure out how much to buy. We knew that some didn't drink. We figured what we could, but the liquor was gone before bedtime the first night. We had to round up some more whiskey. We found a liquor store somewhere. I don't remember where we got it. Oh man, that crowd was really lively.

CJ: I was on detail the next day to take them to Grandfather Mountain out on that bridge.

TR: I was in charge of the golf tournament, too. We had one salesman who came in from Texas about 1:00 or 2:00 in the morning. Calvin, I don't know if you remember it or not. He had $5 million in sales that day, and he was really feeling his oats. Oh, man. Really sales were booming then. Like you talked about, business was good. We had one salesman, Sherrie, that lived in Akron, Ohio. That's where the rubber company, tire companies, were. Burlington made the chafer cloth, they called it. It was for part of the tire, and one salesman that's all that he did. Just stayed there in his town and filled out orders.

CJ: When a supervisor would leave down here, we'd always pitch them a party. Everybody that went would pitch in a certain amount of money. We had a certain amount of money that they spent for liquor and a certain amount for food. We'd go to maybe the Moose Lodge, the Country Club, or just different places to have this going away party. I never did drink, and I was having to pitch in this extra money for whiskey, you know. I complained about it one day. They said, 'Well, you're just in the group, so you can drink it if you want it. It's there for you.' I told them, 'Okay.' So, the first bottle that they emptied, I went over and got that bottle. Every time that they would pass the bottle, I'd pour me a drink in the empty bottle. When I got through, that bottle was full! This was the night that was Feaster Newton's party because he was leaving. Of course, when I got through, I just did it for the heck of it, I gave it to him as a going away present. We had a time. We had some good times.

TR: Yeah, we sure did. It was rough to swallow sometimes. Basically, everything was pretty good. There was a certain amount of calmness if Bill Craven was in the crowd. If they had a boss there, they would respect him and behave.

CJ: One night they roped me into playing poker on a trip. I had never played poker in my life. I said, 'Well, I've never played any poker before.' They said, 'Then you're the one that we want to play.' I sat down there, and I got to playing. Of course, I was sitting next to Bernie, and he would help me along. I was green on it. I didn't know anything about it.

TR: Bernie was sharp.

CJ: Yes, he was. It wound up that I'd lose a little money along the way. I wasn't betting a whole lot of money. It wound up that I got a royal flush. I didn't know what I had. Bernie was about to go crazy sitting next to me. He had already dropped out. He was looking at my hand. J. R. and Estes stayed in there. Bernie kept telling me what to do. J. R. dropped out. Estes kept throwing money in the pot and throwing money in the pot. Staying right with me. I ended up showing that royal flush.

TR: I don't know what that is.

SH: It's the highest hand that you can have.

CJ: He hit the ceiling. I had gotten a big pot beforehand by just staying with it. He thought that I was bluffing. They told me that was beginner's luck.

TR: That's the psychology of poker, isn't it?

CJ: Yeah.[29]

Calvin and Tom were able to discuss entertaining the New York executives who came to the area for business, and Calvin shared other exploits. Rhodhiss was able to entertain the authorities.

Burlington was instrumental in supporting the United Way campaign every year. The office staff was able to get community volunteers to canvas town for their contributions. Rhodhiss United Fund had support from many of the townspeople. Activities and meetings were held at the club house on Magnolia Street, and the organizers were able to help the community with these funds. Similarly, Rhodhiss often had campaigns to clean the town. Cook outs and ice cream socials often kicked off these endeavors. The mill company was behind these clean up days. They got all organizations and the school involved which ensured their success.

Rhodhiss Mayor Cecil "Bud" Munday is shown accepting a check for $10,000. from Martha Yount, Rhodhiss United Fund Secretary-Treasurer. The money was donated to the town's recreation commission Monday afternoon. (GF photo)

UNITED WAY. 1970S. MARTHA YOUNT AND CECIL "BUD" MUNDAY. *GRANITE FALLS PRESS* PHOTO.

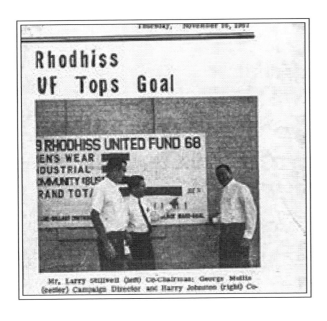

UNITED WAY NOVEMBER 1967. LARRY STILWELL, GEORGE MULLIS, AND HARRY JOHNSTON. *GRANITE FALLS PRESS* PHOTO.

GRANITE FALLS PRESS PHOTO

During the early 1960s office management met and talked about Rhodhiss' image within the tri-county area. Some people often took the attitude of Rhodhiss' citizens being low class because most of the townspeople worked in the plants. With Bill Craven's and Tom Ross' leadership, the management decided that the area merchants needed to see that their revenue came from good, hard-working citizens in Rhodhiss. Tom Ross and Shelley Teague discussed this with me. They said:

> TR: They can say what they want to about Rhodhiss, but Rhodhiss meant a lot
> to this end of Caldwell County.
> ST: You are right. Here is something. They paid off one time down here in $2 bills, just to let others know how much money was coming from Rhodhiss.
> TR: Yes, I was here then. $66,000 in $2 bills. We paid off every 2 weeks.
> SH: And the payroll was $66,000. Can you believe that? $66,000 in $2 bills.
> TR: They found out where their money was coming from. That was a good
> deal.[30]

This was a novel idea, and area merchants had to notice when their patrons came and paid for their merchandise in $2 bills. Carl Compton added to the story:

> I started to work for Burlington in 1961 and was working in the card room when they paid us off with the $2 bills. I'm not sure of the exact year. I'm thinking it was in 1962, but like usual I am probably wrong. I don't know whose idea it was, but I remember Doughton Beshears escorting the strongbox in on a set of hand trucks. I don't remember exactly who paid us off, but I think it may have been Mr. Ross. I know some people didn't really want to take them for payment and some had never seen a $2 bill and were very suspicious of them. I saved one of the actual $2 bills for years but have no idea where it is now.[31]

Doughton Beshears would have guarded the strongbox as it was moving from employee to employee within the mills because he was the police chief at that time. Many former employees walked around for years with a $2 bill in their pockets as a memento. Rhodhiss mill workers were occasionally treated disrespectfully in other communities, and oftentimes they felt the need to speak out. Earl Lingle expressed this sentiment with Tom Ross and me:

> TR: We have come to the conclusion that Rhodhiss was a good place. It was a good community. Everybody enjoyed it just like a big family. It was amazing.
> EL: Yeah. You know, I used to be active in politics. I'd go up to Lenoir. I took it about as long as I could. They'd always refer to us as 'the lower end.' So, we had a great big meeting. I was representing Lovelady as my precinct. I had a good following. I forget who the county chairman was. It was my time to stand up, you know, to tell them how our precinct was going. He introduced me and said, 'Now tell us how the lower end's going.' I could just feel my face.

My friend was looking at me. I looked at the chair, and I said, 'What do you mean by lower end? Would you stand up and explain that, sir?' I saw the veins in his neck. I said, 'What I've heard is that when they discovered this county, they came down the Catawba River or either up the Catawba River, and they had to come through Rhodhiss to get up here to this hole in the ground.'

SH: I love it!

EL: Man, I'm telling you what's the truth. Of course, we had a few words after we got out of there. I told him, I said, 'Now, if you jump on me, you'll have to jump on these fifteen people that I brought. That's the reason that I put you down. I don't want to hear anything about the LOWER end anymore.'

TR: You probably didn't either.

EL: No, sir.

TR: Because there were a lot of voting people at that time.

EL: That's right.[32]

Perhaps Earl's sentiment was because the word "lower" was usually stressed. Millhands were often called "lintheads," even after synthetics became dominant in the textile industry. Exie Hand had the right idea when she commented on working and living in a mill town. "Well, there are not many towns where there aren't cotton mill hills close. What would people have done if hadn't been for cotton mills and mill houses?"[33] Textile towns were widespread across the South, but some people delighted in calling these hard-working employees derogatory names or calling their children "mill hill kids." Yes, the mill workers made an honest living laboring for their wages. My dad always said, "Don't criticize a man that makes a living by the sweat of his brow."

When W. L. "Bill" Craven left Rhodhiss, he went to the corporate office in Greensboro as the Vice President of Burlington Industries. In his new position he announced in the early 1970s that C. B. Sperry who had been a plant manager at Rhodhiss was promoted to Burlington's Industrial Division Headquarters in Greensboro. Sperry started at Rhodhiss in 1964. Craven also announced that Luther Sigmon would become the Rhodhiss' plant manager and Fletcher "Buddy" McLaurin would be superintendent.[34] Butler Monteith and Shelley Teague mentioned other plant managers. They liked Duffie Taylor who later transferred to South Carolina. Shelley said that he was "a good fellow." Butler added, "Duffie Taylor was one of the best fellas that I ever worked for in my life. If you asked him a question, he would say, 'Well, I don't know, but I bet you that I will find out.' He would go find out, and he would come back in the plant and give you the answer, and if he couldn't find out, he would come back to tell you that."[35] Mary Bolick and Tom Ross also discussed Duffie's role as plant manager at Rhodhiss. They stated:

MB: You remember Duffie, don't you?

TR: Yeah.

MB: Well, he's in Texas now, but he called me. It excited me so much when he called. Well, we had the same birthday, and he always sent me a card everywhere that he has been.

TR: Is that right?

MB: So, he called, and he was in New Hampshire the last time that I sent him a card. I went ahead and sent it; then I didn't get one. I said, 'I bet that they's something wrong with Duffie.' The day my birthday was, he called me that morning about 8:00. He said, 'This is Duffie. I've moved, and I lost your address. I just thought that I would call and wish you a happy birthday.'

TR: How about that!

MB: I asked where he was, and he said that he was in Texas, but he didn't tell where in Texas. As I say, I was so excited. He said that he would send me his address. Now there were some people that didn't like him, but I did. Now, I really liked him. Because he straightened out a lot of things that needed straightening out. I told him, I said, 'You'll not make it. That's just all that there is to it.' He said, 'Yes, I will.' I said, 'Well, I just don't think that you're going to make it.' But he did stay a pretty good while. Then he moved. I don't know if they actually moved him, or he moved.

TR: Did they send him to Cheraw?

MB: Yeah, I believe so.

TR: That's when they were trying to do some of the same thing down there, the same weave that they were weaving in Rhodhiss.

MB: But he was a person that you could talk to. He was doing something, and I said, 'I don't know whether you ought to have done that. You'll just never make it. That's all there is to it.' He did though. He must have been there five years or more. Everybody hated to see him leave. Some of them didn't. He'd come in there, and he'd walk up and down 'em aisles, and he could spot that stuff just like that. He would laugh and tell me, 'All that I have to do is stop and look like I was looking at something, and they'd start looking around.' That was the truth. He was something else.

SH: I remember that daddy liked him.

MB: He really was a nice man. He'd tell me sometime, 'I thought that you said that I wasn't going to make it.' I said, 'Well, I didn't think that you were, not at some of the things that you were doing.'[36]

Rhodhiss had plant managers come and go, but their legacy stayed with the company and within the minds of the employees.

Although Burlington was good for the community and the employees, some of the changes were hard. Claude Barker started working there in 1919. He was a weaver, fixer, and overseer. Burlington asked him to shift to the third shift, but he did not want to, so he retired. Claude's wife Gladys worked for Rhodhiss Manufacturing, Rhodhiss Mills, Pacific and Burlington. She fell and broke her arm in the mill in 1963. She was glad to have a job for all those years, but she retired, too. She said that they kept "doubling up, doubling up, cutting out, cutting out, and laying off. It got pretty hard doing things different."[37] Many people discussed the cutting of the workforce and the demand for more production. Arthur and Exie Hand also mentioned this:

SH: What was it like to work down here?

AH: Well, it was just like any other place. It was working.

EH: It was a good place to work.

AH: It was. Now, Pacific was a real company, but when Burlington got it

EH: Well, it was a good place, but they worked you pretty hard.

AH: Yeah, it was a good place. When I quit down here, the first of the next year they had hired twelve on that job. My job. Then they still didn't have anybody on it. I stayed with it, where the rest of 'em just quit, quit, quit, quit, quit on the other shifts.[38]

Several workers discussed that the production quota was oftentimes out of reach. I discussed this with my dad who worked there for 37 years. Daddy said that a joke circulated within the mill when one of Burlington's New York executives died. Supposedly, at the cemetery the executive rose from his casket and asked, "How many are carrying me?" The pallbearers responded, "Six." The executive retorted, "You can do it in four."[39] Some of the employees felt the pressure to "double up, double up."[40] However, my dad loved working there. He was never satisfied with other companies after having worked for Pacific and Burlington. He felt as if his work community was his family. This sentiment was shared by many. Alvis Kelley elaborated, "Burlington Industries as far as I was concerned was as good of a company as you could work for, and most people would go up to the filling station and say how bad they were, and they wouldn't work for them again. I still say that it's the best company that I worked for. I worked for a good company. That's what I always told Joe and them."[41] Alvis is alluding to his son, Joe Kelley, who worked at the mill, too. Working at a place where people feel like a cohesive family unit makes the day go by much faster, and it makes going to work enjoyable. Family can ease many trials, tribulations, and sorrows.

The employees at Rhodhiss wanted to make sure that their products were top notch. Whether they worked for Rhodhiss Manufacturing, Rhodhiss Mills, Pacific or Burlington, they were laborers who gave their best to the job. They were proud of the image that they portrayed to the community and to the company. Hard work built Rhodhiss!

BOYD YOUNT, KURT SMITH, DWIGHT KIRBY, LUTHER SIGMON, JASPER PROPST, VANCE KIRBY, PAUL
WILLIAMS, DOUG TOLBERT, JOE KIRBY, NED BEAN, J. D. GASTON, BILL CRAVEN, BOYD BROWN,
GRADY MASSAGEE, MARSHALL SHORT, EDFIN HOLLAR, JOHNNY PERRY, WAYNE MULLINAX, AND
OTHERS. AT THE CLUB HOUSE ON MAGNOLIA STREET. SHERRIE HARTSOE SIGMON PHOTO.

1963 RURITAN YARDS OF THE WEEK. *GRANITE
FALLS PRESS* PHOTO.

GRANITE FALLS PRESS PHOTO.

1963 RHODHISS' RURITANS' KITE FLYING
CONTEST. JEANNIE KIRBY, ALLEN KIRBY,
BILLY ELMORE, TERRY WILLIAMS, TOM
ROSS, SHELLEY TEAGUE, DOUG MCCALL.
GRANITE FALLS PRESS PHOTO.

1963 JOE KIRBY PAINTING HIS HOUSE ON PARK
AVENUE. SHERRIE HARTSOE SIGMON PHOTO.

GREG KIRBY PAINTING HIS HOUSE. 1963 *GRANITE FALLS PRESS* PHOTO.

1960S CLEAN UP RHODHISS CAMPAIGN WITH RONNIE TUCKER, DAVID JONES, RAY LUNSFORD, STANLEY BROWN, PAUL BROWN, ESTELLE STARNES, CLARA KIRBY, LINDA TRAMBLE, RICHARD DEAL, DOUG TOLBERT, VANCE KIRBY, DEXTER HORNADAY, BILL CRAVEN, DWIGHT KIRBY, BOYD YOUNT. SHERRIE HARTSOE SIGMON PHOTO.

THE RHODHISS GARDEN CLUB'S FLOWERBED NEAR MARION AVENUE. OLD STEEL BRIDGE IN BACKGROUND. ALSO, THIS SHOWS THE PARKING LOT WHEN IT WAS ACROSS THE STREET FROM PLANT 2. SHERRIE HARTSOE SIGMON PHOTO.

MEETING AT THE MAGNOLIA STREET CLUBHOUSE WITH GRADY MASSAGEE, TOM ROSS, MARTHA YOUNT, DEXTER HORNADAY, LUTHER SIGMON, BOYD YOUNT, ARLEY CHURCH, RUTH SIGMON. MANY ORGANIZATIONS MET AT THE CLUBHOUSE ON MAGNOLIA, INCLUDING THE GIRL SCOUTS, LADIES' AUXILIARY, WOMAN'S CLUB, RURITAN CLUB, THE GARDEN CLUB, AND THE SUPERVISORS' CLUB. SHERRIE HARTSOE SIGMON PHOTO.

1960S MEETING AT MAGNOLIA STREET CLUBHOUSE WITH NED BEAN, LUTHER SIGMON, GRADY MASSAGEE, CLARK MCKEE, BOYD BROWN, BEN PEARSON, AND OTHERS. SHERRIE HARTSOE SIGMON PHOTO.

1960S WOMEN MEETING OUTSIDE THE OLD CLUB HOUSE. NELLY MULLINAX, GAIL KIRBY, VIRGINIA HOLLAR, MARTHA YOUNT, RUTH SIGMON, ILZE DEAL, LENA LYLERY, AND OTHERS. SHERRIE HARTSOE SIGMON PHOTO.

PLANT 2 DURING THE 1960S WITH OLD STEEL BRIDGE AND PARKING LOT ACROSS THE STREET. BURLINGTON PHOTO. SHERRIE HARTSOE SIGMON PHOTO.

BURLINGTON'S MAGIC SHOW FOR EMPLOYEES AND CHILDREN. MIDDLE 1960S AT OLD GRANITE FALLS HIGH SCHOOL. SHERRIE HARTSOE SIGMON PHOTO.

CROWD ATTENDING A BURLINGTON FUNCTION AT RHODHISS ELEMENTARY AUDITORIUM IN THE MID 1960S. SHERRIE HARTSOE SIGMON PHOTO.

PARK LAND DONATED BY BURLINGTON. 1970S. DUFFIE TAYLOR, ANN AUSTIN, AND BUD MUNDAY. *HICKORY DAILY RECORD* PHOTO.

TATE WHITTINGTON AND CLARENCE BURNS AT PARK'S OPENING. 1970S. *GRANITE FALLS PRESS PHOTO.*

1963 PLANT 2 GETS PAINTED. SHERRIE HARTSOE SIGMON PHOTO.

Charter Members of Rhodhiss Ruritan Club as taken from Bicentennial pamphlet:

Dwight Kirby, President
Boyd Yount
Luther Sigmon
M. E. Smith
J. D. Gaston
J. E. Propst
Grady Massagee
Clyde Keller
Boyd Hollar
Dyke Annas
George Maddox
Marshall Short
W. E. Parker
Joe Kirby
Harold Brown

P. E. Jordan
Vance Kirby
Paul Williams
Arley Church
John Rhea, Jr.
Earl Bumgarner
S. J. Early
James Walter Fox
Charles Watson
John Laney
William Eckard
John D. Hornaday
Raymond Griffin
Boyd Brown

RHODHISS RURITAN CHARTER MEMBERS

CORA BROWN, RUTH SIGMON, MARTHA YOUNT, JOANNE LONGSHORE WITH GERALD AND
ELIZABETH. 1970S. GUY LONGSHORE PHOTO.

NOTES

1   Elmore, Fred and Martha and Tom Ross.

2   Glass, Brent D. *The Textile Industry in North Carolina: A History*. Raleigh, North Carolina: Division of Archives and History, North Carolina Department of Cultural Resources. 1992, pp. 84-85.

3   Rhodhiss Town Minutes. 16 July 1955.

4   Rhodhiss Town Minutes. 3 August 1955.

5   "Churches Given Land, Houses at Rhodhiss." *Granite Falls Press*. 12 August 1955. Volume IV, Number 24, page 1.

6   Jones, Calvin and Tom Ross.

7   Townsend, Hans and Katherine and Tom Ross.

8   Beshears, Monteith, Ross, and Teague.

9   Laney, Billie Sue. Telephone Interview. 28 December 2021.

10   "Rhodhiss Shows Much Progress." *Lenoir News-Topic*. 26 February 1969, p. B13.

11   Beshears, Monteith, Ross, and Teague.

12   Kirby, Beth.

13   Aldridge, Joe and Olive.

14   Beshears, Monteith, Ross, and Teague.

15   Rhodhiss Town Minutes. 10 August 1970.

16   Beshears, Monteith, Ross, and Teague.

17   Bolick, Mary Starnes and Tom Ross.

18   "240 Rhodhiss Employes (sic) Recognized." *Hickory Daily Record*. 1963.

19   "North Carolina Directory of Manufacturing Firms 1956." *North Carolina Digital Collections*. https://digital.ncdcr. gov/digital/collection/p249901coll22/id/400180/rec/13. Accessed 8 February 2022.

20   Bolick, Mary Starnes and Tom Ross.

21   Townsend, Hans and Katherine and Tom Ross.

22   Compton, Carl. Personal Interview with Sherrie Hartsoe Sigmon. Rhodhiss, NC. 18 July 2019.

23   Hartsoe, Daniel. Personal Interview with Sherrie Hartsoe Sigmon. Gastonia, NC. 11 December 2015.

24   Bolick, Mary Starnes and Tom Ross.

25   Bolick, Mary Starnes and Tom Ross.

26   Jones, Calvin and Tom Ross.

27   "Rhodhiss Shows Much Progress." *Lenoir News Topic*. 26 February 1969, p. B13.

28   Kirby, Beth.

29   Jones, Calvin and Tom Ross.

30   Beshears, Monteith, Ross, and Teague.

31   Compton, Carl. Email Interview with Sherrie Sigmon. 01 January 2015.

32   Lingle, Earl and Tom Ross.

33   Hand, Arthur and Exie.

34   "Burlington Makes Shifts in Rhodhiss Plant Setup." *Hickory Daily Record*. 1972.

35   Beshears, Monteith, Ross, and Teague.

36   Bolick, Mary Starnes and Tom Ross.

37   Barker, Gladys.

38   Hand, Arthur and Exie.

39   Hartsoe, Boyce. Personal Interview with Sherrie Hartsoe. Rhodhiss, NC. 3 April 1988.

40   Barker, Gladys.

41   Kelley, Alvis and Precious and Tom Ross.

CHAPTER 24
RHODHISS VOLUNTEER FIRE DEPARTMENT AND CIVIL DEFENSE

S afety is imperative within a community. Citizens need fire, rescue, and police protection. Rhodhiss provided these for the community, but on various levels throughout the years. Calvin Jones noted in Chapter 21 that the mill company provided fire protection for the town. At one point Granite Falls Fire Department covered the town for a fee in the 1950s. In 1960 the town's citizens met to discuss the formation of a volunteer fire department. Also, in the early 1960s during the Cold War the United States government was concerned about nuclear fallout in the event of an attack, so a civil defense program was implemented in many US cities, and Rhodhiss was designated as an official fallout shelter. Safety was paramount on the minds of the town and mill company.

According to the town minutes, an official from the Town of Granite Falls attended a Rhodhiss board meeting to discuss a contract between the two municipalities which would pay Granite Falls for fire service.[1] The cost for this service was $65 per call, and after much discussion and many negotiations, the agreement was signed.[2] Several years later Mayor Bill Childers mentioned that a volunteer fire department was needed, and he thought that the shop crew would be good men to have in this department since they could leave their jobs in the event of a fire.[3] Four years later the board asked Arley Church to check into the possibility of forming a volunteer fire department. A public meeting was held on Saturday, November 19, 1960 at 10:00 AM at the Rhodhiss Elementary School for any people interested in joining a volunteer fire department.[4] The town accepted a bid of $14,600 from American LaFrance Company for a fire truck, and Arley Church was named the first fire chief.[5] The new fire truck arrived in September and additional equipment, such as signals, radios, coats, helmets, and badges, was purchased at a cost of $1,200.[6] The original fire station was on Caldwell side at the present-day town garage. Eugene and Ellis Glass donated land for a new fire station to be beside their grocery store on Burke Street. This new building housed the fire department, police department, and the town hall.[7] The Town of Rhodhiss needed a way to pay for this new facility. After almost a year of deliberation and ideas tossed about, a group approached the board with their proposal. David Annas was now the fire chief, and he was accompanied by the President of the Ladies' Fire Department Auxiliary, Betty Bowman; the Ruritan President Luther Sigmon; and the President of the Community Improvement Group, Dwight Kirby. These people revealed their plan to borrow money from the Valdese Savings and Loan in the names of their organizations. They would lease the building to the town for the annual cost of the payment to the savings and loan. At the lease's end the organizations would deed the building to the Town of Rhodhiss. The board agreed unanimously.[8] Bids were accepted for the proposed building, and Mackie Building and Supply of Granite Falls with Ernest and Rebecca Marsico as owners won the bid.[9] In the spring of 1965 the fire department, police department, and general government offices moved into the new municipal building on Burke Street. In 1974 a tanker was added to the fire department.[10] The longest serving fire chief was Larry Yount, and in 2000 the town board voted a Resolution of Appreciation for his twenty years of service.[11] At the end of this chapter is a list of all the fire chiefs and a list of the charter members of the Rhodhiss Volunteer Fire Department.

BUDDY AND GENE GLASS LEFT THE MILL COMPANY BUILDING AFTER BURLINGTON ARRIVED AND BUILT THEIR OWN STORE ON BURKE STREET SINCE THERE WAS NO LONGER A MILL COMPANY STORE. THEY DONATED THE VACANT LOT BESIDE THEM TO THE TOWN TO BUILD THE TOWN OFFICE AND FIRE DEPARTMENT BUILDING. 1963. SHERRIE HARTSOE SIGMON PHOTO.

PETE BOWMAN, WHO WORKED IN MAINTENANCE FOR THE TOWN, AT THE VACANT LOT THAT WOULD BECOME THE TOWN OFFICE AND FIRE DEPARTMENT. 1963. SHERRIE HARTSOE SIGMON PHOTO.

THE TOWN GARAGE BURNED IN THE 1970S. *GRANITE FALLS PRESS* PHOTO VIA CARL HOLLAR.

Civil Defense became a huge part of President John Kennedy's agenda. Fallout shelters became commonplace in many areas. Some people even built bomb shelters. *The New York Times* detailed these turbulent times, and how New York was affected. The article stated:

> In the early 1960's, especially after the heightened fears of nuclear attack following the Cuban missile crisis, fallout shelters were believed to be the chief means of defense against the effects of a nuclear blast. They were a civic responsibility patriotically and cheerfully shouldered by both the largest corporations and the smallest suburban householders. More than 230,000 buildings were officially designated as fallout shelters in the metropolitan area, and thousands of these were stocked with basic survival supplies. The cost was immense, estimated at $30 million in the city alone — or $2.92 cents per person: $1.17 for the wheat biscuits, providing 10,000 calories in two weeks; 44 cents for steel water containers with plastic liners, which could be converted to toilets when emptied; 25 cents for medical kits; 17 cents for sanitation kits; 18 cents for radiation-detecting equipment; and 21 cents for warehousing and transportation.[12]

Because of the Cold War during the middle of the twentieth century, the government implemented many programs to deal with nuclear fallout.

Although Rhodhiss was not a big city like New York, it had a fallout shelter at the Burke plant of Burlington Industries. Calvin Jones served as the plant engineer at that time, and he was told that he was to oversee the shelter. Calvin explained to Tom Ross and me:

> CJ: During the early '60s after Bill Craven came, the government wanted to make this mill across the river (Burke) a fallout shelter. I don't know why Bill Craven or ever who it was in the office picked on me.
>
> TR: You were in the shop. Calvin, that had your name all over it.
>
> CJ: They wanted me to take this course and be the fallout shelter manager. I didn't have much choice. They said, 'You're it!' So, I had to go to Morganton. I forgot how many days, once or twice a week for about six months. Took a course up there on fallout shelter management. Had to take a radiation course on how to check radiation in case we had a nuclear bomb to hit here and the fallout from it. I had to learn how to check that. Then I had to go to Asheville several times for classes. Then to get my diploma I had to go to Asheville and spent 36 hours in a fallout shelter there with 50 people, and the thing or the room was about the size of Tom's living room. We had to eat, sleep, and go to the bathroom in that little room.
>
> TR: They were serious.
>
> CJ: Yes, they were serious. The government was pushing this. The government was putting it on. They're the ones that found out about this mill and came in and made it a shelter. They got a hold of the company and wanted to make a fallout shelter, and of course, Burlington went along with it. Because Bill Craven was for it.

TR: Yeah, yeah. Was Lacy involved?

CJ: He finally got Lacy Hodges roped in and got Elmer Yoder roped in, too. The two of them. I had Ruffey Dula roped in. Those were the ones who were to help me if we ever had to go into a fallout shelter. Anyhow after we got it fixed up, the government got it checked out. They sent enough food in here for over 2,000 people.

SH: Would this place have housed over 2,000 people if there had been a bomb?

CJ: Yeah, the mill across the river, Burke County side.

SH: Yeah, I knew that daddy talked about it. When I was in school, I had to take a Civil Defense class. We learned where our nearest fallout shelters were.

CJ: After I got my diploma, we started putting on classes at the mill. I had two doctors to come in and teach the class a medical course. It taught you how to deliver a baby. Of course, when you go into a fallout shelter, you don't know if there's going to be a doctor there. If there's not a doctor, and people have babies, you're going to have to do it. Then you're going to have to deal with deaths. We had to study all of this. What would you do, and how would you handle a death? With radiation at that time, they were teaching us that the only thing that you could do was roll them up into a sheet or blanket and pitch them outside. That's the way that you'd bury them. Because you couldn't get outside to bury them. You couldn't keep them inside because the body would start decomposing. Then you'd be in trouble with diseases, so the only thing that you could do is roll them up and throw them outside. That would be a hard thing because you'd have families there, and they wouldn't go along with this. You had to learn how you'd cope with families that didn't want their loved one pitched outside. So, it would be a problem. I can see that.

SH: So, did you have to keep this place stocked all the time with food and everything?

CJ: The government sent it in here, and it stayed stocked till I retired in '75. Then after I retired, I resigned the job as fallout shelter manager because I wasn't going to be down there. Civil Defense people, I think was it C. B. Sperry talked them into taking that food out?

TR: You had water, too, didn't you?

CJ: I had water because the water coming in would be contaminated. These tanks that we had weren't completely sealed off. We had to have the water tanks and have chlorine. We had it stored in tanks in drums over in the industrial mill.

TR: Didn't you find a spring underneath the mill?

CJ: We did when we were building that last section on the end.

SH: Was that at number two?

CJ: Yeah. Found a spring that was beautiful. I bet that it ran 100 gallons a minute. A beautiful spring. So, we had that in the back of our minds in case we ever had to go in there that we would be able to pick up water.

TR: Yeah, fresh water.

CJ: Because it was directly under the mill. It wasn't outside, so it wouldn't be contaminated. In this fallout shelter where we went there and spent the 36 hours, Lacy Hodges and I are the only ones that went. We went in there. We had to sleep and eat, and they just roped off a place for the curtain for us to use the bathroom right in the same room. This thing had to be real. We had men, women, and children in the same area. Had one little boy who was the most inquisitive boy that I have ever seen in my life, and he would just worry you to death about everything. I think that they planted that boy in there intentionally, just to aggravate us. I was the one responsible for checking radiation, and of course, they had planted cobalt around at different places on the outside. I'd have to find that thing with this monitor that I had, and it was kind of like a Geiger counter. I had earphones on, and it would detect radiation. I knew that they had planted radiation, and I found out about where it was planted. I had to move the people back away from the area where I found it. This little boy was pulling on my coattail and saying, 'Let me listen to that. I want to listen.' He just worried you to death, and I was trying to do a job. If it had been the real thing, it would have been worse. We knew that all of this was just a mock type thing. Anyhow we got by that 36 hours, and we ate these K rations. That's all that we had. Boy, when we got out of there, me and Lacy and this boy from Hildebran from over there were taking it, we all took off to Buck's Steak House.

TR: Everybody knew about Buck's in Asheville.

CJ: Yeah, we headed there and got a big steak as soon as we got out of there.

TR: Obviously, the government really thought that we were going to be attacked.

CJ: Yeah, they did. I really enjoyed it though. Another thing that I don't know if Sherrie remembers or not because she may not have been old enough, after we had this fallout manager's course, and I studied radiation and all of that stuff, Burke County wanted us to put on a mock nuclear accident. We settled on the Valdese General Hospital as the place to have it. Dr. White, the radiologist, taught the radiation course. He was handling it, and he wanted me to be in charge of the thing to set it up over all of Burke County. I don't know why they picked on me. Anyhow I set the thing up, and I think that Martha Yount did most of my typing. She typed up the pretend amounts of radiation that we were going to have at different places all over the county. We had people calling in with these 3-way radios telling about the mock accident and how much radiation they had there. They were reading off this little card that I had given them with the amount of radiation. We were telling them what to do from Valdese General Hospital. Then we were having people that were in mock accidents and having to bring them into the hospital. The rescue squads were involved in this thing. They were going out and bringing people in. I remember that we had Norma Kirby. They brought Norma in over at the hospital on a stretcher. Vance was in on this thing. I forgot what Vance did. We had people here at Rhodhiss. We had people at Glen Alpine, just all over Burke County in this thing. It proved to be very successful.

TR: I don't remember that. I do remember that the White fella was really involved in this thing, wasn't he?

CJ: Yeah, he was the radiologist over at Valdese. He did all the teaching of the radiation courses. Then we had the county doctor. What was his name? Burke County.

TR: I don't know whether I ever knew that.

CJ: He came down and taught the ladies in the medical course. They called it a Medical Self-

Help course. I was trying to think of it a while ago. We taught the men separate from the ladies. It was very interesting, I will tell you. It was just something good to know in case you ever have to use it. Like in the fallout shelter, I didn't mention you might have fights. Of course, when you go into a fallout shelter, you want to make sure that you take away all weapons, knives, guns, or anything that they might try to bring in. It was just a big job thinking about something like that.

TR: That thing was overwhelming.

CJ: Yes, it was.

SH: That was a big responsibility initiating it.

TR: You didn't think so much about it in that way.

SH: From what you were told, it was part of your job.

CJ: That's right.[13]

Calvin's leadership in implementing the fallout shelter was amazing. This was certainly indicative of the times, and the town took it quite seriously.

In an article in the *Hickory Daily Record* by Wake Bridges, he outlined Burke County's role in Civil Defense. It stated:

> J.C. Sossoman of Morganton, director of Civil Defense in Burke County, said that tractor-trailer deliveries of supplies for fallout shelters were sent to Burlington Mills in Rhodhiss and then to Valdese General Hospital. The other designated shelters are at Morganton Furniture Company and Broughton Hospital. The food and water will be put in storage in the designated shelters for the basic needs of those housed for a two-week period, based on the maximum number of persons that the space can house. 'The shelters have been set up and are being stocked for use in the event of a nuclear attack or natural disaster,' the Burke County civil defense director pointed out. Mr. Sossoman said today that 'personnel is being trained for monitoring radiation from the shelters, also for shelter management.'[14]

Burke County even hired a Director of Civil Defense. Four fallout areas were designated in Burke County: Burlington Industries, Valdese Hospital, Morganton Furniture, and Broughton Hospital.

The *Granite Falls Press* also printed an article regarding Rhodhiss' role in the government's Civil Defense program. The article was entitled "Rhodhiss Citizens Complete Civil Defense Class." It noted:

> Men completing the class were: Arley Church, Mayor of Rhodhiss, Franklin Benfield, Jerry Bogle, R. A. Bowman, Jr., Boyd L. Brown, David Annas, James W. Fox, Bobby Lee Gregory, Willard W. Herman, Lacy Hodges, Dexter Hornaday, J. Calvin Jones, Vance A. Kirby, Al Lowdermilk, Frank McNeil, Marshall E. Short, Baine L. Smith, Walter J. Starnes, Elmer R. Yoder, Boyd Yount, John E. Bolan, Kenneth Hatch, Blaine Hollar,

Dwight Kirby, Earl Lingle, and Luther P. Sigmon. Many of the men are employed at Rhodhiss Mills. On September 25, twenty-five ladies from Rhodhiss, many of them wives of the Burlington Industries employees, completed the Medical Self-Help class also. The instructor for these two classes has been John B. Harris, who gives his time voluntarily to the work of civil defense. These classes consist of a 16 hour period, two hours a week for 8 weeks. Assisting Mr. Harris, also voluntarily, were Dr. Emmett White of Valdese General Hospital, Dr. G. F. Reeves, head of the Burke County Health Center, the Burke County Rescue Squad, Elmo Pascal from the Burke County Health Center and Mrs. Harry Feimster, registered nurse, who taught the class on Nursing Care of the Sick and Injured. The Medical Self-Help classes are sponsored by the Burke County Civil Defense Agency and are free for all civilians of Burke County. Rhodhiss is very proud of it's (sic) accomplishments in Civil Defense during the past 18 months. The Rhodhiss people are constantly reviewing what they have been taught in the Fall out (sic) Shelter Managers Class, the Radiological Monitoring Class, the Medical Self-Help classes. The community is now asking the Burke County Civil Defense Agency to arrange a class on Adult Education in Civil Defense.[15]

Rhodhiss' fallout shelter would have housed over 2,000 people. The provisions were provided by the government, but Burlington Industries spent many man hours getting the facility ready for a potential nuclear war.

Fire protection and Civil Defense were big issues during the 1960s in Rhodhiss. A new volunteer fire department along with a Ladies Auxiliary were formed. A fire truck and equipment were purchased, and a new building was erected. The Rhodhiss Volunteer Fire Department is still active and serving the community today with approximately twenty members. The Burke County Burlington plant was prepped with all the essentials for a fallout shelter for the citizens of Rhodhiss and others within the surrounding area. This facility has since been abandoned as a fallout shelter. Safety was on the minds of the town, and the strong work ethic of its citizens ensured that the fallout shelter would be successful if needed.

Rhodhiss Fire Chiefs (list obtained from Town Minutes)

Year	Name
1961	Arley Church
1964	David Annas
1968	Walt Fox
1976	Larry Nichols
1979	Allen Kirby
1980	Walter Biddix
1982	Larry Nichols
1983	Larry Yount
2006	Michael Bailey, Interim
2007	Larry Yount
2009	Will Dennis
2017	Jimmy Drum

Charter Members of Rhodhiss Fire Department 1961
(list obtained from Bicentennial pamphlet)

Pete Bowman	Doug Cowick
R. A. Bowman	Thad Elmore
Bill Eckard	Cyrus Yates
Thad Martin	Dillard Church
James Munday	Arley Church
James Buckner	R. D. Beshears
Walter Fox	Wayne Mullinax
Larry Nichols	Dave Annas
Vance Kirby	Paul Williams
Roy Tucker	John Rhea, Jr.
Harold Hollar	Homer Goodman
Ralph Settlemyre	Harry Lowman
Hub Eller	Joe Aldridge

THE FIRETRUCK THAT WAS PURCHASED IN 1961. RHODHISS FIRE DEPARTMENT PHOTOS.

DILLARD CHURCH, WALTER BIDDIX, JIM BROWN, AND JOE ALDRIDGE. 1960S RHODHISS FIRE DEPARTMENT PHOTO.

RICHARD DEAL, DAVE ANNAS, BILL ECKARD.
RHODHISS FIRE DEPARTMENT PHOTO.

CARL DEWEY IN 1979. RHODHISS FIRE
DEPARTMENT PHOTO.

LARRY YOUNT WITH NEW FIRE TRUCK IN
1992. *HICKORY DAILY RECORD* PHOTO.

THE RHODHISS FIRE STATION IN 2005. RHODHISS
FIRE DEPARTMENT PHOTO.

IN 2015 THE LEGENDARY SUPERINTENDENT HOUSE BURNED. *LENOIR NEWS-TOPIC* PHOTO.

RHODHISS' CIVIL DEFENSE TEAM IN 1963. *GRANITE FALLS PRESS* PHOTO.

EVEN IN THE EARLY 1970S, CIVIL DEFENSE WAS STILL IN THE THOUGHTS OF RHODHISS SCHOOL PERSONNEL. *GRANITE FALLS PRESS* PHOTO.

NOTES

1   Rhodhiss Town Minutes. 10 June 1953.

2   Rhodhiss Town Minutes. 1 February 1954.

3   Rhodhiss Town Minutes, 14 February 1956.

4   Rhodhiss Town Minutes. 10 October 1960.

5   Rhodhiss Town Minutes. 4 May 1961.

6   Rhodhiss Town Minutes. 11 September 1961.

7   Rhodhiss Town Minutes. 2 September 1963.

8   Rhodhiss Town Minutes. 22 September 1964.

9   Rhodhiss Town Minutes. 9 November 1964.

10   Anderson, pages 181-182.

11   Rhodhiss Town Minutes. 11 September 2000.

12   "Civil Defense Fallout Shelters: Relics of the 60's." The New York Times. 21 November 1979, Section C, Page 9. https://www.nytimes.com/1979/11/21/archives/civil-defense-fallout-shelters-relics-of-the-60s.html. Accessed 4 July 2022.

13   Jones, Calvin and Tom Ross.

14   Bridges, Wake. "More Goods Due to Come During Week." Hickory Daily Record. 18 February 1963.

15   "Rhodhiss Citizens Complete Civil Defense Class." Granite Falls Press. 12 December 1963.

CHAPTER 25
MOON FLAG AND OTHER MATERIALS

Brent Glass discussed the prominence of textiles throughout North Carolina in his book, *The Textile Industry in North Carolina: A History*. Burlington Mills started in 1923 and continued to grow as other textile companies declined. In the late 1930s Burlington produced rayon in eighteen plants, and in 1938 Burlington was one of the nation's top hosiery manufacturers. Over fifty products were made for the government during World War II. In 1952 they were the largest producer of synthetics in the world, with 73 plants in 8 states and 4 foreign countries. They employed 31,000 and had a payroll of $93 million. Burlington purchased Pacific Mills in 1954. Burlington Mills changed their name in 1955 to Burlington Industries and had nine separate divisions. By 1967 they had grown to 130 plants in 15 states and 11 countries and 83,000 employees. In North Carolina almost 20 percent of textile workers were employed with Burlington Industries for a total of 40,000 workers. Burlington's president, J. Spencer Love, was credited with these successes. He was a Gaston County native who attended Harvard and returned to work in Burlington, North Carolina.[1] All of this relates to Rhodhiss because many people wonder why Rhodhiss' plants were so successful. Their triumph is most probably because Burlington was known worldwide, and Rhodhiss was often used as a pilot for materials that made their mark. For example, Ned Bean discussed Kevlar: "We helped Dupont develop Kevlar."[2] During the 1960s any child whose parent worked at the Industrial Division Plant at Rhodhiss knew that Rhodhiss made the bullet proof vests for the American troops in Vietnam and that the Rhodhiss plant wove materials that were used in the Apollo lunar landings.

Rhodhiss' forte was not limited to Kevlar. There were so many other products in their stock. Joe Aldridge explained:

> We made tent material for years. We wove the flag that's on the moon. We made the nose cones for the missiles. The heat shields on those shuttles, we made that. We made underwater parachutes for the government. They put those bombs in them. They hid

them from place to place. We made the bullet-proof material. One type of it, nothing could shoot through it, not even a cannon. What they called Kevlar. You couldn't cut it. A string the size of a pencil lead, there wasn't any way of breaking it. Any kind of automobile tire. We made snow fences. We made a lean one. Every thread it in was a quarter inch. They used that for contractors. They put a plastic coating on it. In the wintertime, well summer, too, they'd haul the framing up on the house and take that stuff and cover it up. If you were working, you never got too cold, too rainy, or anything else. All kinds of vacuum for carpets.[3]

Rhodhiss' products were of top-notch quality, and the millhands had pride in their work.

Beth Kirby gave more details in her paper regarding Burlington Industries in Rhodhiss. In 1964 to change the Burke plant to an industrial fabrics division the company installed huge steel beams to support the machinery's weight. The old machinery (cards, spinning frames, winders, twisters, and looms) was transferred to other plants and new machinery was installed. In 1965 this plant was remodeled with 150 new looms, 1 warper, 1 winder, 4 twisters, and auxiliary equipment. The warehouse got an addition; another boiler was added, cloth storage bins were implemented, and the cloth room was air conditioned. At this plant their final products included "tire cord, flag material, bulletproof and fireproof material, scrim material, material used for runways for airplane landings, nose cones for missiles, chafer and bead wrap, snow fencing, and grass catcher fabrics." These materials were sent to Greensboro or Kernersville for finishing.[4] Carl Compton worked at this plant when the mill company added the heavier machinery. Carl wrote:

THIS POST WAS IN THE INDUSTRIAL FABRICS PLANT (BURKE) UNTIL THE COMPANY DISCARDED THE ORIGINALS TO INSTALL STRONGER BEAMS FOR NEWER MACHINERY IN THE 1960S. SIX OF THESE ARE STILL IN EXISTENCE IN A CALDWELL COUNTY FARM. THEY ARE ABOUT 12 INCHES IN DIAMETER. SHERRIE HARTSOE SIGMON PHOTO.

I remember very well when they replaced the posts. The plant continued to operate while the renovation was going on. They replaced every other post with steel beams and dug the footing for the steel about 10 foot deep and poured concrete. They built wood frames and surrounded the work area with plastic, to keep dust and debris from getting on the looms and warps. One of the main reasons they put the stronger support in the building was the new and much, much larger and VERY HEAVY slasher they put on the upper floor, along with the warper and all those very heavy warps. The old slasher was small and in the slasher room at the back end of the weave room. When the renovation was complete, they moved all the warps and empty beams into the old slasher room on the ground floor at the back of the weave room.[5]

Carl's firsthand recollection of the mill's changeover adds depth to the story. Rhodhiss continued its successful history as an article in the *Hickory Daily Record* detailed:

Even though the general economy was not good in 1969 the 2 Rhodhiss Burlington plants had a good 1969. The corporate outlook for 1970 appears to be good, also. Burlington's goal in 1970 is to maintain job security and to strengthen profit-sharing. The two Rhodhiss plants contribute strongly to the economies of Burke, Caldwell and Catawba counties. Both plants employ approximately 450 people and the payroll exceeds $2.5 million. Both plants have been expanding and improving their facilities with new equipment, air conditioning, and new square footage. The Men's Wear Division in Caldwell County has converted from weaving to yarn manufacture. This plant supplies other plants yarn for men's and boys' suits, slacks, and sportswear. Burlington's Men's Wear is the country's largest producer of synthetic and synthetic blends. Burlington's Industrial Division in Burke County produces fabrics of man-made fibers and blends. Industrial products are used in the military for tenting, packs, cartridge bags, bullet-proof vests and more glamorous uses such as fabrics for space suits. Burlington has more than 130 plants in the US and in 11 foreign countries; 76 of those plants are in NC. Although Burlington is less than 50 years old, it is the largest textile firm in the world with 86,000 employees.[6]

Burlington's name was known worldwide. The Rhodhiss employees held their heads high because they knew that their products were of superior quality and that the demand was high.

In the early 1970s the Caldwell Plant changed from Men's Wear to House Division. They produced draperies, upholstery material, bedspreads, sheets, pillowcases, towels, and rugs.[7] Calvin Jones and Tom Ross discussed some of the changes implemented. They stated:

CJ: A dust collection was put in. You know how dust and lint would fly around in the mill. We put in a dust collecting system that would pull all the dust out. It had ducts. On the cards you could see it just flying in the air. It would pull that stuff off the card and take it through to a collection system. We'd empty it about once a day. It would take all that lint out of the air, and there wasn't any lint flying in the air at that time. We did that in the spinning room where you had a lot of lint and in the card room. It just pulled that lint out. We put that in after we got rid of the looms on this side (Caldwell). That's when we went to an all-spinning mill here, to a yarn mill, so to speak, instead of a weave room.

TR: They put twisting in the bottom floor.

CJ: Yes, they took the looms out and put twisting in the bottom floor. Was that after Craven turned this thing over to the different managers? After Craven left here and Charles Grady was here? What year was that?

SH: Craven left in '70.

CJ: It was about '70 or '71 when they put that in. I'll tell you when they changed it. When they brought Eddie Cook up here. That's when it was changed. Do you remember when they brought in Eddie Cook that morning? They put Eddie in and said that they were changing it to a spinning mill, a yarn mill.

TR: That was the director's division people.

CJ: Yeah. House fabrics. Burlington House Fabrics.

TR: Oh, man. They couldn't make enough then to sell. It's amazing how that business was booming. They just made the yarn.

SH: Did it decline and that's why they closed plant 1?

TR: Yeah, people quit buying the drapes and other materials.[8]

Change is inevitable, and Burlington moved to making houseware materials believing this would be the best avenue for sales; however, within five years the demand decreased.

Burlington Industries in Greensboro wrote an article on the products that were manufactured at the Rhodhiss Industrial Division Plant (the Burke plant) in their 1981 in-house magazine, *The Burlington Look*. It stated that when the space shuttle Columbia launched, it carried 33 tons of Burlington Industrial fabric with it into space. More details follow:

Woven from rayon yarn at the Rhodhiss, N. C. plant, the fabric was used to make a carbon and resin composite that protects the rocket booster system during lift-off, when temperatures from the rocket blast reach 6000 degrees Fahrenheit. At the Rhodhiss plant, quality control manager, Gene Mull, noted that the rayon fabric was very tough to make, but added that 'we've mastered it over the years.' Weavers and loom fixers at the Rhodhiss plant were unanimous in describing the difficulties of weaving the fabric, but all agreed that they had the know-how to do it right. 'It's a hard running style to get the quality they want,' said loom fixer Carl Compton. 'But knowing where it ends up sure makes you work a little harder.' While on a trip to Kennedy Space Center with his daughter, Compton saw some of the Burlington fabric on display. 'You could see how it was charred from reentry,' he said. Employees' children have been especially proud that their parents contributed to the successful flight of the space shuttle. 'My kids told all their friends at school,' said weaver Linda Shelton. 'It's a hard style to get started up when you first put it on the loom,' said weaver Maxine Carver, 'and you need experienced weavers to run it.' Carver's children were also excited about her important contribution to the space program. 'Actually, we've been making fabric like this for the military and NASA (the National Aeronautics and Space Administration) since

1961,' said Jack Leach, technical specialist for the Industrial Division. 'Our rayon fibers have been used in practically all space shots since 1965. But before it can be used in outer space, the industrial fabric undergoes a series of dramatic changes. First the woven rayon is 'carbonized.' This is a process in which the rayon fabric is heated to over 2000 degrees Fahrenheit until all the non-carbon atoms in its molecules are 'smoked off,' leaving only the pure carbon backbone of the rayon. After it is carbonized, the rayon is treated with an epoxy resin so it can be formed into a hard, tough shape for use in the spacecraft. When the process is complete, the fabric composite is so heat resistant it actually absorbs heat and energy. That's why rayon is used rather than metal.' According to Leach, Burlington's aerospace material has been used in nose cones and heat shields of the Navy's Polaris and Trident missiles, as well as in space crafts for the Mercury, Gemini and Apollo programs. 'Without this material,' he explained, 'missiles would disintegrate when coming back into the earth's atmosphere. Missiles plunge directly into and through the earth's atmosphere and reach temperatures as high as 20,000 degrees Fahrenheit,' Leach said. 'But the space shuttle uses a different system of reentry where temperatures do not exceed 2500 degrees Fahrenheit.' In order to make sure that the aerospace fabric performs perfectly, it's tested about 10 times more than most ordinary industrial fabrics. 'Every yard has to be identical to every other yard and it can't get wet or it's no good,' Leach added. But in spite of the difficulties involved the Industrial Division is proud to have a hand in the nation's space program. As weaver Maxine Carver explained, 'It just makes you feel good to know you're involved in something worthwhile.'[9]

The Rhodhiss Industrial Division plant made a name for itself. In the 1995 NASA came to town and presented Rhodhiss a plaque commemorating all the assistance that the employees gave to the space program. Not many communities can boast that they made materials that were used by NASA. As one former employee, Roy Whisnant, stated to the news media, "I never thought that I would make something out of this world!"[10]

Mary Settlemyre Darty worked at Rhodhiss all her working life. She retired prior to the closing of the Industrial Division Plant. Mary stated, "Did anybody tell you that the material was made down here at Rhodhiss for the flag on the moon? That was something that we were proud of. Isn't it something that our material was picked from that plant?"[11] Any person who lived or worked in Rhodhiss in 1969 knew this story. The town was abuzz talking about this major accomplishment. Edward Phifer also mentioned this in his Burke County history. He wrote, "According to a company official, 'The list of products woven at Rhodhiss Industrial Fabrics, a part of Burlington Industries, challenges the imagination…. The first flag on the moon was woven at Rhodhiss and placed there by American astronauts.'"[12] Caldwell County also noted the accomplishment as Norma Kirby stated, "Burlington Industries here has the distinction of weaving the material that produced the flag placed on the moon by our astronauts in 1969."[13] Everyone in Rhodhiss lived this, and they knew that it was a part of the town's heritage.

In the late summer of 1969, the mill company announced to the employees that the flag that was placed on the moon on July 20, 1969, was woven at the Rhodhiss Industrial Fabrics Division. They planned a celebration party for the employees that was held on an August Friday. Don Hartsoe, who had worked at the plant that summer, recalls that he had graduated from high school that spring, and he was a freshman at Gardner Webb that fall. He came home that Friday in August to attend the celebration.[14] Around the same time an article appeared in the local newspaper, the *Granite Falls Press*, and was entitled "First Flag on Moon Woven at Rhodhiss." The article noted:

> The list of products woven at Rhodhiss Industrial Fabrics, a part of Burlington Industries, challenges the imagination. In fact, a product woven at the plant is resting snugly 240,000 miles away. The first flag on the moon was woven at Rhodhiss and placed there by American astronauts. Besides marking one of our nation's greatest endeavors, Rhodhiss flag fabrics are found in many other places from golf courses to flag ships. They are woven from spun and filament yarns representing many different fiber blends and constructions. The plant continues to produce many interesting fabrics. In fact, Indianapolis 500 winners have ridden on tires containing materials woven at Rhodhiss Industrial. All of the major tire producers are utilizing chafer and bead wrap fabrics woven at the local plant. One of the company's newly developed and initially successful products is a woven fence fabric. It has been used for crowd control in sporting events, for marking ski trails, to build sand dunes for beach erosion control, and a number of other applications. Substrate fabrics for the coating and laminating market are also of great importance, as well as filter fabrics used in the filtration industry, cloth for specialized uniforms, special fabrics for aerospace industry and protective fabrics for the military. The division is continually evaluating new fibers as they become available, in an effort to constantly upgrade and expand the utilization of manmade fibers in the industrial market. Nylon continues to be the major man-made fiber utilized in the industrial products.[15]

Rhodhiss made all types of materials that were used by major corporations and the United States government.

Burlington's in-house magazine also published an article describing the success of the Industrial Fabrics Division at Rhodhiss. This same article was reprinted for the *Rhodhiss Bicentennial Times* newsletter that was written on several occasions in 1976. The article was entitled, "It's a 'Grand Old Flag' That's Woven by Industrial." It stated:

> The mayor of Rhodhiss, N. C., is particularly proud of the new American flag which flies above the city's municipal building. He received the flag as a gift from the Burlington Industrial Fabrics Rhodhiss Weaving plant, where the fabric was woven -- and where Mayor Cecil 'Bud' Munday works as supply supervisor. 'So, the flag has extra significance to me,' the mayor said. 'And it's appropriate that plant management

presented it to the city as we start the Bicentennial Year, because Rhodhiss has been designated a Bicentennial community.' Plant management also gave five other U. S. flags to officials in nearby Granite Falls and Hudson, as well as local school systems. Each flag measures 5-by-8 feet. Duffie Taylor, Rhodhiss plant manager, said: 'We wanted to do a little something to show our appreciation to the local governments and schools for their support over the years.' While these flags will all be flown close to home, plant management likes to point out the flag that's farthest away. The first U. S. flag planted on the moon by American astronauts (in 1969) was made of fabric woven at Rhodhiss. 'Actually, you would probably find flags made from Burlington fabric all around the world, because the Company has been manufacturing flag fabrics for more than 20 years' said Raymond Ronan, division planning manager in New York. 'Today, Burlington is the largest supplier of fabrics to the flag manufacturing industry.' Burlington sells fabrics of 100 percent nylon, 100 percent acrylic and 100 percent cotton to flag manufacturers who cut and sew flags for all kinds of organizations. 'The Company's Dillon, S. C. plant and the Plaid plant in Burlington are also running flag fabric,' Mr. Ronan said. 'All three constructions -- nylon, acrylic and cotton -- are made to U. S. government specifications for manufacture into flags for federal, state and local governments, as well as for commercial sales to companies and individuals.' Ronan added that because of the Bicentennial the demand for flags has risen.[16]

Again, another periodical saluted Rhodhiss for its accomplishments. The hearts and souls of the Rhodhiss people resonate with pride, knowing the town's role in NASA's history.

Rhodhiss was featured in many local and state newspapers throughout the years for the moon flag story. Many former employees discussed the big picture in the lobby with the American flag on the moon that was housed at the Burke County Burlington plant. Rick Justice and I spent one entire year looking for this picture to no avail. It is like seeking the Holy Grail. During a lunar landing anniversary, the town council decided that Rhodhiss needed to commemorate this accomplishment. The board voted in May 1995 to obtain town limit signs with a decal of the moon flag from NASA.[17] Then later that year the board voted to make the moon seals the official town emblem and to have fourteen seals made for the town vehicles.[18] A brief article ran in the *Hickory Daily Record* on the twenty-sixth anniversary. It stated, "History was made 26 years ago in Rhodhiss when weavers wove the flag material for the moon missions. Ruby Walden, a former employee of the plant said, 'they knew they were making flag material, but didn't know what it would be used for.'"[19] Employees were not told prior to the moon landing that their materials were aboard the Apollo 11 flight; however, later the news spread throughout the plant after corporate informed the executives.

In January 1996 the Hickory paper wrote an article regarding the moon flag. It noted:

The dream is still alive for people in this small community which straddles the Catawba River in Burke and Caldwell counties. Here is where the materials for the U. S. flags on the moon were manufactured in the late 1960s and early 1970s and residents are still proud of that accomplishment. Some 25 years after the moon flags were erected by the astronauts, Rhodhiss town officials decided to use NASA's theme 'Keep The Dream Alive,' and replaced the town limits sign with a picture of the astronaut and flag on the moon. Last month, Acting Director George W. S. Abbey of Lyndon B. Johnson Space Center in Houston, Texas presented the town of Rhodhiss with a plaque containing a North Carolina state flag which was flown aboard the Apollo 16 mission to the moon April 16-27, 1972. The plaque was personally signed by the space flight Commander John W. Young and contains a photograph of Capt. Young on the moon doing the 'Jumping Salute.' Abbey said, 'The townspeople of Rhodhiss should take great pride in their many contributions to this nation's space program, and I hope this flown memento will serve as a reminder of the part your community has played. Your interest and support of the United States space program is truly appreciated.' The Rhodhiss Town Council voted recently to adopt the moon flag and astronaut as the official town seal and seals are being made by the city of Hickory to be placed on all Rhodhiss town vehicles in the near future. The N. C. Department of Transportation has also announced it will place Rhodhiss directional signs on Interstate 40 at the Icard Exit in Burke County. Flag materials were woven in the Old Burlington Industries plant on Burke Street in Rhodhiss at the bridge. That plant also manufactured other items for the U. S. government including parachutes, bomb blankets and crowd control fencing.[20]

NASA came to Rhodhiss and presented a plaque to the town commemorating their accomplishments in the aerospace industry. Rhodhiss' success makes many present and former citizens smile with delight and pride.

On the forty-year anniversary another *Hickory Daily Record* article was written about Rhodhiss. An excerpt from it reads:

> Calvin Jones, a former plant engineer for Burlington Industries, said that the Burke County plant primarily made synthetic materials. The plant on the Caldwell side made men's wear. Jones, who is 94, says that he was honored to work at the place that has its materials on the moon. 'We were all excited -- all of Rhodhiss was excited when it happened.' Rick Justice, Rhodhiss' Mayor, says, 'When I was a young man, there was big talk that the town had the privilege to do that. It could have been done anywhere in the world, but it wasn't. It was done in Rhodhiss.'[21]

Rhodhiss' story kept being reported. On Sunday, March 20, 2016, Rick Justice and I met at the old Rhodhiss Methodist Church with over twenty former employees and several citizens to discuss the moon flag. These people were present: Robert and Susan Wilson, Jack Griffith, Linda Shelton, Gerald Crunkleton, Ted and Dorothy Hartley, Roy and Anita Whisnant, David and Ester Smith, Marshall Fairchild, Blayne E. Hollar, Betty Adkins, Gwynne Lunsford Baker, Maxine Carver, Floyd Pope, Carl and Brenda Compton, Wanda Walsh, Nellie Thomas, Morris and May McCourry, Bob Szalanski,

Rick Justice, Sherrie Hartsoe Sigmon, Debbie Phillips, Michael Sigmon, and Bruce Hartsoe. Some of the information obtained includes that Burlington dealt with the Reeves Brothers, Dupont, Firestone, Good Year, Uniroyal, the U. S. government, and over 200 companies all over the country. The 50-inch machines were sent to South Carolina when the plant closed in 1983. In the late spring of 1968 to early 1969 the 210-denier nylon was woven. One of the style numbers was 441 and another style was 300 something. As per the people meeting on this day, they confirmed that they were told by the Burlington Industrial Fabrics Division executives that the flag on the moon was woven at Rhodhiss, and a picture hung in the plant noting that the moon flag was indeed made there.[22]

In 2019 the Town of Rhodhiss celebrated the fiftieth anniversary of the Apollo 11 lunar landing. In the Morganton paper an article entitled "Lunar Pride: Residents, Plant Workers To Celebrate Part Played in Inaugural Moon Landing," Carl Compton was quoted first and then Mayor Rick Justice. They stated:

> 'When we were weaving the flag material, we made thousands of yards of it. The employees actually didn't know that it had anything to do with the moon flag until about a week after the lunar landing. Management put a notice up on the bulletin board telling that they had used our fabric to make the flag. Everybody was really excited about it…. At that time, Burlington Industries was the largest textile company in the world. Even then, they had plants in four or five different countries…. I've got a feeling of great pride of being able to actually work with the material that's on the moon. As we had one person say before, 'That is out of this world!' The material was finished at another plant in Kernersville and then sent to a facility in New Jersey, which made the flag. Mayor Rick Justice said, 'After they found out (about the flag), it spurred such a great pride in the workers. Everybody stepped up their game once they found out the importance of what they were doing.'[23]

Rhodhiss' claim to fame has been covered through various media outlets throughout the last half century and by word-of-mouth from the citizens who feel it in their souls.

At the 50th anniversary of the moon landing celebration in Rhodhiss on July 20, 2019, more former employees voiced the same sentiments as those that met in 2016. Rick Justice and I interviewed these people. They all agreed that a picture of the moon flag was in the entry area of the Burlington Industrial Fabrics Plant in Burke County, and the workers were informed by management a few weeks after the July 20, 1969, moon landing that the flag placed on the moon was woven at Rhodhiss. Many of these Burlington employees were attendees of the meeting in 2016, but some new faces were able to attend. They were videotaped and their enthusiasm for Rhodhiss was obvious. Mack and Yvonne Hentschel, Ruth Kiziah, Joe and Ila Kelley, Larry Nichols, Maxine Carver, Gary McCourry, and Marvin Buchanan offered their thoughts on the NASA materials and the moon flag's origination at their plant.[24]

Rhodhiss, North Carolina is a small town that has a lot of pride. The townspeople can see the image of the moon flag on the town's seal, the town's entry from both the Caldwell and Burke sides, and the town vehicles. NASA visited in 1995 to honor the village with a plaque that represents the town's place in aerospace history. Burlington Industries did well by using Rhodhiss as the pilot program for many of their innovative ideas. Mary Fagerstrom stated in Chapter 11, "I tell you that Burlington was the lifeblood of that community." Perhaps that works two ways. Rhodhiss' employees were the lifeblood of Burlington Industries because of their hard work, dedication, and commitment to making superior products.

THIS 1960S ADVERTISEMENT AND TAG CITE RHODHISS' NOTORIETY IN MEN'S FASHION. SHERRIE HARTSOE SIGMON PHOTO.

THE *GRANITE FALLS PRESS'* ARTICLE IN AUGUST 1969 DETAILING RHODHISS' MOON FLAG STORY. SHERRIE HARTSOE SIGMON PHOTO.

IN 1976 BURLINGTON'S ARTICLE DETAILING THE MAKING OF THE LUNAR FLAG MATERIAL AT
RHODHISS. CARL HOLLAR PHOTO.

THE TOWN OF RHODHISS DONATED FLAGS. *HICKORY DAILY RECORD* PHOTO.

1981 *BURLINGTON LOOK* MAGAZINE'S STORY OF FLAG AND AEROSPACE MATERIAL. SHERRIE HARTSOE SIGMON PHOTO.

SOME RHODHISS EMPLOYEES WHO MAKE AEROSPACE MATERIALS. CARL COMPTON, LINDA SHELTON, AND MAXINE CARVER, 1981.

THIS PHOTO HANGS IN THE TOWN OFFICE. THE PICTURE HOLDS THE LUNAR FLAG PICTURE, A PIECE
OF THE MATERIAL, THE NASA LETTER, AND THE DESCRIPTION. CARL COMPTON PHOTO.

THIS IS AN ENLARGED PICTURE OF NASA'S LETTER
TO THE TOWN IN 1995. CARL COMPTON PHOTO.

THIS IS THE PLAQUE GIVEN TO
THE TOWN BY NASA IN 1995. CARL
COMPTON PHOTO.

1995 THE RHODHISS TOWN EMPLOYEES INSTALLED THE SIGN INDICATING RHODHISS' NASA TIES. TOWN OF RHODHISS PICTURE.

THIS SIGN GREETED PEOPLE AS THEY ENTERED RHODHISS IN 2013. SHERRIE HARTSOE SIGMON PHOTO.

THESE PEOPLE MET IN 2016 TO DISCUSS THE FLAG MATERIAL BEING MADE IN RHODHISS. JACK GRIFFITH, ROBERT WILSON, AND BETTY ADKINS. SHERRIE HARTSOE SIGMON PHOTO.

ATTENDEES TO THE FLAG MATERIAL MEETING IN 2016. BRUCE HARTSOE, CARL AND BRENDA COMPTON, MAXINE CARVER, AND OTHERS. SHERRIE HARTSOE SIGMON PHOTO.

MORE ATTENDEES. CARL AND BRENDA
COMPTON, FLOYD AND LIBBY POPE, ROY
WHISNANT, ESTER SMITH, BLAYNE HOLLAR,
AND OTHERS. SHERRIE HARTSOE
SIGMON PHOTO.

THE MEETING PROVED TO BE INFORMATIVE
AND A REUNION. LINDA SHELTON, WANDA
WALSH, MORRIS AND MAY MCCOURY, CARL
AND BRENDA COMPTON, AND OTHERS.
SHERRIE HARTSOE SIGMON PHOTO.

ROBERT AND SUSAN WILSON, JACK GRIFFITH,
LINDA SHELTON, GERALD CRUNKLETON, BOB
SZALANSKI, AND OTHERS. SHERRIE HARTSOE
SIGMON PHOTO.

MAYOR RICK JUSTICE SPEAKING TO THE
FORMER WORKERS. SHERRIE HARTSOE
SIGMON PHOTO.

THE NEW SIGN UPON ENTRANCE TO RHODHISS FROM CALDWELL COUNTY.
CARL COMPTON PHOTO.

NOTES

1   Glass, pp. 79-81.
2   Bean, Ned and Elvie and Tom Ross.
3   Aldridge, Joe and Olive.
4   Kirby, Beth.
5   Compton, Carl. Email Interview with Sherrie Hartsoe Sigmon. 4 September 2022.
6   "Burlington Industries Plants Report Good Year During 1969." Hickory Daily Record. 28 February 1970.
7   Kirby, Beth.
8   Jones and Ross.
9   "Industrial Div. Plays Key Role in U. S. Space Program." The Burlington Look. Vol. 6. No. 6. June 1981.
10   Whisnant, Roy. 20 July 2016. https://www.wfmynews2.com/article/news/local/origin-of-moon-landing-flag-still-a-mystery/83-278257596.
11   Darty, Mary Settlemyre and Tom Ross.
12   Phifer, pp. 247-248.
13   Anderson, pp. 181-182.
14   Hartsoe, Donald. Personal Interview with Sherrie Hartsoe Sigmon. Granite Falls, NC. 20 March 2016.
15   "First Flag on Moon Woven at Rhodhiss." Granite Falls Press. August 1969.
16   "It's a 'Grand Old Flag' That's Woven by Industrial." The Burlington Look. 1976.
17   Rhodhiss Town Minutes. 8 May 1995.
18   Rhodhiss Town Minutes. 11 December 1995.
19   "Town Celebrates Giant Leap into History." Hickory Daily Record. July 1995.
20   "Rhodhiss Recognized for Efforts." Hickory Daily Record. 29 January 1996. Page 2A.
21   Williamson, Sarah Newell. "Lunar Legacy: Rhodhiss Flag Leaves Mark on Moon." Hickory Daily Record. 21 July 2009. Pages A1 and A3.
22   Former Burlington Employees. Personal Interview with Sherrie Hartsoe Sigmon and Rick Justice. Rhodhiss, NC. 20 March 2016.
23   Gercken, Tammie. "Lunar Pride: Residents, Plant Workers To Celebrate Part Played in Inaugural Moon Landing," The News Herald. Vol. 133, Pub. No. 174. 19 July 2019, pages A1 and A3.
24   Former employee Videotaped Personal Interview with Sherrie Hartsoe Sigmon and Rick Justice. Rhodhiss, NC. 20 July 2019.

CHAPTER 26
CELEBRATING THE NEW BRIDGE AND THE BICENTENNIAL

I n 1972 the old, dilapidated one-lane steel bridge was no longer the mode of transportation from Burke County into Caldwell County, or vice versa. After years of discussion and political negotiations with the state, a new bridge was erected. This bridge was a cause for celebration. Similarly, the arrival of the country's Bicentennial in 1976 allowed the townspeople to commemorate that event. Great preparation took place for the town to honor these two occasions.

Tom Ross, who served as office manager for Burlington, was instrumental in bringing the new bridge to fruition. Tom and Ned Bean discussed this with Elvie Bean and me:

TR: I had a file on the bridge. That didn't mean anything to anybody else.

NB: Well, that bridge was a long-drawn-out process. I remember working on that .

TR: Everything had to fall into place. Arch Laney found out about it, and the fact that he was working for the state at the time was a great coincidence. Burlington advanced $75,000 footing the bill to move the lines, the road, and things like that even though they were reimbursed later. They had to get approval from Burlington for the $75,000. I called Bill Johnson in Rutherfordton on Monday morning. We had to know by 10 that morning. We were told that if we didn't get the okay that day that there was no telling when we would get the bridge.

NB: You know it was costing Burlington to drive to Hickory to get to the other plant. It was costly all those years.

EB: I don't understand.

SH: The heavy equipment couldn't go across the old bridge.

NB: The old bridge you couldn't drive a transfer truck across it. When they came to Number 1, they had to go back through Hickory to get to Number 2.

EB: Oh, the weight.[1]

Burlington Industries advanced $75,000 to the bridge construction to fulfill the need for this bridge. Prior to 1972 large transfer trucks could not use the bridge because of their weight. A former Rhodhiss citizen, Arch Laney, lived and worked in Raleigh, and with his help, the bridge finally became a realization.

The Rhodhiss minutes indicated that a meeting was held on Monday, May 26, 1969, at 7:00 PM for a discussion of a new bridge. The board indicated that Tom Ross, Charles Grady, C. B. Sperry, all three from Burlington Industries were asked to attend. In addition, the board invited State Highway Commission officials, J. G. Stikeleather, Jr. and F. L. Hutchinson.[2] Several years lapsed before another entry regarding the bridge appeared in the minutes. An announcement was made three years later that the bridge dedication service was held on November 29, 1972, at 11:00 AM.[3] The process took longer than anyone could have imagined, and it was long overdue. The old one-lane bridge was very rickety and dangerous. Tom Ross and Mary Starnes Bolick discussed this bridge with me. They stated:

> MB: When they blew up the old steel bridge, we went outside and watched
> them do that. We kinda hated to see it blown up.
> SH: Mr. Ross was telling me a story about a man that ran a body shop. The man said that he
> wasn't going to make as much money now because half of his income came from the cars that
> hit the holes in the old Rhodhiss steel bridge.
> TR: On frosty mornings there were a lot of bump ups down there.[4]

The old bridge had been in existence for over fifty years when it was replaced, and it needed repairs.

The *Hickory Daily Record* ran an article detailing the history of the old steel bridge in 1972. The article read:

> At one time Burlington considered buying and preserving the old bridge, but the bridge will be destroyed since Burlington decided against retaining it. Tom Ross, office manager at Burlington, said that the bridge will definitely be torn down because of the expense and liability involved in retaining it. He added that Burlington had initially talked of buying the old bridge to serve as a link between the two plants, but the plants are now separate divisions, and there is no need. Mr. Ross said that the town's citizens and the 500+ workers are excited about the new structure along with the much-needed new access road. At this time the only known descendants of Rhodes and Hiss are Mrs. John P. Rabb, who is the great niece of George Hiss and Dr. Voigt R. Cromer, past president of Lenoir Rhyne College, who is a grandson of John Rhodes. The town presently has a mayor and 3 town commissioners, who are elected on a two-year basis. Fire protection is provided by a 27-member volunteer fire department. The fire equipment was updated recently with the purchase of a $4,500 communications system. Hillside Beach is also a popular recreational site within the

town. The clubhouse is available for indoor activities. The close-knit community of Rhodhiss is still changing. Many believe that its vitality is because of the people who live there. The school (grades 1-8) is one of the finest in the area. The churches provide refuge and strength to both members and the community; civic groups like the Boy Scout troops are vital within the town. All these factors contribute to the history being made within the town.[5]

The old bridge had served its purpose and was no longer needed because of its condition. The two Burlington plants considered purchasing it to transport materials between the two mills; however, since the plants were separate divisions within Burlington Industries, the need was no longer valid. In her article Nell Greene praised Rhodhiss for its vitality, strength, and fine school. She was correct in her assessment.

After the dedication, the *Hickory Daily Record* ran another article detailing the festivities. The article noted:

Governor Bob Scott did not keep his scheduled appointment to dedicate the new bridge. Tom Ross, general manager for Burlington Industries, replaced Scott as the principal speaker. Present for the dedication were Robert G. Barr of West Jefferson, one of the highway commissioners; Highway Commissioner Jack Kirksey of Morganton, who cut the ribbon; Rhodhiss Mayor Cecil Munday. More than 100 people gathered for the dedication. At first the crowd was told that the Governor would be at least an hour late because of airplane engine trouble at Raleigh; however, minutes later, the crowd was told that he would not attend. Tom Ross, who had given the Governor the history of the old bridge, spoke briefly about the pride that Burlington took in replacing the old bridge. Mayor Munday introduced Ross and Kirksey. Kirksey praised the work of Arch Laney, highway commission public relations director and former Rhodhiss resident. Kirksey said that Laney was instrumental in the building of the new bridge. Laney was not present. A number of other highway engineers and state officials were introduced to the group that included Granite Falls High School Band members, Rhodhiss school students, press members, and local citizens. A ribbon cutting ceremony was also held. After that, the highway officials left for a dinner meeting in Hickory with Governor Scott. The new bridge was contracted in November 1970, and the approaches in July 1971. The bridge opened earlier this year. It replaces a 1916 one-lane steel structure with a roadway of only 15.3 feet. The new bridge is 36 feet wide and over 650 feet long. The total cost for right of way and construction for the bridge and its approaches is in excess of $1 million.[6]

As the article stated, Tom Ross replaced the Governor that day. Tom had already gotten the history together for Governor Scott, so he knew the material; however, Mr. Ross said, "My knees were shaking when I made that speech."[7] Prior to the new bridge's construction, the main road, Caldwell Street, through Rhodhiss went between the Caldwell plant and the old post office/Company Store building. During the completion of the bridge, the road was changed to go behind the old building. The bridge's cost was over $1 million.

The *Granite Falls Press* also provided an article detailing the old bridge and the new one. This article stated:

> The new two-lane bridge in Rhodhiss was constructed by Triplett and Rhyne Construction Company of Chester, SC. Construction workers used 210 pounds of dynamite in the pillars to destroy the old bridge. The construction company employees placed four cases of dynamite in drilled holes of the four old piers. Many people gathered around to watch the old bridge being demolished. Some took movies and pictures of the explosions, and some news media were there. After 1:00 PM workers cleared the parking areas in Caldwell and Burke counties, and traffic was stopped at a safe distance. Two piers were demolished in the first blast while two piers and one section of the bridge remained. Shortly after 3:00 PM the workers readied the site for another explosion. When the detenator (sic) was set off, small pieces of concrete began to fly. The last section of the bridge slammed into the water. The concrete from the pier next to the bank flew in small pieces all over the parking lot on the Caldwell side. Three windows were broken out of Burlington's office building and a car was hit with flying debris which went a tenth of a mile in all directions. Then as things quietened and smoke cleared there was the old bridge, laying (sic) quietly partially submerged in the Catawba River, totally obliterated. Construction of the new bridge began in June 1971 and was completed on June 3, this year.[8]

After years of negotiations and planning, the new two-lane bridge was dedicated and opened to the public, and the old bridge was demolished.

In 1976 many cities and towns across the nation celebrated the Bicentennial of America, and Rhodhiss was no exception. The planning started in 1975 when the Reverend E. Guy Longshore approached the town board. Preacher Longshore discussed the need to begin planning for a Bicentennial celebration, where all town organizations would join efforts, churches, school, Scouts, and Ruritan. Mayor Munday appointed Ben Pearson and Charles Beshears to co-chair this committee. Ben Pearson later became the sole chairman because of Mr. Beshears' health.[9] According to the Bicentennial Program the town's population in 1976 was 800. A flagpole was erected in 1975 in memory of Homer Goodman, and the American flag was donated by the Granite Falls chapter of the American Legion and Veterans of Foreign War. The North Carolina flag was donated by Ralph Adcock of the chapter of the Hickory American Legion. A bicentennial flag was presented on September 29, 1975, by the American Revolution Bicentennial Administration. Flags hold importance to the town because the flag on the moon placed by the astronauts in 1969 was woven at Rhodhiss Industrial Fabrics.[10]

The town not only celebrated the Bicentennial on Saturday, May 22, 1976, but they also planned an event that would be on the minds of attendees for years. The celebration included a parade (starting on Duke Power Road and ending on Burke Street), an official program, games, contests, prizes, and a memorial service. The lineup for the parade started at 8:30 AM on the Powerhouse Road, and the parade started at 10:00 AM with Kit Carson as the parade marshal. At 11:00 AM the Bicentennial Commission Chair, Ben Pearson, spoke, and he was followed by the presentation of colors and the national anthem. At 1:00 PM Ben Pearson spoke again and then came the invocation by the Rev. E. Guy Longshore and a greeting from Rhodhiss' Mayor Cecil "Bud" Munday. The Master of Ceremonies was Mike McKay from WBTV. The founding of Rhodhiss was discussed by John Rhodes' grandsons, Dr. John Rhodes from Raleigh and Dr. Voigt Cromer from Hickory. Bill Craven, the Vice President of Burlington Industries in Greensboro, spoke about Burlington's role in Rhodhiss. Several politicians were on hand to speak, Senator Wade Walsh, Senator Don Kincaid, NC Representative James Edwards, and US Congressman James T. Broyhill. The official program ended with a prayer by the Rev. Don Ingle from Dudley Shoals First Baptist Church. At 3:00 PM a long list of games began including bingo, horseshoes, checkers, chess, apple bobbing, sack races, three-legged races, egg tosses, spoon races, and the 100-yard dash. Prizes were awarded for these events.[11]

At 6:00 PM Jack Edwards welcomed everyone to the memorial service. Eugene Walsh had the invocation, and the Rev. Zeno Wright led the Pledge of Allegiance. The Baptist Church Quartet sang two songs, and the Methodist Church Quartet sang two songs. A prayer was given by the Rev. D. J. Brooks. The Rev. E. Guy Longshore introduced the speaker for the event, the Rev. Dr. Thad Dowdle from College Avenue Baptist Church in Lenoir, NC. Dr. Dowdle also led the benediction. The Pastors taking part in the memorial program were the Rev. D. B. Alderman from the First Methodist Churches in Granite Falls and Rhodhiss, the Rev. D. J. Brooks from Granite-Rhodhiss Church of God, the Rev. E. Guy Longshore from the First Baptist Church in Rhodhiss, and the Rev. Zeno Wright from Friendship United Methodist Church.[12] The churches were well represented at the Bicentennial celebration.

In 1976 the Rhodhiss Town Council included these people: Cecil "Bud" Munday, Mayor; Benjamin S. Pearson, Commissioner; Arley Church, Commissioner; Noah Lunsford, Commissioner; Charles Beshears, Commissioner; and Norma L. Kirby, Town Clerk. These individuals were part of the Bicentennial festivities. The 1976 Bicentennial Commission Chairs were Ben S. Pearson, Chairman; Walter Biddix, Co-Chairman; David C. Hollar, Festivities Chairman; Johnny Reece and Boyd Brown, Finance Co-Chairmen; Jerry Hedrick, Heritage Chairman; and Ann Austin and Jack Hendrix, Co-Chairmen Horizons. The Commission Chairs carried out their jobs to the fullest. These people served as 1976 Bicentennial Commission Members: Cecil Munday, Ben Pearson, Arley Church, Noah Lunsford, Charles Beshears, Norma Kirby, Jack Hendrix, Coy Long, David Hollar, Boyd Brown, Johnny Reece, Ann Austin, Clara McLean, Jerry Hedrick, Larry Nichols, Shanda Nichols, Vance Kirby, Dillard Church, Mrs. Richard Deal, Eugene Walsh, the Rev. Guy Longshore, Clarence Burns, Mrs. Clarence Burns, Tammy Burns, Harry Williamson, Drenda Burns, Renita Compton, Doug Crump, Terry Rash, Kathy Cannon, Kathy Biddix, Jeff Brittain, David Dewey, Danny Minton, Walter Biddix, Johnny Biddix, Delores Biddix, Betty Biddix, Loran Owens, Frank Ball, Jimmy Brown, Cindy Kirby, Mrs. Boyd Yount, Jerry Elmore, Joe Fowler, Joe Kirby, and Arthur Edwards.[13] The committee did an excellent job. The fire department in 1976 included these members: Allen Kirby, Jimmy Brown,

Vance Kirby, Joe Kelley, Jerry Hedrick, Jack Hendrix, Joe Helton, Harry Lowman (Honorary), Thad Martin, Coy Long, James Mundy, Larry Nichols (Fire Chief), Walter Porch, Paul Williams, David Hollar, James Church, Arley Church, Joe Aldridge, Walter Biddix, and J. W. Fox.[14] The firemen were on duty the day of the event in order to provide safety and leadership.

The parade was quite a procession through town. The parade lineup according to the program follows: Police Escort, Rhodhiss Police Department; Rhodhiss Boy Scout Color Guard; Caldwell County Sheriff; Burke County Sheriff; Parade Marshal, Kit Carson; Bicentennial Chairman Ben Pearson and Vice Chairman Walter Biddix; Festivities Chairman D.C. Hollar, Finance Chairmen Johnny Reece and Boyd Brown; Heritage Chairpersons Jerry Hedrick and Debbie R. Haynes; Granite Falls High School Marching Band; Rhodhiss Mayor Cecil Munday; Rhodhiss Town Commissioners; Past Rhodhiss Mayors; Dr. John Rhodes and Dr. Voigt Cromer; Caldwell County Commissioners Earl Land and Alden Starnes; Lenoir Mayor Robert Gibbons; Rhodhiss Fire Chief Larry Nichols; Bicentennial Commission Float with King and Queen Contestants; Granite Falls JC President John Corpening; Antique Car; American Legion/VFW Granite Falls Chapter; Cedar Valley Boy Scouts; Rhodhiss Fire Truck; Rhodhiss Ruritan Club President; Rhodhiss Cub Scouts' Float; Rhodhiss Elementary School Cheerleaders; Granite Falls High School Homecoming Queen; Congressman James T. Broyhill; Bazaar Granite Float; Rhodhiss Cub Scouts; Antique Cars; Bicentennial Horseman (Scout); Dudley Shoals Scouts' Float; Dudley Shoals Boy Scouts; Granite Falls Boy Scouts; Junior Troop Girl Scouts; Brownie Troop 93; Christmas Queen, Granite Falls High School; Granite Falls High Varsity Cheerleaders; Winkler's Nationwide Insurance Float; Settlemyre Sportster; East Burke High School Band; Open East Burke Entrants; Burlington Industries Vice President Bill Craven from Greensboro; Burlington Float; Four Church Buses; Antique Cars; Lake Hickory Campground Unit; Tammy Lunsford Dance School; Rhodhiss Softball League; Bob's Snack Shack Float; Mayor Huffman's Antique Fire Truck; Granite Falls Teen Queen; Historical Lincoln Continental; NC Representative James Edwards; Foster Cloggers; NC Emergency Patrol; Bicentennial Fishing Tournament Winner; Rhodhiss Ruritan Club Float; Hickory Girl Scouts; Catawba County Girl Scouts; Granite Falls Fire Department Antique Fire Truck; Senator Don Kincaid; Granite Falls Lions Club President; Bicycle Riders; Two National Guard Jeeps; Granite Falls Press Float; Twirling Suzettes; Senator Wade Walsh; Gamewell-Collettsville High School Band Float; Hickory Speedway Pace Car and Miss Hickory Speedway; Gatorade 88; Two Antique Cars; Northside Minit Mart Float; Lovelady Rescue Squad; Caldwell County Ambulance Service; Icard Fire Truck; Valdese Fire Truck; horses and wagons; horse and hearst; and horses.[15] The streets were lined with spectators trying to get a glimpse of their friends, family members, celebrities, or politicians.

The Bicentennial Day in Rhodhiss needed sponsors who were willing to donate their time, merchandise, and labor. These people and organizations comprised the list of sponsors: Burlington Industries, Rhodhiss; Town of Rhodhiss; Granite Falls Press; Granite Falls Insurance Agency; Granite Falls Savings and Loan; Owens Service Station and Grocery, Rhodhiss; Rhodhiss Bait Shop; S&T Grocery, Hickory; Foster's Beauty Salon, Hickory; Bazaar Granite; Bob's Snack Shack, Granite Falls; Dana's Florist, Granite Falls; Floyd's Variety, Granite Falls; Northside Minit Mart, Granite Falls; Drexel Heritage, Drexel; Rhodhiss Furniture; Rhodhiss Gulf; Doug's Nik Nak, Rhodhiss;

Glass' Supermarket, Rhodhiss; John's Automotive, Rhodhiss; Charles Beshears; Shelley Settlemyre, Hickory; Oyama Cabinet Shop, Conover; Winn Dixie, Granite Falls; Shuford Mills, Granite Falls; Shanda Nichols; Main Food Center, Granite Falls; Granite Falls High School; Starnes Brothers, Granite Falls; Lumbo's Lumber Company, Icard; Town of Granite Falls; Caldwell County Board of Education, Lenoir; Granite Electric and Merchandising Company; Lovelady Rescue Squad, Granite Falls; and Rhodhiss Upholstery.[16] With the help of these people and companies, the day was one to remember.

FEBRUARY 28, 1970, *LENOIR NEWS-TOPIC* AERIAL VIEW OF RHODHISS. *LENOIR NEWS-TOPIC* PHOTO.

The Rhodhiss Bicentennial was very successful, and many people attended this celebration. As the Rev. E. Guy Longshore had suggested to the town in 1975, the event should include all organizations and the town, and with the cooperation of all these entities, the Bicentennial fulfilled all the requirements needed. When the citizens of Rhodhiss came together, they made festivities enjoyable and memorable, whether it was the dedication of the bridge or an event to honor America's 200th birthday.

SLIGHT AERIAL VIEW OF RHODHISS WITH THE BAPTIST CHURCH IN THE BACKGROUND IN THE EARLY 1970S. GWEN LONGSHORE GEDDINGS PHOTO.

TOM ROSS WAS THE KEYNOTE
SPEAKER AT THE BRIDGE
DEDICATION SINCE GOVERNOR
SCOTT COULD NOT MAKE IT. TOM
ROSS PHOTO.

THE NEW BRIDGE FINALLY BECAME A REALITY IN 1972.
TOM ROSS PHOTO.

MANY PEOPLE CAME FOR THE BRIDGE DEDICATION IN NOVEMBER 1972. BUD MUNDAY IS
SPEAKING. TIM HARTSOE AND HIS RHODHISS ELEMENTARY CLASSMATES ARE IN THIS PHOTO.
TOM ROSS PHOTO.

TWO BRIDGES IN RHODHISS FOR A SHORT WHILE. VAN HURLEY PHOTO.

THE CONSTRUCTION PHASE. VAN HURLEY PHOTO.

THE PROCESS OF DEMOLISHING THE OLD BRIDGE. VAN HURLEY PHOTO.

DEMOLITION OF THE OLD BRIDGE. VAN HURLEY PHOTO.

DEMOLITION OF THE OLD BRIDGE. VAN HURLEY PHOTO.

VIEW OF DAM AND BRIDGE. VAN HURLEY PHOTO.

THE NEW BRIDGE. TOM ROSS PHOTO.

BRIDGE COMPLETED. VAN HURLEY PHOTO.   THE NEW BRIDGE. VAN HURLEY PHOTO.

PLAQUE DEDICATION HELD AT RHODHISS — A memorial plaque was dedicated in honor of and in memory of Homer Goodman, who served as Assistant Fire Chief and as a commissioner in Rhodhiss. The dedication was held Saturday, Oct. 26 at the Rhodhiss Fire Department. Flags were flown at half mast during the ceremony and until the plaque was unveiled by Mayor Cecil Munday. Goodman was killed in a tractor-trailer accident last year in South Carolina. Friends and relatives of the Goodman family were present for the dedication along with town officials and

OUTSIDE THE TOWN OFFICE IN BURKE COUNTY A FLAGPOLE PLAQUE WAS DEDICATED AND INSTALLED IN MEMORY OF HOMER GOODMAN IN 1975. *GRANITE FALLS PRESS* PHOTO.

STUDENTS AT RHODHISS SCHOOL PARTICIPATED IN THE BICENTENNIAL FESTIVITIES. TIM HARTSOE AND HIS CLASSMATES ARE IN THIS PHOTO. CARL HOLLAR PHOTO.

APRIL WAS DESIGNATED A BEAUTIFICATION MONTH FOR THE BICENTENNIAL. ANN AUSTIN AND JACK HENDRIX. CARL HOLLAR PHOTO.

BEN PEARSON HOLDING THE BICENTENNIAL FLAG WITH
ANOTHER MAN. BURLINGTON PHOTO.

THE STATIONERY THAT WAS USED FOR
THE BICENTENNIAL. CARL
HOLLAR PHOTO.

THE *HICKORY DAILY RECORD* REPORTED THAT THERE WAS
A PARADE BREAKDOWN. *HICKORY DAILY RECORD* PHOTO.

THE BICENTENNIAL PARADE IN RHODHISS. GUY LONGSHORE PHOTO.

THE PARADE ROUTE IN FRONT OF THE OLD JOE CHURCH'S STORE. GUY
LONGSHORE PHOTO.

THE PARADE ROUTE GOING ACROSS THE BRIDGE. GUY LONGSHORE PHOTO.

JOE MUNDAY, GAIL KIRBY, VIRGINIA HOLLAR, AND OTHERS WATCH THE
PARADE. GUY LONGSHORE PHOTO.

GAIL KIRBY, VIRGINIA HOLLAR, RAYMOND MUNDAY.
GUY LONGSHORE PHOTO.

THE CROWD DISPERSED AS THE PARADE ENDED.
GUY LONGSHORE PHOTO.

PATSY POARCH, JAN PENDERGRAST, ANNE MARIE LONGSHORE, VIRGINIA BUCKNER, EULA CHURCH. GUY LONGSHORE PHOTO.

FAYE AND EARL BUMGARNER. GUY LONGSHORE PHOTO.

BICENTENNIAL PARTY. GUY LONGSHORE PHOTO.

DANCING AND CELEBRATING THE BICENTENNIAL. GUY LONGSHORE PHOTO.

RHODHISS MEN CELEBRATING. GUY
LONGSHORE PHOTO.

JOHN RHODES' GRANDSON AS KEYNOTE
SPEAKER AT BICENTENNIAL WITH HIS WIFE.
BOTH GRANDSONS, CROMER AND RHODES
WERE PRESENT, NOT SURE WHICH ONE THIS IS,
BUT PROBABLY CROMER.

GAIL KIRBY, VIRGINIA HOLLAR, BOYD YOUNT,
CINDY KIRBY PROVIDED ENTERTAINMENT. GUY
LONGSHORE PHOTO.

NOTES

1   Bean, Ned and Elvie and Tom Ross.

2   Rhodhiss Town Minutes. 12 May 1969.

3   Rhodhiss Town Minutes 13 November 1972.

4   Bolick, Mary Starnes and Tom Ross.

5   Greene, Nell. "Old Bridge To Become Rhodhiss History Soon." *Hickory Daily Record*. November 1972.

6   Teague, Kermit. "New Rhodhiss Bridge Dedicated." *Hickory Daily Record*. November 1972.

7   Ross, Tom.

8   "Last Look At The Old Steel Bridge." *Granite Falls Press*. December 1972.

9   Rhodhiss Town Minutes. 10 February 1975.

10   "Bicentennial Program." 22 May 1976. Produced by the Rhodhiss Bicentennial Committee.

11   "Bicentennial Program." 22 May 1976. Produced by the Rhodhiss Bicentennial Committee.

12   Bicentennial Program." 22 May 1976. Produced by the Rhodhiss Bicentennial Committee.

13   Bicentennial Program." 22 May 1976. Produced by the Rhodhiss Bicentennial Committee.

14   Bicentennial Program." 22 May 1976. Produced by the Rhodhiss Bicentennial Committee.

15   Bicentennial Program." 22 May 1976. Produced by the Rhodhiss Bicentennial Committee.

16   Bicentennial Program." 22 May 1976. Produced by the Rhodhiss Bicentennial Committee.

CHAPTER 27
BURLINGTON PLANTS LEAVE TOWN

Burlington Industries came to Rhodhiss in 1954 with innovative ideas that energized the workers. This company offered insurance, vacation pay, and profit sharing, too, and the employees were excited to keep these benefits. However, in 1975 the first plant which had formerly been the Men's Wear Division and then Burlington Housewares announced that it was closing. This was quite a blow to the workers and the community. For the next seven years the workers at the Industrial Fabrics Division lived in fear that their plant, too, would be closed. That became a reality with the announcement in the fall of 1982 that the plant would cease production the next year. The hard-working people in Rhodhiss found themselves without jobs.

According to the *Charlotte Observer* from 1982 to 1985, "textile mills in the Carolinas closed at a rate of one every 11 days."[1] In addition, one in every three textile jobs were lost in the Carolinas from 1973 to 1985.[2] These statistics are astounding. The mill companies of prior generations were leaving the Carolinas at a staggering rate. Towns across the South were losing their identities and revenue. The 1975 closing of the Caldwell County Burlington plant brought sadness to all of those involved. Many employees had worked there their entire lives. Tom Ross said that this plant employed 250, plus salaried employees when it closed.[3] The *Hickory Daily Record* quoted Carl T. Purdee, the plant manager. He attributed the plant's closing to "'excess spun yarn capacity in the company... We have been in a curtailed situation for a number of weeks, dating back to early winter, and market conditions indicate the likelihood of further curtailment making it necessary to close the Caldwell Plant.'"[4] The Housewares Division was going well until the need for draperies, sheets, and bedspreads leveled off in the middle 1970s. When the plant first started making these products, they were selling their merchandise profusely, but then the decline came. Employees were given severance pay based on the number of years of employment. Tom Ross and Mary Starnes Bolick discussed this with me. Mary worked at the Burke plant, so her severance pay didn't take effect until that plant's closing in 1983.

They stated:

Burlington Mills Begins To Close 1 Rhodhiss Plant

THE *HICKORY DAILY RECORD* ARTICLE DETAILING PLANT 1'S CLOSING IN 1975. *HICKORY DAILY RECORD.*

MB: I got a year's severance pay. I got paid for a year just like I was working. I guess because of my age and as long as I worked there. I believe that I was 67 whenever the mill quit. Well, I mean closed.

TR: Yeah, I had 20 months of severance pay.

MB: I was doing pretty good. I was drawing Social Security and severance pay both. A lot of people couldn't believe that I got that severance pay.

TR: I forgot what it was, but I did know what it was totally in the Caldwell plant for severance pay. When they shut that one down, I knew the figure, but I've forgotten it now.

MB: But I was satisfied to work if I hadn't gotten it. You know because I enjoyed working there.[5]

Mary and Tom both received severance pay from Burlington, but both wished that they could have retired from the company instead of their leaving because of a shut down. When the Caldwell plant closed, almost 400 people were out of work, and the building was sold to Chadwick Furniture in 1976.[6] One of the cornerstones of Rhodhiss left.

In October 1982 the second mill announced its departure. Employees would work on a seniority basis with the last hired being the first to leave. Mary Settlemyre Darty discussed leaving before the plant's closing. Mary elaborated to Tom Ross and me:

SH: Did you stop working when they closed the plant or before?
MD: Before. See they cut my job out. Well, they offered me a job in the cloth room, and I had

always worked with yarn. They said that I could go upstairs. It never did come about because they were in the process of closing it down, but nobody knew it then. I would have been old enough to retire at 62 in July. The last day that I worked was the last of February of '81, I believe. It was about a year and something before they closed it down. So, I just put in to retire.

TR: I never thought that they would close that plant. It was too good of a plant.

MD: It didn't surprise me because I had heard so much about it. It was an old plant, and Burlington was closing its oldest plants.

TR: The fact that it was three floors didn't help it a bit. New plants are being built on one floor.

MD: They had done away with the spinning. I don't know how many years before that was, you know. They took it on across the river, and then took all of it out. So, it didn't surprise me.

TR: We've seen a lot of changes at Rhodhiss, good and bad.

MD: Yeah, I saw a lot. They put that steel in and went down in the ground about 15 feet with cement. They did that to reinforce the card room, spinning room. They built on both ends. Took the cloth room and made offices out of that. Really, it seemed like a new place every so often down there. To pass by, you just don't realize all the changes.[7]

Mary seemed to feel that the company knew for over a year that the closing was inevitable. The end of the Burke plant left quite a void in the hearts of the employees and within the community.

Ned Bean was one of the last to leave on the seniority basis. He left in late summer 1983. Ned and Elvie Bean discussed this with Tom Ross and me:

NB: When we closed the plant, it was like a long-drawn-out funeral to me. It seemed like it was never going to end. They shut down a little bit now. Then a few would leave. A few days later there would be a few more leave. It was just a long-drawn-out funeral.

TR: There was so much invested in that thing that I didn't think that they would ever close it.

NB: Well, I didn't either.

EB: People had their whole lives invested in that plant.

NB: The bad part about it was that they never made money at Cheraw, and we made money. We made money every year.

EB: Ned felt like for four years he was a sitting duck. He would say, 'We are going out. They are going to sell our little plant over there, and we have the best operation.' He was so proud of that company. He knew that they made money compared to what they had to do with the equipment, the machinery. Ned said that they wouldn't spend any money on that plant because they knew down the road what they were going to do with it.

NB: They didn't spend money on that plant for years.

TR: It was the same way with the Rhodhiss plant on the Caldwell side. They spent $4 million dollars on new machinery and everything like that. Cloth was low per pound. We didn't see any reason for them to close it, but when you don't have any demand for the product, you have to stop.

NB: The thing that got us though was that glass business. They had that big modern plant down at Cheraw. The glass business was gone, so they just moved ours there. Then Cheraw couldn't get it off the ground.[8]

Ned described the closing as a funeral. Many others used that same analogy. Ned and Tom both elaborated on the company not spending money on the plant because they knew its demise. Ned, Tom Ross, and I also discussed the plant's destroying all the files that pertained to Rhodhiss' history:

SH: I have no way of getting that material because I wrote a letter to Bryant
Haskins at the Greensboro corporate office. He said that all of that was
destroyed.
NB: Yeah, a lot of that stuff was burned at the mill. They had barrels out there to burn them.
They decided what they wanted to keep and what they didn't want to keep.
TR: It doesn't sound as if there was a lot of heartfelt interest in it.
NB: No, none at all. They had about a dozen barrels out behind the mill, and they just kept them stirred up with papers. We had files there at the plant with things from the beginning of the company.[9]

The histories of both mill companies were destroyed when the Burke plant closed. The library burned!
    Mary Starnes Bolick also mentioned that she felt that the closing of the plant was like a funeral. She discussed this with Tom Ross and me:

SH: Ned Bean said that it was one big funeral watching everybody leave.
MB: Well, it was. Everybody was just about crying. I don't care who knew it, but I did! That was just like home.
TR: You didn't have a place to go the next day, did you?
MB: That's right. I'll tell you that was just about the biggest change that I've ever seen. To be used to getting up every day and going to work. Then you get up, and there's nowhere to go.[10]

Mary worked at Rhodhiss for 48 ½ years. That was her life! Several people commented that Mary volunteered after her job ended to go make coffee in the mornings for the few employees that were left because she was so accustomed to working; however, she was told that insurance would not allow her to do that. Joe Aldridge also worked at Rhodhiss for over 30 years. He noted, "Good Lord, people would leave there just crying. We were one big happy family, and I miss them."[11] Joe also told me something that my dad (Boyce Hartsoe) had said about the closings. This was the conversation among Olive, Joe, and me:

JA: Did anybody tell you what your daddy said about that?
SH: What my daddy said?
JA: Yeah, about moving Rhodhiss School.

SH: No, but knowing daddy, it could have been anything.

JA: He said, 'Well, the first thing that they did, they moved the school out of Rhodhiss; now they are closing our plant down and moving it to Cheraw, and the next thing that you know they will be moving the damn river.' I laughed at him.

OA: Joe was telling someone that interviewed him that, and he said, 'I wish that I could get somebody to say that.'

JA: He said, 'I would love to meet that man.'

SH: He said that about daddy.

JA: Yeah.

OA: He said, 'I would just give anything to get somebody to say that.'

JA: Yeah, but you know we couldn't say anything though.

SH: Well, that's true because you were in a situation where you weren't able.

JA: Because if the company heard you say that they might fire you right then, and you lost everything that you had with them. That's the reason they wouldn't say anything.[12]

Rhodhiss School closed in 1982, and yes, the closing of the mills was a gut punch. People had worked there their entire lives, and suddenly they had to find another job. They were leaving more than a job. They were leaving their work family.

Many newspapers covered the story of the Burke plant's closing. The *Lenoir News-Topic* and The *Hickory Daily Record* had stories published in October 1982. The *News-Topic's* story stated:

> Burlington Industries has announced the closing of their Industrial Fabrics Plant In Rhodhiss. The plant will be phased out during the next 6 to 8 months because of 'economic conditions which require consolidation and cost control.' Fifty-seven percent of the employees live in Caldwell County though the plant is located in Burke (25% are from Burke). The plant was built in 1914. The plant became the industrial fabrics division in 1965. In 1975 the Burlington plant in Caldwell County closed because of poor economic conditions. John Allen, the plant manager said that operations will be moved to newer and better equipped plants. Allen adds that is the Cheraw, SC plant. Betsy Chester, office manager for the Caldwell County Employment Security Commission in Lenoir, said that she thinks that few employees will choose to move to Cheraw and that many of the employees have been at the plant for 45 years, yet there are a few with less than a year's experience. John Allen said, 'These people have a lot of pride and independence you don't find other places. We manufactured the flag which was placed on the moon and the people in our plant have seen many other accomplishments.... This decision in no way reflects on the performance of the plant. Rhodhiss employees have a long-standing record of excellent performance. We also had good support from the community.' Allen added that the plant will be advertised for sale, but definite plans for the building are not available.[13]

John Allen, the plant manager, praised the Rhodhiss employees because their work ethic was beyond reproach, and as an executive he was aware of the flag material that was on the moon. The employees' years of service to the mill company were commended. The Hickory paper's article had most of the same information as Lenoir's article, but a few variances. The *Hickory Daily Record* added, "The plant--maker of the fabric for the flag which flies on the moon--will be phased out." The Mayor R. A. Bowman stated that approximately 700 to 900 people are citizens of Rhodhiss, and 250 people worked at the plant. Burlington gave the town 17 acres of land for a park in 1976. John Allen mentioned that only four people worked there for less than a year, and most were there for decades. One employee worked there for 48 years. John Allen, too, again mentioned the moon flag material as woven at Rhodhiss.[14] The mill that wove the material for the flag on the moon was soon to be history.

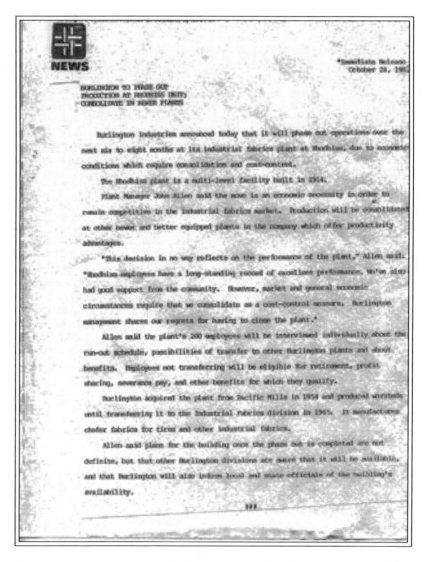

WHEN I TRIED TO OBTAIN INFORMATION FROM BURLINGTON'S CORPORATE OFFICE IN GREENSBORO, THEY HAD ONLY THESE 2 ITEMS IN THEIR FILES: THE PRESS RELEASE AND THE SALES BROCHURE FOR PLANT 2. BURLINGTON PHOTO.

THIS IS THE SALES BROCHURE THAT WAS STILL
IN THE CORPORATE FILES IN GREENSBORO.
THEY MAILED IT TO ME IN 1988.
BURLINGTON PHOTO.

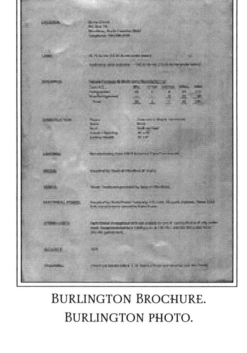

BURLINGTON BROCHURE.
BURLINGTON PHOTO.

BURLINGTON BROCHURE.
BURLINGTON PHOTO.

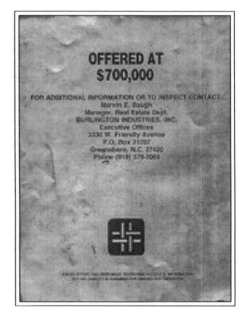

BURLINGTON BROCHURE.
BURLINGTON PHOTO.

The *Granite Falls Press* was a weekly newspaper, and their article did not appear until the first week of November. Their coverage was quite lengthy, and it shared more of the raw emotions felt by the workers and citizens. John Allen was described as the plant manager for two years, and he noted that interviews for transfers to other Burlington plants and retirements were taking place.

Allen indicated that "'the plant would have been closed years ago, but the employees kept up such a remarkable quality product. Their work made a reputation for them. You have a good caliber of people here. We have already had several inquiries from other area plants about our people.'"[15] The hard-working employees had a reputation that preceded them. "Billy Bryant, personnel manager, said the plant has been a 'measuring stick' for other Burlington plants... 'We have had customers to specifically ask for Rhodhiss-made materials.'"[16] Mr. Bryant expressed that various companies requested Rhodhiss made products. Rhodhiss employees made all the materials for the Goodyear Blimps, and rayon made in Rhodhiss was used in the booster rocket walls that lifted the space shuttle off the ground at Kennedy Space Center. In addition, Rhodhiss wove material for the US flag on the moon, for bomb blankets, bullet-proof vests, and snow screening. The town lost about $30,000 in taxes from the plant's closing. As per the town's records, the town received $3,882 in property taxes from the plant.[17] Retiree Charlie Kirby, who worked for Burlington for 48 years, said that he went to work when the Burke plant was built in 1914.[18] Boyd Brown said that he worked at Rhodhiss for 20 years before he retired. He said, "'Burlington treated me good.'" He added that the town would not die because the good people within the town would not allow that to happen.[19] Ossie Crunkleton, an employee, said that she was 58 and with the plant 28 years. Crunkleton added, "'When I go to work now, I see the plant, and know it's dying, it reminds me of a funeral.'"[20] Ticketing Clerk, Gerald Crunkleton, worked at the plant for 9 years, and he said that he is young and can find another job, but not one that will pay his present salary.[21] People of all ages were forced to find work elsewhere with the closing of the Industrial Fabrics Division Plant.

The *Hickory Daily Record* wrote a second article explaining the impact on the town and the employees. It noted:

> Rev. James D. Cool said, 'It's like a death that you know will come and you are never really prepared to accept it.... Knowing the people of Rhodhiss and our church (Rhodhiss First Baptist), I think they will bounce back. These people have great intestinal fortitude. They will bounce back. In the final analysis, it will make our church stronger. I think it's a time of travail, so to speak, that will draw us closer together.' Bud Munday, a 25 year Burlington employee, added 'It's just like somebody that's been sick for a long time and you're expecting them to die. When they do, you're not really prepared for it.... That plant's been really good to me.' Dawn Harris, an employee of Rhodhiss Grocery, says, 'The older people are having fits over that plant closing because they say it's like part of history because the flag was made there.' Harris adds that the grocery business where she works will suffer without Burlington employees. Harris added that the plant cut timber on their wooded lots and burned a house that it owned two weeks ago.[22]

Burlington got rid of most of their property before making the announcement of the closing. They were starting to sever ties with the community before they made the move to cease their time in Rhodhiss. The workers at Rhodhiss felt lost and unsettled with the company's leaving town. Studs

Terkel wrote a book entitled *Working: People Talk About What They Do All Day and How They Feel About What They Do*. It states, "'The working man has but one thing to sell, his labor. Once he loses control of that, he loses everything.'"[23] The labor was gone in Rhodhiss.

In 2005 the former Caldwell County plant burned. A few pictures of this fire were included in Chapter 2. Many people were emotional about the destruction of their former workplace. The *Lenoir News Topic* reported:

> Firefighters were able to get a huge blaze at the old Burlington Mills plant on Lake Rhodhiss under control by 1 a.m. Saturday morning, but the county fire director will have to wait until Monday before he has a chance to start digging for evidence to either confirm or contradict his suspicions. Fire marshal Brown won't be able to start digging in the debris until Monday because of the heat. He believes because it is a vacant building with no heat and security the cause is suspicious. Some of the walls have already caved in and others are leaning. The remaining walls will have to be knocked down before an investigation can take place. Firefighters were able to stop the spread of the fire to a second building. The SBI was asking questions of the town's citizens who live nearby to see if they noticed any activity at the building. The destroyed three story building was approximately 80 feet by 306 feet. Assistant Rhodhiss Fire Chief, Jimmy Drum, was one of the first there on Friday night, and he said that the fire spread quickly. The alarm came in at 9:00 p.m. As the firefighters arrived, they saw heavy smoke and flames on the first floor. Then the second floor fell in. They were able to get a 2,400 pound oxygen tank out of the building before the firefighters had to get out. Back up came from Sawmills and Granite Falls; twelve other agencies answered the call to help fight the fire. By 1:30 a.m. the fire was under control. The building was probably 50 to 60 feet tall according to Drum, and the flames were 100 feet high. No one was hurt. The fire department had been called to the same scene in August for a suspicious fire. Not much was damaged then. These groups responded: Rhodhiss, Granite Falls, Sawmills, Drowning Creek, Icard, Grace Chapel, Hudson, Lovelady, Caldwell County Sheriff's Office, Lovelady Rescue, Caldwell County Emergency, and Burke County REACT.[24]

Later, the reason for the fire would be determined as arson. Several months later the *News-Topic* wrote that the old mill would be demolished, and the bricks and timber would be sold to support charities.[25] Bricks were purchased by several former citizens as souvenirs of their time in the community or as workers in the mill.

The Rhodhiss millhands endured many hardships and tribulations throughout their years at the plant; however, most considered themselves to be the ones who benefited from this labor. They put their heart and soul into the products that they wove. They were married to their jobs and did not seek employment elsewhere until the mill company forced them to do so. They lived their work, and their work lived in them.

FIRST SHIFT WHEN THE INDUSTRIAL DIVISION CLOSED IN 1983.
CHARLES ADKINS, LEONARD MCCALL, NED BEAN, TROY HARDING, DENNIS RAY, TRUETTE CRUMP, RALPH KELLER, BILLY ANDERSON (2) LEVI BROWN, ANDERSON TEAGUE, HAROLD KALE, GERALD CRUNKLETON, RICK BENFIELD, ROGER KIRBY, BILLY BRYANT, GENE MULL, MAX CROWDER, RICHARD "BOLO" WHISNANT, FRED ELMORE, CHARLES A. MYERS, WALTER BIDDIX, LESTER "SHORTY" MCKINNEY, (3) JUDY THOMAS, MARY BOLICK, PEGGY PENNELL, JANET SELLS, ROSS DULA, BILLIE SUE LUNSFORD, LENNIS FOWLER, LORETTA BROWN, NADINE DULA, EDNA STILWELL, BETTY LYNN, MARY ENGLAND, WILLIE DENNIS, BEULAH LUNSFORD, LINDA SHELTON, JAN MURPHY, RITA YOUNT, DELAINE CLINE (4) HAROLD BOWERS, ELMER YODER, RUBY WALDEN, DEAN PAIGE, FRANCES STEPHENS, THELMA MCRARY, CAROLYN BOWMAN, SUE LUNSFORD, CLARA WARD, SELMA ROBERTS, PEGGY CONNELLY, YVONNE HENTSCHEL, EUNICE HARPER, OSSIE CRUNKLETON, ORA BELLE RICHARDS, GWEN JOHNSON, DIANE KIRBY, ERNESTINE GREENE, REVONDA BOWMAN, MARLENE BUCKNER, PAT WHITE, FRED BRIDGES, BLAYNE HOLLAR, (5) MAXINE CARVER, TED HARTLEY, MORRIS "MOOSE" MCCOURRY, LLOYD CHILDERS, BOYCE HARTSOE, DONALD BALL, JOHN AGNER, CLYDE WINKLER, ROBERT WILSON, CARL COMPTON, PAUL CLINE, PERRY BRYANT, RICHARD DRUM, ROBERT "BUCK" TEAGUE, GLENN PRICE, EDDIE LUNSFORD, CARROLL JUNIOR JACKSON, (6) JERRY MYERS, ARTHUR EDWARDS, LEWIS ALDRIDGE, OLIN CRAFTON, ALLEN HAMBY, PAUL BUMGARNER, JOHNNY LUNSFORD, DOYLE HARRIS, FLOYD POPE, LARKIN HORTON, MACK HENTSCHEL, ARLEY "RED" CHURCH, JOHN MESSICK, DAN HARTSOE, JOHN WINN, JAMES REID, BOBBY WEBB, JOHN ALLEN. BOYCE HARTSOE PHOTO.

SECOND SHIFT WHEN THE PLANT CLOSED IN 1983.
(1) SHIRLEY BERRY, SHERRY DEAL, LOIS DULA, LARIE CORPENING, ROBERTA "ROBIN" EDMISTEN, CAROL ALDRIDGE, CATHY HERRING, ESTER SMITH, MARIE SMITH, LILLIE MACKEY, RUBY EDWARDS, KAY CLARK, DAVID CLARK, JOE ALDRIDGE, TOM RAY (2) DAVID BYRD, LAWRENCE COLEY, ROY BUMGARNER, JOYCE SMITH, ELAINE HAYNES, DORIS JACKSON, CYNTHIA TRIVETTE, PAM LUNSFORD, JAMES COGDELL, JAMES WEBB, JIMMY F. BROWN, D. W. CHILDERS, HOMER HERRING, MARVIN BUCHANAN, JIMMY A. BROWN, C. R. BRADSHAW, RICHARD DEAL, JUDY LEWIS, (3) RONALD CARSWELL, JOE BILL EARLY, JOHNNY PARLIER, ALBERT STORY, REECE CLARK, ZENO HUBBARD, RONNIE PARLIER, REGNAL HUFFMAN, ROBERT BALL, CHARLES ENGLAND, CLARENCE "BUD" ROLAND, JACK EDWARDS, JAMES WILLIAMS, DAVID SMITH, ROBERT COLE, DALLAS HARDING. JACK EDWARDS PHOTO.

THIRD SHIFT WHEN THE PLANT CLOSED IN 1983.
BILLY BRYANT, ERNEST THOMAS, ARCHIE HENDRIX, CARL DEAL, SCOTTY BOWMAN, PATTY
BOWMAN, LYNN KIRBY, RENITA COMPTON, MARY LANEY, STELLA BARR, LOUISE RANDALL (2)
JACK GRIFFITH, JOE PRICE, GEORGE BURTON, DONALD BROWN, JERRY ALDRIDGE, BOYD YOUNT,
CHARLES ADKINS, DWIGHT HELTON, JONATHAN GEOUGE, GREGORY EARLEY, BYRD FOWLER
(3) DONALD ALDRIDGE, CHARLES FOWLER, WILLIE JOE LUNSFORD, BILL LANEY, TED FOWLER,
JAMES CANNON, LEONARD CHAMBERS, GREGORY ESTES, DWAYNE BURGIN, DAVID HICKS, KEITH
BUCKNER. RENITA COMPTON HARTSOE PHOTO.

1983 PAUL BUMGARNER. LARKIN
HORTON PHOTO.

1983 MAXINE CARVER. LARKIN
HORTON PHOTO.

1983 PAUL CLINE. LARKIN HORTON PHOTO.

1983 CARL COMPTON. LARKIN
HORTON PHOTO.

1983 OLIN CRAFTON. LARKIN
HORTON PHOTO.

1983 ROSE DULA. LARKIN
HORTON PHOTO.

1983 BOYCE HARTSOE. LARKIN
HORTON PHOTO.

1983 YVONNE HENTSCHEL. LARKIN HORTON
PHOTO.

1983 DIANE KIRBY. LARKIN HORTON PHOTO.

1983 MORRIS MCCOURRY. LARKIN HORTON PHOTO.

1983 DEAN PAIGE. LARKIN HORTON PHOTO.

1983 ROY WHISNANT. LARKIN HORTON PHOTO.

1983 ROBERT WILSON. LARKIN
HORTON PHOTO.

1983 CLYDE WINKLER. LARKIN
HORTON PHOTO.

1983 BOYD YOUNT. LARKIN HORTON
PHOTO.

NOTES

1   Eichel, Henry. "2 Cornerstones of the Carolinas Begin to Slip." *Charlotte Observer*. 15 September 1985, pp. 1A and 15A.

2   Eichel, p. 1A.

3   Jones, Calvin and Tom Ross.

4   Pegram, Charles B. "Burlington Mills Begins To Close 1 Rhodhiss Plant." *Hickory Daily Record*. Spring 1975.

5   Bolick and Ross.

6   Kirby, Beth.

7   Darty, Mary Settlemyre and Tom Ross.

8   Bean, Ned and Elvie and Tom Ross.

9   Bean, Ned and Elvie and Tom Ross.

10   Bolick, Mary Starnes and Tom Ross.

11   Aldridge, Joe and Olive.

12   Aldridge, Joe and Olive.

13   Reagan, Cleave. "243 To Lose Jobs At Rhodhiss Plant." *Lenoir News-Topic*. 29 October 1982, pp. 1 & 10.

14   Murphy, Joan. "Burlington To Shut Down Plant in Rhodhiss." *Hickory Daily Record*. 29 October 1982, pp. 1A & 10A.

15   "Closing of Burlington Plant Brings Mixed Emotions to Employees." *Granite Falls Press*. 4 November 1982, Page 9A.

16   "Closing of Burlington Plant."

17   "Closing of Burlington Plant."

18   "Closing of Burlington Plant."

19   "Closing of Burlington Plant."

20   "Closing of Burlington Plant."

21   "Closing of Burlington Plant."

22   Lail, Vivian. "Rhodhiss Awaits Loss of Industry." *Hickory Daily Record*. 5 November 1982, pages 1A & 14A.

23   Terkel, Studs. *Working: People Talk About What They Do All Day and How They Feel About What They Do*. New York: Pantheon Books, 1974, p. 191.

24   Harris, Joshua. "Old Mill Fire Cooking Down." *Lenoir News Topic*. 18 December 2005, pages 1A & 9A.

25   Harris, Joshua. "Old Mill Comes Down." *Lenoir News Topic*. 23 February 2006. Pages 1A & 3 A.

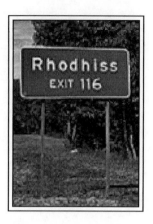

CHAPTER 28
TWENTY-FIRST CENTURY RHODHISS

The first two decades of the twenty-first century have been busy for the Town of Rhodhiss. In 2003 the community celebrated its 100th anniversary. In 2004 another natural disaster hit the town in the form of a flood. In 2010 a group of former Rhodhiss Elementary students held a reunion on the old school grounds. That same year the town started the first annual Grant Wilson Christmas parade which continues each year. A historical marker was placed at the old Methodist Church in 2012 commemorating the location of the original school building. That same year the town was awarded grant money for a new park, and in 2017 this park was completed. In October 2017 another natural disaster hit the town in the form of a tornado. In the summer of 2019, a grant was given to aid the town with water and sewer projects. During this same time the community celebrated the fiftieth anniversary of the lunar landing with a festival. Lastly, the town presently has plans for the development of the old property where plant one stood in Caldwell County. The twenty-first century has brought celebrations and improvements for the town.

The 100th anniversary of Rhodhiss was held on Saturday, September 20, 2003. The event took place in Burke County near the present-day Cooper Penny. A parade started the festivities; Lanny Elmore was the keynote speaker, and the evening ended with fireworks. According to the town minutes the "Celebration by the Lake" committee included Julie Jarvis, Chairman; Debbie Lunsford; Kristi Isenhour; and Wayne Wilson.[1] The next year (2004) in September a huge flood hit the area and several area schools remained closed for days. The crest was 7.41 feet over the spillway in Rhodhiss on September 9, 2004. The only recorded flood to top that was the flood of 1940.[2] The 1916 data was not available. The first few years of the twenty-first century brought celebration and anxiety to the townspeople.

RHODHISS CELEBRATED ITS CENTENNIAL IN 2003. TOWN OF RHODHISS PHOTO.

RHODHISS VOLUNTEER FIRE DEPARTMENT WAS ON DUTY DURING THE CENTENNIAL. RHODHISS FIRE DEPARTMENT PHOTO.

CHILDREN WERE ENTERTAINED BY THE BOUNCE HOUSE AND SPARKY. RHODHISS FIRE DEPARTMENT PHOTO.

Some of the people that helped with the 100th anniversary of the town decided to resurrect the Ruritan Club. According to the town minutes, Billy Propst served as president; Wayne Wilson was elected vice president; Tina McCrary was the secretary; Linda Miller held the treasurer's position; and the board members were Billy Austin and Vickie Morrison.

In 2010 after much discussion that started on Facebook, several former Rhodhiss Elementary School students organized a reunion. They met on Saturdays to give the celebration the foundation that it needed. Many former scholars and teachers attended this event on Saturday, September 25, 2010. The day was full of activities, from hula hooping, dancing, karaoke, tours of the town, and DJ music from Jerry McKee. Even Elvis made a special appearance. The reunion committee included former students who wanted to show their love and dedication to the old red schoolhouse, and several town officials pitched in to make the reunion a reality. Many friends united that day for the first time in years. Here is the list of the day's activities:

Rhodhiss School Reunion -- Agenda
September 25, 2010 -- 11:00 AM -- 6:00 PM

11:00 AM	*Jerry McKee will give the opening remarks and introduce Rhodhiss' Mayor Rick Justice for his comments. *Dan Greene, Pastor of Christian Fellowship Chapel in Granite Falls, opens with prayer.
All day Activity	Roy Whisnant will provide tours of Rhodhiss
11:30 AM	III'n I (Three in One, *Pam Triplett, *Christy Owens, Shirley Roberts) perform.
12:00 PM	Give a door price away -- Music will be playing after the door prize.
12:30 PM	Singer Robert Kincaid -- Karaoke for anyone who wants to sing.
1:00 PM	Give a door prize away. Group photo of Rhodhiss Elementary School students on steps
1:15 PM	Kids' games will be announced and played. Honor oldest living person.
2:00 PM	Give a door prize away. Honor any former teachers who are present.
2:15 PM	Line Dancing. Second group photo of Rhodhiss Elementary School Students on steps with former teachers.
2:30 PM	Kids' games will be announced and played. Karaoke for anyone who want to sing.
3:00 PM	Memorial Service around the flagpole. Releasing the balloons.
3:30 PM	Elvis impersonator, Ed Smith
4;00 PM	Give a door prize away. Kids' games will be announced and played.

4:30 PM　　　　Hula Hoop with music -- Can you, do it?

5:00 PM　　　　Give a door prize away, last door prize. Last chance photo of Rhodhiss Elementary School students on steps.

5:15 PM　　　　Karaoke for anyone who wants to sing.

5:45 PM　　　　Closing remarks.
*Denotes Rhodhiss School student

DAN GREENE, RICK JUSTICE, JERRY MCKEE.
2010 SCHOOL REUNION.
CARL COMPTON PHOTO.

JERRY MCKEE, MASTER OF
CEREMONIES. CARL COMPTON PHOTO.

HOME OF THE WARRIORS. CARL
COMPTON PHOTO.

RHODHISS METHODIST WELCOMED
THE REUNION ATTENDEES.
CARL COMPTON PHOTO.

RANDY AND MARY BUMGARNER, TIM HARTSOE,
JOHNNY ALDRIDGE, MR. AND MRS. JERRY
HERMAN, AND OTHERS. CARL COMPTON PHOTO.

CARL AND BRENDA COMPTON, GERALD AND
VICKI JONES, AND RITA JONES LONGEST.
CARL COMPTON PHOTO.

BARRY GOODMAN. CARL COMPTON PHOTO.

DEAN AND KRISTI ISENHOUR, JOE AND GAIL
KIRBY, JAMES LONGSHORE, TERRY RASH, AND
DANNY GREENE. CARL COMPTON PHOTO.

LEO AND JUDY TUCKER AND VIRGINIA JONES HOLLAR. CARL COMPTON PHOTO.

DANCING AT THE REUNION, CLYDE DAMERON, DIANE TEAGUE CRUMP, TERRY TEAGUE, RITA MORETZ FRITZ, DONNA ABERNETHY PRICE, DEBBIE WALSH HARTLEY. CARL COMPTON PHOTO.

PAM LUNSFORD BROWN AND DONNA ABERNETHY PRICE. CARL COMPTON PHOTO.

MARY LAWS, JOANNE LONGSHORE, ELIZABETH LONGSHORE, PAUL AND ELLEN BRIGHT. CARL COMPTON PHOTO.

RENITA COMPTON HARTSOE.
CARL COMPTON PHOTO.

JERRY MCKEE AND BRENDA COMPTON WITH
EDITH BOWMAN EDWARDS, THE OLDEST
ATTENDEE. CARL COMPTON PHOTO.

CROWD WHICH INCLUDES MARY LAWS, JOEY
KIRBY, TERRY TEAGUE, AND OTHERS.
CARL COMPTON PHOTO.

CARL COMPTON, LIBBY AND FLOYD POPE.
CARL COMPTON PHOTO.

AB AND MELBA JEAN HEAVNER WITH MAYOR
RICK JUSTICE. CARL COMPTON PHOTO.

BRENDA ALDRIDGE COMPTON AND LENNIS
ALDRIDGE SCOTT. CARL COMPTON PHOTO.

CROWD WHICH INCLUDES EUGENE WALSH,
LARRY "COTTON" NICHOLS, AND JOANNE
LONGSHORE. CARL COMPTON PHOTO.

EUGENE WALSH REMINISCES WITH HIS
FRIENDS, JEFF BRADY AND STEVE TUCKER.
CARL COMPTON PHOTO.

JOEY KIRBY. CARL COMPTON PHOTO.

ANDREW TRAMBLE. CARL COMPTON PHOTO.

CHARLES AND BRENDA LANEY.
CARL COMPTON PHOTO.

MR. AND MRS. CHUCK DEMPSEY.
CARL COMPTON PHOTO.

J. L. Curtis, Marvene Curtis, and Eugene
Walsh. Carl Compton photo.

Gwen Longshore Geddings, Donna
Abernethy Price, James Longshore,
Tim Hartsoe, and Wayne Wilson. Carl
Compton photo.

Jeff Kirby. Carl Compton photo.

Joe Kirby and Gene Moffitt.
Carl Compton photo.

BILLIE SUE LANEY, JOE KIRBY, KIM RHEA
BOLICK AND FRANK BOLICK. CARL
COMPTON PHOTO.

GARY HENSON. CARL COMPTON PHOTO.

TERRY RASH, JONES DENNIS DECKER, TIM
HARTSOE, AND ALLIE TURNER. CARL
COMPTON PHOTO.

CATHY ALDRIDGE AND KATIE CHURCH. CARL
COMPTON PHOTO.

DWAYNE PENDERGRAST AND NED FLEMING. CARL COMPTON PHOTO.

RITA JONES LONGEST. CARL COMPTON PHOTO.

LYNDSEY HARTSOE, BRENDA ALDRIDGE COMPTON, AND ELVIS (ED SMITH). CARL COMPTON PHOTO.

ROY WHISNANT. CARL COMPTON PHOTO.

CARL COMPTON. CARL COMPTON PHOTO.

CARL AND BRENDA COMPTON, GERALD AND
VICKI JONES, OTT AND EDITH EDWARDS, JUDY
AND LEO TUCKER, JOHNNY LUNSFORD,
PAM EDWARDS TRIPLETT, CHRISTY OWENS,
WILLIE BROWN, JR., JUDY BROWN, AND
OTHERS. CARL COMPTON PHOTO.

RENITA COMPTON HARTSOE AND KELIA
HARRIS BRIDGES. CARL COMPTON PHOTO.

DUSTY WEAVER AND DAVID CLARK.
CARL COMPTON PHOTO.

DWIGHT KELLEY, ANGIE SETTLEMYRE REID,
DONNA ABERNETHY PRICE, TIM HARTSOE, AND
OTHERS. CARL COMPTON PHOTO.

The winter of 2010 also had a special celebration. For over twenty years Grant and Christine Wilson held an annual Christmas Open House at their home on the Rhodhiss-Airport Road. The town decided to have a parade that would begin in Rhodhiss and end at their house. This activity in 2010 was dubbed the Grant Wilson Christmas Parade. The first annual event was first held on December 5, 2010.[3]

THE PARADE STARTS ANNUALLY AT THE OLD
RHODHISS ELEMENTARY SCHOOL. CARL
COMPTON PHOTO.

DIANE ECKARD AND BARBARA HARMON
REPRESENTED THE TOWN. CARL
COMPTON PHOTO.

GRANT WILSON AS SANTA WITH AUSTIN TURNER AND LANCE SIGMON 2007.

ARTHUR AND EDITH EDWARDS AS RHODHISS SCHOOL'S ELDEST MEMBERS. CARL COMPTON PHOTO.

DONNA PRICE, VICKIE SHOUN, BRENDA COMPTON, GWEN GEDDINGS, ANGIE REID, EUGENE AND LINDA WALSH. CARL COMPTON PHOTO.

ROBERT "SANTA" EGGERS MADE AN APPEARANCE. CARL COMPTON PHOTO.

A PICTURE FROM A PREVIOUS CHRISTMAS CELEBRATION WAS PLACED ON THE RACECAR. 2010 AT GRANT AND CHRISTINE WILSON'S HOME. CARL COMPTON PHOTO.

In 2012 an anonymous donor purchased a state historical marker for the location of the original Rhodhiss School. The dedication ceremony was held on Sunday, April 15, 2012, at the old Rhodhiss Methodist Church. This location housed the original school. A sign still sits in the flowerbed commemorating the school's history. The Reverend Joyce Reynolds, who pastored Rhodhiss Methodist Church at the time, gave the invocation. Rick Justice, the town's mayor, presided and gave opening comments and introduced special guests. Lastly, Joe Kirby, a town commissioner and former Rhodhiss School attendee, gave the closing remarks and prayer. Many Rhodhiss Elementary scholars had their photos taken with the historical marker.

ARTHUR "OTT" AND EDITH EDWARDS, RUTH WALSH KIZIAH, AND JUDY EDWARDS TUCKER. CARL COMPTON PHOTO.

SUSAN YOUNT, RANDY ANNAS, AND MARY ANN BROWN. CARL COMPTON PHOTO.

RUTH WALSH KIZIAH, STEVE AND JANIS
TUCKER, TIM HARTSOE, SHERRIE HARTSOE
SIGMON, PETE SETTLEMYRE, DAVID TUCKER.
CARL COMPTON PHOTO.

PETE SETTLEMYRE. SHERRIE HARTSOE
SIGMON PHOTO.

PRECIOUS KELLEY, BARBARA ROSS, JANIS
TUCKER, ANGIE SETTLEMYRE REID, SHERRIE
HARTSOE SIGMON, RANDY ANNAS, SUSAN
YOUNT. CARL COMPTON PHOTO.

BRUCE AND JENNY HARTSOE. CARL
COMPTON PHOTO.

CARL AND BRENDA COMPTON. CARL COMPTON PHOTO.

CARY ROSS. CARL COMPTON PHOTO.

BARBARA HARMON, ELIZABETH LONGSHORE, GWEN LONGSHORE GEDDINGS, LENNIS ALDRIDGE SCOTT, STEVE TUCKER. CARL COMPTON PHOTO.

DAVID PEARSON, PETE SETTLEMYRE, DWAYNE PENDERGRAST, RANDY ANNAS, SUSAN YOUNT, BUZZIE WINKLER, LEONA BROWN, WAYNE CLINE, ZENO CRUMP, JUDY TUCKER, ARTHUR "OTT" AND EDITH EDWARDS. CARL COMPTON PHOTO.

ELIZABETH LONGSHORE, ANGIE SETTLEMYRE
REID, GWEN LONGSHORE GEDDINGS, ARTHUR
AND EDITH EDWARDS, RENITA COMPTON
HARTSOE, DONNA ABERNETHY PRICE. CARL
COMPTON PHOTO.

ARTHUR AND EDITH EDWARDS, CHARLES
LANEY. CARL COMPTON PHOTO.

PAM EDWARDS TRIPLETT, CARY AND BARBARA
ROSS, ARTHUR AND EDITH EDWARDS, PRECIOUS
KELLER KELLEY, DANNY AND SUSAN KELLER,
WAYNE CLINE. CARL COMPTON PHOTO.

PRECIOUS WHISNANT KELLER KELLEY.
CARL COMPTON PHOTO.

RUTH WALSH KIZIAH.
CARL COMPTON PHOTO.

SHERRIE HARTSOE SIGMON.
CARL COMPTON PHOTO.

TIM AND RENITA HARTSOE.
CARL COMPTON PHOTO.

BRUCE HARTSOE, BUZZIE WINKLER, LEONA
BROWN. CARL COMPTON PHOTO.

GWEN LONGSHORE GEDDINGS, ANGIE
SETTLEMYRE REID, DONNA ABERNETHY PRICE.
CARL COMPTON PHOTO.

JOE AND GAIL KIRBY.
CARL COMPTON PHOTO.

DAVID, LEO, AND JUDY TUCKER.
CARL COMPTON PHOTO.

STEVE AND JANIS TUCKER.
CARL COMPTON PHOTO.

ZENO CRUMP. CARL COMPTON PHOTO.

As a result of the 2010 school reunion the committee discussed what to do with the profit from the festival. It was decided that park benches would be placed at the town park; the benches were installed at the new park which sits on land owned by the town and located behind the old Burke County textile plant, which is now Wipelli. According to the town's minutes on August 14, 2012, Mike Phillips read a letter from Governor Beverly Perdue congratulating the town for being awarded a Parks & Recreation Trust Funds Grant in the amount of $163,750, which the town matched for a total of $327,500 to spend on the Rhodhiss Horseshoe Trail Park located on Carolina Avenue. This grant provided a parking lot, paved walking trails, gravel walking trails, picnic shelter, picnic tables, benches, observation deck, foot bridges, signage, and an information kiosk.[4] Later during the winter of 2017 the town minutes indicated that the Horseshoe Park was completed.[5] Prior to the park's completion in October 2017 another natural disaster hit the town in the form of a tornado. This force came through Burke and Caldwell counties causing extensive damage, and Rhodhiss was not spared. The townspeople did what they had done in previous disasters: pick up the pieces, rebuild, and move forward.

HORSESHOE PARK IN 2016.
SHERRIE HARTSOE SIGMON PHOTO.

THE HORSESHOE TRAIL PARK. CARL COMPTON PHOTO.

THE NEW PARK OPENED.
CARL COMPTON PHOTO.

FALL IN THE NEW PARK.
CARL COMPTON PHOTO.

BRIDGE COMPLETED ACROSS THE PARK
PATHWAY. CARL COMPTON PHOTO.

VIEW FROM THE NEW PARK.
CARL COMPTON PHOTO.

ANOTHER VIEW OF THE PARK:
CARL COMPTON PHOTO.

HORSESHOE TRAIL PARK.
CARL COMPTON PHOTO.

JIM MUNDY SHOWING THE TORNADO DAMAGE
ON PARK LOOP IN OCTOBER 2017.
CARL COMPTON PHOTO.

OCTOBER 2017 TORNADO DAMAGE ON MAPLE
STREET. CARL COMPTON PHOTO.

PARK LOOP DAMAGE FROM 2017 TORNADO.
CARL COMPTON PHOTO.

PARK AVENUE DAMAGE FROM 2017 TORNADO.
CARL COMPTON PHOTO.

PARK LOOP DAMAGE. CARL COMPTON PHOTO.

PARK LOOP DAMAGE. CARL COMPTON PHOTO.

PARK AVENUE DAMAGE.
CARL COMPTON PHOTO.

SHELBY STREET.
SHERRIE HARTSOE SIGMON PHOTO.

CAROLINA AVENUE DAMAGE.
SHERRIE HARTSOE SIGMON PHOTO.

RHODHISS /BURKE COUNTY DAMAGE.
SHERRIE HARTSOE SIGMON PHOTO.

SHELBY OR GARDNER STREET DAMAGE.
SHERRIE HARTSOE SIGMON PHOTO.

SHELBY STREET DAMAGE.
SHERRIE HARTSOE SIGMON PHOTO.

AFTER THE TORNADO, THE DAM'S OVERFLOW.
CARL COMPTON PHOTO.

DAM OVERFLOW SCENE FROM THE BRIDGE.
CARL COMPTON PHOTO.

In 2019 the Town of Rhodhiss was awarded a North Carolina State Reserve Loan of $100,000 and a State Reserve Grant of $300,000 from the Department of Environmental Quality Division of Water Infrastructure.[6] The minutes indicated that the sewer and water project started in October 2020.[7] The year 2019 also saw one of Rhodhiss' biggest celebrations ever. On July 20, 2019, the town's citizens and guests celebrated the fiftieth anniversary of the lunar landing. According to the minutes on July 9, 2019, the board announced the anniversary of the Lunar Landing Celebration.[8] Between 1,500 to 1,800 people attended. It was also held on the hottest day of 2019, on July 20, but everyone enjoyed the event. The evening ended with spectacular fireworks over the Catawba River.

CARL COMPTON WITH RHODHISS' NASA PLAQUE AND A PIECE OF THE FLAG MATERIAL. SHERRIE HARTSOE SIGMON PHOTO.

RICK JUSTICE, MAYOR; SHERRIE HARTSOE SIGMON; BARBARA HARMON, TOWN CLERK; AND CARL COMPTON, FORMER BURLINGTON EMPLOYEE, REPRESENTED THE TOWN AT VARIOUS EVENTS THROUGHOUT JULY'S LUNAR CELEBRATIONS. BARBARA HARMON PHOTO.

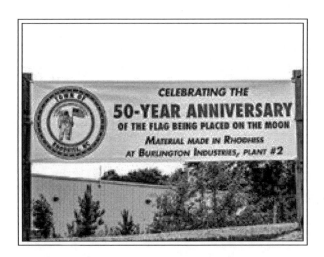

BANNER ANNOUNCING THE RHODHISS' LUNAR
CELEBRATION. CARL COMPTON PHOTO.

THE ARTICLE IN THE MORGANTON PAPER
REGARDING THE 50TH ANNIVERSARY
LUNAR LANDING.

PINK FIRE TRUCK FOR BREAST CANCER
AWARENESS. CARL COMPTON PHOTO.

CROWD AT THE CELEBRATION.
CARL COMPTON PHOTO.

MAYOR RICK JUSTICE ROCKED THE 60S STYLE
DURING THE 50TH ANNIVERSARY OF THE LUNAR
LANDING. SHERRIE HARTSOE SIGMON PHOTO.

REPLICA OF THE APOLLO 11.
CARL COMPTON PHOTO.

A YOUNG MAN DRESSED AS AN ASTRONAUT FOR
THE CELEBRATION. CARL COMPTON PHOTO.

FORMER BURLINGTON EMPLOYEES IN 1969,
MACK AND YVONNE HENTSCHEL. JANIS
TUCKER IS ALSO IN THIS PICTURE.
CARL COMPTON PHOTO.

FORMER BURLINGTON EMPLOYEE, JOE KELLEY.
CARL COMPTON PHOTO.

FORMER BURLINGTON EMPLOYEES, RUTH KIZIAH,
MAXINE CARVER, MARVIN BUCHANAN, GARY
AND LUANNE MCCOURRY, BRUCE HARTSOE, AND
OTHERS. CARL COMPTON PHOTO.

CROWD AT THE CELEBRATION. CARL COMPTON PHOTO.

CROWD AT THE CELEBRATION.
CARL COMPTON PHOTO.

THE EVENING ENDED WITH FIREWORKS.
CARL COMPTON PHOTO.

NIGHTLIFE AT THE CELEBRATION. CARL COMPTON PHOTO.

THE EVENING WAS COMING TO
AN END. SHERRIE AND
MICHAEL SIGMON.
ELAINE ABERNATHY PHOTO.

RHODHISS AWARDED WATER AND SEWER GRANT. *LENOIR NEWS-TOPIC*

MORE INFORMATION ON WATER AND SEWER.
LENOIR NEWS-TOPIC

SEWER AND WATER IN RHODHISS.
CARL COMPTON PHOTO.

SEWER AND WATER IN RHODHISS. CARL
COMPTON PHOTO.

SEWER AND WATER IN RHODHISS.
CARL COMPTON PHOTO.

INSTALLATION OF THE NEW FLAGPOLE. WILL DENNIS, ALLEN SPENCER, CARL COMPTON, AND JOE KIRBY. DALE HAWKINS PHOTO.

In 2021 the town office moved from Burke County to Caldwell County on the old Rhodhiss School ball field. On July 20, 2021, the town erected a flagpole that flies the United States flag, the North Carolina flag, and the Rhodhiss flag. Lastly, the minutes in 2021 give a hint of more to come for Rhodhiss. Rick Justice, the Town Manager, reported to the board that there has been interest in the purchase of the old mill property on the Caldwell County side of the bridge. A plan was provided to the board of what the interested party wants to do with the land.[9]

MAYOR ALLEN SPENCER AND COUNCILPERSON KENDRA EDWARDS IN FRONT OF NEW FLAG AND POLE, JULY 20, 2021. CARL COMPTON PHOTO

INSTALLATION OF THE NEW FLAGPOLE AT THE NEW TOWN OFFICE. JULY 20, 2021.

JULY 20, 2021, FLAGPOLE INSTALLED
FOR THE 52ND ANNIVERSARY OF THE
LUNAR LANDING.
CARL COMPTON PHOTO.

JUNE 2022. THE NEW TOWN OFFICE LOCATED IN
CALDWELL COUNTY ON THE OLD RHODHISS SCHOOL
BALL FIELD. SHERRIE HARTSOE SIGMON PHOTO.

Rhodhiss has for the past 120 years given so much to its citizens and the community. The people of Rhodhiss have a reputation of being hard workers who are proud of their small town, and they continue to weave the threads of love in the hearts of all. Rhodhiss' passageway to the future looks bright. The townspeople give the best of themselves to ensure success for the village, and they do it with love for family.

BEAUTIFUL SUNSET ON DECEMBER 6, 2018, THE DAY PRIOR TO A
BIG 15-INCH SNOW. CARL COMPTON PHOTO.

ANOTHER SUNSET PICTURE THE DAY BEFORE THE BIG SNOW IN 2018.
CARL COMPTON PHOTO.

A DECEMBER SUNSET IN 2017. CARL COMPTON PHOTO.

NOTES

1   Rhodhiss Town Minutes. 11 November 2002.

2   NOAA. https://water.weather.gov/ahps2/hydrograph.php?gage=rhon7&wfo=gsp. Accessed 10 July 2022.

3   Rhodhiss Town Minutes. 9 November 2012.

4   Rhodhiss Town Minutes. 14 August 2012.

5   Rhodhiss Town Minutes. 16 February 2017.

6   Rhodhiss Town Minutes. 3 June 2019.

7   Rhodhiss Town Minutes. 20 October 2020.

8   Rhodhiss Town Minutes. 9 July 2019.

9   Rhodhiss Town Minutes. 8 June 2021.

Index

B

C

F

H

L

M

Q

R

U

Made in the USA
Columbia, SC
22 May 2023

16947802R00322